PRESENCE, POWER AND PROMISE

PRESENCE, POWER AND PROMISE

THE ROLE OF THE SPIRIT OF GOD IN THE OLD TESTAMENT

EDITED BY
DAVID G. FIRTH AND
PAUL D. WEGNER

APOLLOS (an imprint of Inter-Varsity Press)
Norton Street, Nottingham NG7 3HR, England
Website: www.ivpbooks.com
Email: ivp@ivpbooks.com

First published 2011

British Library Cataloguing in Publication Data
A catalogue record for this book is available from the British Library.

UK ISBN: 978-1-84474-534-0

Set in Monotype Garamond 11/13pt
Typeset in Great Britain by Servis Filmsetting Ltd, Stockport, Cheshire
Printed and bound in Great Britain by MPG Books Ltd, Cornwall

Inter-Varsity Press publishes Christian books that are true to the Bible and that communicate the gospel, develop discipleship and strengthen the church for its mission in the world.

Inter-Varsity Press is closely linked with the Universities and Colleges Christian Fellowship, a student movement connecting Christian Unions in universities and colleges throughout Great Britain, and a member movement of the International Fellowship of Evangelical Students. Website: www.uccf.org.uk.

CONTENTS

Part 3: The Spirit and wisdom

Part 4: The Spirit and creativity

Part 5: The Spirit and prophecy

Part 6: The Spirit and leadership

Part 7: The Spirit and the future

Part 8: The Spirit at Qumran

CONTRIBUTORS

Andrew Abernethy is Lecturer in Old Testament at Ridley Melbourne Mission and Ministry College, Melbourne, Australia.

Richard E. Averbeck is the Director of the PhD Program in Theological Studies and Professor of Old Testament and Semitic Languages, Trinity Evangelical Divinity School, Deerfield, Illinois.

Daniel I. Block is Gunther H. Knoedler Professor of Old Testament, Wheaton College, Wheaton, Illinois.

Robert B. Chisholm, Jr is Chair and Professor of Old Testament Studies, Dallas Theological Seminary, Dallas, Texas.

Rosalind Clarke is a PhD student at Highland Theological College.

Daniel J. Estes is Distinguished Professor of Old Testament at the School of Biblical and Theological Studies, Cedarville University, Cedarville, Ohio.

David G. Firth is Director of Extension Studies, St John's College, Nottingham.

Jamie A. Grant is Vice-Principal and Lecturer in Biblical Studies at the Highland Theological College, Dingwall, Scotland.

Richard S. Hess is Earl S. Kalland Professor of Old Testament and Semitic Languages, Denver Seminary.

Robert L. Hubbard, Jr is Professor of Biblical Literature, North Park Theological Seminary, Chicago.

Tremper Longman III is Robert H. Gundry Professor of Biblical Studies, Westmont College, Santa Barbara, California.

Geert W. Lorein is Senior Lecturer in Old Testament at the Evangelische Theologische Faculteit, Leuven, Belgium.

Hilary Marlow lectures in Old Testament and Biblical Hebrew in the Faculty of Divinity of the University of Cambridge.

Eugene H. Merrill is Distinguished Professor of Old Testament Studies, Dallas Theological Seminary, Dallas, Texas.

Erika Moore is Associate Professor of Old Testament and Hebrew, Trinity School for Ministry, USA.

John N. Oswalt is Visiting Distinguished Professor of Old Testament at Asbury Theological Seminary, Wilmore, Kentucky.

Robin Routledge is Academic Dean and Senior Lecturer in Old Testament at Mattersey Hall, England.

Willem VanGemeren is Professor of Old Testament and Semitic Languages, Trinity Evangelical Divinity School, Deerfield, Illinois.

John H. Walton is Professor of Old Testament, Wheaton College, Illinois.

Paul D. Wegner is Professor of Old Testament, Phoenix Seminary, Phoenix, Arizona.

Lindsay Wilson is Academic Dean and Lecturer in Old Testament at Ridley Melbourne Mission and Ministry College, Melbourne, Australia.

ABBREVIATIONS

1QIsa^{a}	Isaiah^{a}, Cave 1, Qumran
4QIsa^{c}	Isaiah^{c}, Cave 4, Qumran
4QIsa^{d}	Isaiah^{d}, Cave 4, Qumran
AB	Anchor Bible
ACC	Ancient Christian Commentary
AEL	*Ancient Egyptian Literature*, Miriam Lichtheim (University of California Press)
AGJU	Arbeiten zur Geschichte des antiken Judentums und des Urchristentums
ANET^{3}	*Ancient Near Eastern Texts Relating to the Old Testament*, ed. J. B. Pritchard, 3rd ed. (Princeton: Princeton University Press, 1969)
AOAT	Alter Orient und Altes Testament
AOTC	Abingdon Old Testament Commentaries
ASV	American Standard Version
ATJ	*Ashland Theological Journal*
AUSS	Andrews University Seminary Studies
BBB	Bonner biblische Beiträge
BBR	*Bulletin for Biblical Research*
BCOTWP	Baker Commentary on the Old Testament, Wisdom and Psalms

BDAG	W. Bauer, F. W. Danker, W. F. Arndt and F. W. Gingrich, *A Greek-English Lexicon of the New Testament and other Early Christian Literature*, 3rd ed.
BDB	F. Brown, S. R. Driver and C. A. Briggs, *A Hebrew and English Lexicon of the Old Testament* (Oxford: Clarendon, 1907; repr. Peabody: Hendrickson, 2005)
BETL	Bibliotheca Ephemeridum Theologicarum Lovaniensium
BHS	*Biblia Hebraica Stuttgartensia*, ed. K. Elliger and W. Rudolph (Stuttgart: Deutsche Bibelstiftung, 1983)
Bib	*Biblica*
BJS	Brown Judaic Studies
BN	*Biblische Notizen*
BST	The Bible Speaks Today series
BWANT	Beiträge zur Wissenschaft vom Alten und Neuen Testament
BZAW	Beihefte zur Zeitschrift für die alttestamentliche Wissenschaft
CAD	*Chicago Assyrian Dictionary*
CAT	*Commentaire de l'Ancien Testament*
CBQ	*Catholic Biblical Quarterly*
CEV	Contemporary English Version
COS	*Context of Scripture*, eds. W. Hallo and K. L. Younger (Leiden: Brill, 2003)
CRINT	Compendia Rerum Iudaicarum ad Novum Testamentum
CSB	Christian Standard Bible
CT	Cuneiform Texts
DDD²	*Dictionary of Deities and Demons in the Bible*, ed. K. van der Toorn, B. Becking and P. W. van der Horst, 2nd ed. (Leiden: Brill; Grand Rapids: Eerdmans, 1999)
DJD	Discoveries in the Judean Desert
DSD	*Dead Sea Discoveries*
DSSSE	*The Dead Sea Scrolls Study Edition,* edited by F. García Martínez and E. J. C. Tigchelaar
EBC	*The Expositor's Bible Commentary*, ed. F. E. Gaebelein, 12 vols. (Grand Rapids, 1976–95)
EQ	*Evangelical Quarterly*
ESV	English Standard Version
ET	English translation
EVV	English versions
ExpTim	*Expository Times*
FOTL	Forms of the Old Testament Literature

GKC	*Gesenius' Hebrew Grammar*, ed. E. Kautzsch, rev. and tr. A. E. Cowley (Oxford: Clarendon, 1910)
HALOT	L. Koehler and W. Baumgartner, *The Hebrew and Aramaic Lexicon of the Old Testament*, tr. and ed. under the supervision of M. E. J. Richardson, 5 vols. (Leiden: Brill, 1994–2000)
HAT	Handbuch zum Alten Testament
HCSB	Holman Christian Standard Bible
Heb.	Hebrew
HSS	Harvard Semitic Studies
HUCA	*Hebrew Union College Annual*
ICC	International Critical Commentary
IDB	*Interpreter's Dictionary of the Bible*
IEJ	*Israel Exploration Journal*
Int	*Interpretation*
ISBE	*International Standard Bible Encyclopedia*
ITC	International Theological Commentary
JANES	*Journal of the Ancient Near Eastern Society*
JAOS	*Journal of the American Oriental Society*
JATS	*Journal of the Adventist Theological Society*
JBL	*Journal of Biblical Literature*
JEBS	*Journal of European Baptist Studies*
JETS	*Journal of the Evangelical Theological Society*
Joüon	P. Joüon, *A Grammar of Biblical Hebrew*, trans. and rev. T. Muraoka, 2 vols. (Rome: Pontificio Istituto Biblico, 1996)
JPS	Jewish Publication Society
JPSTC	Jewish Publication Society Torah Commentary
JPT	*Journal of Pentecostal Theology*
JQR	*Jewish Quarterly Review*
JR	*Journal of Religion*
JSOT	*Journal for the Study of the Old Testament*
JSOTSup	*Journal for the Study of the Old Testament, Supplement Series*
JSPSup	*Journal for the Study of the Pseudepigrapha, Supplement Series*
JTS	*Journal of Theological Studies*
KJV	King James Version
KTU	*Die keilalphabetischen Texte aus Ugarit*, ed. M. Dietrich, O. Lorenz and J. Sanmartín, AOAT 24/1 (Neukirchen-Vluyn: Neukirchener Verlag, 1976)
LHB/OTS	Library of the Hebrew Bible/Old Testament Studies
LAB	*Liber Antiquitatum Biblicarum*
LXX	Septuagint

MT	Masoretic text
NAC	New American Commentary
NASB	New American Standard Bible
NCB	New Century Bible
NCBC	New Century Bible Commentary
NEB	New English Bible
NET	New English Translation
NIB	*The New Interpreter's Bible*, ed. L. E. Keck, 12 vols. (Nashville: Abingdon, 1993–2002)
NIBCOT	New International Biblical Commentary on the Old Testament
NICNT	New International Commentary on the New Testament
NICOT	New International Commentary on the Old Testament
NIDNTT	*The New International Dictionary of New Testament Theology*, ed. Colin Brown (Grand Rapids: Zondervan, 1971)
NIDOTTE	*New International Dictionary of Old Testament Theology and Exegesis*, ed. W. A. VanGemeren, 5 vols. (Carlisle: Paternoster; Grand Rapids: Zondervan, 1996)
NIV	New International Version
NIVAC	NIV Application Commentary
NJB	New Jerusalem Bible
NKJV	New King James Version
NLT	New Living Translation
NRSV	New Revised Standard Version
NT	New Testament
OEAE	*Oxford Encyclopedia of Ancient Egypt* (New York: Oxford University Press, 2001)
OLA	Orientalia Lovaniensia Analecta
OT	Old Testament
OTL	Old Testament Library
OTM	Old Testament Message
OTS	Old Testament Studies
RB	*Revue biblique*
RIMA	*Royal Inscriptions of Mesopotamia, Assyrian Periods* (University of Toronto)
RIME	*Royal Inscriptions of Mesopotamia, Early Periods* (University of Toronto)
RSV	Revised Standard Version
SAA	State Archives of Assyria
SAALT	State Archives of Assyria Literary Texts

SBJT	*Southern Baptist Journal of Theology*
SBL	Society of Biblical Literature
SBLDS	Society of Biblical Literature Dissertation Series
SBLWAW	Society of Biblical Literature Writings from the Ancient World
SBT	Studies in Biblical Theology
SJT	*Scottish Journal of Theology*
SP	Sacra Pagina
STDJ	Studies on the Texts of the Desert of Judah
SVTP	Studia in Veteris Testamenti Pseudepigrapha
TDNT	*Theological Dictionary of the New Testament*, ed. G. Kittel and G. Friedrich, trans. G. W. Bromiley, 10 vols. (Grand Rapids: Eerdmans, 1964–76)
TDOT	*Theological Dictionary of the Old Testament*, ed. G. J. Botterweck, H. Ringgren and H.-J. Fabry, 15 vols. (Grand Rapids: Eerdmans, 1974–2006)
THAT	*Theologisches Handwörterbuch zum Alten Testament*, ed. E. Jenni and C. Westermann (Munich: Chr. Kaiser, 1971–6)
TJ	*Trinity Journal*
TLOT	*Theological Lexicon of the Old Testament*, ed. E. Jenni and C. Westermann, trans. M. Biddle, 3 vols. (Peabody: Hendrickson, 1997)
TNIV	Today's New International Version
TOTC	Tyndale Old Testament Commentaries
TWOT	*Theological Wordbook of the Old Testament*, ed. R. L. Harris, G. L. Archer and B. K. Waltke, 2 vols. (Chicago: Moody Press, 1980)
TynBul	*Tyndale Bulletin*
UF	*Ugarit-Forschungen*
Vg	Vulgate
VT	*Vetus Testamentum*
VTSup	Supplements to *Vetus Testamentum*
WBC	Word Biblical Commentary
WEC	Wycliffe Exegetical Commentary
WTJ	*Westminster Theological Journal*
WUNT	Wissenschaftliche Untersuchungen zum Neuen Testament
YES	Yale Egyptological Studies
ZAW	*Zeitschrift für die alttestamentliche Wissenschaft*

INTRODUCTION

David G. Firth and Paul D. Wegner

The Spirit of God in the Old Testament (hereafter OT) appears to be the energizing force in the lives of people to accomplish God's mission on earth. Eberhard Kamlah describes it like this:

> It can come mightily upon a man (Jdg. 14:6; 1 Sam. 16:13 and passim), can 'clothe' him (Jdg. 6:34 and passim), enter into him (Ezek. 2:2 and passim), descend upon him (2 Ki. 2:9; Isa. 11:2 and passim), impel him (Jdg. 13:25), all of which indicates the powerful operation of God upon a man, enabling him to perform some ecstatic, supernatural deed.[1]

The Spirit of God is an important topic in the OT, and yet there is surprisingly little scholarly work on this issue. To address this, we have assembled some of the best OT scholars to discuss various aspects of this topic, as well as specific exegetical articles on significant passages to provide further insight and depth. Richard Averbeck explores the various nuances of the relationship between wind and spirit in the OT, helping to answer the question of whether or not it is possible to speak meaningfully of the Spirit in the OT. John H. Walton provides an important backdrop to the wider issues by

1. Eberhard Kamlah, 'Spirit, Holy Spirit (*pneuma* [part])', in *NIDNTT*, 3:691.

examining the 'spirit of the LORD' against its Ancient Near Eastern context. After these two context-setting essays, we have major thematic essays, brought together with some studies on specific texts that have been thought relevant to the understanding of the Spirit in the OT related to the general theme under consideration. It should be noted that the conclusion of some of these articles is that specific passages do not contribute to a theology of the Spirit, though even these negative conclusions actually provide an important contribution. But others highlight aspects of the work of the Spirit that might surprise us, demonstrating the value of reflecting on the OT's perspective on the Spirit. The issue of spirit and creation is covered by Robert Hubbard, while Tremper Longman examines the spirit and wisdom. The exegetical discussions on specific wisdom passages (Job 27:3 by Rosalind Clarke; Ps. 51:12–19 by Daniel Estes; Ps. 139:8 by Jamie Grant; Prov. 1:23 by Lindsay Wilson) help flesh out the concept of wisdom and the spirit. Rick Hess discusses the area of spirit and skill (or creativity), centring on passages from Exodus. Daniel I. Block provides an overview of the spirit and prophecy, with specific passages on prophecy covered by John N. Oswalt (Num. 24:2), Hilary Marlow (Isa. 11:2), Paul D. Wegner (Isa. 48:16) and Erika Moore (Joel 3:1–2 [ET 2:28–29]). David Firth provides an overview of the spirit and leadership in the historical books, with specific exegetical articles by Eugene Merrill (Judg. 13:25; 14:6, 19; 15:14), David Firth (1 Sam. 19:23) and Robert Chisholm (2 Kgs 2:16). Willem VanGemeren and Andrew Abernethy and Robin Routledge provide two thematic articles on the spirit and the future, providing a bridge for further development of the spirit in the New Testament (hereafter NT). Finally, Geert Lorein explores the understanding of the spirit in the Qumran materials.

The Hebrew word *rûaḥ* ('spirit') occurs 394 times in the OT, with a range of meanings: 'breeze, breath, wind, spirit'.[2] The research presented in this book focuses more narrowly on the 39 times this word occurs in connection with God ('spirit of God', 11 times; 'spirit of the LORD', 25 times; and 'Holy Spirit' [or 'spirit of holiness'], 3 times[3]), in addition to those times where a pronominal suffix attached to *rûaḥ* refers back to God. With such a broad range of meanings for the word *rûaḥ*, it can be difficult to determine its exact meaning when associated with God. Kamlah notes: 'The idea behind *rûaḥ* is the extraordinary fact that something as intangible as air should move; at the same time it is not the movement *per se* which excites attention, but rather the energy

2. *HALOT*, 3:1197–1201; *NIDOTTE*, 3:1073–1078, para. 8120.

3. Ps. 51:11(13); Isa. 63:10, 11.

manifested by such movement.'[4] When *rûaḥ* is connected with a person, it often refers to one's emotions (Gen. 41:8; Exod. 6:9; 35:21; Num. 5:14; Deut. 2:30; Judg. 9:23; 1 Sam. 1:15; 16:15–16, etc.), or one's being, essence, power or life (Gen. 45:27; Josh. 5:1; Judg. 15:19; 1 Sam. 30:12; 1 Kgs 10:5; 2 Chr. 9:4; Job 10:12, etc.). There are many passages in the OT that use this latter meaning for the 'spirit of the LORD' coming upon a person (Gen. 6:3; Num. 24:2; Judg. 3:10; 6:34; 11:29; 13:25; 14:6, 19; 15:14; 1 Sam. 10:6, 10; 11:6, etc.); however, it is difficult to determine what is actually happening to the person or what exactly is coming upon them. Several passages are quite clear that when God's power comes upon a person, they in turn demonstrate immense power, wisdom, creativity or leadership. Van Pelt, Kaiser and Block describe this well:

> Frequently the Spirit of God represents the agent/agency by which God exercises his sovereign control over individuals. Occasionally the effects are calamitous, as in those instances where the LORD's Spirit is described as destructive or disruptive (not evil in a moral sense; Judg 9:23; 1 Sam 16:14–16, 23; 18:10; 19:9). But usually God's Spirit operates on behalf of his people by energizing them (Ezek 2:2), transporting them (1 Kgs 18:12; 2 Kgs 2:16; Ezek 3:12, 14; 8:3; 11:24; 37:1, though sometimes in visionary form), endowing ('filling') them with his Spirit, and giving them special gifts and power for sacred service (Exod 35:31; Mic 3:8).[5]

To the OT readers, God's spirit emanated from God and came upon people to empower them to do some service for him (i.e. ruling, defeating Israel's enemies, judging, prophesying), though reference to the spirit might also symbolize God's presence. It is interesting that one of the primary roles of the 'Spirit' in the NT is to empower believers to live a godly life. However, there are also significant distinctions between the 'spirit' in the two Testaments. In the OT, the 'spirit of the LORD' was considered more as a force emanating from God, while in the NT the 'Holy Spirit' is a person and part of the Godhead. Also the spirit's role in the OT is centred upon physical empowerment, while in the NT it seems to be centred upon spiritual empowerment. These concepts do not contradict each other, but rather integrate nicely as more detailed information continued to be revealed. In fact, some people believe that they integrate so nicely that the Spirit as the third person of the Trinity must have been its understanding in the OT also. But would the OT

---

4. *NIDNTT*, 3:690.

5. M. V. Van Pelt, W. C. Kaiser and D. I. Block, 'רוּחַ (#8120)', in *NIDOTTE*, 3:1075–1076.

readers have understood the 'spirit of God' as a person? Is it fair to jump directly to the NT's understanding and argue that the 'spirit of God/the LORD' in the OT is indeed the third person of the Trinity? We see the difficulty with this in the basic question of whether to translate *rûaḥ* as 'Spirit' or 'spirit'. One would imply a clearer trinitarian perspective than the other. Should we translate the term from the perspective of a wider biblical theology and in certain circumstances render *rûaḥ* as 'Spirit', or should we leave it as 'spirit' on the basis that no-one in Israel would have thought in trinitarian terms?

While some have done this,[6] and it will quickly be evident that there is considerable diversity on how to resolve this among our contributors, it seems preferable in terms of exegesis to interpret the OT passages as their authors would have intended and not through the lens of their subsequent development in the NT. A primary principle in hermeneutics is that the meaning of a passage is found in what the original author intended it to mean.[7] Klein, Blomberg and Hubbard explain:

> Of course, if we are seeking the meaning intended by the author to the original recipients, that meaning *must* be the meaning they could understand at the time, not the meaning we would determine based on our position of advanced historical developments. Obviously, we have access to the full canon of Scripture. We know how the whole story turned out, so to speak. However, in seeking to understand the meaning of a given text, we cannot impose insight that is based on later revelation . . . At least we must admit that the human author could not have intended in his or her message what we know only from subsequent revelation.[8]

---

6. See Erickson's discussion on Isa. 48:16 (Millard J. Erickson, *Christian Theology* [Grand Rapids: Baker, 1985], p. 866). Wayne Grudem states, 'In fact, from a full New Testament perspective (which recognizes Jesus the Messiah to be the true servant of the Lord predicted in Isaiah's prophecies), Isaiah 48:16 has Trinitarian implications: "And now the Lord GOD has sent me and his Spirit," if spoken by Jesus the Son of God, refers to all three persons of the Trinity' (*Systematic Theology: An Introduction to Biblical Doctrine* [Grand Rapids: Zondervan; Leicester: Inter-Varsity Press, 1994], pp. 228–229).
7. See specifically E. D. Hirsch, *Validity in Interpretation* (New Haven: Yale University Press, 1967) and *The Aims of Interpretation* (Chicago: University of Chicago Press, 1976). An early proponent of applying this type of hermeneutic principle to biblical studies is K. Stendahl, 'Implications of Form Criticism and Tradition Criticism for Biblical Interpretation', *JBL* 77 (1958), pp. 33–38.
8. William W. Klein, Craig L. Blomberg and Robert L. Hubbard, Jr, *Introduction to*

Some scholars have argued that the OT authors may have meant one thing but God intended another. First of all, it is dangerous to make a distinction between what the author meant and what God meant, for if God did not intend what the author meant, then there is a hidden or deeper meaning that we may never know. Second, there is no doubt that God knows everything and that he completely understands how a passage may be developed further, but that is significantly different from arguing that the text has a deeper meaning that God intends in the passage. How could the readers be expected to know the mind of God or how a concept will be developed in the future, unless he tells them? God cannot hold people responsible for not knowing his thoughts unless he has already made them plain.

One good reason for God not to reveal the Trinity or multiple persons in the Godhead to OT Israel is that polytheism was such a significant problem during this period. Deuteronomy 6:4, 'the Shema', was the backbone of Israelite theology; a 'trinity' concept would have been considered polytheism at the time. Even the Jews in Jesus' day considered blasphemous his claim to be the 'Son of God' (Matt. 26:65; Mark 14:64; John 10:33). Celsus, the second-century Roman philosopher and opponent of Christianity, went further and claimed that Christians were not monotheists.[9] It seems reasonable, then, that

---

Biblical Interpretation, 2nd ed. (Dallas: Word, 2004), p. 11. Walter C. Kaiser rejects the idea that the NT writers found additional or different meaning in OT passages, arguing instead that the NT author's meaning was somehow understood or at least latent in the words of the OT author. Kaiser acknowledges that a NT writer may make different applications or develop different implications of an OT text, but he would argue that this is in the area of significance and not meaning (for a full discussion, see *The Uses of the Old Testament in the New* [Chicago: Moody, 1985]).

9. In Celsus's work, called *On the True Doctrine*, he states the following about Christians: 'Now if the Christians worshipped only one God they might have reason to their side. But as a matter of fact they worship a man who appeared only recently. They do not consider what they are doing a breach of monotheism; rather they think it perfectly consistent to worship the great God and to worship his servant as God. And their worship of this Jesus is more outrageous because they refuse to listen to any talk about God, the father of all, unless it includes some reference to Jesus: Tell them that Jesus, the author of the Christian insurrection, was not his son, and they will not listen to you. And when they call him Son of God, they are not really paying homage to God, rather they are attempting to exalt Jesus to the heights' (Celsus, *On the True Doctrine: A Discourse Against the Christians*, trans. R. Joseph Hoffman [Oxford: Oxford University Press, 1987], p. 116).

God could use the fairly broad word *rûaḥ* to signify a power that emanates from him and displays itself in a variety of ways: Samson demonstrates this power by ripping apart Philistines, Jephthah by defeating the Amonites, David by leading his people well, Bezalel by using his creative ability to build the tabernacle, and so on. Later in the NT, the Spirit continues to demonstrate power often in the spiritual arena to help believers live a godly life, but there is also a further development of distinguishing the Spirit from other parts of the Godhead.

While it may be justifiable to admit there is significant overlap in the concept of 'spirit' between the two Testaments and that at least sometimes in the OT the 'spirit of God' may indeed be the third person of the Trinity, this is by no means clear and it is not what God intended to reveal in these passages. The OT Scriptures were divine revelation and thus authoritative long before the NT came and added further enlightenment. In fact, it is possible that God can indeed send out a power from himself to accomplish something without it being the Holy Spirit; for example, Judges 14:19 says that the 'spirit of the LORD' rushed upon Samson and he ripped apart a lion with his bare hands. The implication is that God's power came upon Samson and empowered him to perform a supernatural action, but it is not necessary to think that the Holy Spirit was this demonstration of his power.

There is a significant relationship between the two Testaments; scholars generally view the NT as a 'fulfilment' of the OT. Passages such as Matthew 1:22; 2:15; 3:15; 5:17 and others suggest this type of relationship between the Testaments. But there has always been some uncertainty as to how certain OT concepts or even specific passages have been picked up by NT writers and applied differently or suggested a different meaning than in the OT. And while some have argued that the NT authors do not find further or different meaning than the OT authors intended,[10] most scholars would disagree and have attempted to explain these discrepancies in a variety of ways.[11] It may well be that the NT authors use a variety of ways to advance the meaning of

10. Kaiser, *Uses of the Old Testament.*

11. Douglas Moo, 'The Problem of *Sensus Plenior*', in D. A. Carson and J. D. Woodbridge (eds.), *Hermeneutics, Authority, and Canon* (Grand Rapids: Zondervan, 1986), pp. 175–212; R. N. Longenecker, *Biblical Exegesis in the Apostolic Period* (Grand Rapids: Eerdmans, 1975); D. A. Carson and H. G. M. Williamson (eds.), *It Is Written: Scripture Citing Scripture* (Cambridge: Cambridge University Press, 1988). For a good discussion of various positions, see Klein, Blomberg and Hubbard, *Introduction*, pp. 169–185.

an OT passage and apply it to a new situation. We have argued that Matthew 2:15 picks up Hosea 11:1 and says that it is 'fulfilled' by Jesus coming out of Egypt, but in fact, Hosea 11:1 is referring to a past event – when God brought his people out of Egypt. It is plausible that *plēroō* is being used in the sense of 'to fill (up)' or 'bring something to completion'.[12] If this is the case, Matthew is not saying that the NT event is a direct fulfilment of this OT passage, but rather that it adds new meaning to it. We see a similar type of development in the concept of the 'Day of the LORD' where several OT prophets build upon the 'Day of the LORD' and even add new concepts or further revelation as to what to expect during this day; but it is not until we get into the NT, in several chapters in Matthew and the entire book of Revelation, that the 'Day of the LORD' is fully revealed. If OT passages and concepts are developed and advanced in the NT, then it is certainly reasonable that the concept of the 'spirit of God' can develop.

12. BDAG, p. 678. Moo calls this a typological reading and says: 'New Testament persons, events, and institutions will sometimes "fill up" Old Testament persons, events, and institutions by repeating at a deeper or more climactic level that which was true in the original situation' ('Problem of *Sensus Plenior*', p. 196). Klein, Blomberg and Hubbard explain this concept just a little differently: 'Christ and his Church provided structures and trajectories for a new understanding of the events and texts in the OT Scriptures. They reread these texts and saw patterns and significance not apparent to non-Christians. In their Christian experience they perceived similarities to what God did with his covenant people in previous generations as recorded in the OT. So they interpreted those OT terms in light of their new insight' (*Introduction*, p. 199).

PART 1: ORIENTATION TO THE SPIRIT IN THE OLD TESTAMENT AND THE ANCIENT NEAR EAST

1. BREATH, WIND, SPIRIT AND THE HOLY SPIRIT IN THE OLD TESTAMENT

Richard E. Averbeck

The term 'Holy Spirit' occurs only three times in the Hebrew Bible, written literally 'the Spirit of holiness' (*rûaḥ haqqōdeš*).[1] The Hebrew language often creates adjectival expressions by means of what is known as the construct genitive relationship between two nouns, the latter noun serving as an adjective (also called the bound structure, i.e. the construction 'the . . . of. . .', so 'the Spirit of holiness' = 'the Holy Spirit'). In these three instances the LXX (the Greek translation of the Hebrew OT) translates this combination of words with the same expression the New Testament uses for what we render

1. This chapter is based on and a further development from the initial research published in an earlier article written by the same author, Richard E. Averbeck, 'The Holy Spirit in the Hebrew Bible and Its Connections to the New Testament', in Daniel B. Wallace and M. James Sawyer (eds.), *Who's Afraid of the Holy Spirit? An Investigation into the Ministry of the Spirit of God Today* (Biblical Studies Press, 2005), pp. 15–36, specifically pp. 16–27, used with permission from http://bible.org. Some of the same material reappears here in exactly the same form; other portions are only summarized, while still others are rewritten, reworked, expanded or supplemented. The previous article includes a great deal more about the links between the OT and the NT, while the present one affords an opportunity to focus more intently and in more depth on the details of the Hebrew OT alone.

as 'Holy Spirit' (i.e. the noun *pneuma*, 'Spirit', followed by the adjective *hagion*, 'Holy').

The first occurrence is in Psalm 51:11(13), when David prays in penitence to the Lord, 'Do not cast me from your presence or take your *Holy Spirit* from me' (italics mine).[2] Recall that when Samuel anointed David to be the next king over Israel in place of Saul, 'the Spirit of the LORD came mightily upon David from that day forward', and 'the Spirit of the LORD departed from Saul, and an evil spirit from the LORD terrorized him' (1 Sam. 16:13–14 NASB). Then we read that David himself was the one called to play music for Saul so that 'Saul would be refreshed and be well, and the evil spirit would depart from him' (v. 23). In Psalm 51 David was terrified that, because of his sin, the Lord would take his Holy Spirit from him as he had done with Saul, and perhaps that he himself would be terrified by an 'evil' spirit from the Lord.[3] The term *rā'â* in Hebrew can mean 'evil', but it can also mean 'troubling, difficult'. Here we are talking about a 'spirit' from the Lord that 'troubled' or 'terrified' Saul, not a morally 'evil' spirit (cf. e.g. Judg. 9:23; 1 Kgs 22:19–23).

The two other occurrences of 'Holy Spirit' in the OT occur in Isaiah 63:10 and 11, where the Lord refers to the Israelites as those who had 'rebelled and grieved his *Holy Spirit*' – that is, the Lord 'who set his *Holy Spirit* among them'. Isaiah 63:14 then refers back to the 'Holy Spirit' in verses 10–11 as 'the Spirit of the LORD', who had given them rest in the days of old. The latter expression and its interchangeable counterpart 'the Spirit of God' (see e.g. 1 Sam. 10:6 with 10:10) occur approximately 94 times in the Hebrew Bible;[4] that is,

---

2. All quotations in this article will be from the NIV unless otherwise indicated.
3. See Daniel Estes' paper in this volume for a different view of this passage.
4. The statistics used here are taken from Francis Brown, S. R. Driver and Charles A. Briggs, *Hebrew and English Lexicon of the Old Testament* (London: Oxford University Press, 1906), pp. 924–926; and Abraham Even-Shoshan, *A New Concordance of the Bible* (Jerusalem: Kiryat Sefer Publishing House, 1989), pp. 1063–1066. For helpful surveys of the usage of 'spirit' in the OT, see e.g. Benjamin Breckinridge Warfield, 'The Spirit of God in the Old Testament', in Samuel G. Craig (ed.), *Biblical and Theological Studies* (Philadelphia: The Presbyterian and Reformed Publishing Company, 1952), pp. 149–156; Leon J. Wood, *The Holy Spirit in the Old Testament* (Grand Rapids: Zondervan, 1976), pp. 16–22, 64–77; Gary Fredricks, 'Rethinking the Role of the Holy Spirit in the Lives of Old Testament Believers', *TJ* 9 NS (1988), pp. 81–84; and especially M. V. Van Pelt, W. C. Kaiser, Jr and D. I. Block, 'רוּחַ, *rûaḥ*', in *NIDOTTE*, 3.1076–1077.

if one includes instances where 'the [my, your, his] Spirit' clearly refers to 'the Spirit of the LORD/God' in the context.

Of course, in the Jewish tradition the Holy Spirit referred to in the Hebrew Bible is not taken to be the third person of the Trinity. Therefore, they render *rûaḥ* in such passages as 'spirit', not capitalized. See, for example, the Tanakh translation of the Jewish Publication Society (1985), which renders Psalm 51:13 'Your holy spirit' and Isaiah 63:10–11 'His holy spirit'. According to the rabbis, although the 'spirit of God' is of divine origin, this does not mean that there is a 'Holy Spirit' as a divine person. On the contrary, the holy spirit is a mode of the one and only God's self-expression in word and action. It should be noted, however, that this translation issue is not limited to exclusively Jewish translations since, for example, the NRSV also renders these passages with 'holy spirit' (Ps. 51:11; Isa. 63:10–11).[5]

This chapter will focus on the basic underlying meaning and usage of the main term for 'spirit' in the OT (Hebrew *rûaḥ*), and its implications as they are drawn out in certain specific passages of Scripture. Any meaningful understanding of the Holy Spirit of God in the Bible will need to begin here, and the purpose of this chapter is to capture its importance for the present volume.

Spirit, wind, and breath

To begin with, out of the 378 occurrences of the term 'spirit' (*rûaḥ*) in the OT, it actually means 'wind' or 'breath', not 'spirit', about 140 times (the exact number depends on how one reads certain passages). Thus almost 40% of the time *rûaḥ* refers to the literal movement of air in wind or breath. Sometimes it refers to the wind(s) of nature. For example, in Elijah's confrontation with Ahab, 'In a little while the sky grew black with clouds and wind [*rûaḥ*], and there was a heavy shower' (1 Kgs 18:45, NASB). Psalm 1:4 talks about the wicked being 'like chaff that the wind [*rûaḥ*] blows away'. Ecclesiastes 1:14 describes the futility of so much that we pursue in life as 'chasing after the wind'. Jeremiah 49:36 refers to 'the four winds from the four quarters of the heavens'. These winds are under the control of God and sometimes a means through which he acts in the world. For example, at the turning point in the

5. For an explanation of the Jewish view from a Jewish perspective, see Israel Abrahams, 'God in the Bible', in Cecil Roth (ed.), *Encyclopedia Judaica* (Jerusalem: Keter Publishing House, 1971), 7.643.

flood story, we hear that the Lord 'sent a wind over the earth, and the waters receded' (probably meaning instead that 'the waters calmed' as a result of God's *rûaḥ*, 'wind', moving over them).[6] God brought a locust plague on the Egyptians by making 'an east wind blow across the land' (Exod. 10:13), and in Numbers 11:31, 'a wind went out from the LORD and drove quail in from the sea'.

In some passages the winds are referred to metaphorically as God's 'breath'. In Exodus 15:8, for example, at the crossing of the Reed Sea, God made the way through: 'By the blast [lit. 'wind', *rûaḥ*] of your nostrils the waters piled up' (cf. Exod. 14:21). Similarly, *rûaḥ* sometimes refers to the 'breathing' of air-breathing animate beings, mankind and animal. See, for example, Genesis 2:7, 'the LORD God formed the man from the dust [*ʿāpār*] of the ground and breathed into his nostrils the breath [*nĕšāmâ*] of life [*ḥayyîm*]', and Genesis 7:22b, where all mankind and land animals 'in whose nostrils was the breath [*nĕšāmâ*] of the spirit [*rûaḥ*] of life [*ḥayyîm*], died' (NASB; except those on the ark, of course; cf. 7:15, 'all flesh in which was the breath [*rûaḥ*] of life'). Genesis 2:7 refers only to man and links 'breath' (*nĕšāmâ*) to 'life', but the latter verses refer to both man and air-breathing land animals and, above all, links 'breath' to 'spirit' (*rûaḥ*) and then to animate 'life'.

Moreover, according to Ecclesiastes 3:19–21, both animals and people 'have the same breath [or 'spirit', *rûaḥ*]' (v. 19), and 'Who knows if the spirit [or 'breath', *rûaḥ*] of man rises upward and if the spirit of the animal goes down into the earth?' (v. 21). By and large, the English versions translate *rûaḥ* as 'breath' in verse 19, but, for example, NIV and NRSV switch to 'spirit' in verse 21, while NASB retains 'breath'. Whatever one makes of the theology in this passage (i.e. the fate of people versus animals), the point is that we have trouble with this in the English versions precisely because in our language we do not see the natural link between 'wind/breath' and 'spirit' in the same way and to the same degree as the ancients did when they used the term *rûaḥ*.

---

6. See now the full treatment of this passage in Andrew Sargent, 'Wind, Water, and Battle Imagery in Genesis 8:1–3' (PhD dissertation, Trinity Evangelical Divinity School, 2010), abstract p. v, where he concludes: 'Though the waters are merely waters, no more than material tools in YHWH's cleansing of the earth, Gen. 8:1–3 describes, metaphorically, the turning point in YHWH's battle against the waters of the flood, describing their humbling defeat before the divine *rûaḥ*, the cutting off of their life, and their scattering as YHWH reclaims the dry ground conquered by the waters in his re-creation of the inhabitable world with a new Adam and a new society based on divine law.'

This, in fact, is fundamental to our understanding of 'spirit', including the Holy Spirit, in the Hebrew Bible. Wind, breath and spirit are essential and primal categories of life – animal, human and divine life. The connection between 'wind' and 'breath' seems natural to us even today and appears, for example, in our common expression for having the 'wind [actually the 'breath'] knocked out' of a person, through a physical blow or fall, or in the term 'winded' for a runner who is 'out of breath'. The link between 'wind/breath' as it relates to 'spirit', however, is not so transparent to us. The connection to the Greek *pneuma* is there for us in such words as '*pneum*onia', and even for the English 'spirit' we have words like 'a*spir*ate' and 'a*spir*ator' (cf. also 'aspiration', etc.), but it is not explicit to us on the surface of our language as it is in the Bible. The linguistic data suggests that *in the Bible the link between 'wind' and 'breath' clearly extends also to 'spirit'*. In other words, it is easy for us to see the connection between wind and breath simply by reference to the 'movement of air' that they have in common, but in the Hebrew Bible both wind and breath are just as closely related to 'spirit', because the same term is used for all three. This is important for understanding how 'spirit' is conceived of, whether the spirit of a human person or the Spirit of God.

Wind, breath and the nature of the human spirit

Hebrew *rûaḥ* is often used for elements of the human 'spirit' in Scripture (c. 120 times). As such, it sometimes refers to vitality of life. For example, in Genesis 45:27, 'the spirit of their father Jacob revived [lit. 'became alive']' when he learned that Joseph was still alive. Conversely, when the Amorites and Canaanites heard that the Lord had dried up the Jordan for the Israelites to cross over, 'their hearts failed, and there was no longer any spirit in them' (Josh. 5:1 NRSV; cf. 1 Kgs 10:5). At other times it describes moral and spiritual character, whether positive as in Isaiah 26:9, 'in the morning my spirit longs for you' (cf. Mal. 2:16), or negative as in Isaiah 29:24, 'Those who are wayward in spirit will gain understanding' (cf. Ezek. 13:3). At other times it relates to capacities of mind and will, as in Exodus 28:3, 'the skillful persons whom I have endowed with the spirit of wisdom' (NASB; cf. also Job 20:3, lit. 'the spirit of my understanding'; and Pss 51:12[10], 14[12]; 77:4[6]), or to various dispositions or states of the human person and personality, as in Numbers 5:14, 'and if feelings [lit. 'a *rûaḥ*'] of jealousy come over her husband'. Compare with the latter also, for example, (1) Judges 8:3, 'their resentment [*rûaḥ*] against him subsided' (i.e. 'spirit' = anger, resentment); (2) Proverbs 16:18–19, 'Pride goes before destruction, a haughty spirit before a fall. Better to be lowly in spirit and among the oppressed than to share plunder with the proud' (lit. 'high spirit' = prideful and 'low of spirit' = humble, respectively); (3) Proverbs 17:22, 'A cheerful heart is good medicine, but a crushed spirit dries up the bones' (i.e. 'a crushed spirit' = discouraged, depressed); and (4) Ecclesiastes 7:8, 'patience is better than pride' (i.e. 'long of spirit' = patient), or Proverbs 14:29, 'a quick-tempered man displays folly' (lit. 'short of spirit' = quick-tempered).

Towards the end of Ecclesiastes, at the climax and conclusion of the book, we find the same term used for the immaterial component of a person as opposed to the material in terms that recall Genesis 2:7 (cited above): when a person dies, 'the dust' [*ʿāpār*] returns to the ground it came from, and the spirit [*rûaḥ*] returns to God who gave it' (Eccl. 12:7; cf. also Ps. 146:4; Isa. 42:5). Similarly, but in a context where we once again see the close connection between 'spirit' (*rûaḥ*) and 'breath' (*nĕšāmâ*), Elihu says, 'If it were his [God's] intention and he withdrew his spirit and breath, all mankind would perish together and man would return to the dust' (Job 34:14–15). God is the one 'who forms the spirit of man within him' (Zech. 12:1), so it naturally returns to him at death.

When referring to the human spirit, therefore, *rûaḥ* can refer either to an immaterial element of the human person or personality, or to the whole of the immaterial person. On at least one occasion David expressed his trust in God in the midst of life-threatening circumstances by exclaiming, 'Into your hands I commit *my spirit* [*rûaḥ*]; redeem me, O LORD, the God of truth' (Ps. 31:6[5], italics mine). David was entrusting his spirit to God for deliverance from death. Jesus drew upon this expression at the point of death on the cross, entrusting his spirit to God in death, 'Father, into your hands I commit *my spirit*' (*pneuma*, Luke 23:46, italics mine).[7] Here Jesus, like David before him, was referring to his human spirit (not the Holy Spirit), so we have the OT concept of the 'human spirit' coming into the NT even in regard to the Son of God himself. Jesus was as fully human as he was divine. We cannot pursue this NT discussion any further here, but even in the OT itself the extension of wind and breath to the Spirit of God, in fact, is made explicit in certain passages. We shall say more about this below. Before turning to that discussion, however, there is one particular implication of the discussion so far that requires special attention.

As noted above, the expression 'the Spirit of God/the LORD' and its

---

7. See Peter C. Craigie, *Psalms 1 – 50*, WBC, 19 (Waco: Word Books, 1983), pp. 262–263, for a brief but very helpful explanation of the relationship between the intent of this verse in Ps. 31 and Jesus' quotation from it on the cross.

pronominal equivalents (e.g. 'my Spirit') occur many times in the Hebrew Bible, even though 'Holy Spirit' occurs only three times. Also, as noted, there are many who argue that the term 'spirit' should not be capitalized in the OT as if it teaches that there was a distinct divine person in view when this terminology was used. There is a serious dispute over the interpretation of the Hebrew Bible in this regard. In this debate one of the facts that need to be taken into consideration is that both God and man have a spirit in the OT. What I am suggesting here is that, at least on one level, it seems most natural that since 'the spirit of man' fits his nature as human, similarly 'the Spirit of God' fits God's nature as divine. When we are talking about the Spirit of God, therefore, we are by nature talking about divinity, so 'Spirit' should be capitalized in such expressions. Thus, on certain points at least, we can reason back by analogy from a biblical understanding of the human person as a way of approach to a good biblical understanding of the person of God, especially in terms of the relationship between God and the 'Spirit' of God. This takes us some distance towards the notion of the Spirit of God/the Lord or Holy Spirit as a divine person in the OT, although it does not take us all the way.

Wind, spirit, and the nature of the Spirit of God

If one of the explicitly biblical perspectives from which to approach an understanding of the Holy Spirit of God is through comparison and contrast with the human spirit of people, then another is through the nature and effects of 'wind'. We have already referred to several passages in the OT where *rûaḥ* means 'wind'. Conceptually, 'wind' is closely related to 'breath', since they both involve the movement of air, and both of them are closely related to 'spirit', because if a person stops 'breathing' their life 'expires' and the person's body gives up their 'spirit'. In turn, 'spirit' also sometimes refers to that which constitutes the unique nature of a particular person – their individual personal vitality and personality, character, dispositions and so forth. In the latter sense, the term also applies to the Spirit of God. I am not suggesting that Hebrew *rûaḥ* always means all these things, but that it can potentially mean any of them.

The close connection between 'wind' and 'spirit' comes to the forefront immediately at the beginning of the Bible.[8] In Genesis 1:2b we read that 'the Spirit of God [*rûaḥ ʾĕlōhîm*] was moving over the surface of the waters' (NASB)

8. See also Robert Hubbard's paper in this volume.

before the beginning of God's creative words in verse 3. Some have treated *ʾĕlōhîm* here as an adjective (i.e. its superlative use) meaning 'mighty' or 'terrible', so that the whole expression means 'a mighty wind' or 'a terrible storm'. However, there is no other instance in the OT where *rûaḥ ʾĕlōhîm* or any of its equivalents means anything other than 'the Spirit of God/the LORD' or 'the wind of God/the LORD'. Moreover, the adjectival use of *ʾĕlōhîm* is foreign to this chapter where the term is used so many times to mean 'God' and, in fact, serves as the primary focus throughout the chapter both conceptually and structurally. Recall the repeated formula 'And God said. . .' beginning in verse 3 and running through the whole chapter as the common introduction to each creative movement of God.

The NRSV translates 'a wind from God swept over. . .' rather than the NASB 'the Spirit of God was moving over. . .' (NIV has 'the Spirit of God was hovering over. . .'), reflecting both the Ancient Near Eastern background in which cosmologies sometimes include wind in the creative process, and some translations and discussions in the history of interpretation of Genesis 1:2.[9] The rendering 'wind of God' finds support in Genesis 8:1b where, after the waters of the flood had covered the earth, God 'sent a wind over the earth, and the waters receded' (NIV; probably better, 'the waters became calm'; see the remarks on this passage above). The next two verses refer specifically to the closing up of the flood waters that had burst up from below the ground and the end of the rain from above, and then the actual receding of the flood waters (vv. 2–3).

The context is similar to Genesis 1:2 where waters are also covering the earth and God causes them to recede in the following verses so that the dry ground might appear (later, on the third day of creation). Consider also the watery context in Exodus 14:21–22, 29 where the Lord enabled Israel to cross

---

9. From ancient times until today there has been an ongoing dispute among translators and scholars over the proper interpretation of *rûaḥ ʾĕlōhîm* in this verse. See the helpful review of the debate in Claus Westermann, *Genesis 1 – 11: A Commentary*, trans. John J. Scullion (Minneapolis: Augsburg, 1984), pp. 106–108. He translates 'God's wind was moving to and fro. . .' (p. 76). For a helpful discussion favouring 'the Spirit of God', see Edward J. Young, 'The Interpretation of Genesis 1:2', *WTJ* 23 (1960–1), pp. 174–178. See also James K. Hoffmeier, 'Some Thoughts on Genesis 1 & 2 and Egyptian Cosmology', *JANES* 15 (1983), p. 44, and the literature cited there favouring 'the wind of God'. For mediating somewhere between the two positions, see Kenneth A. Matthews, *Genesis 1 – 11:26*, NAC, 1A (Nashville: Broadman & Holman, 1996), pp. 134–136.

the Reed Sea on dry ground by sending a strong east 'wind' (*rûaḥ*) to drive the waters back. The poetic account in Exodus 15 refers to this wind as a 'blast' (*rûaḥ*) from the Lord's nostrils that piled up the waters (v. 8), and then he 'blew' again with his 'breath' (*rûaḥ*) to drown the Egyptian army with the same waters (v. 10). There are also a few instances in which the expression 'the *rûaḥ* of the LORD' refers to his 'breath' as 'wind'. See, for example, 'The grass withers and the flowers fall, because the breath [*rûaḥ*] of the LORD blows on them. Surely the people are grass' (Isa. 40:7).

Moreover, the next occurrence of *rûaḥ* in the canon after Genesis 1:2 is 3:8 in reference to the Lord God 'walking in the garden in the cool [lit. 'to the wind'] of the day'. Some would render this differently: 'Then the man and his wife heard the thunder [*qôl*] of Yahweh God going back and forth [*mithallēk*] in the garden in the wind of the storm [*lĕrûaḥ hayyôm*], and they hid from Yahweh God among the trees of the garden.'[10] The word *yôm* usually means 'day', but there are a few instances in the Hebrew Bible where it appears to mean 'storm' (e.g. Zeph. 2:2), and also has support from certain Ancient Near Eastern background sources. This is perhaps a possible rendering in Genesis 3:8, but the man's response to the Lord's question of why he was hiding from him in the garden has to do with the fear of being naked, not with a frightening storm. Moreover, if God was coming in such an intentionally frightful way, why would he himself raise the question of why the man was afraid in the first place? In either case, the term *rûaḥ* most certainly refers to a 'breeze' or 'wind' of some sort in this passage. A variation of this view of Genesis 1:2 is to render the last clause 'the Wind of God hovered' (note the capital W) and treat it as 'a concrete and vivid image of the Spirit of God'.[11] As I see it, the main point is that even if 'wind of God' were to be the best English rendering in Genesis 1:2, which is still very much in doubt, the expression still indicates that God was actively present in the primeval unformed and unfilled, deep and dark, watery abyss into which he spoke his creative words beginning in Genesis 1:3. So there is much to commend the translation 'wind' for *rûaḥ* in Genesis 1:2.

On the other hand, we also need to take seriously the fact that the vast bulk of occurrences of 'the *rûaḥ* of the LORD/God' in the OT refer to God's

---

10. Jeffrey J. Niehaus, *God at Sinai: Covenant and Theophany in the Bible and Ancient Near East* (Grand Rapids: Zondervan, 1995), pp. 155–159; the translation given here is on p. 159.

11. See e.g. Gordon Wenham, *Genesis 1 – 15*, WBC, 1 (Waco: Word Books, 1987), pp. 2, 16–17.

'Spirit' understood in a way that corresponds to the human 'spirit' in people (see the reflections on this biblical analogy in the previous section above). Consider, for example, the third occurrence of *rûaḥ* in the canon (after Gen. 1:2 and 3:8), where the Lord says, 'My Spirit will not contend with man for ever' (Gen. 6:3). 'Wind' would make no sense as an English rendering for *rûaḥ* in this context, and there are many like it. This must be taken into consideration in the translation and interpretation of Genesis 1:2. It is especially significant that this is the third and last of the three clauses in Genesis 1:2 describing the condition of the earth before God's repeated pronouncement of creative words beginning immediately in verse 3. Some have countered that since 'the Spirit of God' does not appear anywhere else in this chapter, translating 'the wind of God' suits the focus on forces of nature throughout the chapter. Translating 'the Spirit of God', however, suits the focus on God 'speaking' (i.e. 'breathing out' his pronouncements) throughout the chapter. In other words, the latter rendering would provide a more natural lead into the 'And God said. . .' sequence of the chapter, beginning immediately after this clause.

In the end it seems to me that our problem in handling Genesis 1:2 arises in the first place because we tend to think that 'wind' and 'Spirit' are mutually exclusive. In my opinion, there is no reason why *rûaḥ* in Genesis 1:2 cannot be a reflection of the power of God present and ready to work through 'wind' in this watery environment (cf. Gen. 8:1; Exod. 14:21–22; 15:8–10, cited above) as well as the work of the 'Spirit' of God in shaping the creation through pronouncements (Gen. 1:3ff.), both at the same time (i.e. an instance of *double entendre*). As I have already explained and illustrated above, there is a very close connection between *rûaḥ* as 'wind/breath' (i.e. the movement of air) and *rûaḥ* as (human) 'spirit' or 'Spirit' of God in the Hebrew Bible.[12] In this regard, one might also consider Psalm 33:6, 'By the word of the LORD were the heavens made, their starry host by the breath [*rûaḥ*] of his mouth' (cf. also Pss 147:18; 104:29–30 in NRSV). The Lord's creative word comes out of his mouth as 'breath', and the English versions vary in how they translate some of these passages because some combination of these meanings might be valid (i.e. wind, breath or spirit/Spirit), not necessarily just one of the possible renderings.

---

12. In my opinion, Meredith Kline's proposal that 'the "Spirit of God" in the creation record [referring to Gen. 1:2] is surely to be understood as a designation for the theophanic Glory-cloud' of the exodus from Egypt has little to commend it; see Meredith Kline, *Images of the Spirit* (Grand Rapids: Baker, 1980), p. 15.

The OT passage in which this relationship between 'wind' and the 'Spirit of God' stands out most clearly is Ezekiel 36 – 37. The well-known vision of the valley of dry bones in Ezekiel 37:1–14 begins with 'the Spirit of the LORD' transporting the prophet to the valley (v. 1).[13] Of course, the dry bones represent the house of Israel as a whole, and the real question was whether or not there was any hope for Israel in the future (v. 11). A valley of dry bones suggests not, but God has something more to say about that. As the vision goes on, God tells Ezekiel to prophesy that God 'will make breath [*rûaḥ*] enter' them so that they 'will come to life' (v. 5). Ezekiel prophesies as he has been instructed and the bones rattle, come together, and receive from the Lord flesh and life-giving 'breath' (*rûaḥ*) from 'the four winds' (i.e. the four *rûaḥ*, vv. 7–10). Note the link between 'breath' and 'wind' here. Finally, in the interpretation of this vision in verses 11–14, God says that he will bring the people of Israel back to the land (i.e. out of their graves, vv. 12–13) in accord with the promise that 'I will put *my* Spirit [*rûaḥ*] in you and you will live' (v. 14). A similar correspondence appears in a pivotal passage in the previous chapter. According to Ezekiel 36:26–27, 'I will give you a new heart and put a new spirit [*rûaḥ*] in you; I will remove from you your heart of stone and give you a heart of flesh. And I will put *my* Spirit [*rûaḥ*] in you and move you to follow my decrees and be careful to keep my laws.' In both instances the first-person pronoun 'my', of course, refers to the Lord himself.

So in Ezekiel 37 the 'Spirit' of God is identified with the 'breath' and the four 'winds' of the vision. The oracle begins with 'the Spirit of the LORD' transporting the prophet to the valley of dry bones and ends with God's 'Spirit' reviving the people (i.e. the dry bones) to bring them back from exile (i.e. the valley of dry bones) into the land of Israel. The close connection here between the four 'winds' and the 'breath' that gives life to the dry bones makes one wonder about the interpretation of the famous theophany in Ezekiel 1. Perhaps there is a similar link between the 'windstorm [*rûaḥ sĕʿārâ*] coming out of the north' in Ezekiel 1:4, 'the spirit' of the living creatures in 1:12 and 'the spirit of the living beings' (probably better rendered 'the spirit of life') that animated the wheels in 1:20.[14]

---

13. See the especially helpful treatment of Ezek. 37:1–14 in Michael V. Fox, 'The Rhetoric of Ezekiel's Vision of the Valley of the Bones', *HUCA* 51 (1980), pp. 1–15.

14. See the discussion in Daniel I. Block, 'The Prophet of the Spirit: The Use of *RWH* in the book of Ezekiel', *JETS* 32 (1989), pp. 36–38; and idem, *The Book of Ezekiel: Chapters 1 – 24*, NICOT (Grand Rapids: Eerdmans, 1997), p. 101.

Conclusion

As others have noted, wind, breath and spirit, including both the spirit of a human person and the Spirit of God, are (generally) made evident only by their effects.[15] They are not things that can be seen. Only the evidences and effects of them can be observed with the naked eye (e.g. the movement of the trees caused by the wind). Their effects are, therefore, fundamental to understanding them and, in turn, the Spirit of God in the OT. The focus of this chapter has been on these three closely related dimensions of the term *rûaḥ* as it is used in the OT, whether alone or in combination with other words. Some passages actually use *rûaḥ* in a combination of ways that show the nature of what we should mean when we say 'spirit' or 'Spirit' in English.

As 'wind', *rûaḥ* is a source of power. It moves things, even dry bones so that they rattle (Ezek. 37:7). But in the same instance, as 'breath', *rûaḥ* is a source of life, animated physical life (Ezek. 37:5–6, 8–10). Moreover, in the same context, as a human 'spirit', *rûaḥ* can be a source of personal human life beyond just the physical, even a certain kind of quality of life (Ezek. 36:26; note how this relates to the heart of flesh versus the heart of stone). Finally, again in the same passage, as the divine 'Spirit', *rûaḥ* is a source of life lived with God's Spirit in the human person (i.e. in the human 'spirit', Ezek. 37:14; 36:27). We need to take seriously these meanings of *rûaḥ*, used in such an extended play on words within this and other passages, for understanding how the human 'spirit' and divine 'Spirit' actually work together in, among, around and through people.

Wind is a mysterious and powerful force. We cannot always predict what it is going to do, and it is not under our control. The same is true of the Spirit (wind) of God. We cannot always predict what the Spirit is going to do, and he is not under our control even if what he is going to do has been revealed to us. He is God. We are not. So yes, there is indeed something mystical about all this in a proper biblical sense. But although we cannot completely understand and certainly cannot control the Holy Spirit, we can draw upon his power. There is energy here for God's powerful and empowering work in, amidst and through people and nature. We must not forget, however, that like the wind, this power is available and we can make use of it, but we cannot make or send the wind. Only God can.

---

15. See Daniel I. Block, 'Empowered by the Spirit of God: The Holy Spirit in the Historiographic Writings of the Old Testament', *SBJT* 1 (1997), p. 54, referring to a work by R. Koch.

We might use the analogy of a sailboat. Wind is what drives it along, as long as the sails are up. Yes, we can put up the sails, but only God can make the wind blow. That is, we are dependent on the Spirit of God to empower and guide us on the path that he has called us to walk. In fact, we could take this analogy further. God has long revealed much to his people about what it means to 'put up the sails' in their lives. The Scriptures, for example, have instructed his people to meditate on the law of the Lord day and night (Josh. 1:8; Ps. 1:2), to pray and worship (see the Psalms overall), and so on. We could even talk about these practices as the way the human spirit 'breathes' in and out (inhaling and exhaling) the 'breath' of the Spirit of God.

2. THE ANCIENT NEAR EASTERN BACKGROUND OF THE SPIRIT OF THE LORD IN THE OLD TESTAMENT[1]

John H. Walton

Since the advent of comparative studies, few have argued for an Ancient Near Eastern background for the spirit of the Lord (SOL) concept in the OT. We can easily identify two good reasons for this. First, comparative investigation generally begins with lexical overlap. However, any investigation using this method will quickly meet a dead end, as there is neither Akkadian nor Egyptian use of the collocation 'spirit of [divine name]' to indicate empowerment by deity. Second, since Yahweh is so different from Ancient Near Eastern deities, superficial parallels quickly diverge into significant differences.

I have nothing new to offer on those two fronts. Nevertheless, if we look at the activity of the SOL in the OT, we will find a distinct familiarity when read in light of other Ancient Near Eastern literature; it is this familiarity that I would like to explore. I will contend that the activity of the SOL in the OT falls into categories quite well known in the ancient world, though lexical expressions differ. Said another way, an Egyptian or a Babylonian from the ancient world reading or hearing the book of Judges, Samuel or Ezekiel would not be baffled about the SOL. They would immediately associate it with their own understanding of the way that their gods worked. My study will examine

1. I am grateful for the aid of my student assistants, Rahel Schafer (research) and Ashley Edewaard (editing).

some of the profiles of divine activity in the ancient world that overlap the activity of the SOL in the OT. Using a heuristic approach, then, I propose examining the role of the SOL in the OT, then looking at divine endowment in the same categories in the Ancient Near East.

Rûaḥ

Two obstacles confound our attempts to clarify the terminology: first, the lexical divide between two possible English translations, 'wind' and 'spirit'. Because Hebrew uses the same word for the English concepts of 'wind' (= meteorological phenomena) and 'spirit' (= supernatural manifestation), one might surmise that these two concepts were less distinct in Israelite thinking than they are to us. The second obstacle arises from the ontological divide between cultures – does 'spirit' in the ancient world mean the same thing as it does in contemporary theology, psychology and anthropology? These both complicate our exegesis and contribute to the controversy surrounding the identification of the SOL. How is a person's spirit different from the person? Or is it the essence of the person? Why did the OT authors feel the need to talk about the SOL rather than just saying 'the Lord'? Such obstacles may be insurmountable, but what resolution there might be must begin within the synchronic textual information available to us.

In this study we are most interested in the divine spirit, usually expressed as the 'spirit of Yahweh' or the 'spirit of Elohim'. W. Hildebrandt gives the statistics concerning lexical occurrences:

- 'spirit of God', 15 times, plus five more in Aramaic;
- 'spirit of the Lord', 27 times;
- references to God's spirit not using these exact phrases, 60 times.[2]

He concludes that the *rûaḥ* is the 'active, creative, and vital presence of God'.[3]

> When Israel thought about the source of the forces that they saw affecting and influencing humankind in creation and in nature, they often pointed to the activity of the *rûaḥ*. This was the way Israel answered the question of how God brought about

---

2. See W. Hildebrandt, *An Old Testament Theology of the Spirit of God* (Peabody: Hendrickson, 1995), p. 18.
3. Ibid., p. 42.

> creation. It was also the way they understood their experience of deliverance, salvation, guidance, and the presence of God. When experiencing various leadership role models in their midst, they attributed many of the externally observable manifestations to the *rûaḥ*, whose internal influence they noted in the lives of various leaders.[4]

This is acceptable at least as a working hypothesis and will provide a basis for examining each of the categories of the spirit's activity.

Creation

Old Testament creation

Interpreters have struggled to identify the role of the spirit of God in Genesis 1. Theologians have been quick to equate the spirit here with the Holy Spirit, explaining the putative anachronism as foreshadowing, while scholars of Ancient Near Eastern literature have been inclined to translate the phrase as 'wind of God' and see it as a feature of the chaotic landscape.

The activity of the *rûaḥ* is explicitly described only by the little-attested verb *meraḥepet*. The NIV translation, 'hovering', is fairly common, not because it enjoys abundant supporting evidence, but because there is insufficient evidence to suggest other plausible alternatives.[5] As a result, interpreters have frequently looked outside Hebrew to related (cognate) languages for lexical help. When we investigate the cognates of the root Hebrew uses here, we discover that Syriac uses the same root for brooding protectively over a nest or incubating the eggs.[6] Ugaritic uses the same root to speak of vultures circling overhead, apparently waiting to devour the scraps of a feast.[7] As we consider a translation that can account for both Hebrew and Ugaritic usage and accom-

---

4. Ibid., p. 18.
5. This form of the verb (piel) occurs in only one other passage (Deut. 32:11). There it refers to the behaviour of a mother bird with regard to her young. It is parallel to stirring up its nest.
6. *HALOT* 3:1219–1220.
7. *Tale of Aqhat*, see *ANET*^{3}, 152 (iv: 20–21). Ugaritic is more likely to be helpful than the Syriac, in that both the language and the literatures are closer to the time of the biblical narrative. Since the root is also used to describe bird behaviour in Ugaritic, there is a good chance that Ugaritic usage and Hebrew usage had not developed in disparate ways. Nevertheless, even the Ugaritic uses are too few and unclear to allow for precise nuancing.

modate both biblical contexts, we might note that the verb in all contexts expresses a state of preparedness. Whether birds are brooding or hovering, they are preparing for what is to take place next. Significantly, in contrast, nothing in this verb could be associated with chaos.

Scholars readily recognize wind as a motif in chaos scenes from both the Ancient Near East and the Bible. In the Babylonian Epic *Enuma Elish*, the sky god Anu creates the four winds that stir up the deep and its goddess, Tiamat.[8] This is a disruptive wind bringing unrest. The same phenomena can be seen in Daniel's vision of the four beasts, where 'the four winds of heaven [were] churning up the great sea' (7:2) and disturbing the beasts in the sea.[9] In the Exodus narrative (14:21; 15:8), God uses the wind to master the waters.[10]

C. Westermann, representing those who translate 'wind', has pointed out that the three phrases of Genesis 1:2 should all be considered descriptions of the chaotic state.[11] The close parallelism of the second and third clauses would support this interpretation.[12] The problem with this suggestion occurs on the semantic level: all of the other uses of the phrase *rûaḥ ʾĕlōhîm* in the OT are translated 'spirit of God' rather than supernatural wind.[13] The fact that the four winds are part of a chaotic landscape in Akkadian literature is not as

---

8. *Enuma Elish* I:105–110.
9. Unless indicated otherwise, Scripture quotations in this article are taken from the NIV.
10. In the Exodus narrative the wind is primarily associated with the breath of God. The connection of *rûaḥ* as the breath of God in creation can be made most easily through Ps. 33:6. For fuller discussion, see Hildebrandt, *Spirit of God*, pp. 41–42.
11. C. Westermann, *Genesis 1 – 11* (Minneapolis: Augsburg, 1984), p. 106.
12. Darkness/wind-spirit; darkness is over the surface (*ʿal pĕnê*) of the watery deep (*tĕhôm*), and the wind-spirit is over the surface (*ʿal pĕnê*) of the waters. Some object to this on the grammatical level in that it would require *ʾĕlōhîm* to be translated as a superlative adjective (e.g. 'mighty' to go along with wind) rather than as a noun ('God' to go along with spirit). It is rare that *ʾĕlōhîm* is used as an adjective, but not unattested (cf. Gen. 23:6, where NIV translates it 'mighty').
13. This is the basis on which evangelical interpreters typically reject 'mighty wind'. See J. Sailhamer, 'Genesis', *EBC*, vol. 2 (Grand Rapids: Zondervan, 1990); K. Mathews, *Genesis 1 – 11:26*, NAC (Nashville: Broadman and Holman, 1996); A. Ross, *Creation and Blessing* (Grand Rapids: Baker, 1988); V. Hamilton, *The Book of Genesis: Chapters 1 – 17*, NICOT (Grand Rapids: Eerdmans, 1990); and G. Wenham, *Genesis 1 – 15*, WBC (Waco: Word, 1994).

significant when we notice that in the chaos scenes the winds are typically acting on something (e.g. stirring up the waters). The winds are not personified, but they work on the personified waters. In the Hebrew text the waters are not personified, though the spirit may be. We should also note that in Akkadian literature the wind is not part of a pre-creation state as it is in Genesis,[14] and in Genesis the *rûaḥ* is not used to roil the waters into aggressive action.

More information from both the OT and the Ancient Near East confirms that the *rûaḥ* is related to the presence of the deity preparing to participate in creation. In the OT we find that, though the spirit is not mentioned in Genesis 1 after verse 2, other passages suggest that the spirit continues to act throughout the chapter. Mark Smith has recently elaborated on this point, though earlier scholars such as Wilf Hildebrandt had also presented the data.[15] Hildebrandt concludes his investigation, saying:

> It is evident that the *rûaḥ ʾelohim* is not only superintending the work of creation but in fact brings creation about through the word. The passage is emphasizing the actual powerful presence of God, who brings the spoken work into reality by the Spirit. Thus, the Spirit and the word work together to present how the one God is responsible for all that is seen in the physical universe.[16]

To summarize the evidence for the above conclusion:

- Psalm 33:6, 'By the word [*dābār*] of the LORD were the heavens made, their starry host by the breath [*rûaḥ*] of his mouth.' God's creative utterances (evident throughout Gen. 1) are here represented by the 'word' (*dābār*).[17] The parallel use of *rûaḥ* suggests that God speaks through the *rûaḥ*. We see the same connection in a bilingual hymn from

---

14. One Sumerian tradition features a great storm that results in the union of heaven and earth and the creation act begins. The text states that 'The storm raged, lightning flashed: [it was] heaven [AN] who spoke with earth [KI].' See R. Clifford, *Creation Accounts in the Ancient Near East and in the Bible* (Washington DC: Catholic Biblical Association, 1994), p. 25. In *Enki and World Order*, Enki identifies himself as the firstborn son of An. He also calls himself the 'great storm' (Sumerian: UD GAL). These contribute little to the discussion at hand.
15. M. S. Smith, *The Priestly Vision of Genesis 1* (Minneapolis: Fortress, 2010); Hildebrandt, *Spirit of God*.
16. Hildebrandt, *Spirit of God*, p. 35.
17. Smith, *Priestly Vision*, pp. 54–55; cf. Hildebrandt, *Spirit of God*, p. 41.

the Ancient Near East: 'Your speech is a sweet breath, the life of the lands.'[18]

- Psalm 104:30, 'When you send your Spirit [*rûaḥ*], they are created, and you renew the face of the earth.' Here the *rûaḥ* is the creative force.
- Psalm 147:18, 'He sends his word [*dābār*] and melts them; he stirs up his breezes [*rûaḥ*; note the singular in Hebrew], and the waters flow.' Though this verse refers to the control of nature rather than its initial creation, it still demonstrates that the *rûaḥ* carries out the divine utterances.[19]
- Job 26:13, 'By his breath [*rûaḥ*] the skies became fair; his hand pierced the gliding serpent.' In this verse the *rûaḥ* parallels God's power (*yād*) rather than his utterance, but still in creative activities.
- Isaiah 40:13, 'Who has understood the mind [*rûaḥ*] of the LORD, or instructed him as his counsellor?' This verse immediately follows a description of God's creative activity – measuring the waters and marking off the heavens – with the *rûaḥ* as the active party. Hildebrandt points out that, in this creation context, the author asserts that none gave counsel to the *rûaḥ* in creation (the way that advisors in the divine council worked with Marduk).[20] These observations establish the *rûaḥ* as God's creative presence in creation.

Thus, as Smith indicates, we should equate the *rûaḥ* in Genesis 1 with the divine speech-acts of creation narrated throughout the chapter.[21] *Rûaḥ* in Genesis 1 is the immanent manifestation of God the Creator. It is by the agency of the wind/spirit that he speaks creation into being. The verb *meraḥepet* reflects preparedness for action – waiting for the right moment.[22] Though typically associated with chaos in the Ancient Near East, the winds of Genesis 1 – along with other traditionally chaotic features, such as *tannin* – are presented as elements of the ordered cosmos. In summary we might adapt the well-known phrasing to formulate an OT affirmation: 'In the beginning was the *rûaḥ*, and the *rûaḥ* was from God and the *rûaḥ* was God. All things were

18. *CAD* Š/2, 138b.
19. Note the association in other non-creation passages such as Prov. 1:23.
20. Hildebrandt, *Spirit of God*, p. 40.
21. Smith, *Priestly Vision*, pp. 54–55.
22. This is true of the mother bird over the nest in Deut. 32:11 and of the birds waiting to swoop down on the remains of the banquet in Ugaritic texts. In Gen. 1, the *rûaḥ* awaits the divine dispatch to bring life to creation.

made by him and nothing was made without him. In him was life and that life was the light of men.'[23]

Ancient Near East creation

Now that we have established the nature and function of the spirit of God in Genesis, we may seek out similarities in the Ancient Near East. Some of the most significant connections appear in an Egyptian demotic cosmogony (from the late second century AD), which draws heavily on a variety of earlier sources.[24]

After the Hermopolitan Ogdoad emerges from Ptah, the eight gods coalesce into the single union called Amun. Fragment four, as interpreted by M. Smith, indicates that the four winds merge into one wind, a manifestation of Amun, that then separates the sky from the earth. Smith suggests that the wind also forms or fertilizes the egg, which releases the solar deity, who in turn becomes the creator. In this account, the wind relates to Amun in much the same way that the spirit relates to *ʾĕlōhîm* in Genesis 1:2. The wind and Amun together initiate the most fundamental acts of creation; this role of the wind, though not foreign to the Genesis context, is not explicitly mentioned.

The very late date of this manuscript would usually position it outside the time period relevant for comparative studies. These data could be utilized only if we found enough evidence to assert that this is simply a late copy of traditions that date considerably earlier. Smith indicates that 'a number of Egyptian sources explicitly ascribe this separation to the agency of the wind or a god associated with that element, most prominently Shu'.[25] The Edfu Cosmogony (Ptolemaic, so still late) recounts the creative power of the wind stirring a reed thicket.[26]

---

23. Interestingly parallel to *logos* as 'spirit' and 'word' are parallel in the OT.
24. M. Smith, *On the Primaeval Ocean*, Carlsberg Papyri 5 (CNI 26; Copenhagen: Museum Tusculanum Press, University of Copenhagen, 2002), p. 194. The following several paragraphs are adapted from my larger work, *Genesis as Ancient Cosmology* (Winona Lake: Eisenbrauns, 2011).
25. Smith, *Primaeval Ocean*, p. 59. He cites D. Kurth, *Den Himmel Stützen* (Brussels: Foundation Égyptologique Reine Élisabeth, 1973), pp. 70–76, 78–80. Smith excerpts several of the texts, e.g. the inscription on the propylon of the temple of Khonsu at Karnak that describes Khonsu-Shu as 'the one who elevated the sky with a blast of air from his mouth'.
26. Smith, *Primaeval Ocean*, p. 60.

> A few sources make explicit reference to the wind's ability to create or fertilize eggs. Thus, in an inscription on the propylon of the temple of Montu at Karnak, the Theban nome is called *swḥ.t pr m swḥ*, 'the egg which came forth from the wind'.[27]

Earlier Coffin texts represent the Heliopolitan tradition of the *ba* of Shu, which is exhaled from the nose of Shu and identified as 'exhale-like of form'.[28] Shu's *ba* says, 'my clothes are the wind of life,' and he claims to be the one who stills the sky and silences the earth in preparation for Shu's acts of creation.[29] This preparatory role of the wind/air is also expressed in the formation of the primeval hillock:

> At first calm and motionless, hovering over the sluggish primeval ocean, Nun, invisible as a nullity, it [the air] could at a given moment be set in motion, apparently of itself, could churn up Nun to its depths, so that the mud lying there could condense into solid land and emerge from the flood-waters, first as a 'high-hillock' or an 'Isle of Flames' near Hermopolis.[30]

Smith summarizes the 'wind' elements included in the cosmogony of the Carlsberg Papyri 5 as follows:

> The four winds of the sky merged into a single high wind which brought the universe into existence by separating the sky from the earth and forming or fertilizing an egg from which the sun (= Pshai) emerged. The wind is personified by a being whose name is nowhere preserved.[31]

Smith identifies the personified deity as Amun, who as early as the New Kingdom is referred to as the wind and as the counterpart to the egg, as well as the one who separates earth and sky.[32]

---

27. Ibid., p. 61. He refers also to S. Morenz's extensive treatment of this aspect of the wind in *Religion und Geschichte des alten Ägypten* (Weimar: Hermann Böhlaus Nachfolger, 1974), pp. 469–476.
28. Comparable to *rûaḥ* since the *ba* is understood as the 'sum of an entity less its material form' (*COS*, 1.5, 8, n.1).
29. CT 75 (*COS*, 1.5).
30. Morenz, *Religion*, p. 176, quoting Sethe, *Amun*.
31. Smith, *Primaeval Ocean*, p. 62.
32. Ibid., p. 63. For another example of personification/deification of the wind(s), see the Egyptian Book of the Dead, spell 161, where each of the four winds are

All of this makes it very interesting that the very verb used of the SOL in Genesis most readily refers to the activity of a bird over its nest. Yet the text of Genesis is at best laconic, as it fails to mention either the separation of heaven and earth by the *rûaḥ* or an egg, which in Egyptian thinking held the sun god (or, alternatively, the Ogdoad). I propose, however, that Genesis is not simply being laconic; the absence of the noted elements should be considered neither accidental nor polemical. Instead, the text demonstrates that this arena of discourse overlaps with the Egyptian environment, even though the particulars have a shape all their own. The ancients commonly spoke of the wind's role in creation and described its preparation for creative activity as brooding. It is no surprise that, in Israelite thinking, the creative role of the wind would inevitably be identified as spirit and subsequently connected to God. R. Luyster summarizes the biblical materials by observing that the wind expresses God's sovereignty over the water and executes his will, whatever it might be.[33]

We can also consider the activity of the *rûaḥ* in relation to the potentiality inherent in the pre-creation state. This potentiality is also seen in the primeval waters of the Egyptian accounts.[34] The potentiality is realized through the *ka* (= vital force) of the creator god which is associated with regeneration.[35] Meeks and Favard-Meeks summarize this belief: 'The totality of creation . . . constituted the sum of the creator-god's vital force.'[36]

Our final point of comparison from the Egyptian literature concerns the

---

identified with a particular deity. These, however, are not winds involved in creation but winds that enter into the nose of the deceased to restore him to life: 'As for any noble dead for whom this ritual is performed over his coffin, there shall be opened for him four openings in the sky, one for the north wind – that is Osiris; another for the south wind – that is Re; another for the west wind – that is Isis; another for the east wind – that is Nephthys' (R. Faulkner, *The Egyptian Book of the Dead: The Going Forth by Day* [San Francisco: Chronicle, 1998], p. 125).

33. R. Luyster, 'Wind and Water: Cosmic Symbolism in the Old Testament', *ZAW* 93 (1981), pp. 1–10; quote on p. 6.

34. J. Allen, *Genesis in Egypt* (YES 2; New Haven: Yale University Press, 1988), p. 57. He points out that dialectic between non-existence and potentiality developed by the Ptolemaic period.

35. See A. Bolshakov, 'Ka', *OEAE*, 2:215–217, for this element in the human *ka*, and D. Meeks and C. Favard-Meeks, *Daily Life of the Egyptian Gods* (Ithaca: Cornell University Press, 1996), p. 71, for the divine *ka*.

36. Meeks and Favard-Meeks, *Daily Life*, p. 71.

triad of *Hu*, *Sia* and *Heka* and their relationship to *Maat*. This triad is connected with the creator god and is also available to the king. J. Assmann indicates that the king was responsible for maintaining the original plenitude of meaning in the cosmos as created by the gods so that *Maat* might be realized.

> To do this he had at his disposal two divine powers that had stood at the side of the creator god himself: *Sia*, 'perception,' and *Hu*, 'utterance.' Sia enabled the king to perceive the plenitude of meaning and to keep it in his mind, whereas Hu gave his word the power to become a reality immediately.[37]

He further explains that 'Hu was the creative will of the creator god, directed toward the plenitude, that expressed itself in words'.[38] Silverman adds the third creative force to the profile.

> Before creation could take place, however, three powers had to be present, all of which together represented the energy necessary for creation: Hu (divine utterance), Heka (magic or divine energy), and Sia (divine knowledge).[39]

Despite their significance, the triad are not treated as separate deities in that they are not worshipped in the cult.[40] Similarly, the spirit is not treated as a divine entity, but as a divine manifestation. In Israel, the SOL could be said to combine all three of these powers – utterance, energy and knowledge – in its creative role.

Mesopotamia provides little that relates to the spirit in creation, except perhaps the *mis pi* ritual describing the great gods; here, life proceeds from their word: 'Your utterance is life, your pronouncement is well-being, the work of your mouth is life itself.'[41]

We can now assess the similarities and differences between the biblical and

---

37. J. Assmann, *The Search for God in Ancient Egypt* (Ithaca: Cornell University Press, 2001), p. 4.
38. Ibid., p. 4; see also p. 57.
39. D. P. Silverman, 'Divinity and Deities in Ancient Egypt', in L. Lesko (ed.), *Religion in Ancient Israel* (Ithaca: Cornell University Press, 1991), p. 33.
40. E. Hornung, *Conceptions of God in Ancient Egypt* (Ithaca: Cornell University Press, 1982), pp. 76, 277.
41. C. Walker and M. Dick, *The Induction of the Cult Image in Ancient Mesopotamia: The Mesopotamian Mis Pi Ritual*, SAALT 1 (Helsinki: University of Helsinki, 2001), pp. 148–149, lines 19–20.

Near Eastern literature. Just as the spirit in Genesis 1 manifests God's utterance, energy and knowledge to creation, the Egyptian creator god carried out his creative work through three entities so designated. As in Genesis 1, the Egyptian text associates the creator god Amun with the wind that is used for creation and portrays creation as an egg being fertilized. The Genesis account differs by lacking much of the detail found in Egyptian literature. Of course monotheism is obvious in Genesis and mythological polytheism pervades the Egyptian texts, but an Egyptian reader would have recognized the spirit's role in Genesis.

Leadership

Old Testament leadership

The spirit of the Lord often legitimized leaders in the OT, whether judges or kings. Various terms express the advent of the spirit and certain actions, such as anointing, symbolize its presence. Once we recognize that legitimation – conferring authority, power and victory – is the issue, we can draw comparisons to the Ancient Near Eastern literature.

Two telling verbal roots describe the advent of the spirit of the Lord: *ṣlḥ* ('rush upon') and *lbš* ('clothe'). The former generally occurs with the preposition *ʿal* (Samson, Judg. 14, 15; Saul, 1 Sam. 10, 11) or *ʾel* (David, 1 Sam. 16; likewise the evil spirit on Saul).[42] Synchronic analysis of contexts suggests that whomever serves as the indirect object of the verb could be understood as 'caught up in a momentum' (for either short-term or long-term goals).[43] This usage would compare well to certain NT passages, as when Jesus was driven by the Spirit into the wilderness, and prophets were carried along by the Holy Spirit (2 Pet. 1:21). It minimally identifies a divine stimulus or prompting. The power of this act is evident by its result: Saul was changed (transformed) into another person (1 Sam. 10:6, 9).

The second verb, *lbš*, has been helpfully elucidated by D. Block, who notes that the qal form of *lbš* means to put on a garment.[44] The object in 76 occurrences is always some piece of clothing, except in the following cases:

---

42. These prepositions are often interchangeable in Samuel.

43. I.e. 'on a roll', a juggernaut.

44. D. Block, 'Judges', in J. Walton (ed.), *The Zondervan Illustrated Bible Backgrounds Commentary: Old Testament* (Grand Rapids: Zondervan, 2009), 2:155–156; cf. N. M. Waldman, 'The Imagery of Clothing, Covering, and Overpowering', *JANES* 19 (1989), p. 165.

- Direct object is people (Judg. 6:34, Gideon; 1 Chr. 12:18, Amasai; 2 Chr. 24:20, Zechariah); in these the spirit is the subject.
- Direct object is metaphorical: salvation (2 Chr. 6:41); often in Job and Psalms, either positive qualities like justice, strength or righteousness; or negative conditions like scabs, disgrace, cursing, despair.

The clothes put on are typically identifying garments (royal, priestly, widow's, sackcloth); the terminology therefore refers to someone stepping into a persona or taking on an identity. From this we might conclude that God's power and presence went about in the guise of Gideon. The point is not Gideon's spiritual experience, but rather Gideon as Yahweh's instrument. It is not so much that the *rûaḥ* empowers the person, but that the person becomes the vehicle for the divine activity.[45] This action of the SOL does not obliterate the personality or will of the person, but overrides selectively, taking on the identity of the person. The SOL is embodied through the person, creating a level of shared identity.

On some occasions in the OT, a person endowed with the SOL would manifest a visible trait. In 1 Samuel 10:10–11 Saul has noticeably been transformed, and in 2 Kings 2:15 the company of the prophets recognized that Elisha possessed the spirit of Elijah. We might infer that, during the times of the judges, tribes would only follow the leader of another tribe into battle if they believed that the spirit of the Lord was upon him.

We could also understand the SOL's connection to leadership in the OT by examining the terms used in parallel with the endowment of the SOL. We will examine three: anointing, the arm of the Lord and the hand of the Lord.

Anointing in the OT conveyed authority and life from the spirit.[46] 1 Samuel 16:13 explicitly connects anointing and spirit-endowed authority: 'So Samuel took the horn of oil and anointed him in the presence of his brothers, and from that day on the Spirit of the LORD came upon David in power.' In Isaiah 61:1–3 the spirit of the Lord anoints the messianic figure who is thereby enabled to perform royal roles. Though anointing is carried out physically by

---

45. Compare to John 13:27, where Satan entered into Judas, or Luke 24:49, where Christ instructed his disciples to wait until they were clothed with power from on high.
46. Connections between anointing and the spirit are so close as to be virtually identical. See F. Hesse, '*chriō*', in *TDNT* 9.502–503; T. N. D. Mettinger, *King and Messiah* (Lund: Gleerup, 1976), p. 207.

the prophets, they act as the representatives of Yahweh. So in 1 Samuel 10:1 Samuel anoints Saul with the words, 'Has not the LORD anointed you leader over his inheritance?'[47]

We also find the 'arm of the LORD' and the 'hand of the LORD' used as expressions parallel to the SOL.[48] The parallel between 'spirit' and 'hand', and the conveyance of both by anointing, indicate that these are homologous: when one is referenced, the others can be inferred. These terms converge most in the archetypal and ideal Davidic king. Psalm 89 evidences this constellation of legitimation language as it identifies the Davidic king as chosen (89:3), given strength (89:19), anointed by God (89:20), sustained by the hand of God (89:21), strengthened by the arm of God (89:21), given victories (89:23), appointed firstborn son (89:27), and established through a perpetual dynasty (89:29). The spirit is not mentioned in this Psalm, but its presence is implied when the psalmist associates all these acts with God's anointing. This association also demonstrates that there is little reason to differentiate between God's endowment and the SOL's endowment. These will be important points as we follow the concepts into the Ancient Near East.

With what does the SOL endow leaders? Besides the aspects suggested in Psalm 89 (authority, victory, familial relationship with deity and dynastic reign), Isaiah 11 richly enumerates the qualities given by the spirit: wisdom, understanding, counsel, power, knowledge, fear of the Lord, justice and righteousness (cf. also the description of the Servant in Isa. 42).

The SOL in Judges is usually associated with the calling up of an army. In a tribal society with no centralized government, individual tribes facing problems had difficulty enlisting support from other tribes. In such situations, a leader was measured by his ability to compel others to follow, though he had no authority to command them. In Israel this ability marked the power of Yahweh, for he alone had the authority to call out the armies of the tribes. Yahweh was the only central authority. Therefore, the Lord's authority was clearly at work when someone exercised Yahweh's authority by calling out the armies (see Judg. 11:29; 1 Sam. 11:6–8). This was one of the distinguishing features of the judges of Israel.

Throughout Ezekiel 37 we see the *rûaḥ* giving life, acting on corporate Israel rather than on the king. Job 33:4 attests to the endowment of life on individuals: 'The Spirit of God has made me; the breath of the Almighty gives

47. Cf. 1 Sam. 15:17: 'The LORD anointed you king over Israel.'

48. Particularly in Ezekiel: Ezek. 1:3; 3:14, 22, et al.; but cf. 2 Kgs 3:15; 1 Kgs 18:46 KJV.

me life.'[49] It is not as easy to find royal rhetoric for the idea that the SOL gives life to the king.[50]

Finally, the spirit gives the king utterance and authorizes him to issue decrees. In 2 Samuel 23:1–3 David takes the mantle of prophet in his final song:

> The oracle of David son of Jesse,
> the oracle of the man exalted by the Most High,
> the man anointed by the God of Jacob,
> Israel's singer of songs:
> The Spirit of the LORD spoke through me;
> his word was on my tongue.
> The God of Israel spoke,
> The Rock of Israel said to me. . .

Here David identifies his anointing with the spirit speaking through him. Though framed as prophetic speech rather than royal decree, the psalm legitimates David's dynasty.[51]

In summary of the biblical information we could offer the following composite profile. Anointing often symbolized the spirit's presence on a leader and its presence often assumed outward manifestation. The spirit embodied God's authority in the leader, thus legitimizing the leader as he exercised his authority. The spirit provides the wellspring of life and effective utterance and brings the king's success. Through the spirit the king is sanctioned to reign as son of the deity and given the wisdom to bring justice and prosperity to the land and its people. We may now turn our attention to the Ancient Near East, where we will find all of these same elements represented in the ways that deity works with kings.

Ancient Near East leadership

In Mesopotamia we find the terminology of a spirit embodied in a human, not in the context of gods and kings, but in the language of demonic oppression:

---

49. Note that NIV actually translates *rûaḥ* as 'life' in Isa. 42:5, where it is parallel to *nĕšāmâ*.

50. Closest: Pss 61:6; 144:10.

51. The spirit manifested as words in the mouth of God's people (as opposed to specifically the king) is also seen in Isa. 59:21.

- 'The *alu*-demon has clothed himself in my body as with a garment; sleep covers me like a net',[52] which some translate as 'The *alu*-demon has wrapped my body as with a garment'.[53]
- 'He [the *asakku*-demon] enveloped the miserable man like a garment.'[54]

Parallels to the clothing metaphor in the realm of kingship are scarce; the best approximation I found appears in the Neo-Assyrian iconography of the king wearing the divine symbols as a necklace.[55] An iconographic variation presents the symbols of the gods above the king; by these he acknowledges the gods, but perhaps the symbols also represent the gods' presence with him, resting on him. These non-anthropomorphic representations of deity emanate from the 'higher' personified deity – 'representing various aspects embedded in the image of a transcendental, conceptually human, multi-faceted, and at times invisible, god'.[56] Such emanations may extend the personality and attributes of deity in ways similar to the SOL in the OT, but since the SOL is not a physical manifestation, it would not be properly designated an emanation of Yahweh.

Just as Israelite judges and kings were led into battle and given victory through divine agency, kings in the rest of the Ancient Near East also believed that the gods acted in this way. Neo-Assyrian kings often speak of the gods going before them into battle, sometimes represented by the divine standard or the divine weapon that accompanies them. These objects are viewed as the source of the king's strength: 'With the support of Aššur my great lord, and the divine standard which goes before me, and with the fierce weapons which the god Aššur (my) lord gave me I assembled (my) weapons . . . with the supreme might of the divine standard which goes before me I fought with them.'[57] Here we find the power of the god being made available to the king through an intermediary manifestation.

---

52. Thus W. G. Lambert, *Babylonian Wisdom Literature* (Oxford: Clarendon, 1960), pp. 42–43, 71–72. *CAD*, A/1, 376a renders the statement, 'The *alu*-demon has put on my body as if it were a garment.'
53. Waldman, 'The Imagery of Clothing, Covering, and Overpowering', p. 165.
54. CT 17, 6, iii, 31–32.
55. S. Holloway, *Aššur is King! Aššur is King!* (Leiden: Brill, 2002), pp. 68–69. See discussion in T. Ornan, 'In the Likeness of Man: Reflections on the Anthropocentric Perception of the Divine in Mesopotamian Art', in B. N. Porter (ed.), *What is a God?* (Winona Lake: Eisenbrauns, 2009), pp. 93–151; see p. 101.
56. Ornan, 'In the Likeness', p. 151.
57. Holloway, *Aššur is King!*, p. 173, from *RIMA* 2 A.0.101.1 ii 25–28 (Aššurnasirpal

We find throughout the Ancient Near East that the gods ordain the king to his position of leadership. In Mesopotamia the terminology *nabu*/PÒD describes the gods calling or appointing a king or priest to office.[58] In the case of Yahdun-Lim, this commissioning includes endowment with power to succeed: 'Dagan commanded that I be king and gave me a powerful weapon which overthrows the kings hostile toward me.'[59] In this we might be reminded of Samson, who receives *koaḥ* (strength) from the *rûaḥ* of the divine warrior Yahweh.[60]

In Ancient Near Eastern texts the divine endowment on the king is considered a visible manifestation, just as the biblical text sometimes alludes to a visible manifestation of the SOL.[61] In Akkadian, divine empowerment is called *melammu* (the visible representation of the glory of deity). This marked the king as the legitimate representative of the gods, one who reigned with their approval and authority.[62]

Much additional information can be found in Dale Launderville's thorough analysis of kingship in the Ancient Near East, *Piety and Politics*.[63] He describes his approach as typological – quite similar to my method in this paper.[64]

From the very beginning of his study, Launderville observes that royal

---

II). For further discussion of these divine weapons, which are occasionally marked with the divine determinative (DINGIR), see B. N. Porter, 'Blessings from a Crown, Offerings to a Drum: Were There Non-Anthropomorphic Deities in Ancient Mesopotamia?', in Porter (ed.), *What Is a God?*, pp. 153–194; P.-A. Beaulieu, *The Pantheon of Uruk During the Neo-Babylonian Period* (Leiden: Brill and Styx, 2003), pp. 351–368.

58. See citations in *CAD*, N/1, 36–38.
59. *CAD*, N/1, 38.
60. Smith, *Priestly Vision*, p. 54.
61. Most similar is the glowing appearance of Moses' face after he has been in the presence of the Lord.
62. An additional correlation may be found in the Akkadian term *baštu*. It refers generally to a sense of dignity, often bestowed by the gods, but it is also personified as a protective spirit. It provides various attributes as here, and gives authority to its recipient.
63. D. Launderville, *Piety and Politics* (Grand Rapids: Eerdmans, 2003).
64. 'Aspects of the dynamics of royal authority can be seen to form types or categories that appear in each of the three cultures at an appropriate level of generalization, but I do not try to prove that one culture was the source of an idea or practice for one of the other cultures compared' (ibid., p. 8).

authority was a gift from the gods rather than an actual possession of the king,[65] such that royal authority involved participation in divine authority.[66] It was essential that the king's endeavours evidence divine authority.[67] The king might adopt various expressions and portrayals to convey the basic idea, and Launderville suggests that 'The ways in which such a divine appearance was described indicated how the author negotiated the embodied yet transcendent character of the divine presence, its visible and invisible dimensions.'[68] In Israel this goal was accomplished through the use of the SOL. This might lead us to consider whether we should interpret the SOL as a metaphor, one of many that could be chosen to convey divine involvement.[69] Hebrew uses the SOL to express the mechanism which actuated a symbiotic relationship between the king and his divine sponsor. The Ancient Near Eastern sources use more direct language of the gods themselves actuating the symbiotic relationship.[70] 'All of these ideal royal rulers claimed special assistance and favors from the gods: it was such divine assistance that enabled them to accomplish heroic deeds for their communities.'[71]

When we look into the royal inscriptions, we can see constant reference to this relationship as the gods provide for the king in the same way that the SOL provides for the Israelite judges and kings. The following sampling (drawn from the third to first millennia) could be multiplied many times over.

---

65. Ibid., pp. 1–2.
66. Ibid., p. 356.
67. 'The physical strength, material wealth, and capacity to inspire a following were concrete, tangible realities, but each of these manifestations of power signified that the king had been destined for his leadership role by forces and circumstances beyond his calculated efforts. He tried to persuade the people that he had been chosen for the kingship by the king of the gods who was revered in their tradition. Such a rhetorical effort was essential for the longevity of the king's rule' (ibid., p. 147).
68. Ibid., p. 134.
69. Launderville observes that 'Metaphors bring us into relationship with important realities but do not supply us with the information that would allow us to control them . . . The knowledge communicated through a metaphor is bestowed upon the receptive listener. Such knowledge is never absolute' (ibid., p. 27).
70. Ibid., p. 337.
71. Ibid., p. 337.

Anointed by deity

In a letter from Nur-Sin to Mari, King Zimri-Lim reports a prophecy of Abiya, in which the god Adad says of the king: 'I restored you to the throne of your father's house, and the weapons with which I fought with Sea, I handed you. I anointed you with the oil of my luminosity, no one will offer resistance to you.'[72]

In Egyptian iconography an oft-repeated type-scene portrays the king flanked by deities who are anointing him with *ankh* signs (symbolizing life) used for the oil.

Manifestation of divine endowment

K. L. Younger has demonstrated that one of the common syntagms of Assyrian conquest accounts is 'the terrifying presence of the deity and/or king expressed through symbolic expressions'.[73] He cites the *melammu* (the divine shining) and the *pulḫu melammu* (terror or fear in response to this manifestation of divine endowment) as associated with the king as well as with the divine weapons that overwhelm the enemy.

Priestly personnel could also evidence the divine endowment in their person: 'En-ane-du, the *en* priestess of the god Nanna, (predestined) from the holy womb (for) the great fate of the office of an *en* (and) the nobility of heaven, beloved of the heart, on whose body the goddess Ningal by (her own) hand has put the radiance of the office of *en*.'[74]

Similarly in Egypt, the pharaohs report that they conquer by manifesting the terror of the god. For example, in the Gebel Barkal Stela of Thutmose III: 'I came south with a joyful heart, having triumphed for my lord, [Amun-Re, lord of Karnak]. It is he who commanded these victories, who gave the terror [of me]. . .'[75]

We see an example of the divine weapon in Aššurnasirpal's Standard Inscription: 'When Aššur, the lord who called me by name and made my kingship great, entrusted his merciless weapon in my lordly arms. . .'[76]

---

72. M. Nissinen, *Prophets and Prophecy in the Ancient Near East*, SBLWAW 12 (Atlanta: SBL, 2003), p. 22.
73. K. Lawson Younger, *Ancient Conquest Accounts*, *JSOTSup* 98 (Sheffield: JSOT Press, 1990), pp. 73–74.
74. *RIME* 4, p. 300, Old Babylonian.
75. Ibid., p. 217.
76. Younger, *Ancient Conquest Accounts*, p. 121.

Chosen by the deity and endowed with authority

The king is 'chosen in the heart of the deity'[77] and therefore described as the 'one after [divine name]'s heart'.[78] The king is specially summoned by the god,[79] who also grants him the sceptre.[80] The god determines the destiny of the king,[81] and calls him by name,[82] even from birth.[83] Deity gives the king the 'lead-rope' of the people[84] and establishes a throne of promise.[85] The endowment of kingship is commonly described as eternal, 'forever'.[86]

Born as son of deity/given life by deity/named

The gods are the parents of the king.[87] They name him, nurse him, and set him on their knees.[88] He is implanted in the womb by the god[89] and begotten by the gods.[90] He owes his very existence to the gods[91] and enjoys the status of favoured son.[92] Gudea's statement to Ningirsu in Cylinder A includes many of these elements: 'I have no mother, you are my mother, I have no

---

77. *RIME* 1, pp. 174, 226; *RIME* 2, pp. 72, 85; *RIME* 3/1, pp. 13, 18, 31, 41, 84; *RIME* 3/2, pp. 302, 303, 306, 308, 311, 314, 315, 317, 321, 322, 323, 325, 326, 328, 329, 330, 331, 332, 334, 336, 342, 357; *RIME* 4, pp. 225, 296.
78. '[Gudea] the one after Enlil's heart', Cylinder A. xvii:11, *RIME* 3/1, p. 79. Compare the description of David in 1 Sam. 13:14.
79. *RIME* 1, p. 206.
80. *RIME* 1, pp. 198, 242; *RIME* 2, p. 77; *RIME* 3/1, p. 92.
81. *RIME* 1, p. 230.
82. *RIME* 2, pp. 73, 77, 272.
83. *RIME* 3/2, p. 157.
84. *RIME* 2, p. 97; *RIME* 3/2, p. 134.
85. *RIME* 3/1, p. 92.
86. *RIME* 4, p. 274, Rim-Sin 'may the goddess . . . determine a destiny for them . . . life with exalted days, long years, a firm reign that makes the nation peaceful, the exercise of kingship forever' (see also *RIME* 4, p. 88).
87. Nissinen, *Prophets and Prophecy*, pp. 116–117 (Esarhaddon); Younger, *Ancient Conquest Accounts*, p. 202 (Aššurbanipal).
88. *RIME* 1, pp. 128–130.
89. *RIME* 1, p. 129.
90. *RIME* 1, pp. 176, 188, 226.
91. *RIME* 3/1, p. 71.
92. *RIME* 2, p. 272.

father, you are my father, you had the seed of me implanted in the womb, made me to be born from the sanctuary.'[93]

Given utterance by deity that enables decrees

The gods of the Near East make decrees as they assign the destinies each year. As B. Albrektson indicates, 'The word of the god was a mighty and terrifying power which could prove effective in all spheres of life, a dynamic force bringing about the death or victories of kings as well as the growth or withering of the crops.'[94] Nevertheless, I found no examples in Sumerian or Akkadian of the king receiving utterance from the gods to make decrees; in contrast, this concept permeates Egyptian literature. Here we find *Hu* as the personification of the creative utterance and *Sia* as the personification of understanding. 'Then spoke the royal companions in answer to their god [pharaoh Sesostris I]: *Hu* is <in> your mouth, Sia is behind you O King! What you plan comes about.'[95]

Led to battle and given victory by deity

Military contexts provide the most prominent occurrence of deity acting in concert with kings. In the OT Yahweh, like the gods in the Ancient Near East, calls to battle, leads into battle, gives battle strategy and brings victory. We observe the SOL active only in one level of military activity – enabling judges to call up an army from tribes over which they have no authority.[96] In the Ancient Near East the gods are directly involved with no qualification as they command the battles, lead into battle, endow the king with divine weapons, stand beside the king, run before the king, strike terror into the heart of the enemy, annihilate the enemy and bring overwhelming victory. Ramesses II acknowledges that Amun's role is more significant than the size of the army: 'I know Amun helps me more than a million troops, more than a hundred thousand charioteers, more than ten thousand brothers and sons who are united as one heart.'[97] The author of Judges advances a similar perspective as he records Yahweh reducing Gideon's army from 20,000 to 300 men; Yahweh does this 'In order that Israel

93. *RIME* 3/1, p. 70. Note the role of the spirit of the Lord in the incarnation as he implants the divine seed within Mary (Luke 1:35).

94. B. Albrektson, *History and the Gods* (Lund: Gleerup, 1967), p. 67.

95. Lichtheim, *AEL* 1, 117.

96. One exception could be in 1 Kgs 22:19–21 when a lying spirit from Yahweh leads Ahab into battle that will result in his death. This is contrary to the normal role of deity in battle.

97. Lichtheim, *AEL* 2, 65–66.

may not boast against me that her own strength has saved her' (Judg. 7:2). In the category of military leadership, divine endowment works the same in both the OT and the Ancient Near East. The fact that the biblical text only marginally involves the SOL in this role is noteworthy and probably significant.

Given wisdom by deity

Just as 1 Kings 3:12 portrays the wisdom of Solomon as an endowment of Yahweh,[98] so the literature of the Ancient Near East considers the wisdom of the kings as a gift from the gods. In the epilogue of his collected legal sayings, Hammurabi notably claims that his wisdom was allotted by Ea and that by it he was able to maintain peace and prosperity for his people.[99]

Enabled to establish justice by deity

The king's possession of divine wisdom enables him to establish justice through the power of the deity. 'Aššur-reša-iši, appointee [of] the god Enlil, vice-regent of Aššur, the one whose dominion the gods Anu, Enlil, and Ea, the great gods, designated for the proper administration of Assyria and whose priesthood they blessed.'[100]

Granted strength

Like Samson, to whom the spirit gave strength, the kings of the ancient world claimed extraordinary strength or power given by the deity. Nabopolassar makes such a claim: 'He (Marduk) had Nergal, the strongest among the gods, walk at my side; he killed my enemies, he felled my foes . . . with the mighty strength of Nabu and Marduk my lords, I chased them (the Assyrians) out of the land of Akkad.'[101] A suppliant requests that Ninurta strengthen Sargon II: 'Grant him unrivaled strength, manly might, make his weapons at the ready that he kill his foes.'[102]

---

98. The SOL is not mentioned in this context, though Isa. 11 mentions the spirit of wisdom.

99. M. Roth, *Law Collections from Mesopotamia and Asia Minor*, SBLWAW 6 (Atlanta: Scholars Press, 1995), p. 133, col. 47. See more examples in *CAD*, Š/1, 359 (*šamu* B). Other references to gods giving wisdom: *RIME* 1, pp. 166, 180, 438; *RIME* 2, p. 272; *RIME* 3/1, p. 18; *RIME* 4, pp. 23, 178.

100. *RIMA* 1, p. 312; *RIME* 4, pp. 159, 254.

101. *COS* 2.121. For other examples, see *RIME* 1, pp. 148, 153, 158, 162, 166, 222; *RIME* 2, pp. 272, 285, 287; *RIME* 3/1, pp. 18, 31; *RIME* 3/2, pp. 297, 303.

102. B. Foster, *Before the Muses*, 3rd ed. (Bethesda: CDL, 2005), p. 787.

Summary
The endowments from the gods and the statements of divine agency through the person of the king stand as the foundation for the rhetoric of kingship in the ancient world. It is therefore commonplace for royal inscriptions to include an extensive listing of all these endowments to evidence the king's legitimacy and success.[103] The SOL in the OT provides many of these functions.

Direct references to 'spirit'
Our next question, then, is whether the Ancient Near East offers any direct references to activity by a 'spirit of [divine name]' in the realm of leadership. The following merit mention and consideration.

Oracle of Kititum (= Ishtar of Eshnunna) to Ibalpiel (OB, 18th c.): 'I, Kititum, will strengthen the foundations of your throne; I have established a protective spirit [*lamassu*] for you.'[104]

In Maqlu VIII 90, *lamassu* is again used, along with other comparable terms: 'You are the shade that covers me, you are my *baštu*, you are my *lamassu*, you are my "shape".'[105]

On occasion the god him/herself is described as the *lamassu*: 'May the goddess Ishtar, mistress of battle and warfare, my benevolent protective spirit [*lamassu*]. . .'[106]

In the Old Babylonian inscriptions of Rim-Sin, the king speaks of requesting or being given a protecting genius (*dlamma*).[107]

When we turn to Egypt we again encounter the three personifications of divine endowment, as in the Admonition of Ipuwer: 'Authority

---

103. *RIME* 1, pp. 200, 203, 206, 209, 210, 212, 218, 220, 222, 225, 228, 230, 235, 238: king is nourished by milk, given a fine name, granted wisdom, chosen in heart, nominated, beloved friend, beloved spouse of the gods/goddesses; *RIME* 1, p. 435: king is chief ruler of the gods, granted wisdom, chosen, vizier of the god, military governor, servant of the god, brought up by the gods; *RIME* 2, pp. 34, 311: 'the god Enlil gave to him the scepter, made his intelligence surpassing, and supported him'; *RIME* 3/2, pp. 302, 307: 'god . . . granted a long life-span, crown, and tiara, a scepter of long days, a royal throne, a firm foundation, years of abundance.'
104. Nissinen, *Prophets and Prophecy*, p. 94, no. 66.
105. *CAD*, B, 143.
106. Hammurabi epilogue, Roth, *Law Collections*, 139, 50.92–97. Further information in *CAD* entries on *lamassu* and *šedu*.
107. *RIME* 4, pp. 275, 308.

[*Hu*], Knowledge [*Sia*], and Truth [*Maat*] are with you' (speaking of the king).[108] Through these, the king was said to have the powers of the gods. Just as the SOL is not a physical manifestation, and therefore not an emanation, so the SOL is not a person, and therefore cannot be a personification. Ancient Near Eastern literature shows emanations and personifications performing some of the same functions of the SOL, but I maintain that the SOL is neither an emanation nor a personification.

In each of the above occurrences, the similarity is a quirk of translation, not a real parallel. The Akkadian *lamassu* and *lamma*, and the three entities mentioned in the Egyptian texts, are separate entities, not an extension of the divine persona. Even the reference to Ishtar as a *lamassu* is simply describing her metaphorically as carrying out the function of a known entity. In contrast, in the OT the SOL is not a separate entity from Yahweh, but represents a modified level of divine agency.

Hand on me

One more set of data to be considered in the leadership category concerns the 'hand' of the deity. This terminology is significant because some contexts in the OT equate the 'hand of Yahweh' with the SOL. Consequently, we may consider whether occurrences of the 'hand of [divine name]' in Akkadian may compare to the function of the SOL in the OT.[109] Statements like Gudea's, 'Indeed you let fall on me, O my lady Gatumundu, the favorable right hand of your lofty hands',[110] indicate little more than the strengthening hand of support as the deity stands by his side. In Egypt, Ramesses II affirms that 'Amun is my helper, his hand is with me'.[111] The hand is not a distinct entity as the *lamassu* were; it is probably more an expression of divine aid than of independent divine endowment.

Conclusions on leadership

One might object that this list shows only that the rhetoric of kingship in Israel overlaps considerably with that of the Ancient Near East – what does

---

108. Lichtheim, *AEL* 1, 160. *AEL* 1, 65 includes Heka (divine energy and knowledge of magic).

109. Right from the start it should be noted that we rule out the idiomatic use of 'hand of [divine name]' that occurs in the medical texts as a designation for epileptic types of illness; for discussion see M. Stol, *Epilepsy in Babylonia* (Groningen: Styx, 1993), pp. 33–38.

110. *RIME* 3/1, p. 71.

111. Lichtheim, *AEL* 2.67.

this have to do with the SOL? As is evident in the survey of the royal rhetoric in the OT and the Ancient Near East, very few of the features of kingship result from the endowment of the SOL. Generally, only Yahweh's endowment is noted. When the SOL is the indicated agency for divine endowment it serves as an additional layer between the deity and the king. So the important question becomes, what made this extra layer desirable in only a few of the royal contexts in Israel, but never in the royal contexts of the Ancient Near East? What theology does it represent?

In the OT, Yahweh unequivocally leads into battle, fights, and brings victory. His involvement is complete and vouchsafes the result. In contrast, when the SOL is invoked, the divine participation is more narrowly focused. The role of deity may be qualified, for the human personality is not totally submerged or inactivated. For this reason, those possessed of the SOL can still manifest human inadequacies and failure, thereby mitigating the results. Kings from the Ancient Near East have no inclination to acknowledge such qualification. Likewise, since the gods in the Ancient Near East make no claim to holiness, as Yahweh does, no theological sensitivities would necessitate establishing levels of involvement. The SOL in the OT expresses God's energizing and motivating role without vouchsafing the outcome or overriding the entire process; it expresses God's work through a human mediator who retains some independent agency. Contrast the Ancient Near East: from the human perspective, kings would never want to admit qualified divine involvement; from the divine perspective, they feel no need to insulate deity.

Prophecy

The prophets in the OT saw themselves as filled with divine power, justice and utterance because they were filled with the SOL (Mic. 3:8; Zech. 4:6). Prophets and kings received overlapping manifestations of divine endowment, but for prophets the emphasis falls on the spoken word (cf. Num. 24:2; 2 Sam. 23:2; Isa. 59:21; Joel 2), while for kings the emphasis falls on actions. The Bible portrays prophets as embodiments of the divine.[112] This portrayal overlaps with the concept of the deity 'putting on' a person (see the discussion of *lbš* above).

---

112. J. Goldingay, *Old Testament Theology* (Downers Grove: InterVarsity Press, 2003), p. 1:675.

Sometimes prophetic contexts speak of the SOL rushing upon someone (e.g., Saul in 1 Sam. 19:23), using language like that found in a few Ancient Near Eastern texts: 'the god (Amon) seized a great seer from among his great seers, and he caused him to be in an ecstatic state.'[113] The ecstatic behaviour brought on by the SOL in the OT characterizes one category of prophet in Mesopotamia (*muḫḫu*). Interestingly, when foreign kings encounter Israelite prophecy or dream interpretation in biblical texts, they name the spirit of God, rather than God directly, as the agent (Pharaoh, Gen. 41:38; Nebuchadnezzar, Dan. 4:8, 18; 5:11–14). Nevertheless, the Ancient Near Eastern texts do not commonly speak of prophecy using the terminology 'spirit of [divine name]'.

Having said this, we need to examine briefly S. Parpola's claim that trinitarian theology derives from Assyria.[114] We will not spend time on his larger proposal, which has not been well received, in spite of his status as a highly respected Assyriologist. Instead we will focus on his conclusion that Ištar is equivalent to the SOL.

Parpola begins by observing that in the Neo-Assyrian prophecy texts the chief god Aššur does not give the messages; instead, this function often belongs to Ištar, whose oracles are called the 'words of Ištar'. He concludes that 'Ištar can be viewed as the "spirit" or "breath" of Aššur (= God)' – a concept he indicates as well attested in Neo-Assyrian texts (using *šaru*). Going a step further, he believes that one can say that 'Ištar of the prophecies is the spirit of God, who, residing in the heart of the prophet, *spirits* him and speaks through his or her lips. In other words, she is the functional equivalent of the biblical spirit of God.'[115] Unfortunately, this stunning proposal is not as thoroughly supported as Parpola implies. For example, the Assyrian prophecies themselves never refer to Ištar as *šaru*. His supporting footnote does not substantiate his conclusion, as his evidence draws from personal names that feature some combination of *šaru* and either *ilani* or the name of a deity. Though Parpola proposes that *šar ilani* = *rûaḥ ʾĕlōhîm*,[116] it is not at all clear that Akkadian *šaru* overlaps with that part of the semantic domain of Hebrew *rûaḥ* that designates the SOL.[117] It comes closest when referring to the breath or

---

113. Wenamon, Nissinen, *Prophets and Prophecy*, p. 220; cf. *COS* 1.41 (90b).

114. S. Parpola, *Assyrian Prophecies*, SAA IX (Helsinki: Helsinki University Press, 1997), pp. XVIII–XXXI.

115. Ibid., p. XXVI.

116. For Akkadian *šaru,* see *CAD* Š/2, 133–140.

117. As 'wind' it can be deified or personified, as are mountains and rivers. As 'breath' it is equivalent to Hebrew *ḥebel.*

emanation of the gods,[118] but in these contexts it is better matched with the Hebrew *nepeš*. It carries none of the functions of the SOL. Parpola's equation must therefore be rejected for lack of evidence.

The research of A. M. Kitz is more productive.[119] Kitz designates prophecy as a sub-category of divination, proposing that its role may be expressed by the term 'anthropomancy' (divine manipulation of human beings). The ancients practised divination because they believed that the gods manipulated a wide variety of things in the physical world. Kitz suggests that, 'As part of the physical world, human beings, like animals and inanimate objects, could be guided by the divine. The results of this encounter could be permanent or transitory and were not necessarily reciprocally restrictive.'[120] Much of the divinatory observation in Mesopotamia focused on the abnormal. Atypical behaviour (whether by stars, animals or people) indicated divine influence in the material realm.[121] Prophetic utterances of an entranced practitioner were one type of observable, atypical behaviour.

In Israelite prophecy, the SOL manipulates the human prophet. This type of manipulation, described as the SOL 'coming upon' the prophets, enables the prophet to deliver the 'Word of Yahweh'. In the Ancient Near East, the prophet is overcome by an ecstatic state, but even that is expressed as the god seizing the prophet. Again then, as in the category of leadership, the SOL represents an additional layer between Yahweh and the human who is being influenced. Kitz's description of the relationship as 'reciprocally restrictive' is intriguingly similar to what we previously termed 'qualified agency'. As best I can tell, by 'reciprocally restrictive' she means that both parties retain the freedom to act independently.

Our study of prophecy therefore reaches a conclusion similar to our study regarding leadership. Divine endowment produces much the same results in both the Bible and the Ancient Near East, but biblical description in certain cases adds an extra layer, the SOL, between deity and the endowed human.

---

118. *CAD* Š/2, 138–139.

119. A. M. Kitz, 'Prophecy as Divination', *CBQ* 65 (2003), pp. 22–42.

120. Ibid., p. 31.

121. Ibid.

Additional categories

We need to address briefly two other areas before drawing conclusions. The SOL in the OT also endows the tabernacle craftsmen.[122] This endowment specifically concerns the construction of sacred space, not art generally.

In a Neo-Assyrian document called 'Esarhaddon's Renewal of the Gods',[123] Esarhaddon undertakes the renewal of the cult images but expresses concern about doing so: 'Whose right is it, O great gods, to create gods and goddesses in a place where man dare not trespass?' Since the making of the gods and goddesses is a divine task, Esarhaddon prays for divine endowment on the craftsmen so that the will of deity is accomplished: 'Endow the skilled craftsmen whom you ordered to complete this task with as high an understanding as Ea, their creator. Teach them skills by your exalted word; make all their handiwork succeed through the craft of Ninshiku [= Ea].'[124]

As in the previous categories, the divine endowment is similar in the OT, except it is attributed to the SOL rather than directly to the deity.

A final category concerns the endowment of the SOL on a corporate group, specifically the Israelites as God's covenant people. This corporate endowment is particularly noticeable in Isaiah and Ezekiel as they discuss God's plan to restore his people. In Ezekiel 36:27 the new covenant includes the endowment of the SOL. Other texts identify the spirit coming upon the remnant to bring restoration, fertility, prosperity and life as they are regathered to the land.[125]

In this category I have found no parallel in the Ancient Near East. The Ancient Near Eastern gods make no covenants with groups of people; the literature contains no concept of divine endowment on a particular chosen people.

---

122. Exod. 31:3–11; 35:30 – 36:1. Note that in Exod. 37:29 even the making of the sacred anointing oil is included.

123. See C. Walker and M. Dick, 'The Induction of the Cult Image in Ancient Mesopotamia: The Mesopotamian *mis pi* Ritual', in M. Dick (ed.), *Born in Heaven, Made on Earth* (Winona Lake: Eisenbrauns, 1999), pp. 55–121, esp. pp. 64–66.

124. Ibid., lines 17–20.

125. Isa. 32:15–20; 34:16; 44:2–3; 59:21; Ezek. 39:29; 37:14. The Exodus narratives do not specifically claim that God places his spirit on his covenant people, but the prophets, looking back, refer to this phenomena (Isa. 63:10–11).

Conclusions

Scholars have long recognized that the SOL in the OT expresses the immanent manifestation of God energizing and motivating (usually select individuals) to execute his plan. By endowing life, authority or strength, the spirit effectuates the kingdom of God, including predominantly God's presence, power and plan.

In the Ancient Near East the gods also endow life, authority and strength. Any given kingdom (e.g. the kingdom of Assyria) is established through divine agency granting the presence and power of deity and carrying the plan of deity – however *ad hoc* it may be – but the literature lacks a more specific agent for this endowment, such as a spirit of the gods.

A good comparative study helps us to understand each culture, literature or idea in light of the other, juxtaposing the data to discern the fine mosaic of continuity and discontinuity established by the hues of similarities and differences. By looking at the Ancient Near East we have found that endowments of the gods – manifested in emanations, personifications and embodied essence – are not present in the OT concept of the SOL. In fact, the SOL may well be used in the OT to avoid such ideas because of their theological overtones. Our research has led us provisionally to accept energizing and limited embodiment for the SOL. These roles characterize divine endowment as a qualified agency (Kitz's 'reciprocally restrictive'), thus introducing a nuance that was both unnecessary and undesirable in the theology of the Ancient Near East. Qualified agency thus stands as yet another distinct aspect of Israelite theology. The Ancient Near Eastern literature has enabled us to propose a more precise theological function and rationale for the SOL. Kings of the Ancient Near East must possess the essence of deity to rule legitimately. Such a concept was not acceptable in Israel, but the agency of the SOL established the necessary theological distance.[126] Consequently we could affirm what was said in the introduction: anyone from the Ancient Near East would understand the divine endowment indicated by the role of the SOL. Nevertheless, revelation to Israel qualified the immanence of God such that it would not have fitted the theology of the Ancient Near East.

If this assessment is correct, one further question would merit further

126. Here we could compare the difference between the role of the ark of the covenant in battle (note its misuse by Hophni and Phinehas) and the role of the divine image or divine standard. Yahweh's presence is not vouchsafed by the presence of the ark.

investigation and discussion: how does the work of the spirit in Genesis 1 express qualified agency?

Postscript: Connection of the spirit of the Lord and the Holy Spirit

Church Fathers and theologians readily identify the SOL with the Holy Spirit (HS), since they are typically more concerned about a canonical view of theology than about grammatical-historical exegesis. The Israelites had sufficient trouble grasping the concept of one God even without the complexity of trinitarian theology. Theologians, however, are often more interested in what might be called God's perspective and meaning, even if it is not unpacked until much later. If we admit, however, that there is authority and significance not just in the author's locution, but in his illocution, we must take the author's understanding seriously. It is our exegetical duty to determine how the Israelites apprehended the phrase, rather than imposing our theology directly onto the text.

Though there is no trinitarian perspective in Israelite theology, we will find both continuity and discontinuity when we compare the SOL from this paper to the HS in the NT and Christian theology. Interestingly enough, we will also find continuity between the HS and some of the ideas that we found in the Ancient Near East that did not apply to the SOL.

Functions	**Ancient Near East**	**SOL – OT**	**HS – NT**
Embodiment	Yes	Yes	Yes (more)
Energizing	Yes	Yes	Yes
Essence	Yes	No	Yes
Emanation	Yes	No	No
Personification	Yes	No	Yes
Qualified agency	No	Yes	Yes

These are the most notable aspects to take from the chart:

- The extent of the HS's embodiment (indwelling) compares more favourably to the Ancient Near East than to the SOL.
- The SOL does not confer the essence of deity, yet this essence is present in the Ancient Near East and in the HS.
- The Near Eastern – and especially Egyptian – literature personifies

the endowing agent of the gods. The OT does not personify the SOL, though the NT presents the HS as a person of the Godhead.

Drawing these significant distinctions between the SOL and the HS does not mean that the SOL was never actually the HS. NT references, such as Peter's Pentecost sermon, identify the work of the HS with certain OT passages concerning the SOL. We have not been discussing phenomenology, but textual interpretation – that is, how the OT audience would have understood the SOL in their context. They occasionally refer to the SOL as the 'Holy Spirit' (Ps. 51:11; Isa. 63:10–11) not through a burst of trinitarian insight, but because in those contexts the SOL is the manifestation of God's presence which is intrinsically holy.

Even in the NT, we might find that the Gospels portray the spirit more in the already established pattern of the SOL in the OT than the yet undeveloped trinitarian doctrine relating to the HS, for in that time Christ had not yet ascended to send the Comforter. Passages for consideration would include Luke 1:35 (Mary), John 1:33 (Jesus), Luke 1:15 (John), Luke 4:1 (Jesus) and perhaps even John 20:22 (the disciples). Just as the spirit in the OT functions much like the endowment of divine power in the Ancient Near East, yet demonstrates theological innovation and sophistication in its differences, so the Holy Spirit (third person of the Trinity) functions much like the endowment of the spirit of the Lord in the OT, yet demonstrates theological innovation and sophistication in its differences.

PART 2: THE SPIRIT AND CREATION

3. THE SPIRIT AND CREATION

Robert L. Hubbard, Jr

In 1972, distinguished OT scholar Gerhard von Rad wrote:

> The declaration [of Gen. 1:2] . . . belongs completely to the description of chaos and does not yet lead into the creative activity; in fact this 'spirit of God' takes no more active part in creation. The Old Testament nowhere knows of such a cosmological significance for the concept of the spirit of God.[1]

Obviously, were von Rad correct, this essay would end right here! Worse, a huge question mark would haunt the validity of major studies of the spirit by leading theologians[2] and by those recently promoting a pneumatological interpretation of creation.[3] Against von Rad's sweeping comment ('the Old

---

1. G. von Rad, *Genesis*, rev. ed., OTL (Philadelphia: Westminster, 1972), pp. 49–50.
2. Cf. the chapter on 'The Holy Spirit and Creation' in T. D. Beck, *The Holy Spirit and the Renewal of All Things: Pneumatology in Paul and Jürgen Moltmann*, Princeton Theological Monograph Series 16 (Eugene: Pickwick Publications, 2007); Veli-Matti Kärkkäinen, 'The Working of the Spirit of God in Creation and in the People of God: The Pneumatology of Wolfhart Pannenberg', *Pneuma* 26/1 (2004), pp. 17–35.
3. E.g. A. Yong, 'Ruach, the Primordial Chaos, and the Breath of Life: Emergence Theory and the Creation Narratives in Pneumatological Perspective', in

Testament nowhere knows. . .'), I observe that the OT 'knows of such a cosmological significance' in two places, Genesis 1:2 and Psalm 104:30. This is not the large lode of biblical texts one usually mines to expound a theological theme, but I will argue that they portray a crucial role of the spirit in creation, both in the beginning and now.

Behind what follows lie several assumptions concerning the larger context. First, I assume that Genesis 1:1 performs a double literary function in the narrative: it serves both as a title for 1:2 – 2:1 and as a summary claim that God created everything (the 'what').[4] This means, second, that what follows (1:2 – 2:1) fleshes out the details of that claim (the 'how'). Third, the repetition of 'the heavens and the earth' in Genesis 1:1 and 2:1 brackets that section with a thematic *inclusio*, thus setting it off as the literary context for Genesis 1:2.[5] As for method, the essay has two parts, each from a different perspective. The first and longest part views Genesis 1:2 as if it were an outdoor scene, seen through powerful binoculars capable of zooming in for closer views. The second look at the same scene is through a large picture window from a short distance. The aim of the first perspective is to familiarize the reader with the details of the landscape and their significance, while the second draws from those details conclusions concerning our topic.

A binocular view: Genesis 1:2

Transition and orientation

The grammar and syntax of Genesis 1:2 effects the transition from verse 1 to verse 2. It opens with a noun ('Now the earth was. . .') rather than a verb – in other words, with a *disjunctive* clause. A *conjunctive* clause (a verb followed by a noun) would signal that verse 2 reports the next event after the event in

---

M. Welker (ed.), *The Work of the Spirit: Pneumatology and Pentecostalism* (Grand Rapids; Cambridge: Eerdmans, 2006), pp. 183–204; D. L. Dabney, 'The Nature of the Spirit: Creation as a Premonition of God', in Welker (ed.), *The Work of the Spirit*, pp. 71–86.

4. This view departs from those commentators who read vv. 1–2 as a protasis for the apodasis (i.e. the main clause) in v. 3; cf. E. A. Speiser, *Genesis*, AB 1 (Garden City: Doubleday, 1964), p. 4; N. M. Sarna, *Genesis*, JPSTC (Philadelphia: Jewish Publication Society, 1989), p. 5.

5. Cf. Yong, 'Ruach', p. 191, who sees thematic 'bookends' in references to God's 'wind' and the 'breath of life' in Gen. 1:2 and 1:30.

verse 1. But the disjunctive clause of verse 2, as it were, hits the 'pause' button, freezing the action so the reader may focus on a single aspect of the cosmos introduced in verse 1, 'the earth'. Indeed, the juxtaposition of 'the earth' – the final word in verse 1 and the first word in verse 2 – connects the two verses. Syntactically, the opening of verse 2 leads the reader to expect to learn about a condition or circumstance resulting from verse 1. In short, verse 1 narrates that God created the universe (earth included), while verse 2 describes earth's conditions immediately after its creation.[6] A modern film-maker would achieve this same effect on screen with a wide shot (v. 1) displaying the vastness of the cosmos ('the heavens and the earth') and then slowly zooming in on the earth (v. 2). The 'heavens' would gradually disappear while the earth would slowly enlarge to fill the screen.[7]

Structurally, verse 2 consists of three lines, each of which sketches in a detail concerning the earth's condition at that post-creation moment.

1. The *tōhû wābōhû* condition (v. 2a, α)
2. The darkness over the deep (v. 2a, β)
3. The *rûaḥ ʾĕlōhîm* over the waters (v. 2b, α+β)

Typically, scholars describe the above situation as 'chaos', but some apply that term only to lines 1 and 2.[8] One obvious stylistic feature is the parallelism between lines 2 and 3:

and	darkness	was	*upon (ʿal) the face of*	*the deep,*
but	the *rûaḥ* of God	slowly moved	*over (ʿal) the face of*	*the waters.*

(Translation and italics mine)[9]

Each line has the prepositional phrase (lit.) 'upon the face of. . .' preceding, respectively, the synonyms 'the deep' and 'the waters'. The key question,

6. In such cases, Hebrew grammarians categorize the function of the disjunctive clause as 'circumstantial' (i.e. it introduces the reader to specific circumstances in play at the time).
7. The translation of V. P. Hamilton, *Genesis 1 – 17*, NICOT (Grand Rapids: Eerdmans, 1990), p. 103, ably conveys the sense: 'And the earth – it was. . .'
8. Later, I will give my own assessment of this well-known 'chaos' interpretive assumption.
9. Heb. *rûaḥ* may be rendered several ways (see below). For now, I use the Hebrew word in order to leave the proper translation an open question to be settled later.

however, concerns whether line 3 simply restates line 2 (synonymous parallelism), or states a contrast (antithetical parallelism). My translation reads the latter as the case. Finally, I observe that, though only one verse, Genesis 1:2 is a canonically programmatic statement. It says something about what the earth was like before divine creation began (v. 3), most importantly, the mention of 'the *rûaḥ* of God' on scene at that time. The implications of this latter statement for our understanding of the spirit and creation will hinge upon what we make of verse 2.

The earth's condition, line 1

The earth, says this line, was (lit.) *tōhû wābōhû*, a much-discussed Hebrew phrase that links two nouns, *tōhû* and *bōhû*, with 'and' (*wā*).[10] The OT attests *bōhû* only three times, twice in the phrase *tōhû wābōhû* (Gen. 1:2; Jer. 4:23) and once synonymously parallel to *tōhû* in a separate poetic line (Isa. 34:11).[11] *Bōhû* never occurs by itself, so clues to its specific meaning or connotations are lacking, as is certainty concerning its etymology.[12] In my view, *bōhû* probably represents either a byword for *tōhû* or a similar-sounding, made-up word paired with *tōhû* to form a rhyming phrase like the English expressions 'even-steven' and 'topsy-turvy'.

Not so with *tōhû*, whose sixteen occurrences make its meaning and connotations much clearer. *Tōhû* often denotes a 'wilderness', 'wasteland', 'desert' (Deut. 32:10; Job 6:18; 12:24; Ps. 107:40), or 'desert-like' terrain (Isa. 24:10; Job 26:7; cf. Isa. 34:11).[13] In three texts, *tōhû* means 'useless' or 'uselessness' – i.e. the uselessness of human-made idols (1 Sam. 12:21; cf. Isa. 41:29) and the

---

10. Sample renderings include 'a formless void' (NRSV), 'formless and empty' (TNIV), or 'unformed and void' (Tanakh). For full discussion, including a possible parallel phrase in Ugaritic, cf. D. T. Tsumura, *The Earth and the Waters in Genesis 1 and 2: A Linguistic Investigation*, *JSOTSup* 83 (Sheffield: JSOT Press, 1989), pp. 17–43.
11. Interestingly, the order of the two words in the latter case matches that of the phrase *tōhû wābōhû*.
12. Tsumura, *The Earth and the Waters*, pp. 21–23, claims to trace it to a Semitic root with a possible Arabic cognate 'to be empty'.
13. Cf. Tsumura, ibid., pp. 30–36. In my view, *tōhû* in Isa. 45:19 probably means 'wasteland', given its parallels 'secret' and 'land of deep darkness'; but cf. 'in chaos' (NRSV), 'out in a wasteland' (Tanakh), 'in vain' (TNIV), 'if I could not be found' (NLT). Alternatively, *tōhû* might intend to contrast the two following parallel lines, 'speak truth' and 'say what's upright'. If so, its sense might be 'in vain', 'with no purpose', etc.

'nothingness' of their makers (Isa. 44:9). Idols are 'useless' because, despite their dazzling appearance, they cannot in reality do anything to benefit their worshippers. More broadly, to Yahweh other nations and their leaders amount to 'nothing' – i.e. *tōhû* parallel to *ʾayin*, 'nothing' (Isa. 40:17, 23). In legal contexts, *tōhû* characterizes false testimony, phoney pleas and spurious arguments as 'empty' – i.e. fantasies without roots in reality (Isa. 29:21; 59:4).[14] 'In vain' is the sense of *tōhû* in Isaiah 49:4, where the speaker vents frustration over great effort expended with nothing to show for it.[15] Of particular interest is the appearance of *tōhû* in cosmological contexts. It designates the 'empty space' in the heavens where Yahweh hangs Zaphon (Job 26:7), while Isaiah 45:18 affirms that Yahweh did not create the earth as *tōhû* – 'to be empty' (TNIV), 'a chaos' (NRSV), 'a waste' (Tanakh), 'empty chaos' (NLT) – but to be inhabited.

Several motifs from Genesis 1:2–3 echo in the prophet Jeremiah's observations:

> I looked at the earth,
> and it was formless and empty [*tōhû wābōhû*]; and at the heavens,
> and their light was gone.
> (Jer. 4:23 TNIV)

Strikingly, the prophet observes that divine judgment has returned the once-beautiful earth to its original state (Gen. 1:2). Even light, God's first creation (Gen. 1:3), is gone, its absence presumably plunging the earth again into its primitive darkness (Gen. 1:2).[16] In short, God's vision of horrible punishment ahead for his people evokes *tōhû wābōhû*, an element of the cosmic language of Genesis 1.

Finally, one striking literary aspect of *tōhû wābōhû* becomes obvious if one reads Genesis 1:2 aloud. The phrase has a rhythmical, sing-song sound,

---

14. Isa. 59:4 offers a significant semantic parallel to *tōhû*, *šāweʾ* ('emptiness, vanity') – in this case, spoken emptiness (i.e. lying testimony).
15. The phrase *lĕrîq*, 'in vain', parallels the word-pair *lĕbōhû wĕhebel* either as two separate nouns (e.g. 'for nothing or vanity' [NRSV]; 'for nothing and to no purpose' [NLT]) or as a hendiadys (e.g. 'for empty breath' [Tanakh]; 'for nothing at all' [TNIV]). See below for discussion of the term hendiadys.
16. For a thorough critique of alleged connections between Gen. 1 and Jer. 4:23 (and its context) – in most points unconvincing, in my view – see Tsumura, *The Earth and the Waters*, pp. 36–40. As I see it, it seems inescapable that Heb. *tōhû wābōhû* and *ʾôr*, 'light', echo the language of Gen. 1:2–3 and, hence, link the two texts.

actually repeating 'o' and 'u' vowels (i.e. *tOhU*, *bOhU*) and featuring similar consonants (i.e. *ToHu*, *BoHu*). Several scholars read the phrase as a hendiadys, a well-known figure of speech in which 'and' links two words ('X and Y') in order to convey a single idea ('X-Y'). For example, in English 'bread and butter' means 'basic food', while 'good and warm' means 'pleasantly warm'. Speiser renders *tōhû wābōhû* as a hendiadys – 'a formless waste'[17] – but from the above discussion I propose that *tōhû wābōhû* be rendered 'lifeless wasteland'. The earth is 'lifeless' (i.e. uninhabited) and 'unproductive' rather than 'disordered' or 'shapeless'.[18]

The earth's condition, line 2

At the time the earth was *tōhû wābōhû*, 'darkness was upon the face of the deep'. Here, Genesis 1:2 shares a motif also found in other ancient cosmologies,[19] and many scholars regard the phenomenon as eerie, ominous and sinister. Its connotations are of 'evil, misfortune, death, and oblivion'.[20] As Wenham remarks, 'If light symbolizes God, darkness evokes everything that is antiGod: the wicked (Pr. 2:13), judgment (Ex. 10:21), death (Ps. 88:13).'[21] In fact, however, in the Bible darkness evokes both benign and sinister associations. It is sinister in that it is the antithesis of light – in modern physics, the default natural state of the world without light – and because it 'conceals the location of a thief'.[22] It is benign in a protective sense – that as a kind of veil for God, it protects humans from seeing him and dying (Deut. 4:11; 5:23; Ps. 18:12). More important, darkness is God's creation (Isa. 45:7) and, thus, subject to his sovereign control (Isa. 42:16; 50:3). The psalmist draws strength from the simple truth that 'even the darkness is not dark to you [God] . . . for darkness is as light to you' (Ps. 139:12 NRSV). Human eyes cannot penetrate darkness, but God's eyes can; it does not obscure his vision or impede his

---

17. Speiser, *Genesis*, p. 5; cf. G. J. Wenham, *Genesis 1 – 15*, WBC 1 (Waco: Word, 1987), p. 15.
18. Tsumura, *The Earth and the Waters*, pp. 30–43, reaches a similar conclusion.
19. For examples, see C. Westermann, *Genesis 1 – 11*, Bk 1/1, 2nd ed. (Neukirchen-Vluyn: Neukirchener Verlag, 1976), p. 144.
20. The quote is from Sarna, *Genesis*, p. 6; cf. N. H. Ridderbos, 'Genesis 1.1 and 2', *Studies on the Book of Genesis*, OTS 12 (Leiden: Brill, 1958), p. 240; Westermann, *Genesis 1 – 11*, pp. 144–145 (an anti-creation condition).
21. Wenham, *Genesis 1 – 15*, p. 16; cf. also Ridderbos, 'Genesis 1.1 and 2', p. 240 ('If unrestricted, no life is possible').
22. Cf. Hamilton, *Genesis 1 – 17*, p. 109, n. 20; cf. Wenham, *Genesis 1 – 15*, p. 16.

protective watch over his own. In short, the mention of darkness in Genesis 1:2 introduces an ambiguous motif: does it symbolize the 'lifeless wasteland' or the cloak of God's hidden presence ready to reveal himself?[23]

The darkness specifically covers the surface of 'the deep' (Heb. *tĕhôm*).[24] *Tĕhôm* lacks the definite article, thus leaving open the possibility that the word might be (or once was) a proper name.[25] An earlier generation of scholars read *tĕhôm* against mythological background, connecting it with the name Tiamat, a primordial goddess in the Babylonian creation account. The latter narrates how Marduk killed Tiamat and cut her body in half to form land and sea. Scholars commonly compared one body part to the 'vault' called 'sky' that God created to hold back the 'waters above' (Gen. 1:6). The present essay, however, shares the recent consensus that *tĕhôm* here is simply a key, ancient cosmological term based on a common Semitic root (*tiham*[*at*], 'sea').[26] Specifically, *tĕhôm* designates 'deep, deep waters' – the cosmic, watery abyss that also appears in Egyptian and Phoenician cosmologies.[27] As Waschke notes,

> Behind all the various cosmogonies stands the shared notion that the world was created from water and that the earth from its beginnings was surrounded on all sides by water.[28]

A few other passages understand that *tĕhôm* comprises both the primeval ocean now above the vaulted sky and the ground water that supplies the earth's surface (e.g. Gen. 7:11; Pss 78:15; 104:6–16).[29] Like darkness, the Bible

---

23. Cf. Wenham, *Genesis 1 – 15*, p. 16.
24. For full discussion, cf. E.-J. Waschke, '*tĕhôm*', *TDOT*, 15:574–581.
25. Westermann, *Genesis 1 – 11*, p. 145.
26. Waschke, '*tĕhôm*', 15:574–575; Ridderbos, 'Genesis 1.1 and 2', p. 238; Westermann, *Genesis 1 – 11*, p. 50; Wenham, *Genesis 1 – 15*, p. 16; Hamilton, *Genesis 1 – 17*, p. 111. By contrast, Sarna, *Genesis*, p. 6, suggests that *tĕhôm* may have been the name of a mythological deity like Tiamat but in Gen. 1 has been 'demythologized' (i.e. emptied of its mythological meaning).
27. Quote Wenham, *Genesis 1 – 15*, p. 16; cf. Waschke, '*tĕhôm*', 15:575; von Rad, *Genesis*, p. 49 (part of priestly learning); Westermann, *Genesis 1 – 11*, p. 147. Sarna, *Genesis*, p. 6, traces the prominence of water in ancient cosmologies to its 'amorphous nature'.
28. Waschke, '*tĕhôm*', 15:575, who conveniently surveys the evidence (pp. 575–577).
29. Ibid., 15:580–581; Wenham, *Genesis 1 – 15*, p. 16. Gen. 1 does not specifically detail the creation of 'the deep', but Prov. 8:22–24 reckons it as one of God's creations.

also pictures deep waters ambiguously. They threaten humans with drowning (Exod. 15:8) – witness the account of Jonah (Jon. 2:6) – but also enable human survival in the arid climate of the biblical world (Gen. 49:25; Deut. 8:7).[30] Certainly, the waters are subject to God's omnipotent sovereignty: he assigned them their place as his servants and as testimony to his wisdom and love (Ps. 33:7; cf. 104:6; Prov. 8:27–28).[31] No biblical text, however, portrays the deep as a power independent of God or as a personified entity capable of creating things on its own.[32]

In short, at this time darkness and deep waters cover the 'earth', but the parting of the terrestrial 'seas' will soon reveal beneath them the 'lifeless wasteland' or 'dry land' hidden there (Gen. 1:9–10).

The earth's condition, line 3

The third and final line of verse 2 pictures something different from the preceding two – something actually moving, not static. It also marks the biblical debut of the *rûaḥ ʾĕlōhîm*, the narrative's only other actor besides *ʾĕlōhîm* (cf. vv. 1, 3–31). Here is where we use the zoom feature of our binoculars. First, one must ask how best to translate *rûaḥ* in this phrase. Basically, the word means 'breeze' or 'breath', but in some contexts it denotes 'wind' or 'spirit'.[33] According to Averbeck, *rûaḥ* as 'breath' and 'wind' occurs in the OT 140 times – 40% of the word's total.[34] In other words, 40% of its occurrences involve the movement of air, whether in weather (Gen. 3:8), in the breath of humans and animals (Gen. 6:17), or metaphorically in God's 'breath' expressed in nature's 'wind' (Exod. 15:8). More important theologically, however, is the fact that in most instances the OT associates 'wind' with God's direct intervention.[35] Thus, whenever *rûaḥ* means 'breath' or 'wind', it still presupposes a connection between the *rûaḥ*-action and God. Finally, in some places to translate *rûaḥ* as 'spirit' fits better than 'breath' or 'wind' (e.g. Gen. 6:3; Pss 139:7; 143:10; Isa. 63:14).

As for *ʾĕlōhîm*, 'God' seems the most obvious translation (*ʾĕlōhîm* is standard

---

30. Wenham, *Genesis 1 – 15*, p. 16.
31. Ridderbos, 'Genesis 1.1 and 2', p. 238; Wenham, *Genesis 1 – 15*, p. 16. Occasionally, the OT personifies the deep (Gen. 49:25; Deut. 33:13; Hab. 3:10).
32. Waschke, '*tĕhôm*', 15:578.
33. For details, cf. S. Tengström, '*ruach*', *TDOT*, 13:365–396.
34. R. E. Averbeck, 'Holy Spirit in the Hebrew Bible and Its Connections to the New Testament', in M. J. Sawyer and D. B. Wallace (eds.), *Who's Afraid of the Holy Spirit?* (Dallas: Biblical Studies Press, 2005), p. 18.
35. Tengström, '*ruach*', 13:382.

for 'God').[36] Some recent scholars, however, read *ʾĕlōhîm* here as a superlative akin to the use of 'God' in the English term 'god-awful', a grammatical usage attested in the OT for several words including *ʾĕlōhîm*.[37] This grammatical practice underlies the translations of *rûaḥ ʾĕlōhîm* as 'terrible storm' (von Rad) and 'awesome wind' (Speiser).[38] It seems improbable, however, that Israel ever used *rûaḥ ʾĕlōhîm* to mean 'mighty wind'. Everywhere else the phrase means 'breath/wind/spirit of/from God', and never 'mighty wind'.[39] Further, the fact that elsewhere in Genesis 1 *ʾĕlōhîm* means 'God' (twenty-nine times) increases the probability that the word in verse 2 has the same sense.[40] Finally, Ancient Near Eastern creation accounts typically portray water and wind as polar opposites, reckoning only the former as part of the primeval 'chaos'. This observation led Ridderbos (among others) to conclude that in Genesis 1 'the deep' (*tĕhôm*) / 'the waters' (*hammayim*) are, in principle, antagonists of *rûaḥ* ('wind'). He thus rightly understood *rûaḥ ʾĕlōhîm* to be 'a wind sent by God'.[41] In other words, the adversative 'but' opens line 3 to signal the contrast between line 3 and line 2: 'but the wind from God slowly moved over the

---

36. E.g., Ridderbos, 'Genesis 1.1 and 2', p. 243; Sarna, *Genesis*, p. 6 ('wind from God'); Wenham, *Genesis 1 – 15*, p. 2 ('wind of God'); cf. Westermann, *Genesis 1 – 11* ('storm of God', my translation); NRSV; JPS Tanakh. Those who prefer the more traditional translation, 'Spirit', include Hamilton, *Genesis 1 – 17*, p. 103; and K. A. Mathews, *Genesis 1 – 11:26*, NAC (Nashville: Broadman & Holman, 1995), p. 130.
37. E.g. for *ʾĕlōhîm*, 'god-awful fire' (Job 1:16, my translation), 'mighty prince' (Gen. 23:6 NRSV), 'terrifying panic' (1 Sam. 14:15, my translation). For discussion, further examples and bibliography, see B. K. Waltke and M. O'Connor, *Biblical Hebrew Syntax* (Winona Lake: Eisenbrauns, 1990), §154, n. 33.
38. Von Rad, *Genesis*, p. 49; Speiser, *Genesis*, p. 4.
39. For what follows, cf. Hamilton, *Genesis 1 – 17*, pp. 111–114; Averbeck, 'Holy Spirit', pp. 24–25. Cf. Speiser, *Genesis*, p. 5, who observes that grammatically *ʾĕlōhîm* in construct may function either as a possessive ('of/from God') or as an adjective (e.g. 'divine, supernatural, awesome' but not 'mighty' [Gen. 30:8]).
40. A further questionable implication also arises for interpreters who assume that v. 2 refers to chaos. As Hamilton notes (*Genesis 1 – 17*, p. 112), the superlative theory yields a confusing juxtaposition of meanings for *ʾĕlōhîm*. It sets in opposition the *ʾĕlōhîm* who creates the heavens and the earth (v. 1) and speaks light into being (v. 3) with the *ʾĕlōhîm* in the superlative 'mighty wind' of chaos.
41. Ridderbos, 'Genesis 1.1 and 2', p. 244, who describes it as battling the hostile primeval waters in order to dry out the earth.

waters'.[42] In sum, while possible, the superlative sense seems the less likely sense than 'God', and that is the view taken here. Shortly, I will suggest that Genesis 1 presents the 'wind' and 'waters' not as 'antagonists' but as simple 'contrasts'.

A review of OT usage of *rûaḥ ʾĕlōhîm/YHWH* is instructive, as the chart below shows.[43]

***Use of rûaḥ ʾĕlōhîm/YHWH* in the Old Testament**

	Text	Verbal formula	Action's recipient	Result
1.	Gen. 1:2	'hover, sweep, move' *raḥap* (pi.) *ʿal*	Waters' surface	N/A
2.	Gen. 41:38	'be in (someone)' (*hāyâ*) *bĕ*	Joseph	Wise leadership
3.	Num. 24:2	'come upon (someone)' *hāyâ 'al* X	Balaam	Spoken prophecy Military victory
	Judg. 3:10*		Othniel	Military victory
	Judg. 11:29*		Jephthah	Prophetic actions
	1 Sam. 19:20		Saul's messengers	Prophetic actions
	1 Sam. 19:23		Saul	Spoken prophecy
	2 Chr. 15:1		Azariah	Spoken prophecy
	2 Chr. 20:14*		Jahaziel (a Levite)	Spoken prophecy
4.	Ezek. 11:5*	'fall upon (someone)' *nāpal ʿal*	Ezekiel	Spoken prophecy
5.	Isa. 11:2*	'rest upon (someone)' *nûaḥ ʿal*	New David	Wise rule
6.	Isa. 61:1**	'(be) upon' (*hāyâ*) *ʿal* X	A prophet	Spoken announcement
7.	Exod. 31:3 Exod. 35:31	'fill (someone) with' (*millēʾ* [pi.])	Bezalel	Artistic work
	Mic. 3:8*	'be full of power' (*mālēʾ* [qal] + *kôaḥ*)	Micah	Spoken prophecy

42. The LXX, also, interprets the relationship between the two lines as adversative; cf. Tengström, '*ruach*', 13:384.

43. Westermann, *Genesis 1 – 11*, p. 148, and Tengström, '*ruach*', 13:382, also conveniently summarize the use of this phrase; cf. R. Ouro, 'The Earth of Genesis 1: Abiotic or Chaotic? Part III', AUSS 38/1 (2000), pp. 59–67.

***Use of rûaḥ ʾĕlōhîm/YHWH* in the Old Testament (continued)**

	Text	Verbal formula	Action's recipient	Result
8.	Judg. 14:6*, 19*	'come upon (someone) in power' *ṣālaḥ ʿal*	Samson	Military victory
	Judg. 15:14* 1 Sam. 10:6*, 10 1 Sam. 11:6 1 Sam. 16:13*		Saul	Prophetic activity
9.	Judg. 6:34* cf. 2 Chr. 12:19	'come upon' (lit. clothe) *lābaš*	Gideon	Military victory Spoken prophecy
	2 Chr. 24:20		Zechariah	
10.	Judg. 13:25*	'begin to stir' *ḥālal* hi. + *pāʿam*	Samson	Military attacks
11.	Isa. 59:19*	'drive' *nûs* (pol.) *bĕ*	Pent-up river	New flow
11.	2 Sam. 23:2*	'speak (through)' *dibbēr* [pi.] *bĕ*	David	Spoken prophecy
12.	1 Kgs 22:24* = 2 Chr. 18:23*	'cross from X to speak to Y' *ʿābar* + *dibbēr* (pi.)	Micaiah	Spoken prophecy
13.	1 Kgs 18:12	'carry' *nāśāʾ*	Elijah	Prophetic relocation
14.	2 Kgs 2:16*	'lift up and throw (someone)' *nāśāʾ* + *šālak* (hi.)	Elijah	Prophetic relocation
15.	Ezek. 11:24	'lift up . . . vision given' *nāśāʾ . . . marʾeh bĕ*	Ezekiel	Prophetic vision
16.	Ezek. 37:1	'bring out by . . . and set down' *yāṣāʾ* (hi.) + *nûaḥ bĕtôk*	Ezekiel	Prophetic commission
17.	Job 33:4#	'made (someone)' *ʿāśâ*	Elihu	Human life
18.	Isa. 63:14*	'give (someone) rest' *nûaḥ* (hi.)	Israel	Rest
19.	Isa. 40:7	'blow on' *nāšab bĕ*	Grass and flowers	Wither, fall
20.	Isa. 40:13*	'fathom' *tikkēn* (pi.)	God by humans	Nothing
21.	Mic. 2:7*	'be short' *qāṣar*	N/A	Judgment

**rûaḥ YHWH*

#*rûaḥ ʾēl*

***ʾădōnāy YHWH*

The chart tells us much about the *rûaḥ ʾĕlōhîm/YHWH*. The recurrence of the preposition *ʿal* ('upon') implies that the *rûaḥ* comes from somewhere else – from God, to be sure – and either hovers overhead, rests invisibly atop, or perhaps envelops its recipients. The *rûaḥ* also seems to arrive on scene unrequested and unexpected; it shows up suddenly and simply takes over. As a result, a human person of very limited power immediately becomes 'clothed' or 'filled' with (also 'full of') decisive divine power. The *rûaḥ ʾĕlōhîm/YHWH* asserts incredible influence on people and nature: it 'stirs', 'drives', 'lifts', 'throws', 'brings out', 'sets down', 'makes', 'blows on' and 'gives rest'. Startling things begin to happen with humans and in nature. The most common phenomenon of *rûaḥ* is spoken or acted prophecy; prophets (and others) speak, are relocated, or act like a prophet. More broadly, Bezalel also designs the tabernacle, judges defeat invaders and human life begins; grass and flowers wither and die, and a river resumes its flow. All these reflect the continuing mastery of God over his creation via the *rûaḥ ʾĕlōhîm*, a mastery we may infer in Genesis 1:2 as well.

Finally, the participle (*mĕraḥepet*) of which *rûaḥ ʾĕlōhîm* is the subject merits close attention. The root *rāḥap* occurs three times in the OT, once in the qal (Jer. 23:9, 'to tremble') and twice in the piel, both with the preposition *ʿal* (Gen. 1:2; Deut. 32:11, 'to hover, tremble').[44] In the former passage, Jeremiah laments the grievous unfaithfulness of his fellow prophets ('My heart is broken within me; all my bones tremble [*rāḥap*]' NIV), while the Song of Moses (Deut. 32:11) compares Yahweh's loving care of Israel to that of an eagle teaching its offspring to fly.[45] He rouses his nestlings, watchfully 'hovers' (*rāḥap* [pi.]) over them, and protectively spreads his wings to take them to safety if they falter. In my view, three things support a preference for a connection between Genesis 1 and Deuteronomy 32 rather than with Jeremiah 23:9. First, the same form of *rāḥap* (piel) + *ʿal* appears in both texts. Second, the cognate root in Ugaritic for *rāḥap* also concerns the movement of eagles, perhaps with the sense 'to soar'.[46] Third, only the root in Deuteronomy 32

---

44. Cf. 'swept' (NRSV), 'was hovering' (TNIV), 'sweeping' (Speiser, *Genesis*, p. 4), 'move' (Westermann, *Genesis 1 – 11*, p. 107, my translation of his German word).

45. In my view, this remains the best reading of the text, despite Hamilton's argument (*Genesis 1 – 17*, p. 115) that Heb. *ʿûr* in Deut. 32:11 compares to Ugaritic *ǵyr*, 'to watch over, protect' rather than 'to hover'.

46. For translation, cf. Hamilton, *Genesis 1 – 17*, p. 115, who rightly points out, however, that thus far scholars have only found the root in a single text. The very rarity of the root in both Hebrew and Ugaritic might imply that the piel is a technical term

concerns the movement of wings and has associations with wind.[47] If so, one must not imagine a stationary 'hovering' like a helicopter but a continuous, probably slow, sweeping movement like an eagle in flight.[48]

Through the picture window: Genesis 1:2, again

Our final look at Genesis 1:2 sets the binoculars aside and views the scene from a distance through an imaginary picture window. Our question is, what does the passage teach us theologically about the relationship of the *rûaḥ* ('breath/wind'/'spirit') and creation? But first, we must ask a fundamental question concerning the context: is the earth's condition 'chaos'? This is important because, if the *rûaḥ* acts towards the waters, rather than simply being present over them, we must decide what those waters represent.

Chaos or what?

For decades scholars have understood creation in Genesis 1 as a process by which God transforms the world from chaos to order. Surprisingly, our binocular study of Genesis 1:2 seems to point us away from that assumption. If by 'chaos' one means an earth in disorder and disarray – that *tōhû wābōhû* is Hebrew for 'helter-skelter' – then 'chaos' would be the appropriate term. In my view, however, Genesis 1:2 portrays the earth's condition not as chaotic but simply as 'an unproductive and uninhabited place'.[49] Deep waters cover it, and darkness enshrouds it – certainly, a condition a great distance from the later positive state that *ʾĕlōhîm* calls 'very good' (Gen. 1:31). But, in my reading, verses 3–31 picture creation neither as the clean-up of a disordered mess nor as the conquest of a rebellious, anarchic power called chaos. Instead, day by day, a series of spoken divine statements transform the empty, lifeless earth

---

for flight typical of eagles. Whether 'the wings of the wind' (Ps. 104:3) alludes to the same metaphor is at least worthy of consideration.

47. Tengström, '*ruach*', 13:384.

48. *HALOT*, 1137–1138; cf. Tengström, '*ruach*', 13:384, who suggests that *rāḥap* may connote aggressive or provocative movement in both Deut. 32 and Gen. 1:2. If so, Gen. 1:2 might evoke the well-known biblical image of the wind driving back, if not drying up, the primal waters so the earth might emerge, grow vegetation and become habitable for humans and animals (Gen. 1:2, 9–12; cf. Isa. 17:13; 50:2; Nah. 1:3–4; Ps. 18:16[15]=2 Sam. 22:16; Ps. 106:9). For my alternative view, see below.

49. Tsumura, *The Earth and the Waters*, p. 43.

into a well-watered, fertile and lush world where humans and animals may thrive (vv. 11–30).[50]

First, the process separates the waters vertically, leaving some above the sky and some below it on earth's surface (vv. 6–8). Then it repositions the terrestrial waters horizontally by collecting them into 'seas' so the 'dry land', heretofore hidden underwater, may debut (vv. 9–10). At that point, the now-visible earth presents a stark, silent scene: a lifeless wasteland, empty of vegetation and human or animal inhabitants. Behind this process stands not chaos *per se*, but the fundamental polarity noted earlier – the primal deep waters over against (but not hostile to) the *rûaḥ* of God.[51] The waters symbolize not an enemy but 'passive, powerless, formless primordial matter, from which nothing can arise by its own power'.[52] They represent lifeless raw materials with potential for creation and life if empowered by divine power. Their opposite, the *rûaḥ* from God, metaphorically represents that kind of primal energy, the embodiment of creation's active potential. The juxtaposition of water and *rûaḥ* signals that a decisive moment of divine empowerment is about to happen.

Rûaḥ ᵓĕlōhîm/YHWH: *its connotations*

What traits does the *rûaḥ ᵓĕlōhîm/YHWH* display that illumine its role in creation? In Genesis 1:2, the *rûaḥ* is completely invisible; it offers no material form to be seen. But were human eyes watching, they might see the effects of its silent movement across the waters. If we are to imagine the *rûaḥ* soaring like an eagle, then in its wake flow gentle ripples or majestic waves rolling across the deep. Were human ears listening, they might hear its rustle or rumble, audible like the wind, as it slowly moves over the waters. Or the presence of the *rûaḥ* may unleash an even louder moment – a raucous, noisy and threatening storm, or even the cacophonous violence of a swirling hurricane – rather than the quiet calm of peacefully undulating waters. In sum, visible signs and audible sounds from an invisible source attest the on-site presence of the mysterious *rûaḥ* in Genesis 1:2. Though invisible, the *rûaḥ ᵓĕlōhîm* is not static.

---

50. According to Dabney, Gen. 1 portrays 'a complex activity of *ordering* . . . *making* . . . *naming* . . . *including* . . . and *blessing* by means of which God fills the empty darkness and makes it light'; cf. Dabney, 'Nature of the Spirit', pp. 80–81. Along the same line, Yong ('Ruach', pp. 193–194) sees a similar pattern through processes of division, distinction, differentiation and particularization.

51. Tengström, '*ruach*',13:384–385.

52. Ibid., 13:385.

Its slow movement across the scene smacks of superhuman power ready to work – or, at least, that is what readers familiar with the phrase elsewhere in the OT imagine. The phrase conjures up images of a powerful force sent by God to influence both humans and nature.

Breath/wind, spirit, or both?

Thus far, I have opted to use the Hebrew *rûaḥ* rather than render it either as 'breath/spirit' or 'wind'. My purpose has been to hold at bay possible misunderstandings that either English rendering might potentially evoke. For example, some readers who understand the spirit to be the giver of life might infer from Genesis 1:2 that the universe already had life in itself – that somehow and in some sense it was already alive rather than lifeless. Others might deduce that the spirit is itself a distinct being alongside *ʾĕlōhîm*. But both ideas are alien to the OT. Some Christian readers might even assume – in my view, wrongly – that the mention of the 'spirit of God' here marks the biblical debut of the third person of the Trinity. Now, however, looking through the picture window at the whole scene, I want to revisit the question by assessing several proposals about how *rûaḥ* as 'breath' and 'spirit' may relate.

In Hamilton's view, for example, if one believes the *rûaḥ* in Genesis 1:2 to be destructive, then 'wind' is the appropriate translation; but if it is thought to be beneficent, then 'S/spirit' is the better translation.[53] There is, however, no biblical reason to think that 'wind' is by nature always destructive rather than at times beneficent. Indeed, if the assumed polarity between *rûaḥ* and water(s) noted above also underlies their relationship in Genesis 1:2, the *rûaḥ* may rightly be read as a potentially positive influence. Also, I believe that the text presents the waters in a more neutral than negative light. Alternatively, Averbeck observes that the distinction between 'breath/wind' (i.e. the movement of air) and the 'S/spirit', whether divine or human, is not as sharp in Hebrew as it is in English.[54] This is simply because the same word (*rûaḥ*) shows both meanings. In other words, *rûaḥ* is inclusive (vice exclusive) of the word's two primary senses, and that implies an underlying connection between them. This is true whether one speaks, for example, of the human 'spirit' or the 'S/spirit' of God.

In my view, this connection is evident in Genesis 2, the narrative about the creation of humans. The lifeless physical form of the Human (*hāʾādām*) becomes a 'living being' when God breathes 'breath' (*nĕšāmâ*) into his nostrils

---

53. Hamilton, *Genesis 1 – 17*, p. 114.
54. Averbeck, 'Holy Spirit', pp. 25–26.

(v. 7; cf. Ps. 104:29).[55] Now, according to the story the Human has two main dimensions, one material (symbol: 'dust') and the other immaterial (symbol: 'breath'). The latter symbolizes both the 'life' that now throbs in the Human and also his personhood. As a person, he has self-awareness, powers of reason and reflection, emotions, a 'spirit' (i.e. outlook, mood, temperament, etc.) and an awareness of God. Since God is invisible, the Human's physical side cannot derive directly from God's being. But the narrative implies that the 'breathy' side of the Human – his personhood – does derive from and correspond to God's nature as a person. This is why in some texts *rûaḥ* is best rendered 'spirit', whether describing the nature of God (Gen. 6:3; Hag. 2:5) or of the Human (Job 17:1; Ps. 31:5).

Indeed, Averbeck suggests that the *rûaḥ ʾĕlōhîm* in Genesis 1:2 may simply be a double entendre, connoting both 'breath/wind' and 'spirit' at the same time.[56] The double entendre idea also connects well with the earlier observation that the OT often associates the *rûaḥ ʾĕlōhîm* with speaking by prophets (see below). In sum, I affirm Averbeck's conclusion that:

> there is no reason *ruakh* in Gen 1:2 cannot be a reflection of the power of God present and ready to work through 'wind' . . . (cf. Gen 8:1 and Exod 14:21–22 and 15:8–10. . .) as well as the work of the 'Spirit' of God in shaping the creation through pronouncements (Gen 1:3ff.), both at the same time. . .[57]

The point is that Genesis 1:2 presents us with 'wind' as a reflection of the 'S/spirit of God' who now speaks.

Spirit and word

What about this intriguing juxtaposition of the *rûaḥ ʾĕlōhîm* (Gen. 1:2) and the subsequent 'words' spoken by *ʾĕlōhîm* (Gen. 1:3–31)? Does their narrative proximity imply a connection between the *rûaḥ* and the following creation? In my view, three things support that assumption. First, the biblical association elsewhere of the presence of the spirit with divine speech at least raises that possibility. The above chart shows that one prominent role of the *rûaḥ ʾĕlōhîm* is to empower spoken prophecy and prophetic actions. The

---

55. Heb. *nĕšāmâ* ('breath') and *rûaḥ* are synonyms; cf. Eccl. 12:7, in which translations divide between rendering *rûaḥ* as 'breath' (NRSV, Tanakh) or 'spirit' (TNIV, NLT).

56. The OT often associates the *rûaḥ ʾĕlōhîm* with wind (Exod. 15:8, 10; Isa. 40:7; 59:19; 1 Kgs 18:12; 2 Kgs 2:16).

57. Averbeck, 'Holy Spirit', pp. 24–25; cf. his discussion of Ezek. 37 (pp. 25–26).

coming of the *rûaḥ* upon a human often produces a prophetic oracle – 'Thus says the LORD', followed by direct divine speech. It is striking, then, that as soon as the *rûaḥ* line concludes (v. 2), the very next words report 'And God said' and divine speech – the command 'Let there be light' (v. 3). The latter marks the beginning of God's creative acts after the preface of verses 1–2.[58] To assume a connection between spirit and word would make good sense.

Second, the narrative's literary flow seems to presume that connection. In my view, to understand that the *rûaḥ* participates in creation makes the best contextual sense. Observe that Genesis 1 reports the active, powerful presence of the *rûaḥ* (v. 2) but not its exit from the scene. The spirit of God typically manifests superhuman divine power and, as noted above, its very mention is reason enough to expect it to act in some way. Further, the alternative reading offers a literarily less credible scenario. It would dramatically introduce the spirit as a contrast, if not a counter-force, to the wasteland, darkness and deep waters, and then have it inexplicably vanish from the story. On the contrary, the narrative seems to say that, once it debuts, the *rûaḥ* fully participates in creation, empowering, if not executing, the series of divine words. The 'breath/wind from God' is not simply a force of nature, a common motif in Genesis 1, but God's power ready to work. More important, Averbeck argues plausibly that 'S/spirit from God' would 'provide a more natural lead into vv. 3–31 than would "breath/wind." If so, Gn. 1 would feature the "S/spirit of God," as it were, "breathing out" his pronouncements.'[59]

Finally, the assumption of spirit participation compares to the understanding of creation elsewhere in the OT:

> By the word [*dābār*] of the LORD the heavens were made,
> their starry host by the breath [*rûaḥ*] of his mouth.
> (Ps. 33:6 TNIV; cf. Pss 147:18; 148:8)

The synonymous parallelism implies a close connection between 'word' and 'breath' and thus lends support to Averbeck's inclusive image of the S/spirit 'breathing out' God's pronouncements. Put differently, God's spoken word

58. Granted, in prophecy the *rûaḥ* prompts a human prophet to speak as if he or she were God himself, whereas here God speaks directly. Nevertheless, the direct juxtaposition of the *rûaḥ* sent by God and directly quoted divine speech is striking.
59. Averbeck, 'Holy Spirit', p. 25; cf. the similar view of Tengström, '*ruach*', 13:385.

'makes the creative energy [of the *rûaḥ*] effectual'.[60] More important, by giving audible substance to the invisible 'breath' of God's mouth, the spoken 'word' probably lays a kind of semantic bridge. The bridge leads from the simple idea of 'breath' through the 'word' to 'a truly spiritualized interpretation of [it], the idea of "spirit" in the strict sense'.[61]

The spirit and creation: summary

Genesis 1:2 presents a very dramatic but ambiguous scene, one fraught with both great uncertainty and also great potential. So what is the *rûaḥ ʾĕlōhîm* doing in relation to creation? To begin, there are two things that, in my view, the *rûaḥ* is *not* doing. First, the divine breath/wind/spirit and the waters are not *warring* antagonists. Genesis 1:2 makes no overt reference to any battle or conflict as do other ancient accounts. Thus the conflict interpretation assumes a more direct connection between the latter stories and Genesis 1 than the evidence supports. Rather, the contrast is between the moving, active, powerful, protective and life-giving 'spirit of God' and the stationary, inactive, powerless, unproductive and inert deep waters. The latter symbolize great potential for life and productivity present in the raw materials of Genesis 1:2 rather than hostile opposition. The divinely sent breath/wind/spirit metaphorically represents what Tengström calls 'primal energy that embodies the active potential of creation'.[62] Second, there is no indication that the *rûaḥ* is 'drying up', 'driving back' or 'subduing' the waters/deep as some scholars claim.[63] Such views assume the popular notion that in Genesis 1 God is bringing order out of chaos, an assumption I do not share. As noted above, I affirm that, without struggle, God's commands lead to a two-stage repositioning of the waters so that the 'dry land' becomes visible for the first time (vv. 6–9; cf. Ps. 104:2b–4).

More positively, the canonical position of Genesis 1:2 is striking. Though only one verse, Genesis 1:2 marks the canonical debut of the *rûaḥ ʾĕlōhîm*, an

---

60. Tengström, '*ruach*', 13:385.

61. J. Hehn, 'Zum Problem des Geistes im Alten Orient und im AT', *ZAW* 43 (1925), p. 220 (quoted from Tengström, '*ruach*', 13:385).

62. Tengström, '*ruach*', 13:385, who elsewhere (p. 381) calls the *rûaḥ* 'God's [pre-existent] creative energy'.

63. Cf. Averbeck, 'Holy Spirit', p. 24 ('drying up'); Tengström, '*ruach*', 13:386 ('driving back'); Dabney, 'Nature of the Spirit', p. 80 ('subduing').

invisible manifestation of God's 'breath' – perhaps as 'wind' – that will later make cameo appearances throughout both Testaments. The verse introduces an important biblical phenomenon tantamount to God's power personified almost as if it were a character in God's cosmic drama. Before creation began (v. 3), Genesis 1:2 claims that 'the *rûaḥ* of God' was already slowly moving across the dark, watery scene. What are we to make of this?

First, simply and subtly the *rûaḥ* *ʾĕlōhîm* symbolically asserts the presence of Almighty God amid the darkness and the waters. That very presence affirms that the wasteland still stands under the sovereign sway of Yahweh. More important, given the use of *rûaḥ* *ʾĕlōhîm* surveyed earlier, the phrase here also asserts the presence of divine power – 'primal energy' sent by God and poised to transform the scene in some obvious way. The spirit is invisible, but the spirit is there to act, not to watch. Its presence goes beyond a simple symbolic claim that God is omnipresent – as if God were saying, 'Yoo-hoo, I'm over here!' The spirit compares to an active player warming up on the field for a game, not a spectator seated passively in the stands. Also, its powerful presence creates reader expectation that through the *rûaḥ* God is about to do something important – and perhaps even to *speak*. The reader knows that, whether stirring humans or nature, the *rûaḥ* always shows up decisively to intervene or effect change.

Second, just as divine 'breath' breathes life into lifeless humans (Gen. 2:7; Job 12:10), so the *rûaḥ* breathes a specifically *life-giving* breath into the scene. Its mention signals that God is about to breathe life into the lifeless wasteland – to cause the barren, empty earth to flower and flourish and become inhabitable by all God's creatures. Made alive, the world will provide a beautiful, bountiful home for the 'living soul' that God will create and place there. As a whole, creation puts God's wondrous revelation on display for all eyes to see and all ears to hear. At the same time, it 'bears witness to the mysterious source in God's invisible, creative energy, God's *ruach*'.[64] The spirit's presence implies what Dabney calls 'the possibility and promise of creation': God will fill the emptiness, dispel the darkness by light and reposition the waters. In the soaring of the *rûaḥ* across the deep lies the hope that 'God's possibility for the world' may become a reality.[65]

Finally, the spirit may contribute to at least two other creation phenomena.

64. Tengström, '*ruach*', 13:386.

65. Cf. Dabney, 'Nature of the Spirit', p. 80, who, however, assumes that the 'possibility' is the divine answer to the disordered chaos, an assumption that I do not share.

The first is what Yong calls 'the interactivity and co-creativity' between God and the creation evident in Genesis 1.[66] In some cases, God 'breathes' out his commands and the creation simply obeys – for example, with light (v. 3) and the separation of the lower waters and dry land (v. 9). But at other times, the narrative portrays God as interactive: he names things (vv. 5, 8, 10), or sees them and responds by declaring them 'good' (vv. 4, 10, 12, 18, 21, 25, 31). And in one case, God seems to concede co-creativity to the earth: rather than act or command action, God calls the earth on its own to produce seed-bearing plants and trees (v. 11).[67] Thus Genesis 1 portrays God as commanding, responding and granting creative agency to agricultural processes, processes that began on Creation Day 3 and still continue today. With the latter, God asks the earth to act as, in essence, co-creator without surrendering his absolute sovereignty as Creator. And Yong's 'pneumatological hypothesis' rightly traces the diverse phenomena back to 'the dynamic, particularizing, relational, and life-giving presence and activity of the Spirit of God'.[68]

The same co-creativity also belongs to all 'en-spirited' living creatures (Yong's term), human and animal – what Yong calls 'the unfinished dimension of the creation'. They have the potential and the God-given freedom 'to fulfill creation's reason for being', on the one hand, or 'to sabotage the divine intentions', on the other.[69] Finally, Psalm 104:30 highlights the role of the divine *rûaḥ* in one specific 'unfinished [creation] dimension' – continuing procreation. Yahweh still sends his life-giving 'breath' to enliven future generations of creatures as he did in Genesis 1 – 2:

> When you [Yahweh] send your Spirit [*rûaḥ*],
> they [all life] are created [*bārāʾ*, ni.],
> and you renew the face of the ground.
> (TNIV)

Surprisingly, the psalmist invokes the word 'create', the same word as in Genesis 1. Apparently, he considers such new life, whatever its temporal distance from the first creation, to be another moment of 'creation'. He

---

66. For what follows, cf. Yong, 'Ruach', pp. 196–198; M. Welker, 'What is Creation? Rereading Genesis 1 and 2', *Theology Today* 48 (1991), pp. 56–71.
67. Other examples featuring the same formula, 'Let creation-part-X produce Y', follow it with reports that God 'made' or 'created' them (vv. 20–22, 24–25).
68. Yong, 'Ruach', p. 198.
69. Ibid, pp. 198–199.

understands that the original creation and later creations belong to a single continuous process, one that continues even to our day – and still involves God's *rûaḥ*. And, of course, that is not all that the spirit is doing!

Conclusion

It turns out that von Rad overstated his case against the relationship of the spirit and creation in the OT. Granted, only two texts (Gen. 1:2; Ps. 104:30) expressly link *rûaḥ* with creation (*bārā*ʾ), but they are telling. Viewed close up through binoculars or at a distance through a picture window, they affirm that the *rûaḥ* as breath/spirit, through the spoken divine word, 'en-spirited' the original creation and 'en-spirits' new births many millennia later. Thus the invisible *rûaḥ ʾĕlōhîm/YHWH*, now as then, asserts the mastery of God over his creation. Whenever the spirit is present, life-giving divine activity is either already in progress or not far behind. Originally a literary preface to Genesis 1:3–31, Genesis 1:2 canonically marks a programmatic statement that launches a long biblical trajectory of the spirit's life-breathing activities (e.g. John. 20:22; Rev. 22:17). And that trajectory still continues; the spirit still breathes life and light to dispel darkness and to empower the powerless.

PART 3: THE SPIRIT AND WISDOM

4. SPIRIT AND WISDOM

Tremper Longman III

The temptation is strong for Christians simply to assume that the '*rûaḥ* of God/Yahweh' in the OT is the same as the Holy Spirit in the NT. Such a view is even forwarded or at least implied by some scholars writing on the subject. Too many books simply assume a connection between the OT 'spirit of God' and the Holy Spirit as the third person of the Trinity.[1]

John Walton, on the other hand, certainly does not err in this way, which is not surprising if one is acquainted with his hermeneutical approach and his deep caution over 'reading the New Testament into the Old Testament'. In Walton's discussion of the 'spirit of God hovering over the waters' in Genesis 1:2, he points out that the spirit of God is not a separate entity or person in the OT but an extension of God himself analogous with the expression 'the hand of the Lord'. On this basis, he denies that one can exegetically justify the idea that the Holy Spirit was involved in the creation of the cosmos in some special way.

1. Christopher Wright's otherwise helpful book *Knowing the Spirit through the Old Testament* (Downers Grove: InterVarsity Press, 2006) can be criticized in this regard. As will become clear, I do not so much disagree with Wright's conclusions, as with the fact that he does not adequately reflect on the OT in its own right before looking at it from the perspective of the fuller theology of the NT.

Walton does note, however, that at least on occasion the NT identifies the 'spirit of God' with the action of the Holy Spirit. He specifically mentions that the anticipation of the pouring out of the 'spirit of God' in Joel 2:28 is said to be fulfilled by the pouring out of the Holy Spirit on the Day of Pentecost (Acts 2:16–17), and he admits that 'the Holy Spirit was behind at least some of the activity attributed to the *rûaḥ* of God in the Old Testament'.[2]

I am largely in agreement with Walton, but not quite, which is also not surprising for those who know my views on the relationship between the Testaments.[3] In other words, I would strongly agree that the OT authors and their original audiences did not have any inkling of the Holy Spirit as a separate person of the Trinity. And we must first of all appreciate, to use Childs's phrase, 'the discrete witness' of the OT.[4] However, also with Childs, as Christians we are invited to read the OT in the light of the fuller revelation of the NT. In the light of Christ's ministry, the OT anticipation of him is much easier to see (Luke 24:25–27, 44–48). So in the light of the experience of the Holy Spirit at Pentecost and after, the role of the Holy Spirit in the OT is much easier to see as well. On a practical level, what this means is that I am more willing than Walton to see continuity between the OT 'spirit of God' and the Holy Spirit. It appears that Walton will only affirm this in a case like Joel 2 if that connection is explicitly made in the NT, whereas I would take such connections as encouragement to see the continuity as broader. Such an approach may bring us close to the view of Wright and others, but rather than assuming the 'spirit' in the OT is a reference to the Holy Spirit, each occurrence will have to be considered on its own merits. The purpose of this volume, though, is to look at the spirit of God in its OT context.

That said, the focus of my chapter is specifically on the spirit and wisdom. When I first received the assignment, I have to say that I was a bit concerned whether or not I would have adequate material to write a substantial contribution to the book. As we will see, there is minimum reference to the 'spirit of God' in the books of Proverbs, Ecclesiastes and Job. However, understanding my topic not as the spirit and wisdom literature, but as the spirit and wisdom

---

2. See his discussion on this topic in *Genesis: The NIV Application Commentary* (Grand Rapids: Zondervan, 2001), pp. 76–77, with the quote coming from p. 77.
3. See my discussion in T. Longman, *Reading the Bible with Heart and Mind* (Colorado Springs: NavPress, 1997), pp. 43–45.
4. B. S. Childs, *Biblical Theology of the Old and New Testaments: Theological Reflections on the Christian Bible* (Minneapolis: Fortress, 1993), p. 76.

provides plenty of material for discussion. Even so, I will begin by looking at the three wisdom books: Proverbs, Job and Ecclesiastes.

The spirit in wisdom literature

The spirit in Proverbs

Proverbs has only one relevant passage for our discussion, but it is a very interesting passage that shows a close connection between wisdom and spirit. The context of the passage is the first speech that Woman Wisdom gives in the book of Proverbs (1:20–33). She is speaking in the street at the entrances to the city gate. She is appealing to foolish men (simple-minded, mockers, fools) who ignore her. In 1:23 she says:

> You should respond to my correction.
> I will pour forth my spirit to you;
> I will make known to you my words.[5]

In other words, here she assures those who do listen to her that they will receive her spirit and her words.

Of course, to understand this passage fully we must explore the significance of the figure of Woman Wisdom in the book of Proverbs. Who is Woman Wisdom?

To answer this question, we are drawn to chapters 8 and 9. Chapter 9 is pivotal to the proper interpretation of the book of Proverbs, since it sets up a choice between dining with Woman Wisdom (9:1–6) or with Woman Folly (9:13–18). Chapter 8 gives the fullest description of Woman Wisdom, and for our purposes perhaps the most salient point is that she was an observer and perhaps even a participant in the creation (8:22–31). However, in terms of recognizing the significance of the figure of Woman Wisdom, the most important indication comes from the location of her house. In 9:3 we learn that she invites men to a meal from her house which is located at the 'pinnacle of the heights of the city'.[6]

Whose house would be found at the heights of the city? God's. The temple

---

5. Translations from Proverbs are from Tremper Longman III, *Proverbs*, BCOTWP (Grand Rapids: Baker, 2006).
6. Taking the plural 'heights' as indicating majesty, thus the highest peak of all. See also comment below on 9:14.

was built on the height of the city. Most will agree that Woman Wisdom is a personification of God's wisdom, but I go further in saying that Woman Wisdom represents God himself, just as Woman Folly, whose house is also on the 'heights of the city' (9:14), represents the false gods that try to lure Israelites away from the true God.[7]

Before returning to 1:23, let me point out that this choice between Woman Wisdom and Woman Folly indicates that wisdom and folly are not just practical categories, but theological ideas. To be wise means to be in relationship with Woman Wisdom, that is God himself, while to be foolish is to be in relationship with false gods. The book of Proverbs presents this choice between the two women at the culmination of the discourses and at the transition to the proverbs *per se* so that the theological significance of wisdom and folly will reverberate in chapters 10 – 31.

But returning to 1:23, we see Woman Wisdom, who represents God himself, assuring those who would listen to her that she will pour out her spirit to them. God's spirit, of course, is the source of life, which is also the destination of those who pursue wisdom. She also promises to reveal her words to them,[8] most immediately the words of the book of Proverbs, which seeks to guide the sage on the right path and to avoid the path of folly.[9]

Proverbs 1:23 shows a clear connection between the spirit and wisdom of God (Woman Wisdom). This connection becomes even clearer in later passages, but first a look at Job.

The spirit in Job

Before looking at particular passages in Job, it is important to orient ourselves to the book as a whole. The main issue in Job is wisdom. Suffering is the foil that allows the discussion of wisdom to take place.[10] Job suffers, and the

7. For the full argument, see Longman, *Proverbs*, pp. 58–61.
8. Notice the close connection between spirit and word in other passages (Isa. 42:6; 49:5; 54:10; 55:5; 59:21; 61:8).
9. See the helpful discussion of this passage by Wilf Hildebrandt, *An Old Testament Theology of the Spirit of God* (Peabody: Hendrickson, 1995), pp. 42–43, where he approvingly quotes McKane as saying, 'The intention here may be to represent Wisdom as a charismatic, spirit-filled person, who pours out on those who are receptive and submissive the spirit of wisdom' (*Proverbs: A New Approach*, OTL [Philadelphia: Westminster, 1976], p. 274).
10. See my more extensive comments in T. Longman and R. Dillard, *An Introduction to the Old Testament*, 2nd ed. (Grand Rapids: Zondervan, 2006), pp. 224–236.

human participants in the story debate the reason why. They all have their own diagnosis and their own prescription for Job's problem. They struggle since they are not privy to the information given to the reader in the prologue (Job 1 – 2). We know beyond a shadow of a doubt that Job is innocent (1:1, 8; 2:3). He is not suffering because of his sin. The three friends' diagnosis of Job's problem is that he is a sinner and their prescription is that he needs to repent (see, for example, Bildad's argument in Job 8). They are fully committed to the idea that sin leads to suffering, so suffering is a symptom of sin. Job also affirms this type of retribution theology, but there is a problem – he knows he is innocent. Therefore, he wants an audience with God in order to set God straight. God is unjust. Elihu comes late into the debate, but he ends up arguing like the three friends. Finally God speaks out of the whirlwind to Job asserting his wisdom and power, but not giving Job an answer to the question of why he suffers (38:1 – 40:2; 40:6 – 41:34).

This description of the book of Job could be expanded and nuanced, of course, but this basic overview is sufficient for the purpose of this chapter. The important point for us to remember as we examine passages in which God's spirit is mentioned is that the book of Job presents a variety of conflicting perspectives on Job's suffering and wisdom and one cannot presume that a statement from one of the human participants in the story is theologically normative. One cannot quote the three friends, Elihu, or even Job himself and say, 'Thus says the Lord.' In short, when they speak of the 'spirit of God', we cannot presume that they accurately reflect the truth of the matter. With that background, let us survey the relevant passages in the book of Job. These are passages that speak of the spirit of God.

Job 4:7–17: authority in spiritual wisdom

In his first speech Eliphaz makes an interesting appeal to divine authority for his argument against Job that suffering is the result of one's sin. After appealing to observation and life experience in 4:7–11, he relates the following episode:

> A word stole over to me;
>   my ears took a whisper of it.
> In anxious thoughts of night visions,
>   when deep sleep falls on people.
> Fear and trembling called to me;
>   my bones trembled mightily with fear.
> A spirit passed by my face;
>   the hair on my skin stood on end.

He stood there, but I could not recognize its appearance.
A form was before my eyes.
Silence, but I heard a voice.
'Can mortals be righteous before God?
Can a man be pure before his Maker?'
(4:12–17)[11]

Eliphaz surrounds the heavenly voice that speaks in verse 17 with great mystery. Verses 12–16 describe the experience and his reaction to it in a way that builds up suspense and intrigue. Though he implies that the speaker is a 'spirit' (v. 15), he never clearly identifies the spirit or the voice. The spirit may be an angel. However, Clines may be right when he argues that the spirit is God himself since 'form' (4:16) is always used of God, and that wind often accompanies divine theophany.[12] Again, the recalled event is surrounded by mystery, though the claim is clearly that the statement is coming with heavenly authority.

The revelatory moment begins with subtlety. The 'word' (*dābār*, which can also mean 'message') 'stole' (from *gnb*) over to him. Like a robber it came by stealth, without warning, unexpectedly. Of course, there is no substantial connection with the description of Christ's coming 'as a thief in the night' (1 Thess. 5:2; 2 Pet. 3:10; Rev. 3:3), but both phrases are communicating the idea of surprise. The message (word) did not come through loud and clear, but just as a whisper, again a description that emphasizes mystery as well as secrecy or privacy.

The description that Eliphaz gives is suggestive of an intuition, an internal moment of insight. Of course, he is claiming more than that, or at least he is claiming that his intuition has the authority of heaven behind it.

Even so, this intuition is disquieting according to verses 13–14. It is like a nightmare, or at least a dream that deeply disturbs. Indeed, Eliphaz says that it came in a dream (a vision during deep sleep). This dream produced deep anxiety and fear. Again, this may be no more than a claim of divine revelation. This spirit comes from the heavenly realm and so disturbs mere humans who are the recipients.

The climax of the claim is that a 'spirit' (*rûaḥ*) passed by him. The

11. The translations of the book of Job in this chapter are all from my forthcoming Job commentary to be published by Baker.
12. David J. A. Clines, *Job 1 – 20*, WBC (Nashville: Thomas Nelson Publishing, 1989), p. 131.

identification is not precise or clear; however, it is clear that whatever the 'spirit' was, it was not of this world. In spite of Clines's comments, it is only possible, not at all certain, that Eliphaz is thinking of the spirit of God here. More likely, the idea is that it is some kind of supernatural, perhaps angelic, being. Even so, the experience is eerie and scary. The spirit is an otherworldly presence, thus lending its message authority.

In the silence, he heard only a voice. The voice speaks a word that at first is hard to penetrate. The claim is that no-one can be righteous before God. And if no-one can be perfectly righteous, then Job is not either and deserves the suffering that is coming his way. Job himself will interact with this claim in chapter 9.

Thus, in a subtle, secretive, yet bold way, Eliphaz is enlisting divine support for his contention that Job is a sinner in need of repentance.

Job 20:2–3

In his second and final response to Job, Zophar prefaces his substantial argument by referring to his motivation for speaking:

> My distress causes me to respond
> due to the agitation within me.
> I hear instruction that shames me
> and a spirit beyond my understanding gives me a reply.

If this is the correct translation of the Hebrew phrase *rûaḥ mibbînātî*, taking the min as a privative, then Zophar is appealing to a spiritual source for his wisdom that comes from outside his own understanding. He is thus making a similar appeal to authority as Eliphaz did in chapter 4. On the other hand, it is possible to understand the preposition as locational, indicating the source of Zophar's understanding. Clines suggests that Zophar 'is not given to supernatural revelations' and thus translates the colon 'an impulse from my understanding prompts my reply'.[13] I disagree and believe that Eliphaz appeals to a supernatural authority.

Job 26:2–4

> What help have you been to the powerless?
> What rescue have you brought to the weak arm?

13. See ibid., pp. 471–472.

> What counsel have you brought to those without wisdom?
> What abundant success do you teach?
> Whose words do you speak,
> and whose breath/spirit has come from you?

Job responds to Bildad by a series of sarcastic rhetorical questions. Bildad and his three friends have held themselves up as sages, able to help Job in his predicament. Job rightly points out that in their insistence that Job's suffering is the result of sin, they have been no help at all.

His final question then attacks the source of their advice and presumes that Bildad is claiming some kind of spiritual authority. Bildad implicitly claims to speak from divine authority, but Job is denying that.

Job 32:6–10

While there is some doubt as to whether Eliphaz is appealing to divine or angelic authority in his reference to a 'spirit' who imparts wisdom, there is much more certainty that Elihu makes an appeal to a divine spirit in the opening of his monologue directed at Job:

> So Elihu the son of Barakel, the Buzite, answered and said:
> I am young,
> and you are aged.
> Therefore, I was very afraid,
> to express my opinion to you.
> I said, 'Let days speak,
> and an abundance of years make wisdom known.'
> However, it is the spirit in a person,
> the breath of Shaddai which gives them understanding.
> The many are not wise;
> the elders do not understand justice.
> So I say, 'Listen to me!
> I will show you my opinion.'

Here the 'spirit in a person' is parallel to 'the breath of Shaddai', thus giving us confidence that Elihu is claiming that his wisdom comes from God himself. He is contrasting this source of authority with the wisdom of experience which is the product of living a long time as embodied by the three friends. However, the three friends have failed in their attempt to lead Job to repentance, so now the spirit-filled Elihu will attempt it.

Conclusion

In these speeches, we see an attempt on the part of Eliphaz, Zophar, Job and Elihu to ground wisdom in the spirit. This spirit is clearly God's in the latter three's speeches and is at least heavenly, if not divine, in Eliphaz's.

How do these texts contribute to our understanding of wisdom and the spirit? We must be cautious here. In the context of the whole book of Job, all the wisdom of the human participants (including Job) is ultimately rejected as illegitimate. As God himself says to Eliphaz at the end of the book, 'you did not speak correctly about me' (42:8). Eliphaz's claim to wisdom is false and his appeal to spiritual authority is bogus. As for Elihu, his status in the book is a bit more ambiguous. How are we to interpret the silence that greets his speech? Some commentators take this as implicit agreement. Eliphaz is simply paving the way for the Yahweh speeches. My own opinion agrees with those who consider the silence as a rejection of Elihu's perspective. Neither Job nor God finds it necessary to address him, since he simply repeats the advice of the three friends. He too thinks that Job's problem is a sin problem (34:10–15). The inclusion of the Elihu speech is to show the inadequacy of yet another human pretension of wisdom, namely those who falsely attribute their wisdom to a spiritual source.

God's spirit as the source of life in the book of Job

God's spirit is also mentioned in Job in reference to the source of life in a person. At least one passage[14] has this significance, Job 27:1–6:

> Job continued his discourse and said:
> By the living God who has turned aside my rights,
> and by Shaddai who has made me bitter,
> as long as my breath is in me,
> and the spirit of God is in my nostrils.
> my lips will not speak falsehood;
> my tongue will not mutter deceit.
> Far be it from me that I should concede that you are right;
> up to the point that I expire I will not turn aside my innocence.
> I will embrace and not weaken my grasp on my righteousness;
> my heart will not reproach my days.

---

14. According to some translations that take *rûaḥ* as spirit, Job 26:13 may be a second example, but I think it is more likely that here *rûaḥ* is a reference to the breath of God that makes the heavens/skies beautiful by blowing away the clouds.

In verses 2–6 Job reaffirms his intention to continue to insist on his righteousness in the face of his friends' arguments. Interestingly, he makes his point by an oath in the name of God. But even in the midst of his oath, he takes the opportunity to express his disappointment and frustration with God. He believes God has denied him his rights with the result of turning him bitter. He promises to continue his resistance against the friends as long as he is alive (v. 3). The 'spirit of God' (*rûaḥ ᵓĕlōhîm*) here should be simply taken as a reference to the breath that God breathed into mortal nostrils (Gen. 2:7;[15] Eccl. 12:7),[16] though breath can also refer to S/spirit (Ps. 104:29–30). To deny his own righteousness would be to lie (v. 4). He refuses to lie simply to cater to the opinions of his friends in order to make them go away. We will soon see that Job's persistence rather than his concession is what makes them go away (though it energizes Elihu to get involved). There has been no softening of Job's position. He is as confident as ever of his righteousness and the fact that God is unjust to let him suffer.

The spirit in Ecclesiastes

Job 27:1–6 is a good introduction to a brief examination of the only passage in Ecclesiastes worth discussion under the topic of God's spirit in wisdom literature, namely 12:7, which culminates Qohelet's reflections on death:

> the dust returns to the earth as it was,
> and the spirit returns to God who gave it.[17]

This passage, even more than the Job passage, shows its connection to Genesis 2:7. There is no optimism here in Qohelet's statement. He is not talking about the human soul going to heaven to live with God, but rather the dissolution of life. God takes back his spirit which is the animating source of life.

Conclusion: the spirit of God in wisdom literature

It would be wrong to characterize 'the spirit of God' as a major theme in wisdom literature. Even so, there is a discernible connection between

---

15. Though there, *nišmat* rather than *rûaḥ* is used.
16. The same may be said concerning the use of 'his spirit and breath' in Job 34:14. The reason why all flesh would expire if he gathered his spirit and breath back to himself is that it would be a reversal of Gen. 2:7 (see comments on Eccl. 12:7 below).
17. Translations from Ecclesiastes come from T. Longman, *Ecclesiastes*, NICOT (Grand Rapids: Eerdmans, 1997).

wisdom and the spirit. Granted the best reading of Job understands the claim of a spirit-inspired wisdom as false claims by Eliphaz (4:7–11), Zophar (20:2–3), Job (26:2–4) and Elihu (32:6–10). Proverbs 1:23, though, is the one clear passage that positively links the spirit with wisdom. Also, the false claims of the human participants of Job to have received their wisdom from the spirit of God only make sense if this was a viable avenue of wisdom at the time.[18]

If this was all we had in terms of the connection between wisdom and the spirit in the OT, that would not be much. But there is more. We turn now to other OT passages outside the wisdom literature *per se* that show a decided connection between wisdom and the spirit of God. After that, we will look at post-biblical developments of this connection that also serve as a background to the fuller revelation of the NT.

The spirit that brings wisdom

Old Testament passages that link the spirit and wisdom

The wisdom of Joseph

> The proposal pleased Pharaoh and all his servants. Pharaoh said to his servants, 'Can we find anyone else like this – one in whom is the spirit of God?' So Pharaoh said to Joseph, 'Since God has shown you all this, there is no one so discerning and wise as you. You shall be over my house, and all my people shall order themselves as you command; only with regard to the throne will I be greater than you.' (Gen. 41:37–40 NRSV)

Joseph has long been recognized as an embodiment of biblical wisdom in his speech and in his actions. Indeed, some scholars have identified the Joseph narrative as a type of wisdom literature, though this has been debated.[19] In this passage, the Pharaoh himself makes a connection between Joseph's

---

18. We have noted that Job 27:3; 33:14 and Eccl. 12:7 refer to God's spirit as the animating force of human life in relationship to Gen. 2:7.
19. See James Crenshaw, 'Method in Determining Wisdom Influence upon "Historical" Literature', *JBL* 88 (1969), pp. 129–142; Michael V. Fox, 'Wisdom in the Joseph Story', *VT* 51 (2001), pp. 26–41; Tremper Longman III, *How to Read Proverbs* (Downers Grove: InterVarsity Press, 2002), pp. 92–95.

wisdom and the spirit of God. Of course, Pharaoh is a pagan king, but God can reveal his truth in the mouth of pagan kings (remember Neco in 2 Chr. 35:22). As Hildebrandt points out, Joseph does not demur from Pharaoh's assessment and actually affirms it in Genesis 41:16 when he attributes to God his ability to interpret Pharaoh's dreams.[20]

The wisdom of Bezalel

> See, I have called by name Bezalel son of Uri son of Hur, of the tribe of Judah: and I have filled him with the spirit of God, with ability, intelligence, and knowledge in every kind of craft. (Exod. 31:2–3 NRSV;[21] see also 35:30–31)

Bezalel was the chief craftsman in the construction of the tabernacle. His ability to do the intricate work necessary to complete the tabernacle and its furniture 'according to the pattern . . . which is being shown you [Moses] on the mountain' (Exod. 25:40) is not a natural skill, but rather a divine gift imparted by the spirit of God. The abilities are here described using terms associated with wisdom, including *ḥokmâ*, which the NRSV renders 'ability', but could equally be rendered 'wisdom'.

The wisdom of Joshua

> Joshua son of Nun was full of the spirit of wisdom, because Moses had laid his hands on him. (Deut. 34:9 NRSV)

Joshua, of course, is the divinely appointed successor to Moses. He is the one who will lead Israel into the Promised Land and fight the battles that will establish God's people there. Deuteronomy 34:9 grounds his ability to accomplish these tasks in wisdom connected to the gift of the spirit, a spirit he received when Moses laid hands on him as recorded in Numbers 27:12–23.

The wisdom of Daniel
Similarities abound between the Joseph narrative and the account of Daniel. Both serve in foreign courts. Both are recognized for their God-given talents and are promoted to important positions within the foreign court. And both

---

20. Hildebrandt, *An Old Testament Theology of the Spirit of God*, pp. 105–106.
21. Adopting the alternate reading provided in the footnote: 'spirit of God' rather than 'divine spirit'.

are recognized by their pagan overlords as possessing a divine spirit that gives them their abilities. Nebuchadnezzar expresses this truth in a typically pagan way in Daniel 4:8 when he says of Daniel that he is 'endowed with a spirit of the holy gods'.[22] Belshazzar uses the same formula in Daniel 5:11. Again, Daniel himself attributes his ability to interpret dreams not to himself but to God, so again we may be seeing a connection between the spirit of God and wisdom in the person of Daniel.

The wisdom of the Messiah

> A shoot shall come out from the stock of Jesse,
> and a branch shall grow out of his roots.
> The spirit of the LORD shall rest on him,
> the spirit of wisdom and understanding,
> the spirit of counsel and might,
> the spirit of knowledge and the fear of the LORD.
> His delight shall be in the fear of the LORD.
> (Isa. 11:1–3 NRSV)

Judgment in Isaiah is often described as a cutting down of trees (see 6:13; 10:33–34). The 'stock [or stump] of Jesse' indicates that the Davidic line has also been cut down.[23] However, the tree is cut down, not dead. The 'shoot' that springs up shows that David's line will have new life. It will be restored and will once again bear fruit. The association of the stump with Jesse rather than David indicates that there is a new beginning here, a going back to origins, and a distancing from the later corrupt kings of Judah. The continuation of the Davidic line is an indication of the grace of God based on the covenant of kingship with David where God said, 'Your house and your kingdom shall be made sure for ever before me; your throne shall be established for ever' (2 Sam. 7:16 NRSV). As redemptive history progresses, the new Davidic dynasty is not realized in later Davidic descendants like Zerubbabel (Ezra 3; Zech. 4), but in Jesus Christ.

The shoot is different in character from other descendants of David. Most of them were self-seeking, fearful and cruel. The 'spirit of the LORD' characterizes this descendant. The spirit fills this leader with 'wisdom', the ability to

---

22. Or, as the NRSV footnote puts it, 'a holy, divine spirit'.
23. For an alternate translation and understanding of this image, see the chapter by Hilary Marlow in this volume.

rule, and strength, the power to rule. Scripture makes it clear that the spirit brings wisdom (Exod. 31:3; Deut. 34:9) and that wisdom leads to productive and just rule (1 Kgs 4:29; Prov. 8:15–16).

The 'fear of the LORD' is the basic characteristic of a wise, godly person (Prov. 1:7). The fear described here is not terror, but more like awe. This wise, Spirit-filled person will not judge according to external appearances, but will cut to the heart of the truth of a matter.

The spirit and wisdom in intertestamental literature

As we study the wisdom literature of the intertestamental period, we take note of any even closer connection drawn between the spirit and wisdom. First, we briefly consider Sirach, or Ecclesiasticus, a book written in Hebrew in the first part of the second century BC, but translated into Greek by the grandson of the original author (Yeshua ben Eleazar ben Sira) in 132 BC. While perhaps the most notable emphasis on wisdom in this book is a closer connection between wisdom and law (19:17–20; 24:22), it is also interesting that the connection we noted between wisdom and spirit receives mention in this book. In his description of the sage, he states, 'if it pleases the Lord Almighty, he will be filled with the spirit of understanding, he will pour forth his words of wisdom and in prayer give thanks to the Lord. . .' (39:6). As Montague says, 'wisdom is not totally identified with meditation on the law, for the "spirit of understanding" is a gift of God to be sought in prayer.'[24]

But it is in the Wisdom of Solomon that 'the understanding of the spirit in the wisdom tradition reaches its high point'.[25] This work, in which the author assumes the persona of Solomon, was written sometime between 100 BC and AD 50.[26] Illustrative of the close connection between wisdom and the spirit, we cite 7:22b–25, a description of Woman Wisdom:

> There is in her a spirit that is intelligent, holy,
> unique, manifold, subtle,

---

24. G. T. Montague, *The Holy Spirit: The Growth of a Biblical Tradition* (Eugene: Wipf and Stock, 2006), p. 100.
25. Ibid.
26. P. Enns, 'Wisdom of Solomon', in T. Longman III and P. Enns (eds.), *Dictionary of the Old Testament: Wisdom, Poetry, and Writings* (Downers Grove: InterVarsity Press, 2008), p. 885, prefers sometime during the reign of Caligula (AD 37–41).

> mobile, clear, unpolluted,
> distinct, invulnerable, loving the good, keen,
> irresistible, beneficent, humane,
> steadfast, sure, free from anxiety,
> all-powerful, overseeing all,
> and penetrating through all spirits
> that are intelligent, pure, and altogether subtle.
> For wisdom is more mobile than any motion;
> because of her pureness she pervades and penetrates all things.
> For she is a breath of the power of God,
> and a pure emanation of the glory of the Almighty;
> therefore nothing defiled gains entrance into her.
> (Wisd. 7:22b–25 NRSV)

While we can clearly see here the influence of Greek philosophy in this description of Woman Wisdom, we can also see a further elaboration of the thought already expressed in Proverbs 1:23 where Woman Wisdom imparts her spirit to those who are wise.

Conclusion

Thus concludes our survey of wisdom and the spirit of God from the OT into the intertestamental literature. The most interesting text within wisdom literature was Proverbs 1:23 which describes Woman Wisdom pouring forth her spirit on those who listen to her. The idea that there was a connection between God's spirit and wisdom likely fuels the pretensions of Eliphaz, Zophar, Job and Elihu in the book of Job. We noted that the idea that wisdom came with the gift of the spirit was articulated in descriptions of Joseph, Bezalel, Joshua, Daniel and the future branch of David. We concluded by looking at further developments in the intertestamental period, particularly in the Wisdom of Solomon.

How does one get wisdom? The wisdom literature, from Proverbs to the Wisdom of Solomon, encourages study and the pursuit of wisdom. However, once wisdom is attained, it must be acknowledged that wisdom is not the result of human effort, but rather it is a divine gift. Our survey has shown that this gift is often described as the gift of the spirit of God.

This background prepares the way for Paul, who well understood the connection between true wisdom and the Holy Spirit, so I conclude with a passage from 1 Corinthians 2:10–16:

> [T]hese things God has revealed to us through the Spirit; for the Spirit searches everything, even the depths of God. For what human being knows what is truly human except the human spirit that is within? So also no one comprehends what is truly God's except the Spirit of God. Now we have received not the spirit of the world, but the Spirit that is from God, so that we may understand the gifts bestowed on us by God. And we speak of these things in words not taught by human wisdom but taught by the Spirit, interpreting spiritual things to those who are spiritual.
>
> Those who are unspiritual do not receive the gifts of God's Spirit, for they are foolishness to them, and they are unable to understand them because they are discerned spiritually. Those who are spiritual discern all things, and they are themselves subject to no one else's scrutiny.
>
> 'For who has known the mind of the Lord
> so as to instruct him?'
>
> But we have the mind of Christ.[27] (NRSV)

27. Note Acts 6:3 where the seven men chosen to serve are 'well respected and are full of the Spirit and wisdom'.

5. JOB 27:3: THE SPIRIT OF GOD IN MY NOSTRILS

Rosalind Clarke

While the Spirit of God is not a prominent theme in the wisdom books of the OT, nevertheless the few references to the Spirit in these books are significant for the insight they provide into the common theological understanding of the OT. In Job 27:3, Job illustrates this by swearing an oath by his own breath and by the Spirit of God in him. This divine *rûaḥ* to which Job lays claim is best understood as the life-giving spirit of Genesis 2:7, which is common to all human beings, and expresses not only physical life but also humanity and personhood.

Genre and the problems of doing exegesis in Job

The book of Job presents interpreters with a notoriously complex set of exegetical and hermeneutical issues deriving from the multiple layers of narrative and discourse within the text. One useful identification of the book's genre is that of the 'frame tale',[1] in which the narrative prologue and epilogue

---

1. See Michael Cheney, *Dust, Wind and Agony: Character, Speech and Genre in Job*, Coniectanea Biblica Old Testament Series (Stockholm: Almqvist & Wiksell, 1994), p. 24.

are understood to provide a framework for the discourse within. The frame tale genre identification highlights the book's 'ability to contain a diversity of material without reducing that material to a single meaning or point'.[2] This characteristic diversity warns the interpreter against a simplistic hermeneutic of harmonization. Instead, Cheney suggests that the frame tale invites an intertextual approach to reading, whereby the book of Job is understood to contain multiple 'texts', i.e. the framing narrative and the central discourse.[3] The genre of the book does not require that these 'texts' present a single, harmonious viewpoint, but it does demand that they be read together, so that the meaning of the book is found in the interaction of the whole, rather than in the separate parts.

This diversity means that it is not a straightforward task to determine what, if anything, the book as a whole affirms to be true. Some clues to this are provided in the divine and narratorial judgments given in the framework sections. In each of these, Job is affirmed in some way, though the extent of this approval is somewhat ambiguous. In the prologue, Job is praised for his uprightness, his God-fearing status and his immediate response to the catastrophes which befall him (1:1, 8, 22; 2:3, 10). In the epilogue, however, Job himself repents of speaking that which he did not understand (42:6–7), and it is possible that God's affirmation of Job in 42:7–8 only relates to this repentance.[4] The framing narrative thus establishes a presumption that Job is a more trustworthy speaker than his friends (who are only condemned for their speech), but it stops somewhat short of offering unqualified approval of all his words. In any case, it is possible that the presumptions of the framing narrative may be subverted by the nature of the discourse, and in fact, this is what happens, for it is the friends who speak in accordance with traditional orthodoxy,[5] and in many respects Job and his friends share a common theology.[6] This suggests that doctrinal correctness is not the primary issue under

---

2. Ibid., p. 284.
3. Ibid. This notion of multiple texts within a text may fruitfully be extended further, to consider each speech within the discourse as a 'text' to be read intertextually with the rest of the book.
4. Edwin M. Good, *In Turns of Tempest: A Reading of Job, with a Translation* (Stanford: Stanford University Press, 1990), p. 382.
5. Marvin H. Pope, *Job: Introduction, Translation, and Notes*, AB, 3rd ed. (Garden City: Doubleday, 1973), p. 350.
6. Duck-Woo Nam, *Talking about God: Job 42:7–9 and the Nature of God in the Book of Job*, Studies in Biblical Literature (New York: Peter Lang, 2003), p. 105.

consideration. In Duck-Woo Nam's careful study of 42:6–7, he agrees that the question here is not one of truthfulness, but one of 'constructiveness'.[7] Job's 'constructive' dialogue led him into direct encounter with God which resulted in his transformed perspective. Thus Nam concludes that although Job's theological presuppositions are essentially the same as his friends', there is a crucial difference of perspective: while the friends argue that God *is* fair and reliable, Job argues that God *should* be those things. And, perhaps most constructively of all, Job speaks *to* God, whereas the friends speak *about* God.[8]

This makes the question of exegesis somewhat simpler, at least with respect to Job 27:3, since Job and his friends do appear to share a common theology of the spirit of God. The terminology used in Job 27:3 and Job's other speeches is found throughout the friends' speeches in similar contexts, indicating a common baseline of understanding.[9] There is no reason to attempt to distinguish an orthodox view of the spirit in Job's speeches from an unorthodox position in those of his friends. Thus, with all the caution due to the genre and peculiarities of this difficult book, it can reasonably be assumed that when Job speaks of the *rûaḥ ʾĕlôah* in his nostrils and the *nĕšāmâ* in him, he does so with the same basic meaning as his friends, and this is presented within the structure of the book as essentially correct.

Context and corrupted text in Job 27

Job 27 occurs within the third cycle of the disputation speeches, where the established pattern begins to break down. The brevity of Bildad's speech (25:1–6), the double introduction of Job's speech (26:1; 27:1), the absence of a speech from Zophar, and the content, style and tone of Job's speech have provided grounds for reconstruction of the text. Although the full extent of the speech including 27:3 is debated, it is generally agreed that 27:2–6 should be reckoned as Job's.[10] Whether as a response to Bildad's final speech, or a

7. Ibid., pp. 23–24. See also Good, *In Turns of Tempest*, p. 381.
8. Nam, *Talking about God*, p. 187.
9. Even where the terminology appears in the parodic speeches of Elihu, challenging the theology of the spirit presumed earlier in the book, it simultaneously confirms that this theology is widely recognized and accepted, in order for the parody to be effective.
10. The main alternatives are: Bildad (25:1–6; 26:5–14), Job (26:1–4; 27:1/2–12), Zophar (27:13–23) (Norman C. Habel, *The Book of Job: A Commentary*, OTL

response to the whole disputation cycle, 27:2–6 sees Job at his most desperate, and yet at his most determined 'not to surrender his position of innocence'.[11] These verses constitute what David Wolfers describes as 'a magnificent oath of moral independence . . . incontestably Job's'.[12]

Job makes his oath invoking God himself as his surety: 'The deity named in the oath formula is called on to curse the speaker if the oath is not true.'[13] The speech begins in verse 2 with the standard formula for an oath, *ḥay-ʾēl*,[14] which would normally be followed directly with the content of the oath. In this instance it is usually presumed that there is an implied relative pronoun following the oath formula, introducing the description of the God on whose life Job swears: 'As God lives, *who* has set aside my right and embittered my soul. . .'[15] For Habel, this oath effectively summons God into the courtroom as an active participant in the dialogue, so that it 'is not just another verbal

---

[London: SCM, 1985], pp. 375–378; Robert Gordis, *The Book of Job: Commentary, New Translation and Special Studies*, Moreshet Series, vol. 2 [New York: Jewish Theological Seminary of America, 1978], pp. 1, 283); Job (27:2–6, probably v. 12 and possibly v. 11), a friend, possibly Zophar (27:7–10, 13–23) (Samuel Rolles Driver and George Buchanan Gray, *A Critical and Exegetical Commentary on the Book of Job: Together with a New Translation* [Edinburgh: T. & T. Clark, 1921], p. 225); Bildad (25:1–6; 26:5–14), Job (26:1–4; 27:1–7), Zophar (27:8–25) (Pope, *Job*, p. 187). For a contrary view, identifying some of the problems with the reconstructive approach, see David Wolfers, *Deep Things out of Darkness: The Book of Job – Essays and a New English Translation* (Kampen: Kok Pharos, 1995), pp. 246–247.

11. David J. A. Clines, *Job 21 – 37*, WBC (Nashville: Thomas Nelson, 2006), p. 644.
12. Wolfers, *Deep Things*, p. 247.
13. Habel, *Job*, p. 379. Habel notes that this echoes Job's wife's suggestion in 2:9, that Job should 'Curse God and die'. Here, he is inviting God to curse him and die.
14. See Joüon 165e for the exclamatory formula: *ḥay* followed by the person or life on whom the oath is taken. A positive oath is introduced with *kî* or *ʾim lôʾ* and a negative one with *ʾim* (165f.). The forms using *ʾim* and *ʾim lôʾ* may indicate an oath intended to reinforce an affirmation. A similar form is found in 1 Sam. 14:39, 45; 2 Sam. 2:27.
15. See GKC 155f. An alternative translation would have Job swearing the truth of what is already past. In this case the oath is not a guarantee of future behaviour but merely an assessment of Job's present condition: 'As God lives, he *has* turned aside my lawsuit and the Almighty *has* embittered my soul.' If this is correct, v. 3 begins a new thought, not with an oath formula but with a conditional phrase that nonetheless takes the force of an oath.

outburst in the speech cycle, but a catalytic action in the narrative plot which is designed to initiate a reaction from God'.[16] Verse 3 continues the oath, in which Job now swears upon his own life, expressed as his 'breath' (*nĕšāmâ*) and as the 'spirit of God' (*rûaḥ ʾĕlôah*). The content of the oath is found in verse 4, that he will not lie. Driver interprets the whole oath in the past, as an assertion from Job that what he has already spoken is true, rather than a promise of how he will speak in the future.[17] Either makes sense in the context, as a reference to Job's earlier speeches or as a reference to his forthcoming summary defence. He may be calling on his friends to admit the truth of what he has already told them, or declaring his promise to make a truthful case before God. What is clear is that Job is at the very end of his tether, he is fed up of being doubted and disbelieved, and he is prepared to stake his trustworthiness on the highest possible authorities: his God and his life.

Job 27:3

Job 27:3 is structured with a form of synonymous parallelism, in which the conditional in the first half is elided in the second, effectively holding the whole verse closely together. The syntax of the conditional phrase is somewhat awkward but it can be resolved if *ʿôd* is understood as a noun, so that the expression translates as something like 'for all existence' or, in more idiomatic English, 'for as long as'.[18] The protasis of the condition consists of two parts, parallel in their form:

For as long as	my breath	is in me
kî-kol-ʿôd	*nišmātî*	*bî*
	and the spirit of God	is in my nostrils. . .
	wĕrûaḥ ʾĕlôah	*bĕʾappî*

The syntactic parallelism is reinforced by the use of the word pair *nĕšāmâ* and *rûaḥ*.[19] The repeated preposition together with the pronominal suffix (attached in the first instance to the preposition and in the second case to the noun) complete the parallel. The elided form of the parallelism suggests that

16. Habel, *Job*, p. 380.
17. Driver, *Job*, p. 226.
18. See Gordis, *Job*, p. 287; cf. 2 Sam. 1:9.
19. See Isa. 42:5; 57:16; as well as Job 4:9; 27:3; 32:8; 33:4; 34:14.

there are not two distinct criteria in view but two different ways of referring to the same criterion: Job's breath will remain in him and the spirit of God will remain in his nostrils, both for as long as he lives. Nevertheless the two forms of expression are not precisely synonymous,[20] and the differences between them are as revealing as their similarities.[21] The nature of parallelism sets up an interaction between the two halves, inviting both comparison and contrast, such that the second form of expression in some way enriches the first.

My breath in me

The first subject of Job's oath is his *nĕšāmâ*, a relatively uncommon word in the OT which usually denotes the breath of a living being (e.g. Isa. 2:22; 42:6),[22] such that the absence of *nĕšāmâ* is recognized as a sign of death, as in 1 Kings 17:17. By metonymy, *nĕšāmâ*, like the more common Hebrew words for breath (*nepeš* and *rûaḥ*), can be used to refer to life itself (Gen. 7:22; Isa. 42:5). This metonymy is strengthened by the association of *nĕšāmâ* with the life-giving act of creation (Gen. 2:7; Isa. 57:16): God's breath (*nĕšāmâ*) is breathed (*nph*) into Adam to make him a living being (*nepeš*).[23] T. C. Mitchell has argued that *nĕšāmâ* may be understood as a specifically human (or divine) phenomenon, and as that which distinguishes mankind from the animals. Mitchell's argument depends on his analysis of the OT use of the term: on eighteen occasions, *nĕšāmâ* is unequivocally applied only to human beings or to God,[24] and of the remaining eight uses, Mitchell suggests that none absolutely require the extension of the term to animals.[25] He also notes the use of *nĕšāmâ* in the crea-

20. Precise synonyms are virtually impossible to find. Robert Alter points out: 'literary expression abhors complete parallelism, just as language resists true synonymity, usage always introducing small wedges of difference between closely akin terms' (Robert Alter, *The Art of Biblical Poetry* [New York: Basic Books, 1985], p. 10).
21. Adele Berlin, *The Dynamics of Biblical Parallelism* (Grand Rapids: Eerdmans, 2008), p. 98.
22. In one instance, *nĕšāmâ* appears to refer to something like 'spirit' or 'consciousness' (Prov. 20:27), though this proverb is difficult to translate with any certainty.
23. God's *nĕšāmâ* is not only evident in the act of creation, but also in his acts of destruction (2 Sam. 22:16 = Ps. 18:16; Isa. 30:33).
24. T. C. Mitchell, 'The Old Testament Usage of *nĕšāmâ*', *VT* 11 (1961), p. 181.
25. The most problematic verse for Mitchell's theory is Gen. 7:22, where it is clear from the context that all kinds of living beings are in view. He suggests that the final phrase of v. 21, *wĕkol hā'ādām*, might be read as the beginning of the following sentence, so that *kol 'ăšer nišmat* refers only to this phrase, and not to the other

tion account as a means by which mankind is distinguished from the animal kingdom. Thus he proposes that it is tenable to claim that *nĕšāmâ* describes the breath of God in the OT, 'which, when imparted to man, made him unique among the animals'.[26] Mitchell does, however, admit that his argument is not conclusive,[27] and this view of *nĕšāmâ* has not been widely accepted. While it is true that *nĕšāmâ* is most frequently used to describe the breath or life of God or human beings, this sense must always be conveyed by the context in which it is used. The specific meaning suggested by Mitchell, that *nĕšāmâ* is the divine creative breath which distinguishes human beings from animals, cannot be presumed.

In the book of Job, *nĕšāmâ* is used on seven occasions, by Eliphaz, Job and Elihu, with a breadth of meaning. Both Eliphaz and Elihu use it only to refer to God's breath, in which context it serves as a metaphor for his creative force (33:4; 37:10), his sustaining power (34:14) and his destructive ability (4:9). In 32:8 it is the breath of the Almighty which gives understanding to human beings (32:8). Although there is a strong focus on the divine *nĕšāmâ*, this aspect is not implicit in the meaning of *nĕšāmâ* but must be specified in each case.[28] In this respect, *nĕšāmâ* is no different from the various other divine anthropomorphisms employed in the book. By contrast, on the two occasions when Job uses the term, it has a human connotation. In 26:4 Job questions his friends, demanding to know with whose *nĕšāmâ* they are speaking. Here, while the breath is associated with human speech, it also has a deeper reference, probing the motivating force behind that speech and indicating that there is some external *nĕšāmâ* prompting the friends. The question is left hanging as to whether this *nĕšāmâ* is divine or has some other origin. Only in 27:3 is *nĕšāmâ* unequivocally human. This breath is Job's own, explicitly located within him, and yet even here the parallel with *rûaḥ* *ʾĕlôah* tantalizingly suggests that

---

kinds of living beings mentioned previously (ibid., p. 181). This seems unlikely, especially given the explicit mention of both animals and mankind in the following verse. Further, if only human beings are in view, it is unclear why it should be necessary to specify that they are *beḥārābâ*, 'on the dry ground'. This only makes sense if it is distinguishing land animals from sea creatures. The related term *tinšemet* is used for a type of bird (Lev. 11:18, 30; Deut. 5:23), though, as Mitchell notes, this does not necessarily imply anything about the use of *nĕšāmâ* with respect to birds or other animals (ibid., p. 185).

26. Ibid., p. 186.

27. Ibid., p. 186.

28. Clines, *Job 21 – 37*, p. 646.

something more than physical human breath may be in view. One possibility suggested by Norman Habel is that, while the primary allusion in the verse is to the creative work of God's breath, the metaphysical sense of *něšāmâ* and *rûaḥ* may also be in view:

> 'Breath' (*něšāmâ*) and 'spirit' (*rûaḥ*) refer to the animating life force from God (34:14 cf. Gen 2:7, 7:22). 'Breath' and 'spirit', however, may also be viewed as the source of insight and intelligence (32:8, 33:4, cf. 20:3, 25:4). Though plagued in body and bitter of soul (v. 26), Job takes his oath of integrity as one 'being of sound mind'.[29]

However, there is nothing in the immediate context to indicate that this metaphysical sense is intended and the parallel is hardly conclusive on this point, since *rûaḥ* can also have a variety of meanings. On the contrary, the context of the oath suggests that it is Job's very life and breath which are at stake, not merely his sanity: his promise stands for as long as he has breath, that is, as long as he lives.

The spirit of God in my nostrils

Job's oath continues by invoking the *rûaḥ ʾělôah* which is in his nostrils. The book of Job attests to many of the wide range of meanings of the term *rûaḥ*. It can be a straightforward reference to the wind (1:19; 15:1; 28:25), a way of describing worthlessness (6:26; 8:2; 16:3; 15:2), a metaphor for the transience of life (7:7) or for the existence of life (10:12; 12:10). It can refer to the breath of a human being (9:18; 19:17) or the breath of God (26:13), or it may have a metaphysical sense, denoting a person's spirit (6:4; 7:11; 17:1; 32:18) or understanding (20:3). It can also refer to God's spirit (33:4; 34:14). When applied to God, the term has a somewhat narrower frame of reference: God's *rûaḥ* destroys (4:9), creates (26:13; 33:4) and is necessary for ongoing existence (34:14). The reference to the divine *rûaḥ* in the context of creation inevitably recalls Genesis 1:2, in which the *rûaḥ ʾělōhîm* is said to hover over the waters of chaos before the creative activity begins.[30] However, the expression

---

29. Habel, *Job*, p. 380. See also E. Dhorme, *A Commentary on the Book of Job* (London: Thomas Nelson, 1967), p. 379.
30. The phrase *rûaḥ ʾělôah* is unique to Job 27:3, though there are also references to the divine *rûaḥ* in 4:9; 26:13; 33:4 and 34:14. This is most commonly conveyed by use of a pronominal suffix, but in 33:4 Elihu uses the more common biblical expression *rûaḥ ʾělōhîm*. Since *ʾělôah* is by far more commonly used in the book of Job than elsewhere in the OT (42 of its 58 uses occur in Job), it is not surprising

is ambiguous in Genesis 1, with the possibility that it refers to an impersonal agent such as an 'almighty wind'. Sinclair Ferguson argues persuasively that the inner-biblical exegesis of Genesis 1:2 in texts such as Job 33:4 presumes a personal divine activity in creation, and thus thinks it is better translated as 'the Spirit of God'.[31] Ferguson stops short of identifying this 'Spirit of God' with the third person of the Trinity, since there is insufficient evidence to demonstrate that the *rûaḥ ʾĕlōhîm* was conceived of as a hypostatically distinct person of the Godhead.[32] Even if Ferguson is correct that the *rûaḥ ʾĕlōhîm* of Genesis 1:2 is interpreted by Job 33:4 (among other texts) as the 'Spirit of God', this meaning cannot necessarily be imported into all instances of this phrase or its equivalent. In some instances, an impersonal meaning (wind) is implied, while in Job 27:3 the specific context with its reference to Job's nostrils suggests that a physical metaphor (breath) rather than a metaphysical one (spirit) is intended.

The personal nature of the *rûaḥ ʾĕlôah* is made explicit if the expression is viewed as an example of a divine anthropomorphism. *Rûaḥ* is an attribute of all human beings, just as much as hands, eyes or feet. People have physical *rûaḥ* or breath, and they have metaphysical *rûaḥ* or spirit. When the term is applied to God it may have either of these senses: 'the breath of God' or 'the spirit of God', or it may carry connotations of both if it is used in a deliberately ambiguous context.[33] In each case, *rûaḥ* is the vehicle in the implied metaphor, and at stake are the particular connotations given to the tenor, that is, God. 'The breath of God' connotes something different from 'the spirit of God'. Breath is external and physical, while spirit is internal and metaphysical. Both physical and metaphysical anthropology are evident in Job 27:2–6: Job speaks of his soul (*nepeš*, v. 2) and his heart (*lēbāb*, v. 6), showing a deep interest in his inner life, but he also refers to bodily features, such as his lips (v. 4), his tongue (v. 4) and his nostrils (v. 3). Both the physical and the metaphysical senses of *rûaḥ* are thus available to Job.

---

that the expression *rûaḥ ʾĕlôah* only occurs in Job. Wolfers notes that the use of the term *ʾĕlôah* by Yahweh himself legitimizes it and removes any previous pagan connotations. On this basis, there is no need to postulate any strong theological distinction between *ʾĕlôah* and the more common terms for God, *ʾēl* and *ʾĕlōhîm* (Wolfers, *Deep Things*, p. 76).

31. Sinclair B. Ferguson, *The Holy Spirit*, Contours of Christian Theology (Leicester: Inter-Varsity Press, 1996), p. 20.

32. Ibid., p. 30.

33. It may also have the impersonal sense 'wind of God' as noted above.

In the context of Job 27:3, the physical metaphor 'breath of God' is preferable for a number of reasons. There is a strong, almost incongruous, physicality in the assertion that the *rûaḥ ʾĕlôah* is located in Job's nostrils. Although the *rûaḥ ʾĕlôah* is not to be identified as Job's physical breath, it makes sense to use a physical anthropomorphism within this physical context, so that Job's breath (*nĕšāmâ*) is paralleled with God's breath (*rûaḥ*). The allusion to Genesis 2:7, through the use of the terms *nĕšāmâ* and *ʾappi*, in the context of human life and divine breath, evokes a physical image of God's creation of mankind as noted above. The parallel with Job 33:4, in which Elihu uses the two expressions *rûaḥ ʾĕlōhîm* and *nišmat šadday* to speak about the life-giving breath of Genesis 2:7, indicates that it would not be idiosyncratic for Job to use *rûaḥ* rather than *nĕšāmâ* in this context.[34] Thus in both 33:4 and 27:3, the divine *rûaḥ* is associated with breath (*nĕšāmâ*) as the source of human life, though in 27:3 Job speaks of his own *nĕšāmâ*, while in 33:4 Elihu attributes it to God, thus forming a more direct parallel with the *rûaḥ ʾĕlōhîm*. In the context of Job's oath, then, if his *nĕšāmâ* represents his physical life, the *rûaḥ ʾĕlôah* in his nostrils is an acknowledgment of his humanity and personhood, dependent on the divine life-giving spirit. The two are not identical, but neither are they separate.

Implications

The basis of the oath, Job's *nĕšāmâ* and the *rûaḥ ʾĕlôah* in his nostrils, is related to its content, that is, the truthfulness of Job's speech. Job has previously questioned his friends, albeit rhetorically, asking whose breath (*nĕšāmâ*) they speak by (26:4) when they give their counsel. He now asserts the truth of his own speech, on the basis that it is God's breath (*rûaḥ*) in him (27:4–6). Job recognizes that having the divine *rûaḥ* makes it inappropriate to speak falsely or to deceive. Instead he declares his integrity and honesty, knowing that he does so in the presence of God, and as one whose very life and breath depend on God. Job's oath is very similar in substance to the claims which Elihu makes about his speech (33:1–4). Elihu claims to speak rightly and sincerely, since the divine *rûaḥ* also made him and the divine *nĕšāmâ* gives him life. While both Elihu and Job begin from the same theological understanding of the creative work of the divine spirit and lay claim to speak truthfully on this basis,

34. *Nĕšāmâ* and *rûaḥ* are also used in Job 4:9 with the same referent, illustrating how similar in scope the two terms are.

it is clear that the content of Elihu's speech is intended to contradict Job's claims of innocence. Thus their application of their theology to the specific circumstances of Job's situation differ, but their theological understanding of the spirit is the same. Both acknowledge that the work of the divine *rûaḥ* in creating and sustaining a person ought to lead them to speak rightly, but the juxtaposition of the two speeches within the book of Job demonstrates that there is no guarantee that they will do so.

The divine *rûaḥ* and the divine *nĕšāmâ* have similar roles in the book of Job, reflecting the fact that both are divine anthropomorphisms, divine 'breath'. The divine *nĕšāmâ* and the divine *rûaḥ* both denote God's activity within his world, and especially his creative and destructive activity. That creative activity is what breathes the spark of life into all men, without which they would be dead, and so when Job swears on the *rûaḥ* *ʾĕlôah* in his nostrils, he swears on the very thing which gives him life. In this sense, the divine *rûaḥ* is common to all human beings. Elihu does not need to tell Job that there is nothing special about him, that they both are formed from a piece of clay (33:6), for Job is not claiming any privileged status here. His oath is not predicated on any special status, but on his humanity, his personhood and, ultimately, his life.

6. SPIRIT AND THE PSALMIST IN PSALM 51

Daniel J. Estes

Introduction

No examination of the subject of the Spirit of God in the OT would be complete without a discussion of Psalm 51.[1] This well-known penitential psalm[2] contains four references to spirit (*rûaḥ*), including one of only three references

1. The most thorough study to date of Ps. 51 is Edward R. Dalglish, *Psalm Fifty-One in the Light of Ancient Near Eastern Patternism* (Leiden: Brill, 1962). After comparing Ps. 51 to parallels in Babylonian and Egyptian literature, Dalglish concludes (p. 277): 'The significance of Psalm li as probably the greatest penitential prayer ever composed lies in its literary qualities and in its theological ideas. If the Hebrews borrowed from their neighbors many of the elements of psalmography, they in turn adapted and perfected them through their own spiritual genius.'
2. The seven psalms typically classified as penitential are Pss 6, 32, 38, 51, 102, 130 and 148. The penitential psalms are often considered a subdivision of the individual lament psalms, with the lament portion filled by the psalmist's confession of sin. It should be noted, however, that Ps. 32 more closely follows the pattern of the declarative praise psalm or song of thanksgiving. Thus it is more accurate to say that penitential is not a form-critical category, but rather it relates to the subject matter of the psalm.

to the term 'Holy Spirit' (along with the two references in Isa. 63:10–11) in the OT. Because many EVV capitalize the expression in Ps. 51:11 (Heb. 13),[3] this verse has often been cited by theologians as OT support for the doctrine of the Holy Spirit that is taught explicitly in the NT.

This chapter will examine the uses of *rûaḥ* in Psalm 51:10–17 (Heb. 12–19) to determine their precise meaning within the context of the psalm, and then discuss how these references relate to the broader subject of the Spirit of God in the OT.

Form of Psalm 51

Psalm 51 adheres to the general pattern of the individual lament psalms. Its penitential tone and theme, however, cause the typical lament form to be adapted at several points. The invocation in verses 1–2 (Heb. 3–4) becomes an appeal for divine grace and cleansing. In place of the complaint against an enemy,[4] verses 3–6 (Heb. 5–8) present the psalmist's confession of sin, which is paralleled in Psalm 38.[5] There is no explicit confession of trust, although the psalmist's faith in God is implicit throughout and quite evident in verse 17 (Heb. 19) when the psalmist declares, 'A broken and contrite heart, O God, you will not despise.'[6] The petition does not appeal for the defeat of enemies, but rather the psalmist calls upon God to cleanse his sin (vv. 7–9 [Heb. 9–11]) and to give him spiritual renewal (vv. 10–12 [Heb. 12–14]). The praise section in verses 13–17 (Heb. 15–19) is a vow of praise that anticipates how the

3. W. Creighton Marlowe ('"Spirit of Your Holiness" [רוּחַ קָדְשְׁךָ] in Psalm 51:13', *TJ* 19 [1998], pp. 45–48) provides a useful chart of how a wide range of versions and commentaries have employed capitalization in their renderings of this verse. Clearly, the decision to capitalize the expression as Holy Spirit implies a theological interpretation about the doctrine of the Holy Spirit in Ps. 51, and more generally in the OT.

4. Frank-Lothar Hossfeld and Erich Zenger, *Psalms 2*, trans. Linda M. Maloney, Hermeneia (Minneapolis: Fortress, 2005), pp. 14–15, refute the claim that Ps. 51 is a psalm of a sick person, concluding that 'one should classify and interpret our psalm, with the majority of exegetes, as a "penitential psalm" or as "prayer petitioning for forgiveness of sins and new creation"'.

5. John Goldingay, *Psalms. Volume 2: Psalms 42 – 89*, BCOTWP (Grand Rapids: Baker Academic, 2007), p. 124.

6. All Scripture quotations in this chapter are taken from the NIV.

psalmist will respond after God has forgiven his sins. The final two verses of the psalm, verses 18–19 (Heb. 20–21), are a prayer for the physical and spiritual restoration of Jerusalem. This section has most often been regarded as a subsequent addition to the original psalm, although some scholars argue that the psalmist desires that his personal restoration may be extrapolated to the whole nation.

Flow of thought in Psalm 51

To understand how the term 'spirit' is used in Psalm 51, it is necessary first to grasp the flow of thought in the psalm. The superscription to the psalm links this lament to David's response to the reproof by the prophet Nathan concerning the king's sin with Bathsheba (cf. 2 Sam. 12:1–14). Although the psalmic superscriptions cannot be proven to be part of the original texts of the psalms, they are at least the oldest extant interpretative comments on the biblical texts, so they may provide clues to how the psalms may be understood.[7] Miller notes well, 'Those superscriptions that allude to specific moments and events in the life of David are a way of saying that the psalm over which the superscription is written makes sense in just such a context. A very obvious example of this is Psalm 51 with its allusion to the Bathsheba incident.'[8] Whether or not that is the historical referent of the psalm, what is evident is that Psalm 51 is tightly unified both in its language and in its logical development. As Dalglish observes, 'The poet tarries at each step only as long as it is absolutely necessary to develop his theme. His delicate poetic artistry and sensibility portray his themes with deft master strokes. When one theme has been executed, he moves at once to the next; at every stage in the development he has his audience intellectually informed and emotionally involved.'[9]

In his appeal for divine grace, the psalmist grounds his plea in the gracious character of God. Alluding to Yahweh's self-revelation to Israel in Exodus 34:6–7, in verse 1 (Heb. 3) he calls upon him to exercise his mercy (*ḥānan*),

---

7. I develop this point more thoroughly in Daniel J. Estes, *Handbook on the Wisdom Books and Psalms* (Grand Rapids: Baker Academic, 2005), pp. 141–144.
8. Patrick D. Miller, 'Trouble and Woe: Interpreting the Biblical Laments', *Int* 37 (1983), pp. 36–37.
9. Dalglish, *Psalm Fifty-One*, p. 278. The expositional treatment of Ps. 51 by Samuel Terrien, *The Psalms and Their Meaning for Today* (Indianapolis: Bobbs-Merrill, 1952), pp. 169–178, does a fine job of tracing the flow of thought throughout the psalm.

unfailing love (*ḥesed*) and compassion (*raḥămîm*). The psalmist does not presume to ask God to overlook his transgressions, but rather he calls upon God to cleanse him from the full extent of his iniquity and sin (v. 2 [Heb. 4]).

His confession of sin flows naturally from his appeal for divine grace. In verse 3 (Heb. 5), the psalmist takes personal responsibility for his sins. Then he admits that as heinously as he has wronged other humans, the ultimate measure of his guilt is that he has violated the character and commandments of God, and therefore God is totally justified in condemning him (v. 4 [Heb. 6]). Oxtoby remarks, 'Men have been wronged, surely, but important as this may be, it is engulfed in the greater implication that all sin is ultimately against God. God would therefore be perfectly justified in pronouncing a well-deserved judgment of condemnation, and only because this is freely admitted can any claim of divine mercy be recognized.'[10] Without minimizing the effect of his sin on others, the psalmist acknowledges its full enormity in God's eyes. As Weiser concludes, 'In the last analysis every sin is directed against God, for it reflects the basic tendency of the human will which accomplishes "what is evil in God's sight" and thereby destroys the living contact with God.'[11]

Sin so controls his life that he states in verse 5 (Heb. 7) that he was conceived and birthed in it. By saying this, the psalmist gets to the root of his problem. He must contend with more than just his acts of sinful behaviour. He must also find a cure for his sinful condition that has prompted the evil he has committed. In the deepest recesses of his being, his sin must be rooted out and replaced by the truth and wisdom that God desires (v. 6 [Heb. 8]). This profound transformation cannot be achieved by human resolution alone, but rather it will require divine intervention in his life. In fact, even this new awareness of his spiritual condition before God is indicative that God has graciously 'led him into the beginnings of an understanding of the truth – the truth about himself. He has seen the radicalness of God's interests in a man, and he is beginning to accept them.'[12]

The psalmist's petition focuses first on his immediate need for cleansing from his past sin. In calling upon God to cleanse him with hyssop

---

10. Gurdon Corning Oxtoby, 'Conscience and Confession: A Study of the Fifty-First Psalm', *Int* 3 (1949), p. 419.
11. Artur Weiser, *The Psalms: A Commentary*, trans. Herbert Hartwell, OTL (Philadelphia: Westminster, 1962=1959), p. 403.
12. John Goldingay, *Songs from a Strange Land*, BST (Downers Grove: InterVarsity Press, 1978), p. 159.

(v. 7 [Heb. 9]), he uses the language of purification from ritual defilement in Leviticus 14:1–7 and Numbers 19:14–19. By this means, 'he asks for a cleansing that is analogous to the sprinkling rite prescribed by the law'[13] due to leprosy or contact with a dead human body. If God will wash him, then his uncleanness will be removed and he will be made whiter than snow, and therefore he will be able to celebrate life once again (cf. Eccl. 9:8). He has experienced the heavy hand of divine retribution (cf. Ps. 32:4), so he appeals to God in verse 8 (Heb. 10), 'Let me hear joy and gladness, let the bones you have crushed rejoice.' As in Psalm 30:5 (Heb. 6), the psalmist longs for the restoration of joy after sorrow due to his sin and its painful consequences. In the Psalter, usually the innocent psalmist entreats God not to hide his face from him (cf. Ps. 13:1; 27:9), but in Psalm 51 the psalmist is guilty. Therefore he pleads with God to be merciful and to hide his face from the psalmist's sins and to blot out all his iniquity (v. 9 [Heb. 11]).

In verses 10–12 (Heb. 12–14), the psalmist turns from his sinful past to request from God a spiritual renewal for the future. Because this passage contains three of the four uses of *rûaḥ* in the psalm, it will be discussed in more detail in a subsequent section of the chapter.

As the psalmist envisions the spiritual renewal that he has requested from God, his thoughts advance to the time when his deliverance has become a reality. His vow of praise, then, will take the form of activities that function as the overflowing of his appreciation of God's grace to him. He resolves to teach transgressors the ways of God, so that others will turn back to God (v. 13 [Heb. 15]). This would have special significance if the psalmist were indeed David or another Davidic king, because divine forgiveness would enable him to exercise the spiritual leadership that God requires of him.[14] In Psalm 32 the psalmist expresses the happiness that he has experienced after his confession of sin. The similarity of language in Psalm 51 and Psalm 32, and especially the same terms used for sin, raises the possibility that the later psalm is the fulfilment of the vow expressed in Psalm 51.

In verse 14 (Heb. 16), the psalmist entreats God to deliver him from bloodguilt (*dāmîm*). This expression has been interpreted in several different ways. Mays views it as a comprehensive term for guilt, as in Isaiah 4:4; Ezekiel 18:13; 22:1–16 and Hosea 12:14, and thus a strengthening of the appeal in

13. Ibid., p. 162.

14. Seizo Sekine, *Transcendency and Symbols in the Old Testament: A Genealogy of the Hermeneutical Experience*, BZAW 275 (Berlin: de Gruyter, 1999), p. 166; cf. the royal resolution in Ps. 101.

verse 9 (Heb. 11).[15] Weiser focuses on the legal provision for avenging a crime to a relative, and thus construes the psalmist as asking God to rescue him from an act of human retribution for his sin, and which would prevent him from teaching transgressors.[16] Goldingay reads this verse through the lens of Ezekiel 33:1–9, and he concludes that 'in the context the psalm's language more closely recalls the way Ezekiel speaks of the fatal consequences of failing to tell people how to escape from the danger they are in if they fail to turn to Yhwh for restoration'.[17] Although each of these suggestions has some merit, Zenger may well be closest to the mark as he reads the psalmist as calling on God to forgive him and to deliver him from the divine penalty of death that his sin deserved.[18] Only then would he be able to praise God in the future as he vows to do in this psalm.

As in Psalm 30:12 (Heb. 13), the psalmist's sin had stolen his song, and only divine deliverance could restore it. If God would deliver him from his *dāmîm*, then his tongue would be able to sing of God's righteousness (v. 14b [Heb. 16b]). Continuing his thought in verse 15 (Heb. 17), the psalmist calls on the Lord to open his lips so that his mouth could declare God's praise. The psalmist readily acknowledges that there is no sacrifice or burnt offering adequate to atone for his sin (v. 16 [Heb. 18]). Therefore he humbly casts himself upon God's mercy, offering to God his broken spirit and contrite heart, which he is confident will not be despised by God (v. 17 [Heb. 19]).

Although most scholars view the final two verses of Psalm 51 as an unrelated or even subversive addition to the original psalm, Goldingay argues that the final lines indicate that the psalm was not intended to speak of the sin of a private individual, but instead to refer either to the king or to the community as a whole.[19] Similarly, Mays reasons from the parallels to the language of a new heart and spirit in Jeremiah 24:7; 31:33; 32:39–40 and Ezekiel 36:25–27 that the entire text of Psalm 51 may have been composed for liturgical use by the community, and thus the concluding two verses 'form an appropriate conclusion rather than a contradictory addendum'.[20]

This interpretation is exegetically possible, but it must be admitted that if verses 1–17 (Heb. 3–19) are read alone, it is unlikely that a corporate subject

15. James L. Mays, *Psalms*, Interpretation (Louisville: John Knox, 1994), p. 201.

16. Weiser, *The Psalms*, pp. 408–409.

17. Goldingay, *Psalms*, pp. 136–137.

18. Hossfeld and Zenger, *Psalms 2*, p. 13.

19. Goldingay, *Psalms*, p. 125.

20. Mays, *Psalms*, p. 199.

would be immediately apparent. In particular, the psalmist's admission of his sinful condition from the time of his conception in verse 5 (Heb. 7) and his aspiration to teach transgressors the ways of the Lord (v. 13 [Heb. 15]) seem to fit better an individual referent. If this is the case, then the final two verses can reasonably be viewed as the communal application of the experience of the psalmist that has been described in the preceding portion of the psalm.

Uses of *rûaḥ* in Psalm 51:10–17 (Heb. 12–19)

In Psalm 51:10–17 (Heb. 12–19), the term for 'spirit' (*rûaḥ*) occurs four times, three times in the psalmist's petition for spiritual renewal in verses 10–12 (Heb. 12–14) and once in his vow of praise in verse 17 (Heb. 19). Each of the four uses of *rûaḥ* will be examined in turn, and then the data will be synthesized to determine its relevance to the biblical teaching concerning the Spirit of God.

Psalm 51:10 (Heb. 12)

> Create in me a pure heart, O God,
> and renew a steadfast spirit [*rûaḥ nākôn*] within me.

In calling upon God to perform a work of creation in him, the psalmist employs a verb (*bārāʾ*) that is used in the OT only of divine activity. Just as God called the physical world into existence (Gen. 1:1) and he will create a new heaven and a new earth (Isa. 65:17–18), so God alone can create in the psalmist a pure heart. By appealing to God, the psalmist implicitly acknowledges that he is unable by his own resolution to do what is right before God. He needs a new nature.

The parallel terms, heart and spirit, may well function as a merism to speak of the total inner person.[21] If that is the case, then *rûaḥ* here likely refers to the human spirit, rather than to the Spirit of God. In his confession, the psalmist has evidenced his past inability to counter the power of sin in his life. As he looks ahead, he recognizes that he will need to be able to resist temptation that has previously defeated him. Therefore he asks God to renew in him a spirit 'that is firm and reliable, determined and committed, prepared and set to go

21. André Caquot, 'Purification et expiation selon le psaume LI', *Revue de l'histoire des religions* 169 (1966), p. 134.

God's way. The sinner is aware of his fickleness and unfaithfulness, and his deliverance from this must also be God's achievement.'[22]

It is likely that his reference to a *nākôn* spirit should be read in the light of verse 17 (Heb. 19), where the psalmist says that the sacrifices acceptable to God are a broken spirit. His spirit that has been crushed by divine discipline leading to repentance must then be recreated by God. What God produces in the contrite psalmist is 'a mind and will fixed and steady toward God – ready to praise (57:8), true to God's covenant (78:37), and trusting during evil times (112:7)'.[23] By asking God to do this transforming work in his spirit, the psalmist anticipates what Yahweh promises to do for the nation of Israel in the future (Jer. 31:31–34; Ezek. 11:19–20; 36:25–27). Tate, however, seems to take Psalm 51:10 (Heb. 12) a step too far in the direction of NT pneumatology when he states that this verse refers to 'God's steadfast and reliable spirit, which is given to those who serve him'.[24] The juxtaposition with 'heart' and the connection with the 'broken spirit' (v. 17 [Heb. 19]) more easily support a human referent to *rûaḥ* in this verse.

Psalm 51:11 (Heb. 13)

> Do not cast me from your presence
> or take your Holy Spirit from me.

This verse, with its reference to 'your Holy Spirit' (*rûaḥ qodšĕkā*), has prompted a wide variety of renderings. Two questions in particular present themselves. (1) What is the identity of the psalmist? (2) Who or what is *rûaḥ qodšĕkā*? The various answers to these questions have led to four major lines of interpretation.

The first interpretation takes *rûaḥ qodšĕkā* as referring to the Spirit of God. Then, noting that Nehemiah 9:30, Zechariah 7:12 and many of the historical and prophetical texts portray God's Spirit coming upon the prophets to equip them for ministry, it concludes that the psalmist was a prophet. Neve contends that 'the spirit appears to have departed from the monarchy at the time of Solomon and moved to the prophetic movement'.[25] According to this rendering, the psalmist was a prophet who had sinned and thus compromised his

---

22. Goldingay, *Songs from a Strange Land*, p. 167.
23. Mays, *Psalms*, p. 203.
24. Marvin Tate, *Psalms 51 – 100*, WBC 20 (Dallas: Word, 1990), p. 22.
25. Lloyd Neve, 'Realized Eschatology in Psalm 51', *ExpTim* 80 (1969), p. 266.

ministry to speak for God to the people, so he pleads for the Spirit of God to remain with him so that he would be able to teach sinners the ways of God.[26]

The second line of interpretation views the psalmist as a royal figure, sometimes but not always accepting the superscription as an accurate pointer to David. Dalglish argues that the prophets received the Spirit of God only intermittently, but that the king permanently possessed God's Spirit.[27] Goldingay suggests that if the final two verses are considered part of the original psalm, then 'the psalm does not originally relate to the sin of a private individual but to that of a leader such as the king or of the people as a whole'.[28] This reading clearly echoes the tragic example of Saul, from whom Yahweh withdrew his Spirit in 1 Samuel 16:14. Tate, however, rightly counters that the Spirit of God was possessed by non-royal individuals in Numbers 11:25, 29. Also, the Spirit of God is not prominent in the royal psalms, and never are the OT kings described as possessing him.[29]

The third line of interpretation does not specify the identity of the psalmist, but it focuses on construing *rûaḥ qodšĕkā* as the Spirit of God. Although it acknowledges that it would be anachronistic to read into this expression the NT theology regarding the Holy Spirit as the third person of the Trinity, it nevertheless insists that this rare combination of terms refers to God. Read this way, in the first line of verse 11 (Heb. 13) the psalmist asks that God not cast him away, and in the second line he pleads that God not take himself from the psalmist. In essence, he realizes that his sin has caused a breach with God (cf. Ps. 66:18; Isa. 59:2), so as he confesses his sin he appeals that God's spirit or presence might remain with him.[30] It is the presence of God that

26. Cf. Aubrey R. Johnson, *The Cultic Prophet and Israel's Psalmody* (Cardiff: University of Wales Press, 1979), p. 418.

27. Dalglish, *Psalm Fifty-One*, p. 159. He cites as evidence 1 Sam. 10:6, 9; 16:13–14; 2 Sam. 23:1–2.

28. Goldingay, *Psalms*, p. 125.

29. Tate, *Psalms 51 – 100*, p. 11. Neve, 'Realized Eschatology', p. 266, notes: 'It is not at all certain that the spirit was considered to be the permanent possession of the Davidides. In spite of the assumption on the part of many scholars, it must be observed that never in the Bible is the spirit associated with a reigning Davidic king subsequent to David, neither in the historical books, nor in the prophetic books, nor is it ever found in the royal psalms where it would be most expected.'

30. Goldingay, *Songs from a Strange Land*, p. 168, comments: 'It is because there is a real two-way relationship between God and man that there is something that can be broken. It has to be kept up, to be fostered. The psalmist knows that the way

empowers the psalmist to desire and do God's will, and thus it is foundational to a holy life and ministry. As Weiser expresses it, the psalmist longs for 'a living communion with God'.[31]

Although this view is undoubtedly the majority position, and it is reflected in numerous translations that capitalize the expression as 'Holy Spirit', some important objections have been raised against it. The rare phrase *rûaḥ qodšĕkā* is not the typical OT expression to refer to the Spirit of God. Rather, in passages such as Isaiah 63:14, 'the Spirit of Yahweh' is typically used. Moreover, it seems peculiar that a plea for God not to take his Spirit from the psalmist would occur at this place in Psalm 51. As Neve observes,[32] it would be expected in the initial appeal for divine grace, the confession of sin or the petition for cleansing from his past sin, but it is a bit jarring as the psalmist turns to request God for future spiritual renewal.

Several recent scholars have pointed in a different and more likely direction as they interpret Psalm 51:11 (Heb. 13). Noting that *rûaḥ* in verses 10, 12 and 17 (Heb. 12, 14 and 19) probably refers to the human spirit, they suggest that verse 11 (Heb. 13) should be construed in the same way. As VanGemeren observes, 'These verses say little about the doctrine of the Holy Spirit in the OT but much about the necessity of spiritual renewal.'[33] By this reading, *rûaḥ qodšĕkā* refers to the psalmist's inner desire for God's holiness, thus a life truly centred on pleasing God. It could then be read 'a desire for your holiness'. This inner commitment to God's holiness, which implicitly must be prompted and energized by the Spirit of God rather than by human resolution alone, will enable the psalmist 'to maintain fellowship with God and minister to other sinners'.[34] This spiritual commitment will preclude the psalmist from being

---

he is inclined to treat God imperils the very existence of it. God could withdraw his presence, and yet that very presence is needed if he is to get anywhere near spiritual renewal.'

31. Weiser, *The Psalms*, p. 407.
32. Neve, 'Realized Eschatology', p. 265.
33. Willem A. VanGemeren, *Psalms*, EBC 5, rev. ed. (Grand Rapids: Zondervan, 2008), p. 438. He continues to say, 'Spiritual renewal leads to godliness and wisdom (cf. Dt 5:29; 30:6; Isa 59:21; Jer 31:33–34; Eze 36:26–27).'
34. Marlowe, 'Spirit of Your Holiness', p. 44. This article does an excellent job of building a strong case for this approach to the verse. It should be noted that in contrast to the sense of Ps. 51:11 (Heb. 13) the other two uses of this phrase in Isa. 63:10–11 are better viewed as references to the Spirit of Yahweh than to the human spirit.

banished from the presence of God due to his sin, as the nation of Israel was exiled (cf. 2 Kgs 17:20; 24:30; Jer. 7:15; 52:3).

Psalm 51:12 (Heb. 14)

> Restore to me the joy of your salvation
> and grant me a willing spirit, to sustain me.

The last of the three consecutive uses of *rûaḥ* occurs in verse 12 (Heb. 14), where the psalmist asks God to sustain him by granting him a willing (*nĕdîbâ*) spirit. The Hebrew adjective 'connotes an uncompelled and free movement of the will unto divine service or sacrifice',[35] and it is used in Exodus 35:5, 22 and 2 Chronicles 29:31 for those who gave generously for the construction of the tabernacle and the temple. Unlike the previous verse, there is no pronominal suffix in verse 12b (Heb. 14b), so translations such as the LXX and KJV that insert 'thy/your' mistakenly introduce a reference to the Spirit of God. In his 1978 book, Goldingay argued that this verse refers to God's generous Spirit, but in his recent 2007 commentary he corrects himself when he observes that 'here the context suggests that the word offers another way of characterizing the spirit that God needs to create within the suppliant, a spirit that will in the future maintain its enthusiastic commitment to God'.[36] By this request the psalmist asks God to transform him so completely that he freely and willingly lives for him. As Psalm 143:10 and Ezekiel 36:27 state, it is the Spirit of God who transforms the spirit of the worshipper, but in Psalm 51:12 (Heb. 14) the human spirit is in view.

Psalm 51:17 (Heb. 19)

> The sacrifices of God are a broken spirit;
> a broken and contrite heart,
> O God, you will not despise.

In light of the parallelism with the final line of the verse, clearly the sense of 'the sacrifices of God' must be construed as 'the sacrifices acceptable to God'. What God delights in is a broken spirit, that is to say, a heart that has been broken and made contrite by God's judgment that humbles the sinner.[37] The

35. Leonard J. Coppes, *TWOT*, 2:554.
36. Goldingay, *Psalms*, p. 135.
37. Mays, *Psalms*, p. 203.

OT often speaks of a will or spirit that is hardened against God (cf. Ps. 95:8 of the Israelites, and often of Pharaoh in Exod. 4 – 14), but 'the stubborn will has to be shattered if a man is to be led back into the ways of God, if he is to be open to God's voice'.[38] The Niphal participles translated 'broken' and 'contrite' have a passive force, as they depict the psalmist as the object of God's discipline, as he was in verse 8b (Heb. 10b): 'let the bones you have crushed rejoice'. As Psalm 34:18 (Heb. 19) notes with the same vocabulary as in this verse, Yahweh is near to the broken-hearted and he sees those who are crushed in spirit.[39] Weiser insightfully expounds on the sense of this verse: 'God has delight in a broken spirit and in a contrite heart; that is to say, he has delight in human beings who do not seek by the use of material means to exert an influence on him, be it ever so refined, but who take the reverse course in that they give up all claims to him and face him with a broken spirit – entirely depending on his grace, completely giving themselves up to him and whole-heartedly submitting to him.'[40]

The spirit of God in Psalm 51:10–17 (Heb. 12–19)

Despite the long history of interpretation and translation that regards *rûaḥ qodšěkā* in Psalm 51:11 (Heb. 13) as an OT reference to the Holy Spirit, and reflects that understanding by capitalizing the expression in many EVV, a careful analysis of Psalm 51 does not support that conclusion. The use of *rûaḥ* in verse 17 (Heb. 19) definitely has a human referent, particularly when it is read together with verse 9 (Heb. 10). In verse 10 (Heb. 12), the parallelism between 'pure heart' and 'steadfast spirit' also supports a human referent. In verse 12 (Heb. 14), 'willing spirit' is best read as the psalmist's desired willingness and commitment to God, in contrast to his previous sinful rebellion against God. When *rûaḥ qodšěkā* in verse 11 (Heb. 13) is interpreted within this context in the psalm, it is best rendered as 'a desire for your [God's] holiness'. The psalmist realizes that he will face the ongoing threat of sin that endeavours to subvert his aspiration to live for God. Therefore he calls upon God who has previously crushed his wilfulness to so work in the future in his inner person that he will be able to maintain a firm, focused and free allegiance to him. Although other OT passages such as Psalm 143:10 and Ezekiel 36:27

---

38. Goldingay, *Songs from a Strange Land*, p. 171.
39. Cf. similar statements in Isa. 57:15; 61:1.
40. Weiser, *The Psalms*, p. 409.

demonstrate that the Spirit of God will be the agent of transformation in his life, in Psalm 51 attention is centred on the *rûaḥ* of the psalmist and only faintly does it anticipate the fuller NT doctrine of the Holy Spirit.

7. SPIRIT AND PRESENCE IN PSALM 139

Jamie A. Grant

Introduction

In Psalm 139:7, the poet asks the rhetorical question: 'Where shall I go from your Spirit? And where can I flee from your presence?'[1] The fact that the question is rhetorical becomes clear in the following verses, but the mention of Yahweh's 'Spirit' in verse 7 is interesting and worthy of further investigation in a work that seeks to discuss the idea of the Spirit in the OT. The questions to be addressed in this particular study are: what does the psalmist have in mind when using this term 'your Spirit' (*rûḥekā*)? And how does the use of spirit language here in Psalm 139 complement or nuance the presentation of the Spirit in the Psalter and the OT? In order to answer these questions, Psalm 139:7 needs to be examined in its various contexts. First, the parallelism itself needs to be unpacked in order to assess just what the poet has in mind when using the vocabulary of the Spirit of God. Second, this specific parallelism must be read in the context of the poem as a whole. Third, just as the Spirit language of Psalm 139:7 is influenced by the context of the psalm in its entirety, so Psalm 139 is influenced by its broader context, namely the 'Davidic' collection of Psalms 138 – 145. Therefore it is important to see how

1. All scriptural citations are my own translations, unless otherwise indicated.

the idea of God's Spirit unfolds within this sub-collection of psalms. Then, finally, it will be important to try to draw some theological conclusions from this discussion of the Spirit in Psalm 139.

Psalm 139:7 – the voice of the verse

Context is always important when it comes to accurate interpretation. How often do we hear politicians and sportspeople alike saying that some controversial comment was 'taken out of context'? Their defence, of course, implies that hearing the comment *in context* would change our perception of it. The same applies to the biblical text where context is also essential to accurate interpretation. However, defining context is not always as straightforward as one might think, because each text will have varying degrees of 'autonomy' and a variety of potential contexts. This is particularly true of the Psalms, where context can be defined in terms of the paired lines of a parallelism, the strophe or stanza in which a verse is found, the psalm itself and, perhaps, also the collection of psalms within which a particular composition is located. Clearly, many levels of 'context' apply in the case of Psalm 139:7, but the tight parallelism of Hebrew poetry gives us the first setting that sheds light on the concept of Yahweh's Spirit in Psalm 139.

For the most part, each verse of Hebrew poetry consists of what is called a parallelism. The most common form of parallelism consists of two or more lines which are held together in some sort of creative tension. Where semantic parallelism exists, the parallelism is often enlightening for unpacking what an author might intend when using particular terminology. However, there is some discussion amongst the scholarly community as to how we should understand the relationship between the two lines of a semantic parallelism, and this may impact our understanding of the Spirit of Yahweh in Psalm 139:7.

Traditionally, semantic parallelism is divided into three categories: synonymous, antithetical and synthetic parallelism. Broadly speaking, this implies that the second line of a parallelism essentially either repeats, contrasts with or adds to the information contained in the first line of the parallelism.[2] Following this categorization, Psalm 139:7 would be described as a synony-

---

2. An approach first advocated by Robert Lowth in 1753 that dominated study of the Psalter for over two hundred years. See Jamie A. Grant, 'Scripture and Biblical Criticism', in Michael Bird and Michael Pahl (eds.), *The Sacred Text: Excavating the*

mous parallelism: each of the lines begins with the question 'where' (*ʾānâ*), each includes a first-person singular motion verb ('shall I go' [*ʾēlēk*] and 'can I flee' [*ʾebrāḥ*]), each indicates the idea of separation through the *min* preposition with the possessive 'your' (second masculine singular) appended to each line's object ('Spirit' and 'presence'). What does that communicate about the identity of Yahweh's 'Spirit' in this verse? If we take the traditional reading of Psalm 139:7 as a 'synonymous' parallelism, then the interpretative effect is that the terms 'Spirit' and 'presence/face' have a broadly similar meaning. The logical conclusion would be that the psalmist's understanding of Yahweh's Spirit is roughly equivalent to the concept of divine presence (that is, Yahweh's 'face').

However, another approach to parallelism arose in the 1980s. Scholars such as Kugel, Alter and Berlin suggested that the threefold description of parallelism was overly simplistic and failed to account for the diversity of relationships that might exist within a parallelism.[3] This new approach highlights a range of interactions within the parallelism, but the fundamental dynamic is that the second line of the parallelism somehow heightens the effect of the first. Kugel explains, 'Parallelism employs a complex of heightening effects used in combinations and intensities that vary widely from composition to composition even within a single "genre".'[4] But the basic effect is that the second line of a parallelism is always 'doing' something – it intensifies, specifies, contradicts, heightens, hyperbolizes, elaborates by way of intensified imagery, and so on.[5]

With this in mind, it seems important to ask: does the second line of Psalm 139:7 heighten our understanding of the Spirit language of the first line? Is the idea of the 'presence/face' of God an expansion or elaboration of 'Spirit'? Intensification clearly occurs between the first and second lines, but it is found not in the object of each sentence but in the verbs. In the first line the psalmist asks, 'Where shall I *go* from your Spirit?' but in the second inquires, more

---

Texts, Exploring the Interpretations, and Engaging the Theologies of the Christian Scriptures (Piscataway: Gorgias Press, 2010), pp. 101–118, for further discussion.

3. James L. Kugel, *The Idea of Biblical Poetry: Parallelism and Its History* (New Haven: Yale University Press, 1981); Robert Alter, *The Art of Biblical Poetry* (New York: Basic Books, 1985); Adele Berlin, *The Dynamics of Biblical Parallelism* (Bloomington: Indiana University Press, 1985).

4. Kugel, *Idea of Biblical Poetry*, p. 94.

5. See Jamie A. Grant, 'Poetics', in David G. Firth and Jamie A. Grant (eds.), *Words and the Word: Explorations in Biblical Interpretation and Literary Theory* (Nottingham: Apollos, 2008), pp. 212–221, for summary discussion of these changes.

intriguingly, 'Where can I *flee* from your presence?' It is through the verbs ('going' and 'fleeing') that we see the heightening effect, not in the nouns ('Spirit' and 'presence/face') from which the poet might remove himself. Therefore we can conclude that, irrespective of which approach to parallelism is adopted, the terms 'Spirit' and 'presence/face' broadly correspond in the mind of the psalmist. These two concepts are strongly related. The next step in our discussion is to consider how these terms are normally associated in psalmody.

'Spirit' and 'face' in the Psalms

Following on from the observation that Psalm 139:7 presents 'Spirit' and 'face' as explanatory parallels, we then have to ask how these paired terms inform our understanding of each other. In particular, a superficial reading of the use of these terms in parallel quickly gives rise to the question of *personality* or the lack thereof with regard to the identity of the 'Spirit' from the psalmic perspective. When we look at other passages where these terms appear in parallel, it is possible to chart two quite different understandings of the imagery conjured up by the poetic association of 'spirit' and 'face' in consort. One association seems to point clearly to the 'Spirit' as the personal Spirit of God. However, other psalmic associations of these words point to a concept more like an attribute of God's being rather than a personification of his identity, much like his power or justice – that is, his 'spirit'.[6] Let me illustrate with the help of a couple of examples.

---

6. I should be clear here: there is no concept of multiple personality in the essential being of God in the OT. As Bruce Waltke comments regarding Gen. 1, 'The Old Testament never clearly uses *rûaḥ ʾĕlōhîm* ("spirit of God") with reference to a personal hypostasis of God. On the trajectory of "spirit of God" in the Old Testament to "Spirit of God" in the New Testament, the author would not have had much of the later sense in mind' (*Old Testament Theology* [Grand Rapids: Zondervan, 2007], p. 213). However, as Waltke implies, the more developed trinitarian theology of the NT does not spring from nowhere. There is a process of development in this direction throughout the OT and the intertestamental period arising out of such concepts as the Word, the Angel and the Spirit of Yahweh as they are described in the OT. These phrases are sometimes used to describe Yahweh (see e.g. Gen. 16 or Exod. 3, where the 'angel of Yahweh' is clearly a manifestation of Yahweh himself) yet, at the same time, they are somehow

Psalm 51:11 (MT 51:13) uses the same words for Spirit and face (*rûaḥ* and *pāneh*) in parallel and the connotations seem to point to a personalized understanding of Spirit. 'Do not cast me away from your presence or take your Holy Spirit from me,' is the poet's plea. In the broader context of the poem, and given the use of *Holy* Spirit in this verse, it seems most likely that the psalmist here is talking, albeit in still vague terms, about the divine personality – that is, the Spirit as a representation of Yahweh himself.[7]

Psalm 104:29–30, however, uses plays on these two words somewhat differently. When God hides his 'face' (*pāneh*), the animals of the created order are terrified, and when he takes away 'their breath' (*rûaḥ*), they die (104:29). But when he sends his 'Spirit' – or, as probably better reflects the relationship with the preceding verse, his 'breath' (*rûaḥ*) – the animals are created and the 'face' (*pāneh*) of the earth is made new (104:30). He breathes out his breath/spirit of life and creation comes into being, but he can equally remove that breath/spirit from created beings and their lives expire. Reading these verses in parallel, therefore, the psalmist here seems to be speaking about God's spirit (with a small 's'). Therefore it seems he is not referring to a personification of the divine being, but rather to an attribute of God's being, namely his life-giving, creative power.

A question therefore naturally arises: which understanding of the spirit of

---

distinct from Yahweh. Obviously, this is not as fully orbed as the NT but it is 'a representation of the metaphysical or numinous' (M. V. Van Pelt, W. C. Kaiser and D. I. Block, 'רוּחַ' in *NIDOTTE*, vol. 4, p. 1075). Van Pelt et al. go on to comment that, 'Often the divine *rûah* functions as the alter ego of Yahweh, dwelling in the midst of Israel like the divine Glory (Hag. 2:5)' (p. 1075). So we see both *association* with and *distinction* from Yahweh in the OT's use of the idea of 'the spirit of Yahweh'. This is not as clearly developed as the NT's explicit teaching regarding the Holy Spirit as the third person of the Trinity, so it is probably somewhat anachronous to use Spirit (i.e. with a capital 'S') in reference to Psalm 139, but I do so here for the sake of clarity in distinguishing between the use of 'spirit' language as a reference to a divine attribute and 'spirit' language associated with Yahweh's being.

7. Of course, the Hebrew could also be read as, 'Do not cast me away from your presence or take your spirit of holiness from me,' so that the poet acknowledges that any holiness found within him is not inherent to his own being but ultimately comes from Yahweh. Thus if Yahweh removes his presence then any hope of holiness is removed from the poet with that departure. See Daniel Estes' essay in this volume for a fuller discussion.

God does the poet imply in Psalm 139:7? Are we in fact talking about the Holy Spirit at all in this particular verse? In order to answer this question, it seems helpful to examine this verse, first, in the flow of the psalm as a whole and, second, in the context of the collection of Davidic psalms where Psalm 139 is placed (Pss 138 – 145).

'Your Spirit' in the context of Psalm 137

The question of whether or not the psalmist is referring to the Holy Spirit in Psalm 139:7 is an issue that we must first address in the context of the psalm itself. Psalm 139 is an immensely personal and relational poem. This is clear from the first stanza (vv. 1–6) where every verse contains either an address to Yahweh or the pronouns 'you' or 'your'. This opening stanza focuses on Yahweh's intimate knowledge of the poet in every way. God knows the psalmist's every action, thought, word and motivation – there is a prevailing sense of the intimacy of God's knowledge of the poet. However, grammatically, it is worth noting that whenever the poet refers to God he uses direct speech – 'you [*ʾattâ*] know my sitting and my rising' (v. 2), etc. A scan of the pronouns used in verses 1–6 shows the preponderance of 'my' pronouns with the psalmist referring to God's intervention in his life – 'my sitting . . . my rising . . . my thoughts . . . my ways', etc. In this setting there is only a single use of 'your' language referring to Yahweh: 'your hand' in verse 5.[8] So where does that leave us as we move into the second stanza and the occur-

8. The Hebrew here uses more uncommon *kappekâ* ('your palm') rather than *yādkā* which is an anthropomorphic metaphor referring to God's powerful activity that one encounters much more frequently in the OT. However, in the context of Psalm 139, *kappekâ* is used instead of *yādkā* because the imagery speaks of divine protection rather than divine power. The idea is of the psalmist finding protection in Yahweh's palm. A. F. Kirkpatrick comments, 'God holds him fast in his grasp' (*The Book of Psalms* [Cambridge: Cambridge University Press, 1910], p. 787). One contemporary English version (NET) and some of the commentators (e.g. John Goldingay, *Psalms, vol. 3: Psalms 90 – 150*, BCOTWP [Grand Rapids: Baker, 2008], p. 631) carry forward the effect of '*your* hand' into the next verse, offering the translation '*your* knowledge is too wonderful for me'. Clearly, this is the implication of the knowledge referred to in Ps. 139:6, and it is also the translation option adopted in the Greek of the Septuagint (*hē gnōsis sou*), but no pronominal suffix is actually present in the MT.

rence of 'your Spirit'? 'Your hand' is an anthropomorphic metaphor referring to divine protection, so up until this point in the psalm the only instance of 'your' language refers to an attribute of God's activity rather than to God himself.

However, we see a marked change in the psalmist's use of pronouns as we move into the second stanza. Rather than a preponderance of 'my' pronouns, we see more of tendency towards 'your' pronouns – alongside the continuing use of 'my' pronouns – in the rest of the psalm (vv. 7–24). As well as the 'your Spirit' and 'your presence' under discussion in verse 7, we see 'your hand' and 'your right hand' (v. 10); 'your works' (v. 14); 'your eyes' and 'your book' (v. 16) and 'your thoughts' (v. 17). Superficially, the most obvious thing to note is that each of the objects of the pronoun 'your' refers to attributes of God's character and being. Yahweh's 'hand, right hand, works, eyes, book, thoughts' are, obviously, not the same as Yahweh himself. None of these nouns could be read as representations or personifications of Yahweh. In this vein, Goldingay translates 'your spirit' in Psalm 139:7 with a small 's' – that is, as an attribute of God's being – and interprets this verse as suggesting that:

> [I]t is impossible to escape from Yhwh, and specifically to escape from Yhwh's spirit or face (EVV 'presence'). The former suggests Yhwh's dynamic power; the latter suggests the look that generates blessing for people who belong to Yhwh but trouble for people who do not.[9]

Therefore, are we justified in reading 'your Spirit' as a manifestation of God's very being when the other objects of the pronoun 'your' are clearly concepts separate, or at least in some way distinct, from Yahweh's personal identity?

Again, it is the flow of the poem as a whole that helps answer this question. The poem transitions from a focus on Yahweh in relation to the psalmist in the first stanza to a focus on the psalmist in relation to Yahweh in the second stanza (vv. 7–12). We move from poetic discussion of Yahweh's intimate knowledge of the psalmist (vv. 1–6) to the latter's consideration of himself in relation to God's omnipresence. Throughout almost all of the remainder of the psalm, 'your' language is associated with objects clearly separate from the divine essence, but Psalm 139:7 should be read in the light of the following verse:

---

9. Goldingay, *Psalms 3*, p. 631. This is, perhaps, not surprising as he has elsewhere said that reference to the 'spirit' in the OT never implies more than 'presence' (see John Goldingay, *Isaiah*, NIBCOT [Carlisle: Paternoster, 2001], p. 87).

Where shall I go from *your Spirit*?
  And where can I flee from *your face*?
If I ascend to the heavens there *you* are;
  And if I make my bed in Sheol behold *you* [are there].
(vv. 7–8)

The rhetoric of these verses tells readers that it is folly to flee from God. This provides great assurance for those who follow Yahweh's paths (v. 16), but should fill Yahweh's enemies with great fear (vv. 19–22). However, the rhetorical questions of verse 7 make most sense if we read the indirect objects ('from your Spirit' and 'from your face') as synonyms of 'you' (*ʾattâ*) in verse 8. From the literary perspective – while these phrases *could* refer to abstract qualities of God's power and presence – they make the most sense and communicate most effectively when read as reflecting the concept presented in the following verse: namely, that *Yahweh* is present everywhere. In that sense the immediate context seems to point to the psalmist's understanding of 'the Spirit' as being equivalent to Yahweh in Psalm 139:7. In the same way that the poet's God is present everywhere (v. 8), so the *Spirit* of his God is everywhere. So, while we are not talking about a fully evolved trinitarian theology, it does seem that the psalmist is referring to the Spirit in Psalm 139:7 as a personal representation of the very essence of Yahweh's being. The ancient reader would not have seen the Spirit as being apart from Yahweh, but this poetic expression presents the concept of Yahweh's presence in the sort of personified form which is quite common in the poetic texts and which finds later development into a more rounded concept of divine hypostasis in the NT.

'Your Spirit' in the context of the Davidic collection

So on balance it seems that verse 7 *is* speaking of Yahweh's Spirit as a personal manifestation of Yahweh's being. This message is reinforced from the broader context of the 'Davidic' collection of which Psalm 139 is a part. There is one further occurrence of Spirit language in this collection which also appears to speak of God's Spirit in a personalized manner. Psalm 143:10 reads:

Teach me to do what is pleasing to you
  for you are my God.
May your good Spirit lead me
  on level ground.

This is an interesting and unusual turn of phrase. The only other reference to Yahweh's 'good Spirit' (*rûḥăkā ṭôbâ*) in the OT is in Nehemiah 9:20, which speaks about God's faithful leading of his people through the desert during their flight from Egypt and journey towards the land of promise. Although the theological contexts are somewhat different, the imagery of Psalms 139:7 and 143:10 (and Neh. 9:20, for that matter) speaks of divine presence both to instruct, protect and – importantly for each psalm it seems – to vindicate. Psalm 143:10 is grounded in the Exodus tradition that is so formative for Israel's national and religious identity,[10] but Psalm 139 derives very similar lessons from its creation theology which became equally important to the community's self-understanding.[11] The prayers of each speaker seek a similar end: that Yahweh's real presence would guide, inform and protect those praying as they face difficult present realities and, more specifically, that God would vindicate the speakers in the face of opposition from enemies (Pss 139:17–24; 143:9–10).

This tone of lament[12] and prayer concerning one's enemies is relatively unusual in the context of Book V of the Psalter and is more reminiscent of the type of psalms that we commonly see in (the predominantly 'Davidic') Books I and II. The secondary literature frequently comments on the broad

10. Susan E. Gillingham, 'The Exodus Tradition and Israelite Psalmody', *SJT* 52/1 (1999), pp. 19–46.
11. Klaus Seybold, 'Zur Geschichte des Vierten Davidspsalters (Pss 138 – 145)', in Peter W. Flint and Patrick D. Miller (eds.), *The Book of Psalms: Composition and Reception*, *VTSup* XCIX (Leiden: Brill, 2005), p. 388.
12. Ps. 139 is not a classical 'lament' in terms of its genre, but the closing verses add an interesting and concrete overtone of lament regarding enemies to an otherwise quite contemplative composition. The context for this psalm *may* be one of false accusation against the psalmist to which the poet responds by reflecting on the omniscience, omnipresence and omnipotence of Yahweh. His conclusion is: 'If I have done wrong Yahweh sees, knows *and will respond* to that wrong.' This call for testing is seen most clearly in the language of 'searching' (*ḥāqar*) and 'testing' (*bāḥan*) in v. 23, although it is always difficult to be certain of any psalm's setting. As some commentators point out, this call to 'search' and 'test' the poet may respond to false accusations laid against the poet, or the call to be examined may well be his heart response to the fears that gave rise to the 'vitriol' of his own prayer in vv. 19–22. See Jan Holman, 'The Structure of Psalm CXXXIX', *VT* XXI/3 (1971), pp. 298–310, for the former view, and Th. Booij, 'Psalm CXXXIX: Text, Syntax, Meaning', *VT* LV/1 (2005), p. 15, for the latter.

movement from 'lament to praise' in the Psalms, whereby we see a preponderance of lament psalms of the individual in Books I – III (Pss 1 – 89) and greater dominance of community praises and festal psalms in Books IV – V (Pss 90 – 150).[13] So it is (at least somewhat) surprising to see compositions of this type in this part of the Psalter. Yet the final Davidic collection of the book of Psalms is marked by prayers that seek divine intervention, including Psalms 139 and 143.[14]

In these intercessory psalms, both implicitly and explicitly, the Lord's presence is essential to the psalmist's expression of hope in the face of personal challenge and crisis. Psalm 139 may lament false accusation and certainly calls upon Yahweh himself to judge the integrity of his inner being (Ps. 139:23–24). Similarly with Psalm 143, the poet is dependent upon the reality of God's presence if his prayers are to be answered regarding his enemies. It is in this context that the speakers mention God's Spirit. In Psalm 139 the poet appears to offer a kind of self-imprecation: where can anyone flee from God's presence? For the enemies of God, the reality of his presence is to their great cost. For those who walk in his ways, this is their great affirmation – regardless of the circumstances they face, Yahweh's Spirit is near, hearing and responding. The prayers in this section of the Psalter are fully rooted in the reality of the divine presence and that presence is described as the Spirit of Yahweh.[15] It is God himself who is near, hearing and answering prayers, and the 'lament' psalms in this sub-collection are rooted in that underlying awareness.

The 'spiritual' theology of Psalm 139

So, having established that the reference to 'your Spirit' in Psalm 139 is – most likely – a synonym for Yahweh's divine being, it is important to consider the theological significance of the statement found in Psalm 139:7. What does

---

13. Gerald H. Wilson, 'The Structure of the Psalter', in P. S. Johnston and D. G. Firth (eds.), *Interpreting the Psalms: Issues and Approaches* (Leicester: Apollos, 2005), p. 231.
14. Pss 140 – 142 also show several typical characteristics of lament. So this Davidic collection has the voice of individual intercession at its centre but begins and ends with psalms of confidence in Ps. 138 and Pss 144 – 145 respectively.
15. Seybold describes Ps. 139 as a *Beichtspiegel*, a confessional reflection, and comments that Ps. 139 'is of great theological significance because of the theology of creation and of the *praesentia Dei* implied in it' ('Zur Geschichte', p. 386, translation mine).

it tell us about the poet's understanding of the Spirit of Yahweh from his perspective in the history of salvation?

The obvious aspect to consider with regard to Psalm 139:7 is the commonality between 'Spirit' and 'face/presence'. In the psalmist's mind the Spirit of Yahweh is concomitant with his universal presence throughout all of the created order. The concept of the Spirit of God in part refers to the aphysicality of Israel's God – a notion that was relatively uncommon in the Ancient Near East. Most Ancient Near Eastern religions believed in an essential deity existent beyond the idols that were worshipped, but some physical manifestation in the here and now was seen as essential to religious practice. However, *the spirituality* of God in his essence is key to the psalmist's thought in Psalm 139. Since Yahweh is spiritual by nature, he can be present *everywhere*. There seem to be two conclusions from this understanding of the omnipresence of the Spirit of God, one positive and one negative from the perspective of humanity, and this is seen in the two lines of Psalm 139:7. First, and more neutrally, the poet asks: 'Where can I go from your Spirit?' The overtone here is one of comfort and security. Nowhere is the poet beyond the care of his God who is spiritually present everywhere throughout the created order. There is comfort to be found in this thought. Second, however, the concept of 'fleeing from your face' in the second line adds a cautionary tone to the universal, spiritual presence of God, at least for those who reject his justice.[16] If,

16. Some commentators try to apply the tone of Ps. 139:7b as the overarching voice of the composition and, therefore, read the discussion of divine presence throughout as a threatening reality that intimidates the psalmist (see e.g. Erhard S. Gerstenberger, *Psalms, Part 2; and Lamentations*, FOTL XV [Grand Rapids: Eerdmans, 2001], p. 402). The poet Francis Thompson entitled his re-rendering of this psalm as 'The Hound of Heaven', presenting the wayward speaker chased by a relentless God. Now this may well have been Thompson's experience of God seeking him with a compassionate relentlessness while he rebelled, but those who see the divine presence as predominantly threatening do not seem to do justice to the comfort that the poet expresses elsewhere at the presence of God (vv. 11–12) and the wonder that he voices regarding the fact that he is completely known by God (vv. 13–16). There is a threatening implication to the presence of Yahweh, but that threat extends to his enemies and reflects the inescapable ultimacy of divine justice. Yahweh is ever present both to protect his people in darkness (vv. 11–12) and also to judge those who would slander his name by bringing injustice to his created order (vv. 19–22; this can apply to Israel and Israelites as much as it does to people of other nations, as is made clear in Hab. 9:2–4).

as seems possible, the psalmist is calling upon God to judge him with regard to false accusations, the awareness of the omnipresence of God's Spirit is an awareness of his inescapable justice. Regardless of the accusations of other people, the poet knows that if he has sinned against God he cannot escape *Yahweh's* ultimate justice. He cannot 'go' anywhere beyond divine protection, nor can he 'flee' anywhere to escape divine judgment. This is the dual essence of the psalmist's prayer: the Spirit of Yahweh is both Refuge and Judge on the earth. Hence he makes his plea for a divine declaration of his own righteousness (or otherwise) in the concluding verse of the psalm. God's spiritual presence brings comfort to his people by ensuring protection, but also by guaranteeing that he will outwork his just purpose in present historical reality – both aspects are the work of God's Spirit on the earth. William Brown summarizes this duality, and the psalm itself, well:

> The prevailing image of God is that of judge, impartial in judgement yet passionate in concern. God is called upon to test the mettle of the psalmist's integrity as well as to befriend without compromise. God is both judge and advocate . . . There are no moments, distant and dark as they might be, in which God is absent. There are no traumas in which the psalmist does not own God's mercies. This psalm is an intimate, retrospective look at the fullness and mystery of one's life, a prism, imperfect as it is, through which the fullness and mystery of God are beheld. It is an intimate testimony that God is indeed 'all in all' (1 Cor. 15:28).[17]

17. William P. Brown, 'Psalm 139: The Pathos of Praise', *Int* 50/3 (1996), p. 283.

8. SPIRIT OF WISDOM OR SPIRIT OF GOD IN PROVERBS 1:23?

Lindsay Wilson

The 'slippery' meaning of *rûaḥ*

Some words are slippery in their meaning due to their wide semantic range. Often little rides on the precise nuance, and commonly the wider context will clarify their force. But the Hebrew word *rûaḥ* slides between quite discrete meanings (among others) of wind, breath, spirit and Spirit. Its translation value is affected by its immediate context (e.g. the surrounding verbs, any parallelism) as well as the wider setting of a biblical book or literary genre.

The use of *rûaḥ* in Proverbs 1:23 has not been subject to extensive exploration, but is an interesting case study given Tremper Longman's exploration of 'spirit and wisdom' in this volume.

English translations of Proverbs 1:23

The dominant use of the KJV over so many years has brought this text into play as referring to the Holy Spirit. In searching online, I found that you are able to get the key parts of this verse in the KJV on a 'teatime scroll' (a pottery plaque with a metal symbol of a teapot on it, presumably for you to reflect upon as you have a cup of tea) for hanging in your house.[1] The KJV translates it as 'Turn you at my reproof: behold, I will pour out my spirit unto you, I will make known my words unto you.'

The variety of English translations can be seen in the table opposite. Some, like the ASV, NKJV and NASB, make only slight variations from the KJV, and they all understand *rûaḥ* to mean 'spirit'. While they, and the KJV, do not capitalize the word 'spirit', this is the way that the Spirit of God is referred to in the KJV of the OT (e.g. Gen. 1:2; Joel 2:28; Ezek. 37:1). However, the translation itself could imply either the Holy Spirit or 'the spirit of wisdom'. It is interesting that the ASV changed the preposition from 'unto' to 'upon', and the NKJV and NASB changed it to 'on'. Such changes conjure up a stronger parallel with the pouring out of the Spirit on all flesh in Joel 2:28. (The KJV used the preposition 'unto' in Prov. 1:23 and 'upon' in Joel 2:28.)

In the second half of the twentieth century there was a movement from 'spirit' to 'thoughts' (or something equivalent). Thus the RSV (followed by the NRSV, TNIV) opted for 'I will pour out my thoughts to you'. The NIV moves further away from a literal translation by rendering it as 'I would have poured out my heart to you'.[2] What these translations have in common is that *rûaḥ* is no longer understood as a personal yet unseen force, but now thoughts or longings that can be put into words. This makes a neat parallelism with what follows: 'I will make my words known to you.' Such a trend is also echoed in the paraphrasing translations such as the NLT ('I'll share my heart with you') and the CEV (where the last two clauses are reduced to 'tell you what I think').

Against this trend stands the ESV, which reverts to 'I will pour out my spirit to you', retaining the word 'spirit' but choosing the preposition 'to'. It does not capitalize the word 'spirit', which may be significant in that the ESV (unlike the KJV) uses the capitalized form 'Spirit' in Genesis 1:2, Joel 2:28 and Ezekiel 37:1.

Proverbs 1:23 in theologies of the Holy Spirit

Another useful source of information is the extent to which systematic or biblical theologies of the Holy Spirit refer to Proverbs 1:23. Of particular interest here is whether or not they provide any rationale for the inclusion or exclusion of this verse in developing an OT theology of the Spirit. The

1. Scrolls Unlimited, Inc., www.scrollsunlimited.com/store/index.php?productID=16, accessed 29 October 2010.
2. P. E. Koptak, *Proverbs*, NIVAC (Grand Rapids: Zondervan, 2003), p. 86, notes that the NIV has also moved to a past tense here.

KJV	Turn you at my reproof: behold, I will pour out my spirit unto you, I will make known my words unto you.
NKJV	Turn at my rebuke; Surely I will pour out my spirit on you; I will make my words known to you.
ASV	Turn you at my reproof: Behold, I will pour out my spirit upon you; I will make known my words unto you.
NASB	Turn to my reproof, Behold, I will pour out my spirit on you; I will make my words known to you.
RSV	Give heed to my reproof; behold, I will pour out my thoughts to you; I will make my words known to you.
NRSV	Give heed to my reproof; I will pour out my thoughts to you; I will make my words known to you.
NIV	If you had responded to my rebuke, I would have poured out my heart to you and made my thoughts known to you.
TNIV	Repent at my rebuke! Then I will pour out my thoughts to you, I will make known to you my teachings.
ESV	If you turn at my reproof, behold, I will pour out my spirit to you; I will make my words known to you.
The Message	About face! I can revise your life. Look, I'm ready to pour out my spirit on you; I'm ready to tell you all I know.
NLT	Come and listen to my counsel. I'll share my heart with you and make you wise.
CEV	Listen as I correct you and tell you what I think.

overwhelming response is that this passage is ignored entirely, though it is occasionally used as a prooftext. Thus, in response to Question 32 of the Westminster Larger Catechism (1648), it is used to reference the proposition that God 'promiseth and giveth his Holy Spirit', though no supporting argument is given. Similarly, A. W. Pink includes it 'among the principal pledges which God made that the Spirit should be given unto and poured out upon His saints',[3] but no further argument is made. Thomas Oden uses this verse to prove that the Spirit is active in Israel through proverbs, but also fails to explain why this verse should be read in that way.[4]

The most promising discussion is found in Wilf Hildebrandt's 1995 study

3. A. W. Pink, *The Holy Spirit* (Grand Rapids: Baker, 1970), p. 32.

4. T. C. Oden, *Life in the Spirit. Systematic Theology: Volume Three* (San Francisco: Harper, 1992), p. 38.

of the Spirit in the OT.[5] He includes a section on 'the role of wisdom personified in creation: Proverbs 1:23'. However, there is only a weak argument for identifying *rûaḥ* as Spirit. He simply cites McKane's translation and observes that it has 'credence', suggesting that wisdom is being represented here as a person who pours out, on those willing to receive it, the spirit of wisdom.[6] While quoting McKane, however, he does not explain how he moves from spirit to Spirit. He then moves on to the links between Spirit and wisdom in the rest of the OT, noting that it is often the Spirit who gives wisdom (e.g. Gen. 41:38–39; Exod. 31:3–4; Deut. 34:9; Isa. 11:2; Job 32:7–10). He suggests that wisdom has more affinities with the work of the *rûaḥ* in creation than with the pre-incarnate second person of the Trinity, and that the intertestamental period also shows the links between wisdom and creation.[7]

A survey of commentaries on Proverbs

There is greater consideration of this issue in commentaries and articles on Proverbs. However, even here several simply do not explore the meaning of *rûaḥ*.[8] Others only indicate their view by their translation. So Scott translates *rûaḥ* as 'thought' but adds a translation note that it is literally 'spirit'.[9] Van Leeuwen simply suggests a translation 'I poured out my thoughts to you'.[10] Similarly, Clifford, although he wishes to reconstruct the text of verses 22–23, translates this portion as 'I have been disclosing my thoughts to you'.[11]

Several commentators, however, develop their reasoning more explicitly.

---

5. W. Hildebrandt, *An Old Testament Theology of the Spirit of God* (Peabody: Hendrickson, 1995).
6. Ibid., p. 43.
7. Ibid., p. 44.
8. E.g. D. A. Garrett, *Proverbs, Ecclesiastes, Song of Songs*, NAC (Nashville: Broadman, 1993); K. A. Farmer, *Who Knows What is Good?: A Commentary on the Books of Proverbs and Ecclesiastes*, ITC (Edinburgh: Handsel, 1991); D. Cox, *Proverbs*, OTM (Wilmington: Michael Glazier, 1982); L. G. Perdue, *Proverbs*, Interpretation (Louisville: John Knox, 2000); Koptak, *Proverbs*; J. R. Wright, *Proverbs, Ecclesiastes, Song of Solomon*, ACC (Downers Grove: InterVarsity Press, 2005).
9. R. B. Y. Scott, *Proverbs, Ecclesiastes*, AB (New York: Doubleday, 1965), pp. 34, 40.
10. R. C. Van Leeuwen, 'The Book of Proverbs', in *NIB* 5 (Nashville: Abingdon, 1997), p. 40.
11. R. J. Clifford, *Proverbs: A Commentary*, OTL (Louisville: John Knox, 1999), p. 40.

Rûaḥ = *thoughts*

Norman Whybray notes that *nbʿ* (to pour out) in the *hiphil* is commonly used for the 'verbal communication of a person's mind or thoughts' (citing Ps. 94:4; Prov. 15:2, 28) and opts here for *rûaḥ* meaning 'thoughts' since it is paralleled with 'words'.[12] Alden suggests that the precise nuance of *rûaḥ* here is determined by 'rebuke', which indicates that they are words of reprimand, reproof, advice or counsel.[13] Reyburn and Fry note that it is best understood to refer to 'what characterizes Wisdom, who is the speaker here'.[14] Since her essential characteristic is wisdom, *rûaḥ* here means 'wisdom' or good advice. Similarly, Yoder suggests that here Wisdom is exhorting her listeners to return to her counsel, words and *rûaḥ*, and comments that *rûaḥ* is 'a term used to refer broadly to a person's frame of mind, temperament or spirit (e.g., 11:13; 14:29; 16:19, 32; 18:14)'.[15]

The most detailed exponent of this view is Bruce Waltke, who builds on an earlier article by John Emerton. Emerton argued that the phrase is not likely to be rendered 'I will pour out my spirit unto you' since it would be more natural to use the preposition *ʾel* rather than *lĕ* for this. He notes that 'it is more likely that the *hiph'il* of *nbʿ* has its usual sense of giving utterance in speech'.[16] He argues that *rûaḥ* means 'breath' in the sense of 'utterance, word' as in Psalm 33:6 and Isaiah 11:4 (and perhaps also in Isa. 34:16). In Psalm 33:6 it is in parallel to *dbr*, as here in Proverbs 1:23.

Waltke translates verse 23 as 'I will pour forth my thoughts to you'. In referring to Emerton, Waltke thinks that he has shown persuasively that *rûḥî* means 'my breath' as a metonymy for 'utterance or word'. He notes that the *hiphil* of *nbʿ* normally pertains to speech and that this best fits the parallel in verse 23b. He thinks that to translate this as 'pour out my spirit' would mislead many English readers into associating the thought with Isaiah 44:3 and Joel 2:28.[17] 'My thoughts' would therefore be a good parallel to 'my words' in the next line.

---

12. R. N. Whybray, *Proverbs*, NCB (London: Marshall Pickering, 1994), p. 47.
13. R. L. Alden, *Proverbs* (Grand Rapids: Baker, 1983), p. 28.
14. W. D. Reyburn and E. McG. Fry, *A Handbook on Proverbs* (New York: United Bible Societies, 2000), p. 47.
15. C. E. Yoder, *Proverbs*, AOTC (Nashville: Abingdon, 2009), pp. 17–18.
16. J. A. Emerton, 'A Note on the Hebrew Text of Proverbs i. 22–3', *JTS* 19 (1968), p. 611.
17. B. K. Waltke, *The Book of Proverbs Chapters 1 – 15*, NICOT (Grand Rapids: Eerdmans, 2004), p. 199.

Rûaḥ *is translated as 'spirit'*

Some scholars translate *rûaḥ* as 'spirit' but mean something closer to 'thoughts' than 'Spirit'. Murphy, for example, translates this clause as 'I will pour out my spirit to you', but suggests that 'her "spirit" is really the anger that is manifest in the threatening "words" that follow'.[18] Fox translates it as 'I pour out to you my spirit', but explains this as I will 'let you know how I feel'.[19] Although such writers formally translate *rûaḥ* as 'spirit', they appear to be working with an actual understanding of *rûaḥ* as 'thoughts'.

Rûaḥ = *Spirit*

McKane translates verse 23 as 'If you return when I reprove you, I shall pour out my spirit for you, I shall divulge my words to you.'[20] He relies on Ringgren's view that this may be an echo of the prophetic promise of the pouring out of the spirit (Isa. 44:3). McKane suggests that 'the intention here may be to represent Wisdom as a charismatic, spirit-filled person, who pours out on those who are receptive and submissive to the spirit of wisdom'.[21]

Most recently, Longman translates verse 23 as 'You should respond to my correction. I will pour forth my spirit to you; I will make known to you my words.' Later he notes that Woman Wisdom has offered to give to the foolish people 'her spirit'.[22] He does not explain how we are to understand this term, but slips into a discussion of the Spirit by observing that elsewhere connections are made between God's Spirit and wisdom (e.g. Exod. 31:3; Isa. 11:2–3a). He cryptically adds that 'this connection between Wisdom and spirit and God will become even clearer when we explore the relationship between God and Wisdom in chaps. 8 and 9'.[23] Thus he seems to have hinted at the identification of *rûaḥ* as 'Spirit' rather than simply 'spirit', without offering any substantive arguments at this stage.

Later he identifies Woman Wisdom (e.g. 9:1–6) as a poetic personification of Yahweh's wisdom, so that Wisdom finally represents Yahweh himself. In relation to chapter 8, he notes that while later Jewish interpretations identified Torah with wisdom (e.g. Sirach and Wisdom of Solomon), the NT identified Christ as 'the embodiment of God's wisdom', presumably in the sense that he

---

18. R. E. Murphy, *Proverbs*, WBC (Nashville: Thomas Nelson, 1998), pp. xxxii, 7, 10.
19. M. V. Fox, *Proverbs 1 – 9*, AB (New York: Doubleday, 2000), pp. 95, 100.
20. W. McKane, *Proverbs*, OTL (London: SCM, 1970), p. 212.
21. Ibid., p. 274.
22. T. Longman, *Proverbs*, BCOTWP (Grand Rapids: Baker, 2006), pp. 92, 112–113.
23. Ibid., p. 113; see also pp. 97–98 in this volume.

embodies or fulfils Wisdom. He argues that Wisdom is not only a personification of an attribute of Yahweh, but also a personification of Yahweh himself.[24] However, despite the tantalizing hint in his commentary on 1:23, Longman does not appear to have established the connection between *rûaḥ* and Spirit.

A closer look at Proverbs 1:23

Clearly a re-examination of this clause in verse 23 is in order. The two key issues are, first, the implications of the verb 'to pour out' and, second, the nature of the parallelism with the following clause 'I will make my words known to you'.

First, the verb 'to pour out' is used eleven times in the OT, all but one in Psalms and Proverbs (the exception is in Eccl. 10:1). The overwhelming image is of 'pouring out words'. In Psalm 19:2, it outlines the heavens *pouring out* speech, declaring God's glory. Psalm 59:7 has the enemies thinking or saying, 'Who will hear us?' and this is described as having swords in their lips or uttering (ESV, 'bellowing') with their mouths. In an historical recital psalm (Ps. 78:2), the psalmist introduces his account by saying that he will *utter* dark sayings. Psalm 94:4 has the wicked/evildoers boasting or exulting, and this is another way of describing them *pouring out* arrogant words. Psalm 119:171 announces that 'my lips' will *pour forth* (words of) praise, while Psalm 145:7 speaks of a generation who will *pour forth* (words about) the fame of your abundant goodness. The parallels in Psalm 145:6–7 (speak, declare, sing) all make it clear that words are in view.

In the three references in Proverbs (other than 1:23), the verb 'to pour out' is connected to the mouth in each case. Thus in Proverbs 15:2 it is the mouth of the wicked which *pours out* (presumably 'words of') folly. The ESV renders 'pours out evil things', but this unhelpfully raises the possibility not present in the Hebrew text that it is something other than words. In Proverbs 15:28, in parallel to 'answering', it is said that 'the mouth of the wicked *pours out* evil things' (or could be 'words'). Finally, in Proverbs 18:4 the spring of wisdom – parallel to 'the words of a man's mouth' – are pictured as a *bubbling* brook, with the participial form of the verb 'to pour out' being used as an adjective meaning the 'pouring out' (i.e. bubbling or bursting forth) brook.

The only time that the verb is used without words being in view is in Ecclesiastes 10:1 where it describes ointment *giving off* a bad odour.

---

24. Ibid., pp. 196, 213, 222.

These uses of this verb in connection with words are an important context for understanding its meaning in Proverbs 1:23, and it is significant that here words are also in view. The phrase 'I will *pour out* my *rûaḥ* to you' is in parallel with 'I will make my words known to you'. What is being made known is either words which come from Wisdom's *rûaḥ*, or words which are uttered by a person who has been shaped by Wisdom's *rûaḥ*. Thus it could mean words expressing Wisdom's thoughts, or perhaps words which come from one who has embraced wisdom.

Waltke notes that *rûaḥ* is used twenty-one times in Proverbs, but that 'Proverbs, unlike other biblical authors, does not associate *rûaḥ* with the Lord.'[25] In his section on *rûaḥ* in the introduction, Waltke does not consider 1:23. It is also important to realize that *rûaḥ* is commonly used in the book of Proverbs to refer to the essence or core of an idea or person. There is reference to a haughty spirit (Prov. 16:18), a lowly spirit (Prov. 16:19), a cool spirit (Prov. 17:27) and a crushed spirit (Prov. 17:22; 18:14). People can be trustworthy in spirit (Prov. 11:13) or lowly in spirit (Prov. 29:23). At times it is simply another way of referring to a person, and especially what they are like on the inside. So it is 'his spirit' in Proverbs 16:32; 29:11, or a person's spirit in Proverbs 18:14; 20:27. Sometimes it is simply 'the spirit', but refers to a person not the Holy Spirit as this spirit can be broken (Prov. 15:4), crushed (Prov. 15:13) or weighed (Prov. 16:2). It can also refer at times simply to wind (Prov. 25:14, 23, 28; 27:16; 30:4). Apart from this use, at least in chapters 10 – 31, it apparently refers to a person or the core or typical attitude of a person.

Proverbs 1:23 in the context of the book of Proverbs

Proverbs 1:23 is part of a wider speech not by God, but by Wisdom personified as a woman. Lady Wisdom is calling out for followers in the market place, busy streets and city gates (vv. 20–21). Her invitation is essentially to the 'simple ones' (v. 22a), which is not a description of those with intellectual limits, but rather those whose moral direction in life is not yet formed. Waltke colourfully describes them as 'the heretofore-unresponsive youths'.[26] There are rival voices calling for young men starting out in life, and this is displayed most clearly in the twin invitations of Proverbs 9. Lady Wisdom calls to the 'simple' to eat at her banquet (9:4–5), while Dame Folly also invites

25. Waltke, *Proverbs 1 – 15*, p. 92.
26. Ibid., p. 203.

the 'simple' to dine with her (Prov. 9:16–17). The question concerns which location a morally unformed person will choose as their home base, and the two invitations to the 'simple' are framed around the motto of the book: 'the fear of the LORD is the beginning of wisdom' (Prov. 9:10). Proverbs 1:20–33 is therefore a more extended form of the foundational invitation that will be made by Lady Wisdom in 9:1–6.

If this youth is at this stage in need of moral formation (he 'loves being simple' in 1:22a), this accounts for the reference to reproof in 1:23a. He needs to embrace wisdom, personified as Lady Wisdom, in order to find success in life, which is the *kerygma* of the book of Proverbs. In the context of this choice, Wisdom offers to pour out her spirit to the youth. Spirit here seems to refer to the essence or core attitude of wisdom, building your life on the foundation of the fear of the Lord. This could happen by Wisdom making known her words of reproof and instruction (the counsel and reproof of v. 25) to the youth. However, it is also possible that this is a two-stage process. First, there is the fundamental choice to embrace wisdom by building your life on the fear of the Lord. This is the essence or core attitude of wisdom. Once this fundamental stance has been adopted, the next stage is to have your character shaped by words of wisdom. This is the very process that is adopted in chapter 2.

In 2:1–4 there is a need to receive wisdom's words and commands, striving for insight and understanding as if they were valuable treasures. This will lead to a deeper understanding of the fear of the Lord (2:5) and the development of a wise character (2:9–11) which will then guard and protect those who have embraced wisdom. Lady Wisdom has called in 1:23 for the 'simple ones' to take her reproof seriously, so that she will ground them in the fear of the Lord, the core attitude of wisdom, and then begin to instruct them.

Waltke points out that their failure to embrace wisdom is the reason why she now resolves to deliver her harsh sermon found in 1:24–27.[27] He understands that these words in verses 24–27 are what is poured out by wisdom's *rûaḥ*. Alternatively, and I think more likely, these are words urging them to embrace wisdom so that she can pour out her spirit on them. In any event, their response of ignoring her words of counsel and reproof will lead to terrible disasters and anguish. Verses 28–31 explain this lack of life or success as due to their wrong foundational choice (they 'did not choose the fear of the LORD', 1:29) and their ignoring of wisdom's words of reproof and instruction (1:30). They have brought this upon themselves, and are stuck with the consequences of their choice (1:31).

---

27. Ibid., p. 204.

The passage in 1:20–33 comes to an end with a clear choice. There are two ways to do life. Life without wisdom's foundation and instruction is the path to death and destruction (1:32). But those who have embraced the spirit or core attitude of wisdom and keep on listening to the words of wisdom will have security and be at ease (1:33). Trible suggests that there is a strong parallelism between wisdom's reproof and offer of 1:22–23 and the contrasting outcomes for the secure wise and dying fools in 1:32–33.[28] Similarly, Nel points out that verse 23 is 'clearly an admonition, directly followed by a motivation in a promissory form'.[29] After the account of the rejection of wisdom by many in verses 24–31, there is a final exhortation to base their future on wisdom and find life (vv. 32–33). Thus the whole speech from 1:20–33 is 'an invitation and exhortation of personified wisdom'.[30] In every part of the speech, including the pouring out of wisdom's *rûaḥ* in verse 23, the real concern is that the morally unformed hearers will turn to wisdom, embrace her core commitments and allow themselves to be shaped by her instruction.

Thus Waltke is right to caution that translating verse 23 as 'pour out my spirit' would mislead many English readers into associating the thought with passages like Joel 2:28 (3:1). In its context, he suggests that Lady Wisdom is giving a sermon in verses 22–27 (with vv. 22–23 as a rebuke of the unresponsive, gullible person), followed by reflections on her sermon in verses 28–33. On this break-up, verses 31–33 are summarizing reflections on the destinies of fools and the wise.[31]

However, Waltke's view needs some modification in the light of the passage and the book as a whole. The language of 'pouring out my spirit' can be retained if 'spirit' is not capitalized. *Rûaḥ* here is not just Wisdom's 'thoughts' which are made known through the words of the rest of the passage. Rather, it describes the essence or core commitment of wisdom. This is seen in Proverbs 1 – 9 to be a reference to the fear of the Lord, outlined in the foundational mottos of 1:7 and 9:10. As chapters 1 – 9 are the way in for the reader to the individual proverbs beginning in chapter 10, they are bracketed by these 'fear of the Lord' sayings. The first saying is found in 1:7, immediately after the prologue of 1:2–6. The second is located in the middle

---

28. P. Trible, 'Wisdom Builds a Poem: The Architecture of Proverbs 1:20–33', *JBL* 94 (1975), p. 517.

29. P. J. Nel, *The Structure and Ethos of the Wisdom Admonitions in Proverbs*, BZAW 158 (Berlin: Walter de Gruyter, 1982), p. 58.

30. Ibid., p. 58.

31. Waltke, *Proverbs 1 – 15*, pp. 199–200.

of the twin invitations by Lady Wisdom and Dame Folly in 9:1–6 and 9:13–18. Grounding your life on the fear of the Lord ('respecting God for who he is'), coupled with Wisdom growing her character in a person, are prior steps to receiving wise instruction. This may be what is meant by Wisdom pouring out her essence or core stance or attitude – her spirit.

Links with other 'Spirit passages'

One further argument may need to be considered. Given that there are a number of passages in the OT which speak about God pouring out his spirit, might not the language used in Proverbs 1:23 be read canonically in this way? The NASB, for example, gives cross references from 'pour out my spirit' in this passage to Isaiah 32:15; Joel 2:28 and John 7:39. More recently, the ESV connects the phrase 'pour out my spirit' to Joel 2:28 (= 3:1 in MT) and Acts 2:17.

Yet these possible connections are far from obvious. In Proverbs 1:23, the verb 'pour out' is a *hiphil* form of the root *nbʿ*. In Joel 2:28 (3:1) it is a *qal* form of the root *špk*. In Isaiah 32:15, it is a *niphal* form of the root *ʿrh*, 'to empty'. The similarity is only at the level of our English translations, not the underlying Hebrew text.

Furthermore, the LXX versions of these other two passages do not use the same Greek verb used in the LXX of Proverbs 1:23. This means that Acts 2:17, which simply quotes Joel, uses the same word as the book of Joel, but not the verb used in the LXX of Proverbs 1:23. In relation to John 7:39, there is no mention of the Spirit being 'poured out'. Instead, it simply says that the Spirit was not yet (given) because Jesus was not yet glorified.

Conclusions

If this argument is correct, what are the implications for the connection between this 'spirit' and the Holy Spirit?

First, it is evident that this is not a simple echo of the outpouring of the Spirit promised in Joel 2:28 and which happened in Acts 2. The language is different, and the flow of the argument leads in another direction entirely. It is also the spirit of Wisdom, not the Spirit of God, which is in view. It is not surprising, therefore, that most studies of pneumatology do not use this verse to support the view that the Spirit will be poured out on believers. That concept needs to be grounded in other parts of the OT, such as Joel 2:28.

However, this does not mean that this passage has no implications for understanding the Spirit and his role. Since the spirit in Proverbs 1:23 is the 'spirit of wisdom', then the identity of wisdom in the book is important. Proverbs 8:22–31 makes it clear that wisdom, as one of Yahweh's attributes, is personified and described in exalted terms. Wisdom is depicted in the book of Proverbs as the wisdom of God, and so the spirit of wisdom is not far from the Spirit of God. In NT terms, Christ is described as the wisdom of God (1 Cor. 1:24). This passage continues by describing the work of the Spirit who searches out the depths of God, since no-one comprehends the thoughts of God except the Spirit of God (1 Cor. 2:10–11). Thus the role performed by wisdom in the OT is to some extent made explicit in the NT as the work of the Spirit.

Indeed, it is worth reflecting on the fact that Proverbs 1 – 9 provides the key to reading the book as a whole, and therefore how to live life as God's creature in a way that makes sense. The emphasis in Proverbs 1 – 9 on the fear of the Lord as the foundation and starting place, and the need for the development of a godly character, have clear NT trajectories. For believers in the NT era, the only foundation and starting place is faith in Christ. However, living God's way also requires the development of a godly character, which is at least in part the fruit of the Spirit working in our lives (Gal. 5:22–23). All of this is not explicit in Proverbs 1:23, but the base is laid there for the Bible as a whole to build on Lady Wisdom's call to get the core commitment right and to be shaped by words of wisdom.

PART 4: THE SPIRIT AND CREATIVITY

9. BEZALEL AND OHOLIAB: SPIRIT AND CREATIVITY

Richard S. Hess

At creation the Spirit of God was present (Gen. 1:2) to bring about the order, beauty and life of creation. The high point of creation came about on the sixth day with the climactic emergence of humanity. The distinctive aspect of creation in the image of God was the rule and dominion over everything that God had made.

It is important to understand that humanity's home is the Garden of Eden and that this is where their care for the land and the animals takes place. If this was the first home of humanity, it was also the place where God met with the man and woman. Indeed, this observation reinforces the rest of the description as that of a prototypical sanctuary. All of these elements appear in both the wilderness tabernacle (Exod. 25 – 31, 35 – 40) and the temple of Solomon (1 Kgs 6 – 9). The construction materials for these holy sites include precious stones and gold. Much water is required for the sacrifices and this is most evident in the presence of the great 'Sea' that stands in front of the Holy Place of the temple (1 Kgs 7:23–25). The incense of these holy places recalls the aromas of Eden. Both the tabernacle and the temple open towards the east and include images of cherubim in the Most Holy Place where the ark of the covenant lies. The tree of life is remembered in the multi-branched menorah.[1]

---

1. Gordon J. Wenham, 'Sanctuary Symbolism in the Garden of Eden Story', in

The Bible identifies God as the Creator of the 'temple of the cosmos'. However, in accordance with the decision to give to humanity the ongoing work of creation and dominion over the earth (Gen. 1:26–28), the divine decision was made to appoint human agents to build the tabernacle and the temple in Jerusalem. For the tabernacle Bezalel was appointed by God and given divine skill. His name occurs six times in the Exodus accounts of the tabernacle and twice again in Chronicles.[2] Oholiab is also appointed by God and five times mentioned as Bezalel's assistant.[3] The same appears to be true of the construction of the temple. Solomon brings a figure named Huram from Tyre and has him construct the various items for the temple.[4] The name occurs four times in 1 Kings and twice in 2 Chronicles.[5] It is noteworthy that Huram is assigned his role by Solomon and that he comes from Tyre, where the text relates that he had his origins. He is thereby distinguished from Bezalel and Oholiab in three significant ways. First, Bezalal and Oholiab are explicitly named and appointed by God, according to the text of Exodus. Huram is not. Instead, Solomon seeks him out and he comes and does 'for Solomon' all the required labour. Second, the genealogies of both Bezalel and Oholiab are directly and only connected with Israel. Their patronymics are given and they are related to the tribes of Judah and Dan, respectively. Thus they are pure Israelite and from the people of God. On the other hand, Huram is half-Israelite. His mother was from the tribe of Naphtali, but his

---

Richard S. Hess and David T. Tsumura (eds.), *'I Studied Inscriptions from before the Flood': Ancient Near Eastern, Literary, and Linguistic Approaches to Genesis 1 – 11*, Sources for Biblical and Theological Study, vol. 4 (Winona Lake: Eisenbrauns, 1994), pp. 399–404. See also Mark S. Smith, *The Priestly Vision of Genesis 1* (Minneapolis: Fortress, 2010), pp. 14–15, 19, 30, 32, 36, 69–71, 75–76, 92–93, 107–108, 127, 137, 178, 185, 212, 244, 253; and John H. Walton, *The Lost World of Genesis One: Ancient Cosmology and the Origins Debate* (Downers Grove: InterVarsity Press, 2009), pp. 72–107.

2. Exod. 31:2; 35:30; 36:1, 2; 37:1; 38:22; 1 Chr. 2:20; 2 Chr. 1:5. A post-exilic figure by the same name appears in Ezra 10:30.
3. Exod. 31:6; 35:34; 36:1, 2; 38:23.
4. The name is identical to Hiram, king of Tyre, in its Hebrew spelling. However, he is distinguished from the king of Tyre by his Israelite mother.
5. 1 Kgs 7:13, 14, 40, 45; 2 Chr. 4:11 (*bis*). The Huram of 1 Chr. 8:5 is a different person whose name is spelled differently in the MT, like the spelling of Huram in its first appearance in 2 Chr. 4:11 (*ḥûrām*). The second appearance in this verse follows the spelling of 1 Kgs in the *ketib* but that of the first spelling in the *qere*.

father was a citizen of Tyre. Third, Yahweh called Bezalel and Oholiab by name and, along with the other skilled experts, gave them wisdom for their task. This again contrasts with Huram, whose skill is attributed to his father, a citizen of Tyre who was a bronze worker. Huram is described as skilled in the area of metallurgy. However, he did not receive this skill directly from Yahweh, as did Bezalel, Oholiab and the others who constructed the tabernacle. For this reason, it is of special interest to understand the nature of Bezalel and his companions. They create the tabernacle with skill that comes from God's direct endowment.

The value and role of the one who creates the world of worship and encounter with the living God can be traced in three directions. One has to do with the exegesis of the text itself so as to ascertain the nature and context of Bezalel's gift of the Spirit of God. A second must consider the Ancient Near Eastern context of literature that describes the construction of temples. There are consistent forms in these accounts and these forms may include a type of figure like Bezalel who appears in Exodus 31:1–3 and again in Exodus 35:30–31 as the one divinely appointed and empowered by the Spirit of God to build the tabernacle in the wilderness. The third direction examines the biblical theology of beauty and creativity that will form an essential part of the picture and role of the Spirit of God.

Exegesis

First, it is important to identify the particular role of Bezalel in the context of God's spirit and in the context of the grand gesture of generosity from the people as well as from God. In Exodus 24:1–11 the people voluntarily accept God's covenant mediated through Moses. They twice proclaim their willing acceptance of this book of the covenant. God brings their representatives into his presence where they see God and they eat and drink with him. This unrepeatable event is possible only because the people have entered into covenant with God and remain unsullied by sin. They are perfectly in covenant relationship with God and thus able to enjoy the divine banquet that for later generations would be fulfilled only in the world to come. However, even in Exodus 24 it is not possible for Israel to remain at Sinai permanently. They must move forward and obtain the promise of the land. To do this they must leave Sinai, but they do not leave without God. Indeed, even in the midst of the sin of the golden calf and its consequences, when God tells Moses to lead the people but warns that he will not go with them, he promises to send his angel to drive away the Canaanites who inhabit the land (Exod. 33:2). Moses' intercession proves effective so that God will join Israel on their journey. The tabernacle will become both the residence of the divine presence and the place of atonement.

The description of the construction of the tabernacle begins in Exodus 25 with the promise that this will be the means by which God will dwell among his people (v. 8). In order to affect this, Israel must bring the gold, silver, bronze and all kinds of special fabrics, gems and special wood that they possess so as to construct this place for God to live. This is the beginning of the building of the tabernacle (Exod. 25:1–8). The whole of the construction is based on the assumption that the people will bring this offering. According to Exodus 28:3, God gives his spirit (*rûaḥ*) to each of those engaged with the construction of the tabernacle. In fact, he 'fills' (*mlʾ* in the Piel) each one with the divine spirit so that they can make the garments for the priest in the correct manner. This filling with the spirit appears again when Bezalel is named in Exodus 31:2–3. There he is filled with the spirit of God and with all the necessary wisdom and skill for every task assigned to him.

The spirit appears again in Exodus 35:21, after the story of the sin with the golden calf, and at the beginning of the description of the actual construction of the tabernacle. Here, however, it is not connected with God or with Bezalel and the other workers. Instead, it is 'his willing spirit' (*nādbâ rûḥô*), that is, the willingness of all the people who come forward with their gifts for the construction of the tabernacle. It is followed by the identification of Bezalel and a repeated statement of how God has filled him with his Spirit to perform the work (Exod. 35:30–31), just as in Exodus 31:2–3. These are all the occurrences of the term for 'spirit', *rûaḥ*, in the entire text concerning the tabernacle and the golden calf. The term appeared before this in Exodus 14:21 and 15:8 and 10, where it described God's actions at the Red Sea. It will not occur again until Numbers 5, where it describes a 'spirit of jealousy' that a husband has for his wife (vv. 14, 30).[6] In the tabernacle story, the text juxtaposes God's spirit with that of the people who willingly present their gifts for constructing the tabernacle. Indeed, it seems that the willing spirit of the people in giving leads to the coming of the divine spirit to create the tabernacle and all its accoutrements for the priests.

The people's spirit reveals an abundant generosity that exceeds the needs of the tabernacle and requires prohibition against any further gifts (Exod. 36:6). Interwoven with the spirit of the people is their willing 'heart' that provides

6. The next reference to God's Spirit appears in Num. 11:25–31 where it rests on the seventy elders, and on Eldad and Medad, who all prophesy.

the source of their gracious gifts. Corresponding to this is the understanding and skill that the spirit provides to Bezalel and his assistants to construct all that is necessary for the tabernacle. The willing spirit of the people that leads them to lavish an abundance of riches upon the tabernacle also leads to the spirit filling Bezalel and the artisans. As John Levison observes, this is more than a momentary event.[7] The filling by the spirit (using the Piel of the Heb. *mlʾ*) emphasizes that every area of the person is full of God's presence. No area is withheld. And so every part of the skill and understanding becomes divinely endowed and, even more, fully endowed with the full presence of divinity. Further, this filling, repeated multiple times, is shared by Oholiab and communicated to the remaining skilled workers. These latter may, as Levison suggests, receive their skills from the instruction of Bezalel and Oholiab. That is, the two named workers are specifically 'filled' with the divine spirit and are 'filled' in their hearts so that they are fully competent in every area required for the construction of the tabernacle. The other artisans, on the other hand, have specific skills that God gives them through the instruction and teaching of Bezalel and Oholiab.[8]

There remains the examination of the personal names themselves. Bezalel is best analysed as a Semitic name composed of three elements: the initial *bêth* preposition, the root *ṣll*, and the noun *ʾl*. The preposition means 'in'. The root is normally understood as 'shade' or 'shadow'. The final noun *ʾl* refers either to El as head of the Canaanite pantheon or to the title for 'god'. If the latter is true, then this name means 'In the shadow of God'. While accepting this interpretation as a possibility, Zadok also suggests that the first element might be *ben* or 'son', where the final *nûn* was assimilated.[9] This would have the advantage of using a more common element in this name, rather than the rare use of a preposition beginning a name. However, the use of the preposition *bêth* is not unheard of. Indeed, Noth found a precise parallel to *bêth* plus *ṣll* followed by a divine name in an Akkadian personal name.[10] Further, the use of *ben* is more common with the patronym, which here is Uri, not Zalel. In addition, it would be most unusual for the *nûn* in *ben* to assimilate; something

7. John R. Levison, *Filled with the Spirit* (Grand Rapids: Eerdmans, 2009), pp. 52–58.

8. J. P. Hyatt, *Exodus*, NCB (London: Marshall, Morgan & Scott, 1971), p. 297; Levison, *Filled with the Spirit*, pp. 60–67.

9. Ran Zadok, *The Pre-Hellenistic Israelite Anthroponomy and Prosopography*, OLA 28 (Leuven: Peeters, 1988), pp. 56–57, 59.

10. Martin Noth, *Die israelitischen Personenamen im Rahmen der gemeinsemitischen Namengebung* (Hildesheim and New York: Georg Olms, 1980), p. 152.

that is not done, for example in the *ben* names of many of the Solomonic governors in 1 Kings 4:9–13.[11] The *ṣll* is indicative of West Semitic personal names from early Akkadian and Amorite on into the first millennium BCE.[12] More than any other location, however, are those personal names from Late Bronze Age Alalakh where the *ṣll* may appear by itself, as in *zi-il-lu*, or with a hypocoristic or divine name following the root, as in *zi-li-ia* and *zi-il-la-nu*.[13] The sense of the name as 'In the shadow of God' implies one who is under divine protection or care.[14] Not only does this name fit within the context of ancient West Semitic names in Israel and the surrounding cultures, it also serves as a marker of the character of the name bearer. Here is someone who is especially cared for by God. He is prepared and filled with the divine Spirit to accomplish the tasks that he has been given.

In a similar manner, the name Oholiab carries a special sense. The name is composed of two elements: *ʾhl*, 'tent', and *ʾab*, 'father'. The term for 'father' is a theophoric element often used to describe a deity. It occurs in all periods and places in West Semitic personal names. The term for 'tent' is one that seems most prominent in the early Amorite attestations, where Gelb lists it in as many as fourteen names. It also occurs later in the first millennium BCE in Phoenician names where it can be preceded or followed by a theophoric element, as in *ʾhlbʿl*, *ʾhlmlk* and *grʾhl*.[15] In biblical names it appears in

---

11. See J. Naveh, 'Nameless People', *IEJ* 40 (1990), pp. 108–123; R. S. Hess, 'The Form and Structure of the Solomonic District List in 1 Kings 4:17–19', in G. D. Young, M. W. Chavalas and R. E. Averbeck (eds.), *Crossing Boundaries and Linking Horizons: Studies in Honor of Michael C. Astour* (Bethesda: CDL, 1997), p. 287.
12. The evidence is conveniently collected under my study of Zillah, which, however, I analyse as from a different root. See R. S. Hess, *Studies in the Personal Names of Genesis 1 – 11* (Winona Lake: Eisenbrauns, 2009), pp. 48–49. Martin Noth, *Exodus*, trans. J. S. Bowden, OTL (Philadelphia: Westminster, 1962), p. 240, cites post-exilic examples for biblical names with this *ṣll* element, as the Bezalel of Ezra 10:30. However, he does not deny the numerous attestations in West Semitic names of the pre-exilic period.
13. See Daniel Sivan, *Grammatical Analysis and Glossary of the Northwest Semitic Vocables in Akkadian Texts of the 15th – 13th CBC from Canaan and Syria*, AOAT 214 (Kevelaer: Butzon & Bercker; Neukirchen-Vluyn: Neukirchener, 1984), p. 295.
14. Jeaneane D. Fowler, *Theophoric Personal Names in Ancient Hebrew: A Comparative Study*, *JSOTSup* 49 (Sheffield: JSOT, 1988), p. 127.
15. Frank L. Benz, *Personal Names in the Phoenicial and Punic Inscriptions*, Studis Pohl 8 (Rome: Biblical Institute Press, 1972), p. 262.

Oholibamah in Genesis 36:2 and in the names of Judah and Israel in Ezekiel 23:4, Oholibah and Oholah.[16] As has been observed, the sense of a 'tent' here is one of shelter or protection. The meaning of this name could be either 'tent/protection of God' or 'God is my protection'. Even though the name uses elements that are distinct from Bezalel and a different structure, the sense of one who is divinely protected and cared for occurs in the meaning of both terms and would have been readily perceived by ancient Israelites. Thus both the exegesis of the larger text and the context of the names themselves attest to the particular blessing of intimacy between God and these two artisans.

Building accounts

There is a long history of temple building accounts in texts from ancient Mesopotamia and the West Semitic world. These have been collected and studied, with important conclusions regarding common literary patterns and structures noted, by Hurowitz.[17] He has observed that the style of the tabernacle construction account in Exodus 25 – 40 and that of the temple in 1 Kings 5 – 6 participate in this same overall pattern.[18] Not only do the actual command to build and the subsequent actions parallel Ancient Near Eastern accounts, but even the golden calf incident finds similarities in accounts where the building process is interrupted by a rebellion against the designated builder of the temple. Given strong and numerous parallels, we may also ask whether the artisan designed to build the temple is also identified and given special consideration as is the case with Bezalel and Oholiab. Of course, we have seen this with Huram in the account of 1 Kings 5 – 9. Elsewhere a parallel exists only in the case of the palace of Baal as preserved on tablet four of the Baal cycle from Ugarit. There the god Kothar-wa-Hasis is enlisted to build the temple.[19] This form does not occur in Mesopotamian

16. R. Alan Cole, *Exodus*, TOTC (Downers Grove: InterVarsity Press, 1972), p. 210.
17. Victor (A.) Hurowitz, *I Have Built You an Exalted House: Temple Building in the Bible in Light of Mesopotamian and Northwest Semitic Writings*, *JSOTSup* 115, JSOT/ASOR Monograph 5 (Sheffield: Sheffield Academic, 1992).
18. Victor (A.) Hurowitz, 'The Priestly Account of Building the Tabernacle', *JAOS* 105 (1985), pp. 21–30; idem, *I Have Built You*, pp. 106–113 et passim.
19. For the connection between Kothar-wa-Hasis and the Mesopotamian creator god Ea, see Manfried Dietrich, 'Der Einbau einer Öffnung in den Palast Baals: Bemerkungen zu RS 94.2953 und *KTU* 1.4 VII 14.28', *UF* 39 (2007), pp. 129–130;

temple building accounts, nor in most West Semitic accounts, nor even in other biblical accounts, such as found in the construction of the Second Temple.[20]

Comparisons and contrasts have already been made between Bezalel and Oholiab, on the one hand, and Huram, on the other. However, it is important to understand the similarities and differences with Kothar-wa-Hasis and to set these in context with Bezalel and Oholiab. The name Kothar-wa-Hasis is constructed of two elements joined by a conjunction. The meaning of this name, 'skilled and cunning', reflects the role of the expert among the pantheon in the creation of arts and crafts. Elsewhere he is also an architect as well as a musician, a diviner and a magician.[21] Kothar-wa-Hasis is a significant recipient of sacrifices in the ritual texts, sixth in line for the number of sacrifices received according to del Olmo Lete's count.[22] Thus the artisan deity appears repeatedly in a variety of genres of the texts from Ugarit. Bezalel and Oholiab contrast with this.[23] Their names occur only in the Exodus account, with Bezalel reappearing twice in the Chronicler's genealogy and rendition.

John Huehnergard, *Ugaritic Vocabulary in Syllabic Transcription*, HSS 32 (Atlanta: Scholars Press, 1987), pp. 139–140; E. Lipinski, 'Éa, Kothar et El', *UF* 20 (1988), pp. 137–143.

20. So Hurowitz, *I Have Built You*, pp. 102–103. Mark S. Smith and Wayne T. Pitard, *The Ugaritic Baal Cycle Volume II Introduction with Text, Translation and Commentary of KTU/CAT 1.3–1.4*, *VTSup* 114 (Leiden: Brill, 2009), p. 553, note Hurowitz's point but emphasize Bezalel, Oholiab and Kothar-wa-Hasis as in charge of the construction. This leads them to replace Huram for Solomon's temple with Adoniram, who appears in 1 Kgs 5:14 as the foreman over the workers. However, this does not appear to be the role of Bezalel and Oholiab, who are involved in teaching other artisans, not in the supervision of workers. Nor is it the role of Kothar-wa-Hasis, who seems responsible for all the construction by himself. Thus Huram remains the closest comparison as the chief artisan.

21. Dennis Pardee, 'Koshar', in *DDD*^{2}, pp. 490–491; Mark S. Smith, 'The Magic of Kothar, the Ugaritic Craftsman God, in *KTU* 1.6 VI 49–50', *RB* 91 (1984), pp. 377–380. See also *KTU* 1.108.

22. Gregorio del Olmo Lete, *Canaanite Religion: According to the Liturgical Texts of Ugarit* (Bethesda: CDL, 1999), p. 78; R. Hess, *Israelite Religions: An Archaeological and Biblical Survey* (Grand Rapids: Baker, 2007), p. 97.

23. Umberto Cassuto, *A Commentary on the Book of Exodus*, trans. I. Abrahams (Jerusalem: Magnes, 1967), p. 402, already notes the obvious distinction that Kothar-wa-Hasis is a deity while Bezalel and Oholiab are human.

Furthermore, unlike Kothar-wa-Hasis, both of the tabernacle figures have multi-element names that relate to their connection with the divine and their concern for the tabernacle. Kothar-wa-Hasis has a name that exalts his personal skill, indeed he seems to be a personification of these elements of skill and cunning. Further, the deity's name is often shortened to Kothar, or divided across two lines of poetry so that Kothar appears on the first line and Hasis occurs as the corresponding word pair on the second. This is different from Bezalel and Oholiab, whose names are always given as they appear and never occur synonymously in parallelism.

This leads to a final contrast. It has been noted that other Mesopotamian and North-west Semitic building accounts do not name the artisans. In most cases this should not be surprising. These accounts are sometimes short and reduce the descriptions to what the author considers essential. More importantly, many of these accounts are first-person narratives of the king's building activities and exalt the royal initiative to the exclusion of recognizing or naming any other humans. In this regard, the omission of a named artisan in *Enuma Elish* is surprising, but perhaps here as well Marduk takes on the self-focus of a Mesopotamian king. Even so, when we turn to those occasions where the artisan is named, it is not as surprising as might first appear. Few texts name more people than 1 Kings 4 – 11. Of the dozens of names that occur in these chapters, it would perhaps be more surprising if the chief builder, Hiram, and the overseer of the corvée, Adoniram, were not named. A similar situation holds for tablet four of the Baal cycle. While not as many names appear as in the context of 1 Kings, the author is free with identifying not only Baal and Anat, but Athirat, Yam and El, and also the various deities that serve as messengers and underlings (Qudsh-wa-Amrar and Gapn-wa-Ugar). Further, other deities are named in Baal's complaint (*KTU* 1.4 i 14–18). The context is filled with named individuals. Again, we should not be surprised to find the well-known craftsman Kothar-wa-Hasis also named repeatedly. This is not the case in Exodus 25 – 40. Other than Yahweh, Moses, Aaron and the four sons of Aaron (who appear once in Exod. 28:1), there are no named figures in these chapters. The reduction in the number of named characters contrasts with the other two texts where the artisan is named. It makes the naming of not one but two figures here all the more surprising. One would not expect to find their names in this account. The fact that one does may be attributed less to some sort of West Semitic style of naming the craftsmen and more to something significant about these figures apart from their being chosen for the purpose described. As already noted, the most significant aspect of these two as attested by the text itself is the presence of the fullness of the divine spirit in both. This special privilege is found in their names, in their tasks in the account, and in their special appearance as named characters in an unexpected context.

Theology of creativity

The story of Bezalel and his partner Oholiab is the story of the spirit of creation. It is no accident that similar vocabulary appears in the creation of the world in Genesis 1 and that of the tabernacle in the second half of Exodus. The writers shared a view that the universe, the Garden of Eden and the tabernacle all functioned as special abodes of God and as distinctive centres for the place of divine encounters with creation, humanity and Israel. For this reason the parallels at the end of the creation and building accounts have been observed as points at which God recognizes the work and dedicates it to his good purpose by blessing it:[24]

> Exodus 39:43: Moses saw . . . behold . . . they had made it . . . so they had made . . . Moses blessed. . .
> Genesis 1:31; 2:3: God saw . . . he had made . . . behold . . . God blessed . . . created for making. . .
> Exodus 40:33: Moses finished the work
> Genesis 2:2: God finished on the seventh day his work
> Exodus 39:32: all the work . . . was finished
> Genesis 2:1: the heavens and the earth and everything in them was finished.

24. Smith, *The Priestly Vision*, pp. 75–76, 107. For earlier identifications of this parallel, see Benno Jacob, *Das Buch Genesis: Übersetzt und erklärt* (Berlin: Schocken, 1934), p. 67; Martin Buber, 'Der Mensch von heute und die Jüdische Bibel', in M. Buber and F. Rosenzweig (eds.), *Die Schrift und ihre Verdeutschung* (Berlin: Schocken, 1936), pp. 40–45; Joseph Blenkinsopp, 'The Structure of P', *CBQ* 38 (1976), p. 280; idem, *Prophecy and Canon: A Contribution to the Study of Jewish Origins* (Notre Dame: University of Notre Dame Press, 1977), pp. 54–79; Peter J. Kearney, 'Creation and Liturgy: The P Redaction of Ex 25 – 40', *ZAW* 89 (1977), pp. 375–387; Moshe Weinfeld, 'Sabbath, Temple and the Enthronement of the Lord – The Problem of the Sitz im Leben of Genesis 1:1 – 2:3', in A. Caquot and M. Delcor (eds.), *Mélanges bibliques et orientaux en l'honneur de M. Henri Cazelles*, AOAT 212 (Kevelaer: Butzon & Bercker; Neukirchen-Vluyn: Neukirchener, 1981), pp. 501–512; Jon D. Levenson, *Creation and the Persistence of Evil: The Jewish Drama of Divine Omnipotence* (Princeton: Princeton University, 1994), pp. 78–87.

Thus we see in both the construction of a sacred space and the parallel between God and Moses as builders. The role of Bezalel and of Oholiab does not correspond to that of God. The divine category in the tabernacle story is occupied by Moses. Instead, the artisans correspond to the word of God that becomes the agent for separation and creation of the cosmos in Genesis 1. In a similar manner Bezalel and Oholiab are endued with the spirit. In light of the parallels, it may not be supposing too much to find here that same wind or spirit that hovered over the waters in anticipation of creation in Genesis 1:2. As Bezalel's name suggests, these builders stand in the shadow of God just as the word of God remained close to its divine origin and yet accomplished its task in the physical world.

Nevertheless, we need to consider one other matter that remains so obvious as to hardly require comment. Bezalel and Oholiab constitute two named individuals. In a passage that hardly can be said to be productive of many personal names, there are two builders so named. In Kings and in the Baal cycle this does not occur. Rather, in both these contexts a single builder is named, despite the presence of many more names in the contexts. Why is that emphasized here and why here in Exodus do these two builders both receive a unique (and for the first time mentioned in the canonical Bible) filling of the divine spirit? Is this some dim reflection of the past, of the dual name Kothar-wa-Hasis? With no such similar type of name, did the tradents split the single deity into two human builders? Perhaps, but perhaps we should rather consider what the dual name of the god itself intended to suggest. Did it not imply that the twofold descriptor-name, skilful and cunning, provided a superlative emphasis beyond what a single name could ever do? As in the poetry where Kothar and Hasis become a word pair in standard bicola describing the deity and his work, so in the name itself the repetitive element serves to reinforce the full implication of the figure as the most skilful, the most cunning of workers. Is this dual element reflected as well in the creation account of Genesis 1? Not just the naming of the *rûaḥ* in verse 2, nor even the repeated use of the divine word, but much more significant is the first common plural 'we' and 'our' in verse 26 that suggests a double intensity. And that double intensity becomes so much greater when the creation/construction account reaches its climax in this verse with the image of God.

If this is the case, then the emphasis on the two characters in Exodus takes on new significance. The answer to the problem as to the presence of two new names finds its solution in the twofold intensity of the presence of the divine spirit for the creativity necessary to appropriate the fullness of the people's spirit in their gifts. Now, corresponding to that fullness, there is the need for a full and running over of the spirit to empower these individuals with the capacity to construct this form of the tabernacle in the manner envisioned by God, the divine *tabnît* of Exodus 25:9 and 40. With equal significance is the presence of these two figures who create and who teach wisdom to the other artisans of Israel as the beginnings of a people established before God. The tabernacle will serve the community of Israel. That community begins here in the creation of the structure and its elements by not one but two individuals who are empowered by the Spirit and who bear the full meaning of the name Oholiab, the tabernacle/tent of the Father.

PART 5: THE SPIRIT AND PROPHECY

10. THE VIEW FROM THE TOP: THE HOLY SPIRIT IN THE PROPHETS[1]

Daniel I. Block

In Christian circles pneumatology, 'the doctrine of the Holy Spirit', is essentially a NT doctrine. Few branches of theology suffer from neglect of the OT like the doctrine of the Spirit. When theologians refer to the OT, the data found there are quickly summarized and often exploited to emphasize the discontinuity between the Spirit's operation in the two Testaments. The relative insignificance of the OT for establishing a biblical pneumatology derives largely from the general denigration of the OT in evangelical Christendom, but more particularly from the paucity of occurrences of the phrase 'Holy Spirit' (*rûaḥ qōdeš*). This expression occurs only three times in the OT, always with a suffix.[2] However, although this phrase is rare, we find many other explicit references to the Spirit of God in the prophetic books: *rûaḥ yhwh* ('Spirit of YHWH', Isa. 11:2; 40:13; 61:1 [*rûaḥ ʾădōnāy yhwh*]; 63:14; Ezek. 11:5; 37:1;

1. I am grateful to Matt Newkirk of Wheaton College for his insightful and helpful response to an earlier draft of this paper. Of course, any infelicities of style and substance are my own. Unless otherwise indicated, the translations are my own.
2. Ps. 51:13 (11), *rûaḥ qodšěkā*, 'your Holy Spirit'; Isa. 63:10, 11, *rûaḥ qodšô*, 'his Holy Spirit'. Hereafter where English and Hebrew versification differs, the English number is bracketed.

Mic. 3:8); *rûaḥ ʾĕlōhîm* ('Spirit of God', Ezek. 11:24);[3] *rûḥî* ('my Spirit', Isa. 30:1; 42:1; 44:3; 59:21; Joel 3:1, 2 [Eng. 2:28, 29];[4] Zech. 4:6; 6:8; Hag. 2:5); *rûḥô* ('his Spirit', Isa. 34:16; 48:16; Zech. 7:12). The purpose of this paper is to explore how the prophets of Israel perceived the operation of the Spirit of God.[5]

Second Peter 1:20–21 asserts that no prophecy of Scripture represents a private interpretation of reality, for no (true) prophecy was 'auto-inspired';[6] true prophets 'spoke from God as they were borne along by the Holy Spirit' (*hypo pneumatos hagiou pheromenoi elalēsan apo theou anthrōpoi*). This accords with the view of prophecy reflected in Jeremiah 23:16–22, namely, that the prophets of the OT spoke *ex cathedra* because they stood in the council (*sôd*) of YHWH. As was the case with other matters, this means that when the prophets spoke of the Spirit of God their statements represented the divine perspective.

The prophetic vocabulary of the spirit

The notion of 'spirit' is represented by three different expressions in the prophets. Isaiah's three references to *ʾôb*, which refers to the spirits of the

---

3. Here we should also note the Aramaic expression *rûaḥ ʾĕlāhîn* [*qaddîšîn*], 'spirit of the (holy) gods/holy God', in Dan. 4:5 (8), 6 (9), 15 (18); 5:11, 14; cf. also v. 12, which has *rûaḥ* alone. Although Daniel and Lamentations are not included in the Prophets, since these books are not covered elsewhere in this volume, we include the information they offer in this chapter.
4. Cf. references to YHWH pouring out a/the Spirit: Isa. 29:10 (*nāsak*); 32:15 (*ʿārâ*); Zech. 12:10 (*šāpak*).
5. This study builds on my earlier published essay, D. I. Block, 'The Prophet of the Spirit: The Use of *rwḥ* in the Book of Ezekiel', *JETS* 32 (1988), pp. 27–50. The prominence of the word *rûaḥ* and its distribution throughout the book suggests that Ezekiel may be characterized as 'the prophet of the Spirit'. The same could be said of the book of Isaiah, whose fifty-one occurrences of the word compares favourably with Ezekiel's fifty-two, but it stands in sharp contrast to the latter's contemporary, Jeremiah, a book that is longer but uses the word only eighteen times. For a more recent and fuller study of the term *rûaḥ* in Ezekiel, see James Robson, *Word and Spirit in Ezekiel*, LHB/OTS 447 (New York: T. & T. Clark, 2006). See also John Woodhouse, 'The "Spirit" in the Book of Ezekiel', in B. G. Webb (ed.), *Spirit of the Living God Part One*, Explorations 5 (Sydney: Lancer, 1991), pp. 1–22.
6. Greek *thelēmati anthrōpou ēnechthē*, 'by human will'; cf. Ezekiel's comment in 13:2 that false prophets prophesied 'from their own hearts/minds (*millibām*)'.

deceased (Isa. 8:19; 19:3; 29:4), obviously have no bearing on our discussion. However, the issue is different with *nĕšāmâ*,[7] which usually means 'breath', and may refer to human breath (Isa. 2:22; 42:5; 57:16; Dan. 10:17) or divine breath (Isa. 30:33).[8] However, according to Isaiah 42:5, people derive their breath from YHWH. This pairing of *nĕšāmâ* ('breath') with *rûaḥ* ('spirit') provides a helpful link to what is by far the most common word for 'spirit' in the Prophets.[9]

The root *rwḥ* appears 378 times in the Hebrew Bible and an additional eleven in the Aramaic parts of Daniel. Various forms of the noun *rûaḥ* occur 170 times in the Prophets (including Lamentations and Daniel).[10] Although usually translated as *pneuma* in the Greek OT,[11] the word exhibits a wide range of meanings and has been the subject of many previous studies.[12] Although the root seems fundamentally to refer to air in motion, the semantic range of this noun in the Prophets may be illustrated diagrammatically as in Figure 1. Of these 170 occurrences, one third may be eliminated from the present consideration, since they do not pertain to the Holy Spirit. These include the ubiquitous references to wind,[13] as well as the use of the

---

7. Related to the verb *nāšam*, 'to pant, puff, breathe deeply', Isa. 42:14.

8. Cf. 2 Sam. 22:16 = Ps. 18:16 (15); Job 4:9.

9. These words are also paired in Isa. 57:16.

10. The word is distributed among the prophetic books as follows: Isaiah 51x; Jeremiah 18x; Lamentations 1x; Ezekiel 52x; Daniel 15x (Hebrew 4x; Aramaic 11x); Hosea 7x; Joel 2x; Amos 1x; Jonah 2x; Micah 3x; Habakkuk 2x; Haggai 4x; Zechariah 9x; Malachi 3x; cf. the tabulation of these and related forms by R. Albertz and C. Westermann, *THAT*, 2.727. A full discussion of *rûaḥ* is provided on pp. 726–753. A verb from the same root, *hărîḥ*, 'to delight in, receive with favour', occurs twice in the prophets: Isa. 11:3; Amos 5:21. Elsewhere this verb means 'to smell', and is used of favourable smelling of sacrifices (Exod. 30:38; 1 Sam. 26:19). See further, *HALOT*, 1196.

11. The remainder alternate among *anemos*, 'wind', *pnoe*, 'wind, vapour', and other anthropological terms such as *thymos*, *oligopsychos*, *haima*, *nous*, *psyche*. See E. Hatch and H. A. Redpath, *A Concordance to the Septuagint* (Grand Rapids: Baker, 1983 reprint), 3.263, for references; F. Baumgartel, *TDNT*, 6.367–368.

12. For fuller discussion see Albertz and Westermann, '*rûah*', *THAT*, 2.726–753; for bibliography, see D. I. Block, M. V. Van Pelt and W. C. Kaiser, *NIDOTTE*, 3.1077–1078.

13. Often rendered *anemos* in the Greek OT, e.g. Ezek. 17:10; 19:12.

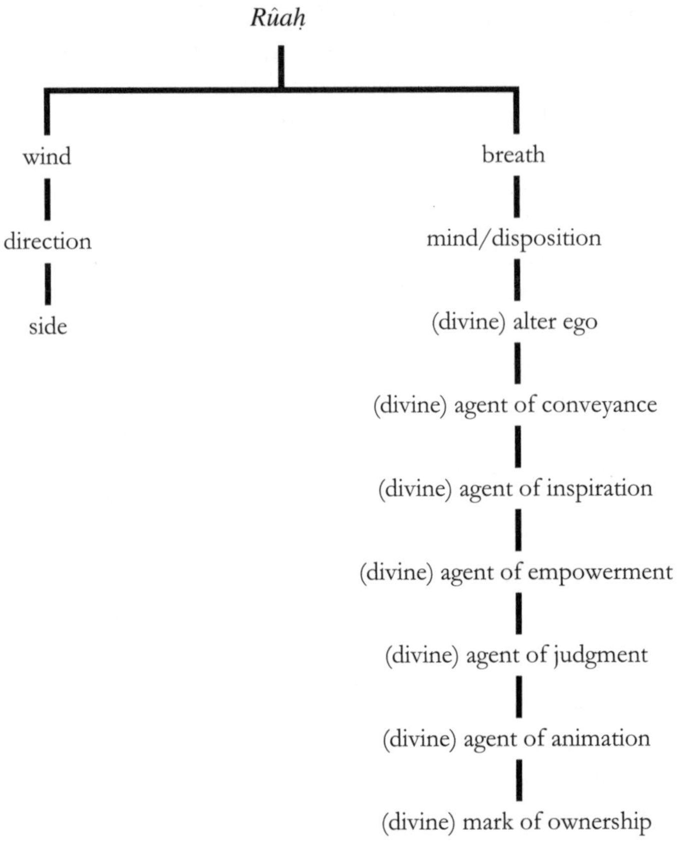

Figure 1: The functions of 'spirit' (*rûaḥ*) in the Prophets

word for direction,[14] side (Jer. 52:23; Ezek. 42:16–20), air (Jer. 14:6), human breath (Lam. 4:20),[15] and human/animal mind/disposition,[16] though in some of these the divine involvement is not absolutely excluded.

---

14. As in 'every wind' (*kol rûaḥ*): Jer. 49:32, 36; Ezek. 5:10, 12; 12:14; 17:21; 21:12; or 'the four winds' (*ʾarbaʿ rûḥôt/rûḥôt ʾarbaʿ*): Jer. 49:36; Ezek. 37:9; Dan. 8:8; 11:4; Zech. 2:10 (6); 6:5.
15. Though even here the *rûaḥ ʾappênû*, 'breath of our nostrils', is associated with YHWH's anointed (*měšîaḥ yhwh*); cf. 1 Sam. 16:13. As we shall see, elsewhere 'breath' usually refers to divine animating breath.
16. Isa. 19:3; 29:24; 54:6; 57:16; 61:3; 65:14; 66:2; Dan. 2:1, 3; 5:20; 7:15; Hos. 4:12; 5:4; Mal. 2:15, 16.

We turn now to a discussion of specific ways in which the prophets employ *rûaḥ* in relation to God.

Rûaḥ as divine breath

The prophets – Isaiah in particular – do not hesitate to attribute breath to YHWH. Isaiah 40:7 speaks explicitly of 'the breath of YHWH' (*rûaḥ yhwh*) that he blows on grass, causing it to wither. In 11:4 the same prophet refers to 'the breath of his lips' (*rûaḥ śĕpātāyw*).[17] As we shall see below, in 27:8 and 30:28 YHWH executes judgment with his breath (*rûḥô*).

Rûaḥ as divine mind/disposition

As noted above (note 16), in the Prophets *rûaḥ* often functions as 'mind', that is the seat of mental activity and emotion.[18] Sometimes YHWH affects the *rûaḥ*, that is, the minds/dispositions of humans.[19] But *rûaḥ* may also be used of the divine mind. Given the emphasis in the broader context on YHWH's obvious intelligence in creating all things, this seems to be the sense of the 'Spirit of YHWH' (*rûaḥ yhwh*) in Isaiah 40:13,[20] though the parallelism suggests *rûaḥ yhwh* could function as a synecdochic expression for YHWH himself. Only Micah uses *rûaḥ* to refer to the divine disposition. In Micah 2:7 the prophet asks, 'Is YHWH's "spirit" shortened?' That is, is he exasperated or impatient? The idiom, *qāṣar rûaḥ*, occurs elsewhere only in Job 21:4, where Job asks rhetorically why his 'spirit' should not be shortened in the face of his struggles. However, this expression functions as a stylistic variant for *qāṣar nepeš*, also 'to become impatient', referring to human impatience in

---

17. Isa. 33:11 is textually problematic; whereas Hebrew reads 'your breath', 'my breath' seems more appropriate. Thus Tanakh, NASB. Isa. 11:15 is ambiguous; *rûḥô* could refer either to YHWH's scorching breath or to the wind with which he dried up the Reed Sea.

18. In this respect it functions as a synonym for *lēb*, 'heart, mind'. On this use of *rûaḥ* in Ezekiel, see Block, 'Prophet of the Spirit', pp. 43–46. Remarkably, in Ezekiel this word never refers to God's mind or disposition.

19. Isa. 19:3, 14; 37:7; Jer. 51:1, 11; Hag. 1:14.

20. Note the references to 'grasping' (*rikkēn*, literally 'measuring') the Spirit of YHWH and 'advising' (*hôdîaʿ*, 'to inform') him as counsellor (*ʾîš ʿēṣâ*).

Numbers 21:4 and Judges 16:16 and to divine exasperation in Judges 10:16 and Zechariah 11:8.

Rûaḥ as a synecdochic expression for YHWH himself

The ambiguity of Isaiah 40:13 characterizes several additional texts that seem to treat the Spirit of YHWH as a synecdochic reference to God himself. This seems to be the case in Isaiah 63:7–14:

> I will recount the gracious deeds [*ḥasdê*] of YHWH, the praiseworthy acts [*tehillōt*] of YHWH, because of all that YHWH has done for us, and the great favour [*rab ṭûb*] to the house of Israel that he has demonstrated for them according to his compassionate acts [*raḥămāyw*], according to the abundance of his steadfast love [*rôb ḥasādāyw*].
>
> For he said, 'Surely they are my people, children who will not deal falsely'; and he became their saviour in all their distress. In all their distress he was distressed, and the envoy of his presence [*malʾak pānāyw*] saved them; in his love and in his pity he redeemed them; he lifted them up and carried them all the days of old. But they rebelled and grieved his *Holy Spirit; therefore he became their enemy; he himself fought against them.*
>
> Then they remembered the days of old, of Moses his servant. Where is the one who brought them up out of the sea with the shepherds of his flock? *Where is the one who put within them his Holy Spirit, who caused his glorious arm to march at the right hand of Moses, who divided the waters before them to make for himself an everlasting name, who led them through the depths?* Like a horse [racing] through desert, they did not stumble. Like livestock that go down into the valley, the Spirit of YHWH gave them rest. So you led your people, to make for yourself a glorious name.

This text is remarkable on several counts. First, verses 10–11 contain two of only three explicit references to the Holy Spirit in the OT.[21] Second, it identifies the Holy Spirit with 'the envoy of his presence' (v. 9), that is, the manifestation of YHWH himself that first appeared to Moses at the bush that did not burn (Exod. 3:2–6), and then guided the Israelites as they made their way through the desert. This interpretation is reinforced by verse 14, which in adjacent lines declares that the Spirit of YHWH gave the Israelites rest and YHWH led the Israelites to make for himself a glorious name (*šēm tipʾāret*).

---

21. The other text is Ps. 51:(13)11. 1QIs[a] reads *rûaḥ qodšô*, 'his Holy Spirit', as *rwḥ qdšyw*, 'Spirit of his holy ones', presumably seeing here a reference to the angelic courtiers of Ps. 89:6, 8.

Here the Holy Spirit personifies YHWH, which means that for the Israelites to rebel against and grieve the Holy Spirit is to grieve the One who had fought for them, but would now become their enemy.[22] The present identification of YHWH's Holy Spirit and his presence (*pānîm*, lit. 'face') recalls Psalm 139:7, where YHWH's Spirit and his presence (*pānîm*) appear in parallel poetic lines, and Nehemiah 9:20, according to which in the desert YHWH gave Israel his good Spirit to instruct them. Similarly, recalling Israel's time in the desert, Haggai 2:5 speaks of the covenant YHWH made (*haddābār kāratti*) with Israel when they came out of Egypt, in which context the promise that the Spirit would be in their midst should have been a source of great confidence. However, the Sinai narratives know nothing of this Spirit; instead the third line of the tripartite covenant formula speaks of YHWH himself dwelling in the midst of Israel: 'I will be your God, you shall be my people, and I will dwell in your midst' (Lev. 26:12).

We observe a similar phenomenon in Zechariah 6:8. Within the broader context we observe several fascinating word plays. On the one hand, the statement *hēnîḥû ʾet rûḥî*, 'he will cause my Spirit to rest', involves two words that rhyme in their basic form: *nûaḥ*, 'to rest'; *rûaḥ*, 'spirit'. On the other hand, the reference to 'Spirit' plays on the same root that had been used in verse 5 of the four 'spirits'/'winds', that is, the horse-drawn chariots that patrol the earth on YHWH's behalf. This *rûaḥ* may be understood in several ways: (1) as the wind as the agent of divine judgment;[23] (2) as a dispositional euphemism for divine wrath;[24] (3) as synecdoche for YHWH himself; the chariot patrols reassure YHWH that the earth is under control, and he may now relax.

Rûaḥ as agent of divine conveyance

We begin our discussion of the functions the Spirit of YHWH plays in the Prophets with a consideration of his involvement in transporting an individual

22. See further, Gary V. Smith, *Isaiah 40 – 66*, NAC 15b (Nashville: Broadman & Holman, 2009), pp. 672–673. John Oswalt (*The Book of Isaiah Chapters 40 – 66*, NICOT [Grand Rapids: Eerdmans, 1998], p. 608) goes too far in recognizing here an approximation of the NT notion of the third person of the Trinity.
23. See further below; cf. Mark J. Boda, *Haggai, Zechariah*, NIVAC (Grand Rapids: Zondervan, 2004), pp. 323–324.
24. Ezekiel uses a similar idiom in 16:42; 21:22 (ET 17) and 24:13, except that he substitutes *ḥămātî*, 'my wrath', for *rûḥî*, 'my Spirit'.

from place to place. Ezekiel uses several figures to describe YHWH's control over him. Perhaps the most graphic is the portrayal of the hand of YHWH coming upon him. Variations of *wattĕhî ʿālāyw yad yhwh*, 'Now the hand of YHWH was upon me', recur repeatedly in the book (1:3; 3:14, 22; 8:1 [with *npl*, 'fell', instead of *hyh*]; 33:22; 37:1; 40:1). In these contexts 'hand' refers metaphorically to power, the overwhelming force with which God operates, as when he rescued Israel from the clutches of Egypt (cf. Deut. 4:34; 5:15; 6:21; Ps. 136:12). It describes the power with which God gripped and energized a person such as Elijah, so that he was able to outrun the chariots of Ahab (1 Kgs 18:46). In Ezekiel the 'hand of YHWH' gains complete mastery over his movements (Ezek. 3:22; cf. 33:22) and transports him back and forth to distant places (8:1ff.; 37:1; 40:1ff.). As Abraham Heschel observes, this expression describes 'the urgency, pressure, and compulsion by which he is stunned and overwhelmed'.[25] Ezekiel was a man seized by God. This more than any other quality distinguishes him from the other prophets and accounts for his mobility and immobility, the apparent lunacy of some of his actions, and his stoic response to rejection, opposition and grief.

But the exilic prophet was also under the control of a *rûaḥ*. No fewer than half a dozen texts describe him being picked up by a *rûaḥ* and wafted away to another location.[26] In 3:12–14 he is picked up and carried off to the exiles at Tel Abib. The additional comment that the hand of YHWH was strong upon him emphasizes the pressure of YHWH upon him. Ezekiel 8:3 portrays Ezekiel lifted up between heaven and earth and borne away to Jerusalem. The additional comment, *bĕmarʾôt ʾĕlōhîm*, 'in divine visions', precludes a literal interpretation. The prophet appears not to have actually left his room. As the vision neared its end he was picked up and brought to the east gate of YHWH's house. When it was over he was raised once more and returned to the exiles in Chaldea. In 43:5 he will be picked up again and brought to the court of the visionary temple.

The anarthrous form of *rûaḥ* in each of these texts reflects the ambiguity of the statements and renders the classification of this use of *rûaḥ* difficult. The effect on Ezekiel might suggest that *rûaḥ* refers simply to a gust of wind that came along (at the command of YHWH, to be sure) and picked him up like a scrap of paper. However, several considerations point more specifically

25. A. J. Heschel, *The Prophets* (New York: Jewish Publication Society, 1962), p. 444. For a full discussion of the expression in its Ancient Near Eastern context, see J. J. M. Roberts, 'The Hand of YHWH', *VT* 21 (1971), pp. 244–251.

26. Cf. Robson, *Word and Spirit in Ezekiel*, p. 92.

to the Spirit of God. The temple vision is framed by references to the locomotion of the prophet by the Spirit (8:3; 11:24) and contains one internal note of this experience (11:1). Moreover, in chapter 8, Ezekiel had witnessed a series of scenes of the abominations being perpetrated in the temple precincts, each of which is introduced with the comment: 'He brought me to. . .' On the basis of verse 3, we should have expected a feminine form of the verb agreeing with the nearest subject *rûaḥ*.[27] But in each instance the verb is masculine (vv. 7, 14, 16), suggesting that the one conveying him about is the same as the person who speaks to him and interprets the observations (vv. 5, 6, etc.). The nearest masculine antecedent is YHWH in verse 1. Similar considerations apply to the broader context of 43:5.

The interpretation of this *rûaḥ* as YHWH's *rûaḥ* is supported by two additional texts. In 11:24b the comment that the prophet was brought back to Babylon in a vision (*bammarʾeh*) is expanded with *bĕrûaḥ ʾĕlōhîm*, 'by the Spirit of God'. However, here *ʾĕlōhîm* need not signify God any more than it does in the expression *marʾôt ʾĕlōhîm* (1:1; 8:3), which simply means 'divine visions'.[28] Nevertheless, even this understanding raises it from the level of an ordinary wind to a gust that is controlled directly by God. If the previous texts leave the question open, the issue seems to be answered in 37:1, which specifies that when Ezekiel felt the hand of YHWH upon him, he was brought out to the valley of the dry bones 'by the *rûaḥ* of YHWH'. Although the expression retains a certain ambiguity, it ties the conveying Spirit directly to YHWH. The phrase *rûaḥ yhwh* occurs elsewhere in the book only in 11:5. However, as we shall see below, its significance in this case is quite different.

---

27. Though *rûaḥ* is occasionally construed as masculine in the Prophets (Isa. 57:16; Jer. 4:12; Ezek. 27:26), as well as elsewhere (Exod. 10:13, 19; Num. 11:31; Pss 51:12; 78:39; Job 4:15; 8:2; 20:3; 41:8; Eccl. 1:6; 3:19).

28. *mrʾwt ʾlhym* is usually translated 'visions of God'. Three considerations argue against this reading, however. (1) In the book *ʾlhym* usually functions as an appellative rather than a proper noun. If visions of God had been intended, *mrʾwt ʾdny yhwh* would have been used. So also M. Greenberg, *Ezekiel 1 – 20*, AB (Garden City: Doubleday, 1983), p. 41. For a full discussion of the names of God in Ezekiel see W. Zimmerli, *Ezekiel*, Hermeneia (Philadelphia: Fortress, 1983), 2.556–562. (2) What the prophet witnesses is not so much a vision of God (only the last few verses of ch. 1 refer to the deity himself) but a vision of divine, heavenly realities. (3) The form *mrʾwt ʾlhym* is not a true plural but a 'plural of generalization'; cf. Joüon 136j; GKC 124e. As in 8:3 the expression is better translated as 'divine visions' or 'supernatural visions'.

Rûaḥ as agent of prophetic inspiration

The involvement of the Spirit of God in the inspiration of the OT prophets is well known.[29] Second Peter 1:21 gives classic expression to this notion: 'No prophecy ever had its origin in the will of man, but men spoke from God as they were carried along by the Holy Spirit.' The involvement of the *rûaḥ* in Ezekiel's prophetic inspiration is hinted at in several places, particularly where his influence is associated with the verbal utterance of YHWH.[30] Examples of this phenomenon occur in Ezekiel 2:2, 'The Spirit entered me as he spoke to me', and 3:24, 'The Spirit entered me and set me on my feet, and he said to me. . .' The most explicit statement of his prophetic inspiration occurs in 11:5a, *wattipōl ʿālay rûaḥ yhwh wayyōʾmer ʾēlay*, 'The Spirit of YHWH fell upon me, and he said to me. . .' Like his comment concerning the hand of YHWH falling upon him (8:1), this expression occurs nowhere else.

The role of the *rûaḥ* as agency of prophetic inspiration receives its most explicit statement in Ezekiel 13. This text is cast as a woe oracle against false prophets, who posed as proclaimers of the will of God. Prophets' authority and credibility as spokesmen for deity depended upon the presence of the divine *rûaḥ*. When their services were required they would employ special techniques and instruments to work themselves into an ecstatic frenzy that was interpreted as seizure by the Spirit of God. Once in this state, whatever utterances they might make would be interpreted as an expression of the will of God.[31]

The great prophets of Israel deliberately rejected all such artificial methods for determining the divine will. Their messages were based instead upon direct and personal encounters with YHWH at his own initiative. Instead of

---

29. On the inspiration of the classical prophets, see Robson, *Word and Spirit in Ezekiel*, pp. 146–170.
30. For fuller discussion of the *rûaḥ* as agent of inspiration in Ezekiel, see ibid., pp. 99–126.
31. The classic texts on the false prophets are 1 Kgs 22:19–23 and Jer. 23:13–40 (also 11:29, though it is silent on the involvement of the spirit). On 1 Kgs 22:19–23, see Daniel I. Block, 'What has Delphi to do with Samaria? Ambiguity and Delusion in Israelite Prophecy', in P. Bienkowski, C. Mee and E. Slater (eds.), *Writing and Ancient Near Eastern Society: Papers in Honour of Alan R. Millard* (New York/London: T. & T. Clark, 2005), pp. 189–216. For a discussion of false prophecy in Israel, see G. V. Smith, 'Prophecy, False', *ISBE*, rev. ed. (Grand Rapids: Eerdmans, 1986), 3.984–986.

emphasizing the role of the *rûaḥ*, whose apparent influence could be manipulated or coerced (cf. 1 Kgs 22), they based their authority on *dĕbar yhwh*, 'the word of YHWH', which came to them almost as an objective concrete entity directly from God himself. However, as Fohrer has pointed out,[32] in his response Ezekiel deliberately distances himself from the false prophets. Being keenly aware of the control of the *rûaḥ* of YHWH over his own life, he dares to challenge head on the fundamental premise on which false prophets operated: their claim to the divine Spirit. We should distinguish genuine and free charismatics from officially accredited announcers. Calling and profession are not the same, though this is not to say that the two were necessarily contradictory. Ezekiel may well have acknowledged some professional prophets as legitimate.

But it is apparent that the prophets addressed by Ezekiel in 13:1–16 were charlatans. First, they are tautologically and sarcastically identified as 'prophets who are prophesying'. As Davidson observed: 'They prophesied and that without limit; their mouths were always full of "Thus saith the Lord."'[33] Apparently the people took their ranting seriously (cf. Jer. 18:18). Second, they are 'prophets from their own hearts'. In verse 2 the preposition *min* on *nĕbîʾê millibbām* is a *min* of source.[34] The expression finds analogues in several OT texts. According to Numbers 16:28, in response to the challenge to his leadership by Korah and his followers, Moses declared: 'Thus you shall know that YHWH has commissioned me to do all these things, for this was not my own idea' (*kî lōʾ millibbî*). Similarly, Jeroboam's religious innovations are described as his own idea (*millibbô*, 1 Kgs 12:33 *qere*). Since Ezekiel's oracle displays many other affinities with Jeremiah, he may have been influenced by his contemporary's own invective against false prophets (Jer. 23:9–40), particularly the latter's use of the phrase *ḥăzôn libbām yĕdabbērû*, 'They pronounce a vision of their own heart' (23:16). In each of these instances *lēb* probably signifies 'mind', suggesting that the false prophets' inspiration was no higher than that of ordinary human wisdom. Their messages were their own concoction, based upon their own evaluation of the situation and their own private

32. G. Fohrer, *Ezechiel*, HAT 13 (Tübingen: J. C. B. Mohr, 1955), p. 69.

33. A. B. Davidson, *The Book of the Prophet Ezekiel* (Cambridge: Cambridge University Press, 1900), p. 84.

34. MT *linbîʾê millibbām* represents an unusual case of the construct form before a preposition. GKC 130a suggests that this is a sign of elevated style. Cf. Gen. 3:22; Isa. 28:9; Jer. 23:23; Hos. 7:5 (all with *min*). The shorter text of LXX reads *pros autous* = *ʾălêhem*, as in 34:2; 37:4, a reading preferred by *BHS* and many commentators.

judgment. While posing as spokesmen for God, they were merely spouting off private opinions.

In the opening volley of the oracle itself, Ezekiel elaborates on this charge (Ezek. 13:3), accusing the professional prophets of being fools. The adjective *nābāl* is used in the wisdom literature of a special kind of fool, who is arrogant (Prov. 30:32), crude of speech (17:7), spiritually and morally obtuse (Job 2:10), and a scoundrel (30:8).[35] Isaiah describes such a person in Isaiah 32:5–6:

> A villain [*nābāl*] shall no longer be called noble,
> Nor a knave be spoken of as a gentleman;
> For the villain [*nābāl*] utters villainous speech [*nĕbālâ*],
> And his mind [*libbô*] plots evil,
> To act impiously and to express deviance [*tôʿâ*] toward YHWH.

Ezekiel's description of the prophets as *nĕbālîm* emphasizes their perverse and impious character.

Third, the false prophets 'walk according to their own "spirit"' (*hōlĕkîm ʾaḥar rûḥām*, Ezek. 13:3).[36] Here *rûaḥ* is employed ambiguously. On the one hand, the reference is to their own 'spirit' that inspires them to prophesy, as opposed to the *rûaḥ* of YHWH, whose inspiration they claim. On the other hand, as we shall see in the discussion to follow, *rûaḥ* may also refer to their minds, functioning as a synonym for *lēb* in verse 2. The expression *hālak ʾaḥar* differs slightly from the more conventional *hālak ʾaḥărê*, 'to walk after' (cf. 20:16; 33:31). Here *ʾaḥar* is used in the sense of norm, standard, yielding 'in accordance with'.[37] Far from taking their cues from YHWH, these

---

35. The classic illustration is found in Nabal, the husband of Abigail (1 Sam. 25:25). In the Psalms the *nābāl* denies God (14:1; 53:2 [1]) and blasphemes him (74:22). Guilt-incurring foolish acts included sexual sins (Gen. 34:7; Deut. 22:21; Judg. 20:6; Jer. 29:23; cf. also Judg. 19:23–24; 2 Sam. 13:12) as well as cultic irreverence (Josh. 7:15).

36. LXX abbreviates and changes *hannĕbîʾîm hannĕbālîm ʾăšer hōlĕkîm ʾaḥar rûḥām* with its rendering *tois prophēteuousin apo kardias autōn*. The last phrase seems to read *lnbyʾmlbm*. Cf. G. A. Cooke, *A Critical and Exegetical Commentary on the Book of Ezekiel*, ICC (Edinburgh: T. & T. Clark, 1936), pp. 138, 142; Zimmerli, *Ezekiel*, 1. 285. For an explanation of how MT might have arisen, see H. van Dyke Parunak, *Structural Studies in Ezekiel* (Ann Arbor: University Microfilms, 1978), pp. 223–224.

37. Cf. *Williams' Hebrew Syntax: An Outline*, 3rd ed. (Toronto: University of Toronto, 2007), #362. Note also 2 Kgs 13:2; 23:3; Isa. 65:2; Job 31:7.

false prophets were merely giving vent to their own imaginations. Their self-inspired messages were a delusion.

Fourth, they lack divine insight. The expression *lĕbiltî rāʾû* is awkward. It seems to mean something like 'without seeing',[38] which could be interpreted in several ways. Since prophets are identified elsewhere as *rōʾîm*, 'seers',[39] and a vision could be called a *rōʾeh* (Isa. 28:7) or a *marʾeh*,[40] this amounts to another denial of their genuineness. Moreover, the statement may also be an attack against their lack of spiritual perception. However the false prophets 'looked' upon themselves, the present situation, or their answer for it, theirs did not represent the perspective of YHWH.

Other prophets also recognize the involvement of YHWH's *rûaḥ* in prophetic inspiration. Hosea tauntingly refers to a prophet (*nābîʾ*) as a 'man of the spirit' (*ʾîš hārûaḥ*), presumably a man with the divine Spirit (9:7). Ezekiel's diatribe against false prophets in Ezekiel 13 is anticipated by Micah of Moresheth who contrasts starkly false prophets and himself (Mic. 3:5–8). In an oracle directed against the former he accuses them of leading the people astray by declaring what people want to hear and taking payment for doing so, when in fact they have received no word from God. In contrast, Micah is empowered and filled with the Spirit of YHWH, which means that he not only speaks courageously, but he also exposes their rebellion and sin (v. 8). Although the final clause in Isaiah 48:16 is awkward,[41] Brevard Childs captures well the sense of 'The Lord God has sent me, endowed with his Spirit!'[42] Whether the person sent is the prophet or the

38. Apart from Jer. 27:18, which is textually problematic, this is the only occurrence of *lblty* + perfect in the OT. Davidson, *Hebrew Syntax*, #149 r2, suggests the phrase means 'that which they have not seen', equivalent to *lʾrʾw* (cf. the use of *biltî* in 1 Sam. 20:26). GKC, 152x, treats it like a relative clause governed by *lĕ*, 'according to things that they have not seen', which would provide a good parallel for Williams's interpretation of the preceding phrase. G. R. Driver, 'Linguistic and Textual Problems: Ezekiel', *Bib* 19 (1938), p. 63; 'Ezekiel: Linguistic and Textual Problems', *Bib* 35 (1954), p. 150, treats *rʾw* as an abstract noun, 'seeing', comparable to *ḥzw* in v. 6. Cf. *śḥw* in 47:5. Greenberg, *Ezekiel*, p. 236, treats *lblty* like *lbly*, 'in a condition of not'. Cf. Num. 14:16; Deut. 9:28; Job 14:12; Ps. 72:7.

39. Cf. 1 Sam. 9:9, 11, 18, 19; Isa. 30:10; 1 Chr. 9:22; 26:28; 29:29; 2 Chr. 16:7, 10.

40. Ezek. 1:1; 8:3; 40:2; 43:3; cf. Num. 12:6; 1 Sam. 3:15; Dan. 10:16.

41. *ʾădōnāy yhwh šĕlāḥanî wĕrûḥô* translates literally 'The Lord YHWH sent me and his Spirit'.

42. Brevard S. Childs, *Isaiah*, OTL (Louisville: Westminster John Knox, 2001), p. 369.

Servant,[43] the oracular nature of verses 17–19 confirms that in verse 16 the person endowed with the Spirit is inspired to prophesy.[44] In Zechariah 7:12 the post-exilic prophet recognizes the role of the Spirit in inspiring his predecessors when he juxtaposes the Torah and 'the words that YHWH of hosts had sent by his Spirit through the former prophets'. Here we should also mention Joel 3:1–2 (ET 2:28–29), which declares that when YHWH has poured out his Spirit on his covenant people they will all prophesy. However, although the prophecies are symptoms of the presence of the Spirit, as we shall see below, the focus is actually elsewhere.[45]

In this context we should also consider Isaiah 29:9–12. In an ironical twist, instead of inspiring the prophets and revealing a vision, YHWH pours upon them a spirit of deep sleep,[46] shutting their eyes and covering their heads, resulting in utter incompetence in their profession.

Rûaḥ as the agent of divine empowerment

In Zechariah 4:6, the prophet reminds the Davidide Zerubbabel that those who are called of God to exercise leadership in the pursuit of the divine agenda are incapable of doing so in their own strength; they are dependent on the empowering presence of the Spirit of YHWH: '"Not by might, nor by power, but by my Spirit," says YHWH of hosts.' This motif of empowerment through the Spirit to carry out the divine mission surfaces repeatedly in Isaiah, usually with reference to the Davidic ruler, that is, the Messianic Servant. The notion is expressed most explicitly in Isaiah 11:2–5, where through the Spirit of YHWH that will rest on him, the shoot/branch from the stem/roots of Jesse will be endowed with all the mental and spiritual qualities needed to administer justice righteously (*bĕṣedeq*), fairly (*bĕmîšôr*) and with integrity (*ʾĕmûnâ*): wisdom (*ḥokmâ*), understanding (*bînâ*), counsel (*ʿēṣâ*), fortitude (*gĕbûrâ*), knowledge (*daʿat*) and the fear of YHWH (*yirʾat yhwh*). This image

43. For the former interpretation, see Oswalt, *Isaiah 40 – 66*, p. 278; for the latter, see Smith, *Isaiah 40 – 66*, p. 329.
44. So also Childs, *Isaiah*, p. 378.
45. The involvement of the Spirit in prophecy is recognized in the Levitical prayer of Neh. 9, specifically v. 30, which speaks of YHWH admonishing his people by his Spirit through the prophets.
46. As in Gen. 2:21 and 1 Sam. 26:12, Hebrew *tardēmâ* denotes a deep sleep brought on by YHWH.

contrasts sharply with the performance of most of Israel's kings, who typically lacked these qualities, particularly the fear of YHWH, which accounts for their corrupt rule that eventually resulted in the nation's exile. In Isaiah 28:5–6, not only will the remnant of his people have YHWH of hosts as their beautiful crown/tiara, but the one who sits in judgment at the gates will be endowed with the Spirit of justice and strength. The first Servant Song characterizes YHWH's servant as his chosen one, the one he upholds, in whom he delights and on whom he has put his Spirit. It seems the latter in particular empowers him to administer justice for the nations, and to endure until he has established justice in the earth (Isa. 42:1–4). In Isaiah 59:21, the endowment of the Spirit is associated with YHWH putting his words in a person's mouth. The words are probably not a prophetic oracle to be proclaimed, but the fundamental knowledge of the will of God to which the person commits himself and by which he operates. Reminiscent of David's anointing as king in 1 Samuel 16:13, in Isaiah 61:1 the possession of the Spirit of God is associated with the agent of YHWH's anointing.[47] This act and the endowment of the Spirit authorize him to announce good news to the poor and to proclaim the liberation of those held captive. Although his work involves proclamation, which links his tasks with that of prophets, this person does not occupy the prophetic office. Prophets have no authority to release captives. It is as the anointed king that he is endowed with the Spirit, which authorizes him to release captives.[48]

In the book of Daniel, the main human character presents a special case of divine empowerment through the Spirit. In a remarkable public testimony, Nebuchadnezzar characterizes Daniel, whom he had renamed Belteshazzar after the name of his god, as one indwelled by the spirit of the holy gods (*rûaḥ ʾĕlāhîn qaddîšîn*), which enables him to solve any mystery (Dan. 4:5–6, 15 [ET 8–9, 18]). Later the queen tells King Belshazzar that she knows of a man in whom is a spirit of the holy gods (*rûaḥ ʾĕlāhîn qaddîšîn*), who exhibits enlightenment (*nahîrû*), understanding (*šoklĕtānû*), wisdom (*ḥokmâ*) equal to that of the gods, an excellent mind (*rûaḥ yattîrâ*), knowledge (*mandaʿ*), understanding (*šoklĕtānû*) to interpret dreams and explain riddles (*ʾahăwāyat ʾăḥîdān*), and to solve problems (*mĕšārē ʾqiṭrîn*, Dan. 5:11–12; cf. vv. 15–16). Whereas in Daniel 4 and 5 the special endowment of the spirit of the gods enabled Daniel to

47. The identity of the agent is unclear. Is this the Servant of the Servant Songs?

48. See further, Daniel I. Block, 'My Servant David: Ancient Israel's Vision of the Messiah', in R. S. Hess and M. D. Carroll (eds.), *Israel's Messiah in the Bible and the Dead Sea Scrolls* (Grand Rapids: Baker, 2003), pp. 27–28.

interpret dreams and unravel riddles, in chapter 6 he demonstrated that he was indwelled by an exceptional spirit (*rûaḥ yattîrāʾ*) through extraordinary administrative skills and character. Because of his performance Darius intended to promote him, and his colleagues admitted they could find no defect in him.

Rûaḥ as agent of divine judgment

Isaiah 25:4 recognizes the destructive power of human breath – 'The breath [*rûaḥ*] of the ruthless is like a winter storm.' But Isaiah also uses this kind of language for YHWH. In the first occurrence of *rûaḥ* in the book, the prophet speaks of purging Jerusalem of her filth and bloodshed with the 'Spirit of judgment' (*rûaḥ mišpāṭ*) and the 'Spirit of burning' (*rûaḥ bāʿēr*, Isa. 4:4). In the contexts of judgment, *rûaḥ* is often translated as 'breath', but we should recognize that this word may also be translated either 'wind' or 'spirit':

> With righteousness he shall judge the poor,
> and decide with equity for the meek of the earth;
> he shall strike the earth with the rod of his mouth,
> and with the *rûaḥ* of his lips he shall kill the wicked.
> (Isa. 11:4 NRSV)

> YHWH will utterly destroy the tongue of the sea of Egypt;
> and will wave his hand over the River with his scorching *rûaḥ*;
> and will split it into seven channels,
> and make a way to cross on foot.
> (Isa. 11:15)

> By expulsion, by exile you struggled against them;
> with his fierce *rûaḥ* he removed them on the day of the east wind.
> (Isa. 27:8 NRSV)

> His *rûaḥ* is like a raging torrent reaching up to the neck,
> to sift the nations with the sieve of destruction,
> and to place on the jaws of the peoples a bridle that leads them to ruin.
> (Isa. 30:28)[49]

---

49. Except for *rûaḥ*, which he renders 'breath', as translated by Childs, *Isaiah*, p. 223.

Whether one translates *rûaḥ* in these texts as 'breath', 'wind' or 'spirit', they obviously involve the divine *rûaḥ*.

Rûaḥ as agent of animation

According to Isaiah 40:7, the breath (*rûaḥ*) of YHWH may kill: 'The grass withers, the flower fades when the breath of YHWH blows on it; surely the people are grass.' However, this effect is the opposite of the life-giving effect of YHWH's *rûaḥ* being in someone or something. As 'agency of animation', however, the *rûaḥ* operates internally, like the breath of a living creature. But the distinction between 'wind' and 'breath' is not absolute and should not be pressed in each instance. In fact, the process of breathing involves making wind. But our present concern is the effect of this *rûaḥ* upon a recipient.

The notion that the wind or breath of God gives life to creatures is reflected in the expression *nišmat ḥayyîm*, 'breath of life',[50] and finds its anthropological paradigm in Genesis 2:7: 'When YHWH Elohim formed the man of dust from the ground and breathed into his nostrils the breath of life, the man became a living being.' Although the term for breath in this instance is *nĕšāmâ* and not *rûaḥ*, the close semantic relationship between the terms is demonstrated by their frequent conjunction in construct associations[51] and as a coordinate (Job 34:14) and parallel pair.[52] The animating effect of the infusion of the divine Spirit is reflected in several texts. Isaiah 42:5 describes YHWH the Creator as the one 'who gives breath [*nĕšāmâ*] to people on it [the earth] and spirit [*rûaḥ*] to those who walk on it'. In Job 27:3 the beleaguered saint vows to retain his integrity 'as long as breath [*nĕšāmâ*] is in me, and the Spirit of God [*rûaḥ ʾĕlōah*] is in my nostrils', which is clarified in verses 5–6 as 'until I die' and 'all my days'. The notion is expressed negatively in Job 34:14–15:

50. The expression finds its counterpart in Akkadian *šaru balāṭi*. In Amarna Letter 143, Ammuniri of Berytus considers himself to be mere 'dust' in the presence of his Egyptian overlord, who is 'the breath of life'.

51. Cf. Gen. 7:22, *kōl ʾăšer nišmat rûaḥ ḥayyîm bĕʾappāyw*, 'all in whose nostrils is the breath of the spirit of life'; 2 Sam. 22:16, *bĕgaʿărat yhwh minnišmat rûaḥ ʾappô*, 'by the rebuke of YHWH from the breath of the spirit of his nostrils'. Cf. the parallel text in Ps. 18:16 (15).

52. Isa. 42:5; 57:16; Job 4:9; 27:3; 32:8; 33:4. Cf. also Gen. 2:7 and Job 12:10. Neither word appears in Gen. 7:2, and only *rûaḥ* appears in Job 12:10.

If he should decide, he can recall his spirit [*rûaḥ*] – that is, his breath [*nĕšāmâ*].
Then all flesh would expire at once,
And mankind would return to the dust.

Psalm 104:29–30 is even more graphic:

You hide your face, they are terrified;
You recall their spirit [*rûaḥ*], they expire and return to the dust.
You send back your spirit [*rûaḥ*], they are created [*bārāʾ*]
And you renew the face of the ground.[53]

Isaiah 57:16 also alludes to this notion:

For I will not accuse for ever, nor will I always be angry;
for the spirit [*rûaḥ*] would grow faint before me,
and the breathing creatures [*nĕšāmôt*] that I have made.

No prophet exploits the notion of the animating power of the Spirit of God as fully as Ezekiel. This animating sense of *rûaḥ* is frequently signalled by the presence of the preposition *bĕ*, 'in'. When the *rûaḥ* enters an object, it comes to life. Readers of the book are confronted with the animating effect of the presence of the Spirit in the opening vision. The divine throne-chariot is borne by four cherubim, each having eagles' wings and four different kinds of heads (Ezek. 1:5–14). Although the prophet is unable to identify the creatures precisely at first, he is impressed by their vitality and refers to them with the general designation *ḥayyôt*, 'living beings'. These creatures are capable of moving about effortlessly in any direction and without turning in the process. Verse 12 attributes the inspiration and direction for this motion to the presence of the *rûaḥ*: 'Wherever the *rûaḥ* wanted to go, they went; they would not turn as they went.'[54]

The presence of the article on *hārûaḥ* here and in verse 20 raises the question, 'Which spirit?' The only previous reference to the *rûaḥ* is found in verse 4. However, there the word had denoted 'wind', a sense that is impossible here. The *rûaḥ* that animates these 'living creatures' may be the vitalizing principle

53. For further discussion of *rûaḥ* the animating principle of life, see D. Hill, *Greek Words with Hebrew Meanings: Studies in the Semantics of Soteriological Terms* (Cambridge: Cambridge University Press, 1967), pp. 212–215.

54. For fuller discussion of the *rûaḥ* in this chapter, see Robson, *Word and Spirit in Ezekiel*, pp. 86–91.

of life that comes from God himself. This interpretation finds support in verses 19–21, which associate each of the living creatures with a complex system of wheels enabling them to move about in perfect synchronism:

> When the living beings moved, the wheels next to them would move, and when the living beings rose off the ground, the wheels would rise beside them, since the *rûaḥ* of the living being was in the wheels. Whenever the former moved, the latter would move, and whenever the former rose off the ground, the latter would rise alongside them, for the *rûaḥ* of the living being was in the wheels.

The use of the singular *rûaḥ haḥayyâ* is striking in a context in which the creatures have otherwise been consistently referred to with the plural *haḥayyôt*. Scholars have tended to understand *haḥayyâ* either as a collective singular or in a distributive sense, 'each living creature' – that is, the one beside each wheel.[55] Others see here an emphasis on the unity of the entire phenomenon.[56] Remarkably, the singular form *haḥayyâ* is preserved in 10:17. Although the account of the second vision of the throne-chariot in chapter 10 has smoothed out most of the stylistic problems raised by chapter 1, *rûaḥ haḥayyâ* remains in verse 17. This seems intentional, suggesting the expression should be understood as 'the Spirit of life' – that is, the divine animating principle.[57] The twofold occurrence of the explanatory clause, *kî rûaḥ haḥayyâ bāʾôpānîm*, 'for the Spirit of life was in the wheels', in 1:20–21 and again in 10:17, seems to emphasize that these normally inanimate objects appear to the prophet to be alive; they are 'living creatures'. For him the unusual phenomenon may be attributed only to the presence of the life-giving Spirit of God.

This vivifying, energizing effect of the Spirit of God was also felt by the prophet personally. Twice Ezekiel speaks of the Spirit entering him. According to 1:28, he had responded to the vision of YHWH's glory by falling on his face. However, in his state of prostration he heard a voice commanding him to rise in order that he might converse with him (2:1).[58] Even as he spoke,

---

55. Cooke, *Ezekiel*, p. 27; Zimmerli, *Ezekiel*, 1.20.
56. Greenberg, *Ezekiel*, p. 48.
57. Cf. LXX *pneuma zōēs*; Vg *spiritus vitae*. Ezekiel also uses *ḥayyâ* instead of *ḥayyîm* for 'life' in 7:13. Elsewhere this usage occurs only in poetry. Cf. Pss 74:19; 78:50; 143:3; Job 33:18, 20, 22, 28 (as a synonym of *nepeš*); 36:14. Cf. G. Gerlemann, '*ḥjh* leben', *THAT*, 1.553.
58. The ambiguity of *wayyōʾmer* is intentional, making it uncertain whether we should translate 'it [i.e. the voice] said' or 'he said'.

the revitalizing and energizing Spirit entered Ezekiel and set him on his feet (2:2). The fact that the prophet is raised concurrently with[59] the sound of the voice suggests a dynamic and enabling power in that voice. We should probably associate the *rûaḥ* that vitalizes the wheels with the *rûaḥ* that energizes the prophet.

The language of this entire scene derives from the royal court. Having been ushered into the presence of a monarch, a person would signify his subjection with the act of prostration.[60] To fall before a god is appropriate, but to remain on one's face once he has indicated a desire to speak is insulting to the deity. Ezekiel may have been a *ben ʾādām*, 'mere human', but infused with the *rûaḥ* he may – yea he must – stand in God's presence. A second similar experience is recounted in 3:23–24.

No text portrays the vivifying power of the divine Spirit as dramatically as Ezekiel 37:1–14. The unit is dominated by the tenfold recurrence of the *Leitwort rûaḥ*, but the use of the expression is not uniform. Impelled by the *rûaḥ* of YHWH, the prophet is brought to a valley full of very dry bones. The question that YHWH poses to the prophet, 'Human, can these bones live?'[61] signals the central issue in the chapter. In reply to the prophet's agnostic answer, YHWH commands him to prophesy over the bones, saying, 'I will cause *rûaḥ* to enter you that you may live. I will overlay you with sinews, cover you with flesh, and form skin over you. I will infuse you with *rûaḥ* and you shall live. Then you shall know that I am YHWH' (vv. 5–6). Ezekiel complies, and the bones assemble with a mighty rattling, sinews overlay them, flesh covers them and skin forms over them. But alas! The prophet notes the absence of *rûaḥ* (v. 8).

The sixfold clustering of *rûaḥ* in verses 8b–10a suggests that we have now arrived at the heart of the unit. The solution to the absence of the *rûaḥ* is announced in verse 9:

> Prophesy to *hārûaḥ*, prophesy, son of man.
> Announce to *hārûaḥ*, 'Thus has the Lord YHWH declared:

---

59. Note the construction in 2:2: *wattābōʾ bî rûaḥ kaʾăšer dibber ʾēlay*, 'And the Spirit entered me while he spoke to me'.

60. On which see S. Kreuzer, 'Zur Bedeutung und Etymologie von *hištaḥăwā/yšthwy*', *VT* 35 (1985), pp. 39–54; M. I. Gruber, *Aspects of Nonverbal Communication in the Ancient Near East* (Rome: Biblical Institute, 1980), pp. 187–251.

61. For a helpful discussion of the rhetorical strategy employed in the development of this theme, see M. V. Fox, 'The Rhetoric of Ezekiel's Vision of the Valley of the Bones', *HUCA* 51 (1980), pp. 1–15.

> From the four *rûḥôt* come, O *rûaḥ* breathe[62] into these slain that they may live.

At the prophet's word, the bodies are vitalized and, like Ezekiel himself in an earlier context (2:2; 3:24), they rise to their feet. The play on *rûaḥ* in verse 9 is obvious. The *rûaḥ* that the prophet summoned is the breath of life, the life force that animates all living creatures. Here, however, it is summoned from the four *rûḥôt*, which, as observed above, refers either to the four 'winds' or the four 'directions'. The text is intentionally ambiguous. Although the metaphor changes, verses 11–14 provide an interpretation for the dramatic parable. The bones do not simply represent dead persons in general, but the nation of Israel, which YHWH will bring back to life like people resurrected from their graves. They will be reclaimed as YHWH's people and brought back to the land of Israel. Perhaps necessitated by the demands of the figure, in verses 8–10 the *rûaḥ* is portrayed as something external to God and that can be summoned by him.[63] If the role of the prophet had really been to represent YHWH, he should have breathed over them his own breath.[64] By adding the first-person singular suffix to *rûaḥ* in verse 14, Ezekiel produces a significant shift in meaning. The *rûaḥ* that will revitalize Israel is not the ordinary, natural life breath common to all living things; it is the Spirit of God himself. Only he is able to restore to life a nation that has been destroyed and whose remnant now languishes hopelessly in exile.

We turn back now to a related text, 36:26–27. We may readily recognize the parallelism of the first two cola of verse 26 when they are set out as poetry:

wĕnātattî lākem lēb ḥădāšâ	And I will give to you a new heart/mind;
wĕrûaḥ ḥădāšâ ʾettēn bĕqirbĕkem	And a new Spirit I will put within you.

The common elements in the lines are the verb *nātan*, 'to give', and the adjective 'new', which is applied to both *lēb* and *rûaḥ*. The chiastic structure is common in synonymous parallelism and may be merely stylistic. However, when examined more closely the synonymous interpretation may be questioned. As Robert Alter has convincingly argued, in poetic parallelism synonymity is seldom exact.[65] Indeed the prepositions associated with the verbs

62. The same verb *nāpaḥ* is used in Gen. 2:7.

63. Cf. Fox, 'Rhetoric', p. 15.

64. Cf. Ezekiel's role in the sign action involving the steel plate in 4:3.

65. R. Alter, *The Art of Biblical Poetry* (New York: Harper, 1985), pp. 13–26.

are different. Whereas the new mind is given to (*bě*) Israel, the new Spirit is placed within (*běqereb*) her. As we have seen, placing the Spirit within someone or something has an animating, vivifying effect on the recipient. Furthermore, the way the two statements are clarified in verses 26b–27 differs. On the one hand, the provision of the new heart involves removal of the heart of stone and replacing it with a heart of flesh. On the other hand, in verse 27 YHWH announces: *wěʾet rûḥî ʾettēn běqirběkem*, 'And my Spirit I will put within you'. Now we learn that the *rûaḥ* referred to in verse 26 is indeed YHWH's Spirit. Furthermore, the text describes the transforming effect of the infusion of this *rûaḥ*: YHWH thereby causes the people to walk in his statutes and to observe his covenant standards. This suggests a radical spiritual revitalization of the nation.[66] Ezekiel 37:14 repeats the announcement of YHWH's infusion of his own *rûaḥ*, suggesting that the entire unit (37:1–14) is an exposition of the notion introduced in 36:26–27.[67]

But here Ezekiel appears to have been influenced by Jeremiah, who incidentally never mentions the *rûaḥ* of YHWH.[68] By juxtaposing Ezekiel's announcement of the infused *rûaḥ* with Jeremiah's description of the new covenant in Jeremiah 31:33, the similarities between the two texts become obvious:

Jeremiah 31:33	Ezekiel 36:27–28
nātattî ʾet tôrātî běqirbām	*wěʾet rûḥî ʾettēn běqirběkem*
....	....
wěhāyîtî lāhem lēʾlōhîm	*wihyîtem lî lěʿam*
wěhēmmâ yihyû lî leʿām	*wěʾānōkî ʾehyeh lākem lēʾlōhîm*
I will have put my Torah within them,	And my Spirit I will put within you,
....	....
And I will be their God,	And you shall be my people,
And they shall be my people.	And I will be your God.

These texts appear to describe the same event. What Jeremiah attributes

66. See more fully, Robson, *Word and Spirit in Ezekiel*, pp. 242–252.

67. Ezekiel often announces a theme briefly and then drops it, only to return to it later with a fuller development. Cf. 5:11, which is expounded on in 8:5–18; 37:26–28, which is developed in chs. 40 – 48; and 3:16–21, which is expanded in 18:1–32; 33:1–20.

68. In Jer. 51:1, 11, YHWH acts on another person's *rûaḥ*.

to the infusion of the divine Torah, Ezekiel ascribes to the infusion of the *rûaḥ*.[69] In both the action breathes new life into the covenant relationship between YHWH and Israel.

Before we leave this subject, we must ask whether and how Ezekiel's vision of the role of the *rûaḥ* in the future restored Israel differs from the operation of the Holy Spirit under the Old Covenant, as he understood it from his own tradition and experience. Appealing especially to John 14:17, some argue that in contrast to new covenant realities, where the Holy Spirit dwells within believers, under the old order people were never indwelt by the Spirit; he merely came upon and was with them.[70] Accordingly Ezekiel must be predicting a phenomenon of which he had no personal knowledge or experience. While space constraints preclude a full response to this thesis, we may summarize some of its weaknesses.

First, it overlooks the indispensable animating role of the divine *rûaḥ* in effecting spiritual renewal. It seems to assume that an ancient saint became a member of the people of God by merely attending to the Torah. But Israelite religion was from the beginning a heart religion. Jeremiah's call for a circumcision of the heart in Jeremiah 4:4 was not an innovation but a recollection of a notion expressed in Deuteronomy 10:16, where the appeal is made to the Israelites to 'circumcise their heart'. Later, in 30:6, the divine role in this transforming work is emphasized: 'YHWH your God will circumcise your heart and the heart of your descendants, to love YHWH with all your heart and with all your being, in order that you may live.' Ezekiel's anticipation of a fundamental internal transformation – as described in

69. Similarly Robson, *Word and Spirit in Ezekiel*, p. 262.
70. See most recently and most fully, James M. Hamilton, 'Were Old Covenant Believers Indwelt by the Holy Spirit?' *Themelios* 30/1 (2004), pp. 12–22; idem, *God's Indwelling Presence: The Holy Spirit in the Old and New Testaments*, NAC Studies in Bible and Theology (Nashville: Broadman & Holman, 2006). Hamilton summarizes his position as follows (p. 3): 'Here [John 14:17] Jesus encapsulates the Bible's teaching on God's dwelling in relation to believers in the old and new covenants. In the old covenant God faithfully remained *with* His people, accompanying them in a pillar of fire and cloud, then dwelling among them in the tabernacle and the temple. Under the new covenant, the only temple is the believing community itself, and God dwells not only among the community corporately (Matt 18:20; 1 Cor 3:16; 2 Cor 6:16), but also *in* each member individually (John 14:17; Rom 8:9–11; 1 Cor 6:19). This is the overarching thesis this book seeks to establish.'

Ezekiel 36:22–32 – effected by the infusion of the divine *rûaḥ* rests upon ancient foundations.

Second, it discredits the explicit witness of Psalm 51:12–13 (ET 10–11), one of only three OT occurrences of the expression *rûaḥ qōdeš*, 'Holy Spirit':[71]

Create for me a clean heart, O God!
And a steadfast *rûaḥ* renew within me.
Do not cast me out of your presence,
Nor take your holy *rûaḥ* from me.[72]

In the context David stands before God fearing rejection and the joy – if not the loss – of his salvation (*yēsaʿ*, v. 14 [12]; *tĕšûʿâ*, v. 16 [14]), while the sentence of death hangs over him for his bloodguilt (*dāmîm*). YHWH's continued acceptance of David in his presence and the presence of the divine *rûaḥ* represent his only hope.

Third, it fails to recognize what ancient pagans acknowledged: people who exhibit extraordinary mental, administrative, moral and spiritual qualities were thought to be indwelt by the spirit of the holy gods. As noted earlier, significant persons within the narrative attribute Daniel's exceptional qualities to the spirit of the holy gods *within* him.[73] Indeed the narrator attributes Daniel's exceptional character – his integrity and the total absence of corruption – to the indwelling Spirit (Dan. 6:4 [3]).[74]

Fourth, it reflects a fundamental misunderstanding of Hebrew anthropology. If originally a dead piece of dirt could only be brought to life by the infusion of the breath of God (Gen. 2:7), analogically the same must be true of those who are spiritually dead and need to be brought to life (Eph. 2:1). If one rejects the notion that believing Israelites experienced this new life,[75] this transformation must be accounted for some other way. As Ezekiel 36:26–28 and 37:1–14 demonstrate, this revivifying work can be achieved only through the infusion of the Spirit of God. Indwelt by the Spirit, regenerate

71. Cf. also *rûaḥ qodšô*, 'the Spirit of his holiness', Isa. 63:10, 11.

72. The expression *rûaḥ qodšĕkā* is admittedly ambiguous; some prefer to translate 'spirit of your holiness'.

73. *wĕdî rûaḥ ʾĕlāhîn qaddîšîn bēh*, 'For the spirit of the holy gods is in him'. Dan. 4:5, 6, 15 (8, 9, 18); 5:11, 12, 14.

74. Though some would argue that this *rûaḥ* refers to his disposition.

75. Hamilton errs in building a wall between regeneration and the indwelling presence of the Holy Spirit.

individual Israelites enjoyed full covenant relationship with YHWH, were energized and enabled to walk in his statutes and observe his ordinances, and enjoyed the blessing of God. Furthermore, although Ezekiel envisions a future eschatological reality, in order for the metaphors of chapters 36 and 37 to have any rhetorical force for his audience, they had to be connected to present reality and/or perceptions of reality. Daniel was precisely the kind of person envisaged. As Ezekiel himself recognizes (Ezek. 14:14, 20), like Job and Noah he was renowned for his righteousness, apparently exhibiting the evidence of the exceptional Spirit of God within him. The same is true of Caleb, many centuries earlier, whom YHWH himself recognizes as having a 'different Spirit' (*rûaḥ ʾaḥeret*) and being 'filled after YHWH' (*millēʾ ʾaḥăray*).[76] Admittedly the OT does not use 'new-birth language' or speak of the indwelling Holy Spirit in the same way as the NT does. However, this does not mean either that the notions did not exist in people's minds or that genuinely godly people did not experience the reality. To argue otherwise is to argue from silence.[77] Revelation of spiritual realities is progressive; notions latent in the OT are developed and clarified in the NT.

Fifth, the doctrine of *imago dei* requires the concept of the indwelling Spirit of God. The prophets comment on the lifelessness and impotence of idols, noting that 'there is no *rûaḥ* in them':

> Everyone is stupid and without knowledge;
> goldsmiths are all put to shame by their idols;
> for their images are false,
> and there is no breath [*rûaḥ*] in them.
> They are worthless, a work of delusion;
> at the time of their punishment they shall perish.
> (Jer. 10:14–15; cf. 51:19–20 NRSV)

> What use is an idol
> once its maker has shaped it –
> a cast image, a teacher of lies?
> For its maker trusts in what has been made,

76. Josh. 14:14; cf. Num. 32:12; Deut. 1:36; Josh. 14:8.
77. The OT is relatively silent on many subjects that are highlighted in the NT: the devil, resurrection of the body, the Trinity. This does not mean these realities were not operative then and were invented only in NT times. Absence of evidence is not evidence of absence.

> though the product is only an idol that cannot speak!
> Alas for you who say to the wood, 'Wake up!'
> to silent stone, 'Rouse yourself!'
> Can it teach?
> See, it is plated with gold and silver,
> and there is no breath [*rûaḥ*] in it at all.
> (Hab. 2:18–19 NRSV).[78]

Recent advances in our understanding of the process of manufacturing idols in ancient Mesopotamia have clarified the significance of these statements.[79] By definition an image of a god was deemed worthy of worship because it was imagined to be indwelt by the spirit of the gods, which brought it to life and enabled a piece of wood or stone to respond to worshippers. The process of vivifying an object involved an elaborate procedure in a sacred context and according to divinely ordained rites. However, as Isaiah mocks in Isaiah 44:9–20, the entire business was a farce and a delusion. Nevertheless, it reflects the pervasive ancient conviction that concrete objects came to life when the spirit of the god entered them. The notion of humankind as the 'icon of God' in general and Israel as his representatives and deputies in particular required a transformed people, vivified by his Spirit and liberated to walk in his ways.

Sixth, this argument evades the evidence of the NT. When Nicodemus requests of Jesus an explanation for his ministry, the discussion quickly digresses to a lecture on the role of the Spirit in the life of one who would enter the kingdom of God:

---

78. We may recognize a play on this notion in Isa. 57:13: 'When you cry out, let your collection of idols deliver you! The wind [*rûaḥ*] will carry them off, a breath [*hebel*] will take them away. But whoever takes refuge in me shall possess the land and inherit my holy mountain.'

79. See Michael B. Dick, 'The Induction of the Cult Image in Ancient Mesopotamia: The Mesopotamian *mīs pî* Ritual', in M. B. Dick (ed.), *Born in Heaven, Made on Earth: The Making of the Cult Image in the Ancient Near East* (Winona Lake: Eisenbrauns, 1999), pp. 55–121. For a more popular presentation, see idem, 'Worshiping Idols: What Isaiah Didn't Know', *Bible Review* 18/2 (April 2003), pp. 30–37; Daniel I. Block, 'Other Religions in Old Testament Theology', in D. W. Baker (ed.), *Biblical Faith and Other Religions: An Evangelical Assessment* (Grand Rapids: Kregel, 2004), pp. 71–74.

> No one can enter the kingdom of God unless he is born of water and the Spirit. Flesh gives birth to flesh, but the Spirit gives birth to spirit. You should not be surprised at my saying, 'You must be born again.' The wind blows wherever it pleases. You hear its sound, but you cannot tell from where it comes or where it is going. So it is with everyone born of the Spirit. (John 3:5–8)

One could interpret this statement as an innovative description of the work of the Holy Spirit in the new era, except that Jesus rebukes Nicodemus for being ignorant of these principles even though he was one of the leading theologians of the time. As far as Jesus was concerned, he introduced nothing new. His statements were based on Ezekiel 36:25–29, a text with which the rabbi should have been familiar.[80]

Seventh, and most critically, the perception of radical discontinuity between the Holy Spirit's work in the two Testaments misses the point of the present context. It is unlikely that Ezekiel was self-consciously introducing a new notion with his promise of the transforming work of the indwelling *rûaḥ* of YHWH. While he may have known Psalm 51, what concerns him is the fundamental incongruity between the idealistic designation of his own people as 'the people of God' and the reality he observed. The problem was not the absence of the Holy Spirit to transform lives, but that this was not occurring on a national scale. The issue was one of scope. The emphasis in the present text, as in the broader context of Ezekiel 34 – 39 in general, is on national renewal and revival, not individual regeneration. Like Jeremiah in Jeremiah 31:31–34,[81] in Ezekiel 36:25–29 the exilic prophet anticipates the day when the boundaries of physical and spiritual Israel will be coterminous. In his day a vast gulf separated the two.[82]

---

80. So also David Ewert, *The Holy Spirit in the New Testament* (Scottdale, PA: Herald, 1983), p. 66.
81. Similar considerations apply to the 'new covenant' announced by Jeremiah in Jer. 31:30–34, the fundamental features of which include: (1) the Torah on people's hearts; (2) covenant relationship expressed by the covenant formula; (3) knowing YHWH; (4) the forgiveness of sins. The only new element is its scope; finally 'all' Israel will be involved; the ideals of God's covenant with Israel will finally be realized. Since in context the covenant involves Israel and none of the constitutive features is new, this covenant should probably be called the 'renewed covenant'.
82. The focus in the broader context of John 14:17 is the ministry of Jesus himself. To this point he has been the disciples' 'helper' (*paraklētos*). He has in fact been 'with'

Rûaḥ as the seal of covenant relationship

We conclude our discussion of the Spirit of God with a consideration of the outpouring of the Spirit in the Prophets. The liquid idiom involving the Spirit occurs in six contexts in the Prophets, three times in Isaiah (29:10; 32:15; 44:3), once in Joel (3:1–2 [ET 2:28–29]), once in Ezekiel (39:29) and once in Zechariah (12:10). The first of these has been noted above and may be excluded from this discussion, since the poured-out Spirit serves an entirely different function. The other five all represent acts of divine favour affirming God's covenantal relationship with his people. In Isaiah 32:15 the prophet looks forward to a day after the judgment of Israel, when the Spirit from on high (*rûaḥ mimmārôm*) will be poured out (*ʿārâ*) on Israel, signalling a significant turn in their fortunes. Whatever the significance of the outpouring, it will be accompanied by a complete transformation of the people and their environment. In fact, the description of the new realities that follows in verses 15b–20 demonstrates that the tripartite covenant involving YHWH, Israel and the land will be functioning perfectly: the land will yield its abundance, justice (*mišpāṭ*) and righteousness (*sĕdāqâ*) will pervade, and the people will live in their homes in perfect peace and security. These represent the normal and ideal consequences of the covenant relationship functioning as it was designed. The covenantal context is unmistakable in Isaiah 44:1–5:

> But now listen, O Jacob, my servant,
> and Israel, whom I have chosen.
> Thus says YHWH who made you,
> and formed you in the womb,
> Who will aid you:
> 'Do not fear, O Jacob my servant,
> and you, O Jeshurun, whom I have chosen,
> For I will pour [*yāṣaq*] water on the thirsty land and streams on the dry ground;
> I will pour [*yāṣaq*] my Spirit on your descendants,
> And they will spring up among the grass
> Like poplars by streams of water.'

---

rather than 'in' them. But when he leaves he will send the Spirit, to indwell them as his representative, and to authorize/empower them to represent him as they extend Jesus' mission. This is precisely what happens in the book of Acts. Indwelt by the Holy Spirit they extended the active and teaching ministry of Jesus (cf. Acts 1:1–2).

This one will say, 'I belong to YHWH,'
And that one will call on the name of Jacob;
And another will write on his hand 'Belonging to YHWH'
And will name Israel's name with honour.

The situation is similar in Joel's magnificent salvation oracle in Joel 3:1–2 (ET 2:28–29): 'Then afterward I will pour out [*šāpak*] my Spirit on all flesh; your sons and daughters shall prophesy, your old men shall dream dreams, and your young men shall see visions. In those days I will pour out [*šāpak*] my Spirit even on male and female slaves.' While many interpret this as a prediction of a universal outpouring of the Spirit, the context is entirely parochial (cf. 2:18–27), and 'all flesh' should be interpreted as all Israel and/or all inhabitants of the land. As in Isaiah 32:15 and 44:1–4, Joel looks forward to a day after the judgment when the tripartite covenantal relationship involving YHWH, the land and the people will be completely restored.[83] As proof, the land will yield its abundance, the beasts of the field will be tamed and YHWH will be in the midst of his people. The outpouring of the Spirit will be accompanied by special signs: all Israelites will be inspired by the Spirit of prophecy, and the cosmos itself will announce the awesome day of YHWH. In Zechariah 12:10 the pouring (*šāpak*) of the Spirit of grace and supplication occurs in the context of the restoration of the dynasty of David and God's renewed activity on behalf of Jerusalem and, in the broader context, of the renewal of the covenant.[84]

This leaves us with Ezekiel 39:29, which may be the most interesting text

---

83. Cf. Joel 2:18 – 3:2, specifically the first verse, 'Then YHWH will be zealous for his land and will have pity on his people', and v. 27, which immediately precedes the reference to the pouring out of the Spirit, 'Thus you shall know that I am in the midst of Israel, and that I am YHWH your God, and there is no other; and my people will never be put to shame.' H. W. Wolff (*Joel and Amos*, Hermeneia [Philadelphia: Fortress, 1977], p. 67) is correct; the context precludes interpreting *kol bāśār*, 'all flesh', universally, as it is commonly understood. In Peter's Pentecost sermon this original sense is respected. Acts 2:5 notes that the people gathered on the occasion were Jews from all parts of the empire. Peter himself emphasizes that he is speaking to the men/house of Israel; cf. vv. 22, 36. That he understood it in this restricted sense is confirmed by the need for a special revelation in Acts 10 to convince him to go outside the house of Israel.

84. Note the reference to the covenant formula in 13:9, 'I will say, "They are my people," and they will say, "YHWH is my God."' Admittedly there is some distance between these two verses, and it may be argued that originally these were uttered as

of all.[85] To grasp the significance of this statement we need to see its place in the broader context. After a lengthy oracle concerning Gog and his allies from the four corners of the earth, involving eight cartoon-like frames climaxing in a bizarre banquet scene (39:17–20), YHWH declares his goal in bringing Gog and then defeating him: to set his glory among the nations that all may know that he is YHWH the God of Israel (vv. 21–24). But he ends this literary unit with a pastoral promise to Ezekiel's own generation:

> Assuredly, thus has the Lord Yahweh declared: Now I will restore the fortunes of Jacob; I will have compassion on the whole house of Israel, and demonstrate passion for my holy name. They will bear their disgrace and all their acts of infidelity which they have perpetrated against me, when they dwell securely on their own land, with no one frightening them. When I bring them back from the peoples, and regather them from the countries of their enemies, then I will display my holiness among them, in the sight of many nations. And they will know that I am Yahweh their God in that, having sent them off into exile to the nations, I will gather them to their own land. I will never again leave any of them out there. Nor will I ever again hide my face from them, for I will have poured out my Spirit upon the house of Israel – the declaration of the Lord Yahweh (vv. 25–29).[86]

I have provided a full discussion of this text elsewhere,[87] and intend here only to make some observations relevant to the present topic. The idea of pouring out the divine Spirit is rooted in the perception of the *rûaḥ* as a sort of divine fluid that covers the object.[88] In each of the texts cited, the pouring out of YHWH's *rûaḥ* on Israel signified the ratification and sealing of the covenant relationship. While this divine action is probably associated with the transformative act of putting his *rûaḥ* within his people, it represented the guaran-

---

separate oracles. However, the repeated references to 'in that day' (12:11; 13:1, 2, 4) as well as the editorial juxtaposing of the oracles suggest some connection.

85. Like Walther Eichrodt and Leslie Allen, Robson (*Word and Spirit in Ezekiel*, pp. 252–262) argues that the outpouring of YHWH's *rûaḥ* on his people and the giving of his *rûaḥ* within them are essentially synonymous.

86. As translated by Daniel I. Block, *The Book of Ezekiel Chapters 25 – 48*, NICOT (Grand Rapids: Eerdmans, 1998), p. 478. Textual notes are provided.

87. See Daniel I. Block, 'Gog and the Pouring Out of the Spirit: Reflections on Ezekiel xxxix 21–9', *VT* 37 (1987), pp. 257–270; idem, *Ezekiel Chapters 25 – 48*, pp. 485–489.

88. Cf. D. J. A. Clines, 'The Image of God in Man', *TynBul* 19 (1968), p. 82.

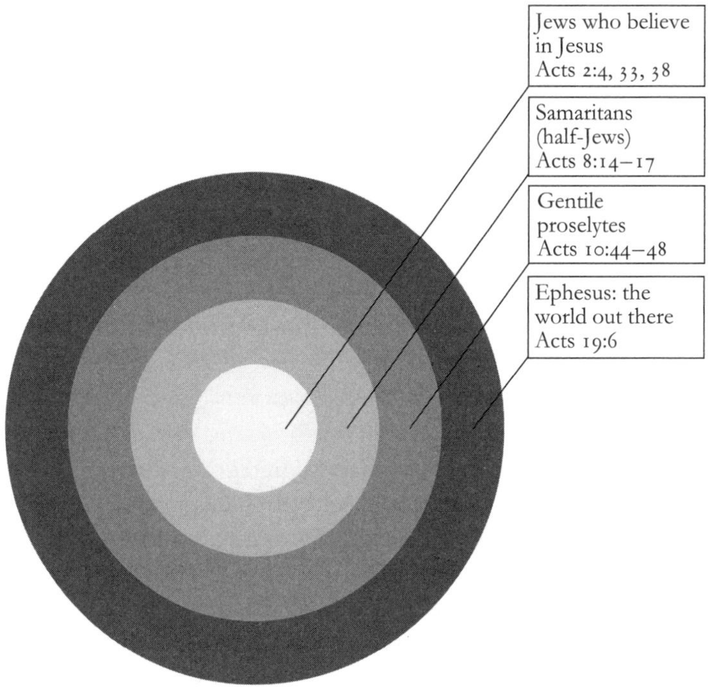

Figure 2: The expanding boundaries of the covenant community as symbolized by the outpouring of the Holy Spirit in Acts

tee of new life, peace and prosperity. It served as the definitive act whereby YHWH claimed and sealed the newly gathered nation of Israel as his own.

In the broader context of Ezekiel 39:29 the causal clause, 'For I shall have poured out my Spirit upon the house of Israel', does not merely explain the events described in the preceding verses, that is, the regathering of the nation. It also explains YHWH's fulfilment of his covenant with his people. The presence of the *rûaḥ* of YHWH, poured out upon his people, served as the permanent witness and seal of the *bĕrît šālôm*, 'covenant of peace', and the *bĕrît ʿôlām*, 'covenant of perpetuity'. By pouring out his *rûaḥ* upon the returned exiles, YHWH seals them as his covenant people and guarantees that he will never again leave any of the house of Israel at the mercy of her enemies and that he would never again hide his face from them, as Ezekiel and his contemporaries had witnessed. In short, Gog becomes the agent through whom YHWH declares concretely that 587 BC shall never be repeated.

The implications of this covenantal interpretation of the pouring out of the *rûaḥ* for the progress of the Holy Spirit's activity in the book of Acts are tantalizing but may be touched upon only briefly. It hardly seems accidental that with the commencement of every new stage in the advance of the gospel and the incorporation of new groups into the covenant people, the narrator refers to the manifestation of the Spirit. (1) The event at Pentecost declared the covenant community to consist of Jews from all over who believe in Jesus (Acts 2:4, 33, 38). (2) In Acts 8:14–17 the Samaritans – half-Jews ethnically and spiritually – were added. (3) Cornelius and his household represent the addition of Gentile proselytes of Judea (10:44–48; cf. 11:16). (4) The Ephesian believers represent those who are far from the holy land, many of whom have no previous ethnic or spiritual tie to Jerusalem (19:6) (see Fig. 2).[89]

Conclusion

In the OT the word *rûaḥ* bears many different meanings. The nuances intended by the authors vary greatly, and the requirements of the context must determine the interpretation in each instance. Fundamentally the term signified 'wind' or 'breath'. But in the hands of Hebrew psychologists (if one may speak of them as such) and theologians, *rûaḥ* seemed to open up numerous possibilities. Attempts to formulate a biblical doctrine of the Holy Spirit demand more careful attention to the OT evidence than has been the common practice, especially since the outlook of the theologians in the NT was determined primarily by their sacred Scriptures, rather than by prevailing Greek notions. This applied to their anthropology and their pneumatology, no less than to their theology, soteriology and Christology.

When we reflect on the OT understanding of the *rûaḥ* of YHWH, of which *to pneuma to hagion* is the Greek counterpart, we should think first and foremost of the divine presence on earth. It was on this basis that the psalmist could cry out: 'Where can I escape from your *rûaḥ* /Where can I flee from your presence?' (Ps. 139:7). The *rûaḥ* is the divine agent through whom God's will is exercised in creation, in dispensing life, in guidance and providential care, in revealing his will, in saving those who are doomed and imprisoned (Isa. 63), in renewing unregenerate hearts and minds, and in sealing his covenant people as his own. However, in the OT the Spirit of YHWH is not a self-existent agent operating independently. Rather, the divine Spirit is an 'extension of YHWH's personality' by which God exercises his influence over

89. Cf. Paul's references to being sealed with/by the Holy Spirit (2 Cor. 1:22; Eph. 1:13; 4:30), which also seem to involve divine confirmation of the covenant.

the world.[90] The *rûaḥ* is the power of God at work in his creation and among humankind. This creating, animating, energizing *rûaḥ* is none other than God himself.

This does not mean that the Hebrews could not speak of the *rûaḥ* as a concrete (or, better, fluid) entity, separable from YHWH, as in Psalm 104:30: 'When you send forth your *rûaḥ*. . .' However, this is anthropomorphic language. YHWH's sending out his *rûaḥ*, 'breath', is analogous to his extending his arm, his smelling of an offering, his utterance of words with his mouth, his seeing and his hearing. Consequently, just as the activity of YHWH's right arm represents YHWH's own actions, so the work of his *rûaḥ* signifies his own direct involvement. If a prophet could be so identified with YHWH that what the prophet said God said, surely we may conceive of an identification between the Spirit and YHWH himself. When the divine *rûaḥ* acts, God acts.

The instruction provided by the prophets concerning God's activity in this world is both rich and complex. However, in serving as model teachers in this regard, they not only spoke of the power of the Spirit, but they also embodied that power in their own person.

90. A. R. Johnson, *The One and the Many in the Israelite Conception of God*, 2nd ed. (Cardiff: University of Wales, 1961), p. 36.

11. IS BALAAM'S DONKEY THE REAL PROPHET (NUMBERS 24:1–4)?

John N. Oswalt

The Balaam narrative (Num. 22 – 24) has long been a source of fascination for students of the Bible. From the talking donkey to the diviner's inability to curse Israel, the account has provided an almost endless fund of data for investigation and speculation. This fascination has only increased since the discovery of the inscriptions at Deir Allah in Jordan in 1967 which refer to Balaam the son of Beor and show him involved in a dispute among the gods. The inscription has been dated to about 800 BC, when the region was still under the control of Israel, and has been used to argue for the essentially pagan nature of Israelite religion at that point.[1]

Within the narrative, the passage under consideration here has been of special interest because of the number of questions it raises. Is this experience to be equated with those of approved Israelite prophets, or is it different in some way? Does the spirit/Spirit come upon Balaam with his permission, or does this experience happen to him against his will? What was the nature of the experience? Was it an ecstatic trance, like that recorded of Saul (1 Sam. 19:23–24) and possibly Ezekiel (8:1ff.), or was it in some way different, as seems to be the case with Micah (3:8)? In that regard, how is the state-

1. For a brief but comprehensive discussion, see B. Levine, *Numbers*, AB (Garden City: Doubleday), 2000.

ment in verse 4 (repeated in v. 16) to be understood when it says that Balaam 'falls down, with his eyes open'? Are we to think of the two statements as complimentary or contradictory? Above all of these, there is the larger issue of the biblical position with regard to Balaam: what sort of person was he, especially given his claim that he could only speak the word of Yahweh (22:18, 38; 23:12; 24:13)? Was he a 'believer', or was he merely a greedy, professional diviner whom Yahweh chose to use? In this regard, does the biblical account actually contain two contradictory assessments of Balaam, betraying at least two or more layers of editing?[2] One could hardly claim to give definitive answers to these questions in a book-length monograph, much less in a short chapter. However, we can at least explore them and seek for some tentative conclusions. We will begin with an investigation of the Hebrew text.[3]

Balaam having seen that it was good in the Lord's eyes to bless Israel.[4] Whatever other questions this verse raises, it is clear that Balaam has learned something from his previous experiences, namely, that any attempts to produce a result that he wished for through the techniques of a diviner were not going to achieve that result. Yahweh would not be manipulated. It is interesting that as the present text presents him Balaam is a very ambivalent character. On the one hand, he was quite convinced that he must say what Yahweh said, but he still cherished the idea that he might be able to influence what Yahweh might say to him. That seems to be the point of 22:18–19. Yahweh had said that Balaam was not to go with the messengers, and that seemed to be that. Nevertheless, Balaam sought a dream, perhaps using some technique, in which God might say something 'more' to him. And God did indeed say something more (v. 20), giving him permission to go.[5] Yet one cannot help but feel that the whole point of the following donkey episode is that the complex diviner's arts are pointless. Even a donkey can see God and his will.

---

2. Two works of interest in this regard are: J. Greene, *Balaam and His Interpreters: A Hermeneutical History of the Balaam Tradition*, BJS 244 (Atlanta: Scholars, 1992); M. Moore, *The Balaam Traditions: Their Character and Development*, SBLDS 113 (Atlanta: Scholars, 1990).
3. The fullest discussion of this text of which I am aware is: H. Rouillard, *La Péricope de Balaam (Nombres 22 – 24): La Prose et la 'Oracles'*, Etudes Bibliques NS 4 (Paris: Gabalda, 1985), pp. 336–354.
4. Translations are the author's own.
5. See R. Moberly, 'On Learning to Be a Prophet', in P. Harland and C. Hayward (eds.), *New Heaven and New Earth – Prophecy and the Millennium; Essays in Honor of Anthony Gelston* (Leiden: Brill, 1999), pp. 6f.

The only question is whether a person's eyes are open to see what is in front of him or her.

He did not go as at other times has been interpreted in two different ways. It seems that the most natural reading is that the reference is to the previous two incidents reported in chapter 23. The references to sacrifices (23:2, 14, 29) and going to a 'desolate height' (where a flight of birds might be seen, 23:3, 'top of Peor', 23:28) strongly suggests omenology, whereby a skilled practitioner might discover an omen favourable to the wishes of the patron.[6] If that is the case, this expression would be saying that Balaam had finally learned that those procedures were not workable in this instance (see 23:23, 'For there is no sorcery against Jacob, nor any divination against Israel'). However, another interpretation suggests that in fact the 'other times' when Balaam went to engage in sorcery did not have to do with Israel because it is not said explicitly anywhere in chapter 23 that this is what he in fact did. Rather, this statement is merely making explicit the implications of the previous chapter that Balaam never engaged in divination in these episodes with Israel.[7] While this point of view is commended by the continual reference to the word of Yahweh in the narrative and the normal biblical condemnation of all kinds of sorcery in connection with Yahweh, it has to be said that this account is hardly normal in any respect. Beyond that, it is hard to understand why 'as at other times' only enters the account here if in fact it had applied to the entire incident.[8]

But he set his face toward the wilderness is even more ambiguous than the previous phrase. Milgrom believes that this is a way of saying that Balaam went to a place where he could look boldly at the entire people of Israel (not only at a part of them, as in 23:13), because he knew now that it would be impossible to curse them, and was ready to pronounce the fullest blessing on them.[9] Gane disagrees, however. Taking a more negative approach toward the diviner, he believes that Balaam, having given up on getting the curse message he

---

6. So J. Milgrom, *Numbers*, JPSTC (Philadelphia: JPS, 1989), p. 201; see also Moore, *Traditions*, pp. 108–109.
7. A. Schüle, *Israel's Sohn – Jahwes Prophet: Ein Versuch zum Verhältnis von kanonischer Theologie und Religionschichte anhand der Bileam-Perikope (Num 22 – 24)*, ATM 17 (Münster: LIT, 2001), p. 46.
8. T. R. Ashley, *The Book of Numbers*, NICOT (Grand Rapids: Eerdmans, 1993), p. 486. It also seems likely to me that the sequence *wyyqtl – wqtl* indicates a protasis-apodosis connection: i.e. as a result of seeing . . . Balaam did not go.
9. Milgrom, *Numbers*, p. 202.

wanted, now abandoned all attempts to get in touch with his divine Source, and went away to the wilderness to craft his own curse message.[10] Undeniably, 'wilderness' is ambiguous,[11] since from the heights of Peor (23:28) one can see wilderness in almost any direction. However, the immediately following statement, that Balaam 'lifted his eyes and saw Israel', seems to support Milgrom. At the same time, Gane's comment that the sight was accidental rather than intentional cannot be denied. The succession of three *wyyqtl* forms, 'he set, he lifted, he saw', does little to resolve the ambiguity.[12]

He saw Israel dwelling according to its tribes is yet another statement that can have a number of differing significances. It may stand in specific contrast to 23:13 where Balak brought Balaam to a place where the diviner could only see part of the people, apparently believing that it would be difficult to produce an effective curse if the entire mass of people was in view. On that understanding, Balaam is here consciously opening himself to giving a blessing.[13] Another possibility is that the phrase speaks of preparedness for battle, which is how Numbers 2 speaks of the tribal organization: 'on the east side . . . those of the standard of the camp of Judah according to their armies. . .' (v. 3). This would suggest the folly of trying to curse such a fully prepared group of people. Yet a third possibility is that the narrator is setting the stage for the oracle itself in which it is said, 'How lovely are your tents, O Jacob, your dwellings, O Israel' (24:5). As is often the case in these kinds of statements, it is well within the realm of possibility that something of all three of these connotations may be intended.

It seems to me that among this welter of possibilities, the most probable scenario is this: Balaam has indeed reached the conclusion that it is useless to engage in any more divination techniques to try to get a curse to pronounce upon Israel. All of the omens have been relentlessly positive. Therefore, though he is not willing to say it to Balak (telling the Moabite king to prepare the sacrifices as before), he submits himself to pronounce a blessing on the

---

10. R. Gane, *Numbers*, NIVAC (Grand Rapids: Zondervan, 2004), p. 709.

11. See Schüle, *Israel's Sohn*, p. 47.

12. Schüle, ibid., p. 46, comments on the irony of Balaam leaving Balak standing beside his costly offerings while Balaam went to some 'other' place than he had before.

13. Rouillard, *Péricope*, p. 343, points out that this phrase 'according to (each of) its tribes' is rare, and specifically calls attention to Josh. 7:16, where Israel is assembled 'according to its tribes' in the attempt to single out the sinner. She says that in both places there is both a literal and a symbolic sense being employed.

camp of Israel. It is in view of the submission that God then sends his Spirit upon Balaam.

The Spirit of God came upon him brings us to the central issue. What is being said about Balaam at this point? What is the nature of the experience which he underwent? And what does this say about his relationship to the classical Israelite prophets? Gane sees this as an entirely involuntary experience: avoiding the previous techniques that had kept producing the wrong message, Balaam had decided to craft his own curse-message without reference to this Yahweh, so Yahweh simply stepped in and 'possesses Balaam as a prophet'.[14] Milgrom is probably at the other extreme among the commentators, seeing Balaam as now being fully willing to become the instrument of Yahweh's blessing.[15] Other commentators fall in between these two. On the more positive side, Cole says, 'seeing and hearing rightly before God must come as the result of divine inspiration and human submission in order for the revelatory process to be effective'.[16] Over against this is R. K. Harrison, who cites M. Unger favourably, '[Balaam was] a pagan magician who fell under the overwhelming influence of the Lord for a short period in his career but served Him from a basic standpoint of greed.'[17] Harrison goes on to say,

> It is important to distinguish this form of ecstatic possession from both the anointing of God's Spirit (Is 61:1) and the bestowal of the Holy Spirit on the Day of Pentecost. Balaam's spiritual experience should instead be compared with periodic gifts of the Spirit that enabled individuals to perform a variety of services to God (cf. Judg 3:10; 6:34; 11:29; 1 Sam 16:13, etc.).[18]

This statement focuses the discussion on three key issues relating to the experience of the Spirit of God in the OT: its duration, its manifestation and its character. First of all, it is too simplistic to suggest that all experiences of the Spirit were episodic (i.e. the Spirit does not remain on a person for an extended time) in the OT whereas this was not true in the NT. Undoubtedly,

---

14. Gane, *Numbers*, p. 709.
15. Milgrom, *Numbers*, p. 195.
16. D. R. Cole, *The Book of Numbers: A Commentary*, NAC (Nashville: Broadman, 2000), p. 418.
17. M. Unger, *Biblical Demonology: A Study of the Spiritual Forces Behind the Present World Unrest* (Wheaton: Scripture Press, 1952), p. 125, cited in R. K Harrison, *Numbers*, WEC (Chicago: Moody, 1990), p. 334.
18. Harrison, *Numbers*, p. 317.

many of the experiences in the OT were episodic, and there is no reason to doubt that this one was, especially if Balaam's advice to tempt the Israelite men with Midianite women came after these events, as they appear to do (Num. 25:1–3; 31:16)! However, there were experiences of the Spirit that were episodic in the NT as well. Note the several occasions where the book of Acts reports the Spirit coming upon or filling someone after the Day of Pentecost (4:8, 31; 7:55; 9:39, etc.). This is not to suggest that the Christian disciples did not experience the fullness of the Holy Spirit in an ongoing way, but only to say that reports of episodes of Spirit-filling in the Bible cannot necessarily be used to argue against a more ongoing experience of such fullness. In that regard, we must take account of the statement that 'the Spirit of the Lord came upon David *from that day forward* . . . But the Spirit of the Lord departed from Saul' (1 Sam. 16:13–14). What can this mean but that the Spirit of the Lord had rested upon Saul for some extended period of time, and that he now rested upon David in a similar manner?[19] All of this suggests that the experience of the Holy Spirit in the OT was not different in quality from that in the NT, but rather different in its availability. Since Calvary, the Holy Spirit is available to all, and not only to a select few as it was before that pivotal event.

A second question which Harrison's comment raises has to do with the manifestation of the Spirit of God. In his discussion of Balaam, Harrison joins with almost all other commentators in labelling the experience one of 'ecstatic possession'. Even Cole, who speaks of the necessity of 'human submission', says that 'he may have entered into an ecstatic trance'.[20] But what is there in the biblical account which points to this assumption? There are two elements that are regularly pointed out. The first is the statement that the Spirit 'came upon' Balaam. So it is said that this is a term for ecstatic possession.[21] But does this phrase by itself imply 'ecstatic possession'? The Hebrew is actually 'was upon', which is even less suggestive than 'came upon'. To be sure, there are instances in the OT where the presence of the Spirit does accompany frantic activity, as, for instance, in the case of Samson (Judg. 14:19; 15:14; but note that the verb in these cases is not merely *hyh*, but is rather *ṣlḥ*, 'to rush upon'; note also that there are other instances of dervish-like behaviour in Samson where there is no mention of the Spirit). But there are other cases where nothing like

19. In fairness to Harrison, he may be including these experiences in the anointing that he differentiates from episodes. It seems to me that it is not easy to differentiate the two in the centre of the spectrum where they overlap.

20. Cole, *Numbers*, p. 416.

21. See Ashley, *Numbers*, p. 487.

ecstatic possession is in view. The Spirit of the Lord 'came upon' Othniel and he judged Israel (3:10). The Spirit of the Lord 'came upon' Jephthah and he passed through Gilead and Manasseh, and advanced on the people of Ammon (Judg. 11:29). There is nothing in either description that even hints of ecstatic possession. So we can hardly say the statement that the Spirit of God came (or, more literally, was) upon Balaam connotes ecstatic possession.[22]

However, there is a second term in this context that could more easily connote such a state. That is the word *nôpēl*, a Qal masculine, singular active participle, 'falling', which occurs in verse 4. The most natural understanding of the term would surely be that Balaam has fallen down in a trance.[23] But when we see it in its larger context, this natural understanding becomes somewhat more complex. The word occurs in the introduction to Balaam's third oracle, given to him by the Spirit, in verses 3–4. The entire introduction reads as follows:

> The declaration of Balaam, the son of Beor,
> and the declaration of the man whose eye is opened;
> the declaration of the one who hears the speech of El,
> who sees the vision of Shaddai, falling and uncovered of eyes.

The burden of this passage is clearly perception: open, uncovered eyes, and sensitive, opened ears. This is so much the case that falling seems distinctly out of place. Thus, there have been several attempts to find alternatives. H. Ackerman proposed that two layers of editing have taken place, with 'falling' having been inserted by an editor who could not believe that this pagan might see the vision of God just like one of the Hebrew prophets might have done (Isa. 1:1; Mic. 1:1), and added 'falling' to make the event appear more pagan. Then a later editor, objecting to that 'slander', corrected it by adding 'with uncovered eyes'.[24] However, there is no textual evidence to support this ingenious suggestion.

John Allegro went in another direction, suggesting that the word be repointed to be read as a Niphal participle of a root *ypl* cognate with Arabic

---

22. The phrase also appears in 1 Sam. 19:23, where the accompanying behaviour certainly suggests ecstatic possession. But there is no such behaviour here. The phrase itself is more neutral.
23. As the LXX takes it, *en hypno.*
24. H. Ackerman, 'Concerning the Nature of Balaam's Vision (Num. 24:3–4)', *Anglican Theological Review* 2:3 (1919), p. 234.

wafala, which means 'peeled, stripped', referring to fruit or bark. Thus instead of being a somewhat incongruous discussion of the 'mechanism of inspiration', the term would work together with the following phrase and the whole would read something like 'pared and peeled of eye' (taking 'eye' as singular with SP).[25] Although, like Ackerman, Allegro must be given high marks for ingenuity, here too the absence of any textual support for such an emendation must be a mark against it.

W. Albright wished to go in the opposite direction from Ackerman and Allegro. He felt that the term was obscure as it stood because its original clarity had been lost. So he proposed that it should be read as an intransitive participle or derived adjective meaning something like 'unconscious'. He cited Akkadian *nabultu* (for *napultu*), 'corpse', and Hebrew *nĕpîlîm*, 'dead hero or shade'. 'The diviner was subject to trances in which he seemed like a corpse but possessed the gift of interior vision.' Once again, while this suggestion is highly ingenious, it is without objective support.[26]

On balance, it seems that all the efforts to correct the text fall short and that the participial rendering 'falling' must be considered original. But that being said, how are we to understand its significance in this setting? Does it imply 'ecstatic possession'? I would argue that it does not. It may well be that it is suggesting that Balaam fell into a trance, as it appears is the case with Ezekiel many years later (3:14; 8:3; etc.),[27] and with John yet many years after that (Rev. 1:10).[28] But a trance is not ecstatic possession, and that distinction is not insignificant. In this regard, Jon Levenson has performed a helpful service in his study of Pseudo-Philo's *Liber Antiquitatum Biblicarum*, a paraphrase and expansion of certain OT passages that dates to the early Christian era.[29] Commenting on Pseudo-Philo's descriptions of the Spirit's work in

---

25. J. Allegro, 'The Meaning of *nophel* in Numbers 24:4, 16', *ExpTim* 65:10 (1954), pp. 316–317.
26. W. Albright, 'The Oracles of Balaam', *JBL* 63 (1944), n. 61, p. 217. Yet another alternative is proposed by Levine, *Numbers*, p. 193, who proposes that the line contains opposing ideas. Balaam is a prophet who can see the visions of God whether 'fallen [asleep] *or* with uncovered eyes'. There is no 'or' in the Heb. text.
27. See D. Block, *The Book of Ezekiel, Chapters 1 – 24*, NICOT (Grand Rapids: Eerdmans, 1997), pp. 278–280.
28. See R. Mounce, *The Book of Revelation*, NICNT (Grand Rapids: Eerdmans, 1977), p. 75.
29. J. Levenson, 'Prophetic Inspiration in Pseudo-Philo's *Liber Antiquitatum Biblicarum*', *JQR* 85 (1995), pp. 297–329.

certain OT figures, such as Kenaz, Joshua and Balaam, Levenson highlights what ecstatic possession actually consisted of in the ancient world. Although he shows that some of Pseudo-Philo's descriptions of Spirit inspiration were drawn from the Bible (in contrast to the conclusions of A. Piñero[30]), particularly the ideas of 'becoming another man' and 'being clothed with' or 'being clothed by the Spirit',[31] he demonstrates that Pseudo-Philo's primary descriptions are drawn from the Hellenistic world. He identifies four characteristics which define the Hellenistic character of inspiration, all of which are prominent in Pseudo-Philo and none of which are to be found in the Bible. They are:

1. Not remembering what had been spoken in the trance.
2. Elevation of the mind beyond normal capacities (being 'out of one's mind').
3. Suspension, or overruling, the rational faculties through sleep or unconsciousness.
4. Frenzied, uncontrolled behaviour in the trance; 'true inspiration leads to frenzy and madness in which the inhibitions of intelligence are cast off'.[32]

These are the characteristics of 'ecstatic possession', and in this light there is no such thing as ecstatic possession in the Bible.[33] Here, no less than elsewhere in the Bible, the prophetic experience does not involve suspension of

---

30. A. Piñero, 'A Mediterranean View of Prophetic Inspiration: On the Concept of Inspiration in the *Liber Antiquitatum Biblicarum* of Pseudo-Philo', *Mediterranean Historical Review* 6 (1991), p. 24, cited by Levenson, *Pseudo-Philo*, p. 299.
31. Levenson, *Pseudo-Philo*, p. 316.
32. Levenson, *Pseudo-Philo*, pp. 314, 319. Interestingly enough, Pseudo-Philo has Balaam actually losing the Spirit: 'and when he saw part of the people, the spirit of God did not abide in him . . . "I am restrained in my speech and cannot say what I see with my eyes, because there is little left of the holy spirit that abided in me. For I know that, because I have been persuaded by Balak, I have lessened the time of my life"' (*LAB* 18:10–12). Levenson says the reason for this is 'probably the ambivalence Psuedo-Philo felt about attributing the oracle of a non-Jewish "interpreter of dreams" (18:2) to the spirit of God' (p. 321).
33. This is contra J. Lindblom, *Prophecy in Ancient Israel* (Philadelphia: Fortress, 1962), who argued at some length that the experiences related by Micah, Isaiah and Ezekiel connoted ecstatic possession (pp. 65–82, 122–137, 173–182).

the rational faculties, abnormal elevation of the mind, inability to remember what was said or wild frenzy under the lash of the god. Whatever falling into a trance meant for the biblical prophet, it did not mean these things. The prophet was not taken out of himself or herself to become merely an unwitting mouthpiece for God. Rather, he or she was taken into fellowship with God whereby the prophet could see things from God's perspective and hear what God had to say about those things. Far from being a mouthpiece, the biblical prophet was invited to become a dialogue partner with God. I do not deny that at times this involved falling into a trance. I only want to insist that this did not involve ecstatic possession on any of the terms that it did elsewhere in the ancient world.[34]

It seems to me that this is the point of the repeated words for perception in Numbers 24:3–4 (as opposed to the single word 'falling', which may imply a trance). The point is that Balaam 'sees' and 'hears', not that he *does not* see or hear, and that point is made no less than four times: he is the man whose eyes are open,[35] who hears the words of El, who sees the vision of Shaddai, who, falling, (nevertheless) has uncovered eyes.[36] None of these, in and of themselves, suggest 'interior vision', as Albright would have it.[37] To be sure, we are not told how the Spirit made Balaam see and hear these things, but it is *not* said that it happened when Balaam was out of his mind.

The declaration of Balaam brings us to a final consideration concerning the

---

34. One of the most famous representations of 'prophetic frenzy' is found in the Egyptian 'Tale of Wen-Amon', where the King of Byblos's page is seized by the Egyptian god Amon-Re and made to speak a message favourable to Wen-Amon. The determinative following the Egyptian word for 'page' is a human stick figure. In this case alone, the arms and legs of the stick figure are drawn with wavy lines. The boy was possessed!

35. Albright wished to divide and repoint *šetum* to *še tāmmâ*, 'which is perfect' ('Balaam', p. 216). This is very plausible, but lacks textual support.

36. Rouillard, *Péricope*, believes that one of the functions, if not *the* function, of the prose section 23:7 – 24:3a is to 'rehabilitate' Balaam after the donkey episode. The narrator is at pains, in this view, to show that Balaam has recovered his 'sight' at least to the extent of that of the donkey, and can now see what is before him (pp. 333–344). In this regard, it is significant that in 22:31, when Yahweh enables Balaam to see the angel, it is the same verb that is used in 24:4, *glh*, 'uncovered'. It is because of the Spirit's action that Balaam is enabled to see the realities of life with regard to Israel.

37. Albright, 'Balaam', p. 217, n. 61.

nature of this experience. Commentators regularly point out that *nĕʾum*, which occurs very frequently in construct with Yahweh (often translated, 'thus says the Lord'), only appears in construct with someone other than Yahweh four times in the OT: 2 Samuel 23:1 (David); Psalm 36:1 (David?); Proverbs 30:1 (Agur); and here. Of these, the one in 2 Samuel holds the greatest interest for this study. The reason for this is twofold: first, because the opening line of the two oracles is very similar ('The declaration of Balaam, son of Beor, the declaration of the man [*geber*] with opened eye'; 'The declaration of David, son of Jesse, the declaration of the man [*geber*] raised up on high'), and second, because both oracles are attributed to the Spirit. When these two points are taken together, the implication seems very clear: the Spirit has enabled these two men to speak as though from God himself. However, as Milgrom points out, both are quite explicit that the declaration *is in their own words*.[38] This is an oracle of Balaam, of David. To be sure, the content has come from God, but the words are their own. This can only underline what has been said above: prophetic inspiration in the Bible is the result of divine/human interaction. How this can be, given divine infallibility and human fallibility, will always be something of a mystery. But surely the Bible so understands the work of the Spirit that in spite of human fallibility he is able to communicate without any error precisely what he wants to communicate. This is the wonder and the joy of the work of the Spirit. This is also the tragedy of Balaam: for one who has known this kind of intercourse with Yahweh to then fall to the level reported of him in Numbers 31:16 is a testimony to how deeply our human fallibility has penetrated us.

This speaks to the issue of the Bible's view of Balaam. It seems to me that any attempt to say that it must have originally been one or the other, positive or negative, is but a manifestation of the tendency of higher criticism to insist on uniformity at all costs. But we need not try to disentangle two supposedly contradictory 'traditions'. We can let the original account be richly ambivalent, as it is with Saul. Saul fits the patterns of Greek tragedy: he is a tragic hero, a man with towering abilities and possibilities, yet beset with a tragic flaw that eventually destroyed him. So it is with Balaam. Here we have something of a tragi-comedy, where we see a man whose donkey is more of a 'seer' than he is, but yet a man who is determined to carry out his task with professional integrity, to say what Yahweh says, and nothing else. Perhaps because of that integrity, he was allowed to experience what it could be to have such a relationship with God as to move beyond technique to fellowship. If in the end

38. Milgrom, *Numbers*, p. 203.

he valued that experience so little as to allow his greed (perhaps) to bring him down, that only highlights the tragedy of what might have been.

12. THE SPIRIT OF YAHWEH IN ISAIAH 11:1–9

Hilary Marlow

Introduction

> A branch will go out from the stem of Jesse,
> a shoot from his root will bear fruit.
> The spirit of Yahweh will settle upon him –
> a spirit of wisdom and understanding,
> a spirit of counsel and strength,
> a spirit of knowledge and fear of Yahweh.
> (Isa. 11:1–2)[1]

These verses from a familiar passage in Isaiah 11 contain probably one of the best-known references to the spirit of Yahweh in the whole of Isaiah and the only place in First Isaiah in which the exact phrase 'the spirit of Yahweh' (*rûaḥ yhwh*) occurs. Although for centuries Isaiah 11:1–9, along with parts of Isaiah 7 and 9, has formed part of Christian liturgy during the season of Advent, the main aim of this chapter is to consider what Isaiah 11 might have meant to its earliest readers, and how it fits into its immediate context and into the contours of the message of Isaiah as a whole. There is a primary intrinsic

1. My translation of the Hebrew unless otherwise noted.

value in the words of the book of Isaiah as they address, say, the threat posed by Assyria or the situation of the exiles in Babylon. This does not mean that it is invalid to read an OT passage like this in the context of anticipating the incarnation. But only once we understand the text in its primary context(s) can we seek to engage with it from our own particular standpoint as readers with hopes and expectations of our own.

Author, dating and other preliminary matters

The secondary literature offers a variety of opinions regarding the origin, author and dating of Isaiah 11:1–9, ranging from the possibility that it is pre-exilic in origin, perhaps even originating from the hand of the eighth-century Isaiah son of Amoz,[2] to the idea that it is an editorial addition from sometime in the post-exilic period.[3] The question of the identity of the recipient of the prophet's message and how or when it was fulfilled is also debated.[4] Within the book of Isaiah as a whole, only First Isaiah exhibits interest in the royal line and its continuation. Second Isaiah makes no reference to the kings of Israel and Judah, and a renewal of the monarchy forms no part of its message of hope. This, Hugh Williamson suggests, is compelling evidence for dating Isaiah 11:1–9 along with other 'messianic' texts in First Isaiah to the pre-exilic period, while the monarchy was still a reality.[5]

Another consideration is the relation of the passage to its wider context. Isaiah 11:1–9 is an important part of the composite literary unit formed by 10:5 – 12:6, which is characterized by detailed descriptions of the downfall of Judah's enemies, particularly Assyria (10:5–19; 11:14–16), and of hope

---

2. Hans Wildberger, *Isaiah 1 – 12*, trans. T. H. Trapp (Minneapolis: Fortress, 1991 [Ger. 1972]), p. 467; John D. W. Watts, *Isaiah 1 – 33*, WBC (Waco: Word Books, 1985), p. 173.
3. Joseph Blenkinsopp, *Isaiah 1 – 39: A New Translation with Introduction and Commentary*, AB (New York: Doubleday, 2000), p. 264; Ronald E. Clements, *Isaiah 1 – 39*, NCB (Grand Rapids: Eerdmans, 1980), p. 122.
4. See Clements, *Isaiah 1 – 39*, p. 122; Marvin A. Sweeney, *Isaiah 1 – 39 with an Introduction to Prophetic Literature* (Grand Rapids: Eerdmans, 1996), pp. 203–204; Watts, *Isaiah 1 – 33*, p. 173; Wildberger, *Isaiah 1 – 12*, pp. 468–469.
5. H. G. M. Williamson, 'The Messianic Texts in Isaiah 1 – 39', in John Day (ed.), *King and Messiah in Israel and the Ancient near East, JSOTSup* (Sheffield: Sheffield Academic Press, 1998), pp. 238–270.

for the remnant of God's people (10:20–23; 11:11–13; 12:1–6). The opening word picture in 11:1 of a tree sprouting contrasts with the judgment oracle at the end of chapter 10 (vv. 33–34), which depicts the downfall of Assyria in terms of trees being felled by Yahweh.[6] The idyllic picture envisaged in Isaiah 11:1–9 whereby an anointed ruler ushers in a reign of harmony in all areas of life presents a stark contrast to the arrogant rule and military supremacy of the Assyrian king.

The remainder of Isaiah 11 comprises a historically specific oracle concerning the gathering of the diaspora community, and is almost certainly an exilic or post-exilic message of hope.[7] The verse immediately following our passage (11:10) is a bridge linking together the two promises of restoration in verses 2–9 and verses 11–18.[8] It develops the theme of the root of Jesse and adds a universal dimension to the ideas of verses 1–9.

One final preliminary comment concerns English translations of the Hebrew word *rûaḥ* and the phrase *rûaḥ yhwh*. Bible versions and commentaries adopt different policies as to whether the word should be capitalized, i.e. written as 'Spirit' rather than 'spirit', and whether to insert a definite article or not in construct phrases such as *rûaḥ mišpāṭ* ('*a/the* spirit of justice'), neither of which can be clearly determined from the Hebrew itself.[9] Seemingly small decisions such as these have significant interpretative consequences, and use of the definite article and capital 'S' may suggest a more definite and concrete understanding of *rûaḥ* than is warranted by the context, and may contribute to the tendency to ascribe later Christian trinitarian understandings of 'spirit' to the prophetic text. In recognition of this issue and of the wide semantic range of *rûaḥ*, this essay will refrain from capitalizing the word 'spirit' when referring to *rûaḥ* in English translation.

The spirit of Yahweh in Isaiah 11

Let us now look in more detail at the passage itself. The imagery of verse 1, as already noted, picks up the tree motif in the preceding chapter: a branch

---

6. See ibid., p. 261.
7. Wildberger, *Isaiah 1 – 12*, pp. 489–490; Clements, *Isaiah 1 – 39*, p. 264.
8. Clements, *Isaiah 1 – 39*, p. 122. He regards it as a rather clumsy attempt at joining the two passages (ibid., p. 125).
9. The exception to the latter point is a construct phrase with a proper noun, e.g. *rûaḥ yhwh*, since proper nouns are determinate (Joüon, 137.b, 139.a).

'will come forth from the stem [*gēzaʿ*] of Jesse' and 'a shoot from his root [*šārāš*] will bear fruit'. Most commentators assume that the picture is of a tree that has died or been cut down to a stump and is now regrowing, and take it to imply that the monarchy has, or will be, destroyed. However, despite English translations such as NRSV and NIV that render the unusual noun *gēzaʿ* as 'stump', the word may not denote a felled tree. In Isaiah 40:24, one of only two other occurrences of *gēzaʿ*, it clearly refers to the 'stem' of a newly planted shrub.[10] The picture painted in Isaiah 11:1 may similarly be that of a stem sprouting rather than the stump of a felled tree regrowing.[11] Given the reference to bearing fruit (*pārâ*), and First Isaiah's fondness for vineyard imagery to describe the people of Israel (e.g. Isa. 5:1–7; 27:2–6), it may call to mind a vine stock that has been hard pruned in the winter months so that the whole plant appears dead, ready for the spring growth. If so, Isaiah is not referring to the impending destruction of the monarchy. Rather, the prophet regards the pressures faced by the Judean monarchs as a form of 'pruning' by Yahweh, akin to the purifying announced in Isaiah 1:25–26, but this pruning will be followed by renewed and vigorous growth. This is particularly relevant to the reign of King Hezekiah, who experienced the pressure of threat from Assyria (Isa. 36 – 37) and grave personal sickness (Isa. 38), but also received a promise of deliverance by Yahweh, itself couched in terms of a plant regrowing, 'The surviving remnant of the house of Judah shall again take root [*šōreš*] downward, and bear fruit [*pĕrî*] upward' (Isa. 37:31).

The reference to Jesse in verse 1 is unusual, since apart from the genealogy in Ruth 4 and a postscript to Psalm 72, the father of King David is not mentioned outside the books of Samuel, Kings and Chronicles. The stories of David's anointing and accession to the throne in 1 Samuel, as well as Yahweh's covenant with him (2 Sam. 7), are so much part of Judah's traditions that merely an allusion is probably sufficient to call to mind the idealized era under King David. Unlike the Northern Kingdom, which was ruled by a succession of non-Davidic kings, Judah maintained the line of Davidic succession in its monarchy, and is here rewarded with the hope of a continuation of the political dynasty, as well as a reminder of Yahweh's faithfulness to his promise to David (2 Sam. 7:16).

The following verses offer a description of the characteristics of the coming ruler (vv. 2–3a) and his actions (vv. 3b–5). The opening line of verse 2,

---

10. The other is Job 14:8.

11. LXX interprets v. 1b in similar way: *kai anthos ek tēs rhizēs anabēsetai*, 'a blossom will go up from his root'.

'The spirit of Yahweh [*rûaḥ yhwh*] will settle upon him', raises the issue of who or what is meant by *rûaḥ yhwh*, and how it relates to the coming king. Is this an aspect of Yahweh himself, or reference to some human quality or qualities that are viewed as emanating from God? Is it a normal part of being a Davidic ruler, or something exceptional and perhaps unexpected? Let us see if light can be shed on this by other references to *rûaḥ yhwh* in First Isaiah.

Yahweh's spirit in Isaiah 1 – 39

There is no single, clear understanding of *rûaḥ* in connection with Yahweh in Isaiah 1 – 39, which is unsurprising given the breadth of meaning of the Hebrew word *rûaḥ* (wind/breath/spirit). Indeed some of the twenty-two occurrences of this word in Isaiah 1 – 39 are not of primary importance to our discussion, since they clearly refer to the physical phenomenon of wind, or to the human spirit or breath. This leaves about a dozen verses in which *rûaḥ* is used either to indicate an attribute or action of Yahweh, or which present him as the agent of *rûaḥ*.

In some instances the *rûaḥ* of Yahweh is the means by which he executes judgment, for example his strong wind (11:15) or the raging torrent of his breath (30:28; see also 27:8). Yahweh alters the course of nations and history by bestowing on human agents a particular 'spirit', which determines their actions, for example 'a spirit of confusion' (19:14) or a 'spirit of blindness' (29:10; see also 28:7). These verses clearly refer to some action or activity of Yahweh, but it seems that *rûaḥ* is somewhat external to Yahweh, evidence of his power as controller of the elements and shaper of human destinies, not a description of Yahweh.

In Isaiah 30:1 the 'rebellious children' of Yahweh are castigated for forming an alliance with Egypt, against Yahweh's 'spirit' and without asking his advice (v. 2). In this instance *rûaḥ* is clearly referring to Yahweh himself – his intention or will for Israel, as the NRSV translates (see also 34:16). The contrast between the power of the Egyptians and that of Yahweh in Isaiah 31:3 implicitly suggests that God is to be regarded as 'spirit' (*rûaḥ*) not flesh (*bāśār*).[12]

The remaining three references are more relevant to Isaiah 11 because they

12. This is not suggesting the kind of ontological, dualistic distinction between spirit and matter that is found in Greek philosophy. Rather what is being stressed is the weakness and impotence of human actions compared with the power of God. See Hans Wildberger, *Isaiah 28 – 39*, trans. T. H. Trapp (Minneapolis: Fortress, 2002 [Ger. 1982]), pp. 211–213.

each link together the coming of *rûaḥ* and the theme of justice or judgment.[13] In Isaiah 4:4, *rûaḥ mišpāṭ* is the means by which Yahweh brings about the purification of Jerusalem's inhabitants, the first part of the verse making clear that this is Yahweh himself at work. Similarly, the hope expressed in 28:5–6 is that Yahweh of hosts himself will become a spirit of justice (*rûaḥ mišpāṭ*) for his people as well as their crowning glory and honour. Although *rûaḥ mišpāṭ* is not one of the specific attributes of the Davidic king in Isaiah 11:2, the idea of the king as guarantor of justice in the land is a key feature of biblical thought and is strongly present in Isaiah 11, as we shall see.

Isaiah 32:14–20 speaks of the changes to be expected in a desolate land when Yahweh's spirit, 'a spirit from on high' (*rûaḥ mimmārôn*), is poured out (32:15).[14] The picture is of harmony in the physical world as the wilderness flourishes and animals live in contentment (32:15, 20; cf. 11:6–8) and of a society in which justice and righteousness reign and people experience safety and peace (32:16–18; cf. 11:4–5). The first part of Isaiah 32 also has themes in common with Isaiah 11, including the picture of an idyllic world in which the king and his princes will rule justly (v. 1; cf. 11:1), and the motif of hearing and seeing so favoured by Isaiah (32:3; cf. 11:3).

To summarize, the *rûaḥ* of Yahweh in First Isaiah expresses something of his action or intention with regard to the world in the context of both judgment and restoration. In some instances *rûaḥ* refers to a somewhat impersonal power of God that sets events in motion, elsewhere it seems to be an attribute of Yahweh himself. It is certain that, as Brueggemann notes, we should not think in terms of 'later trinitarian categories of the church'.[15] What then can we say of *rûaḥ yhwh* in Isaiah 11:2? First, the spirit of Yahweh is important for validating the role of the Davidic ruler, just as the presence and absence of *rûaḥ yhwh* signifies the rise of David and demise of Saul in 1 Samuel 16:13–14. Interestingly, this connection seems unique to Isaiah since there is no indication in Samuel or Kings that any future monarch after David is endowed with *rûaḥ yhwh* in this way, and even in Solomon's dream at Gibeon in which he asks for and receives wisdom, there is no mention of *rûaḥ* (1 Kgs 3). Second, in contrast to other passages in Isaiah, where Yahweh's spirit seems to act without the use of human intermediaries (e.g. 32:15), here it is bestowed on the king, signifying God's willingness to act through a divinely appointed

13. The Hebrew noun *mišpāṭ*, from the root *špṭ* meaning to judge or govern, can be translated as either 'judgment' or 'justice'.

14. Wildberger, *Isaiah 28 – 39*, p. 260.

15. Walter Brueggemann, *Isaiah 1 – 39* (Louisville: Westminster John Knox, 1998), p. 99.

human agent (see also the reworking of these ideas by the author of Second Isaiah in Isa. 61:1–2). The spirit of Yahweh will 'rest' or 'settle' (*rûaḥ*) on the king – an expression found in other significant transfers of power such as Yahweh's spirit empowering Moses' seventy elders in Numbers 11:25, and with reference to the handing on of the divine gift from Elijah to his successor Elisha in 2 Kings 2:15.[16]

The results of Yahweh's spirit

The 'settling' of the spirit is not a passive event; it results in the equipping and empowering of the king to fulfil the responsibilities of his office. Isaiah 11:2 lists a series of six qualities, arranged in three sets of pairs, with which the king will be endowed.[17] The possession of 'wisdom and understanding' will enable him to rule with wise discernment, and to judge righteously on behalf of the poor and afflicted (v. 2a). A 'spirit of counsel and might' will let him plan and act with confidence and strength, ensuring victory over his enemies and adversaries (v. 2b). Finally, he will exhibit the key features consistent with obedience to Yahweh, 'knowledge and fear of Yahweh', suggesting uprightness of character and recognition of his dependence upon God (v. 2b).

Let us now look at each of Isaiah's word pairs in more detail. The qualities of wisdom (*ḥokmâ*) and understanding (*bîn/bînâ/tĕbûnâ*) are clearly associated with the royal office – these same attributes are promised to Solomon in 1 Kings 3:12 (see also 4:29), although, as already noted, without mention of the spirit. They are directly linked with *rûaḥ* in two examples of non-royal individuals who are equipped for a task. In Exodus 31 Bezalel is filled with the spirit of God (*rûaḥ ʾĕlōhîm*) and with wisdom (*ḥokmâ*) and understanding (*tĕbûnâ*) to oversee construction of the tabernacle (v. 3), while in the wisdom tale of Joseph in Egypt Pharaoh recognizes Joseph as one 'in whom is the spirit of God' (Gen. 41:38) and who is discerning (*bîn*) and wise (*ḥākām*) like no other (v. 39). The spirit of Yahweh empowers people at all levels of responsibility for their God-given tasks.

The second word pair, counsel (*ʿēṣâ*) and might (*gĕbûrâ*), suggests both the ability to devise a plan or strategy and the heroic power to carry it out. The sense of 'counsel' is not so much the giving of advice to others but, as

---

16. In the case of Elisha, it is 'the spirit of Elijah' that is passed on (2 Kgs 2:15; see also 2 Kgs 2:9), however the following verse makes a clear link with *rûaḥ yhwh* (2 Kgs 2:16).

17. LXX adds a seventh quality – 'godliness' (*eusebias*).

commentators denote it, 'skill in political diplomacy',[18] or 'the ability to plot comprehensive strategy'.[19] Although in some contexts 'might' has military or warrior connotations, the same word pair occurs in Proverbs 8, along with *bînâ*, 'understanding', and *tûšîyâ*, another word meaning 'wisdom', as part of personified wisdom's self-description (vv. 13–17). Isaiah's picture of the future king incorporates all these qualities and is not merely that of a military conqueror akin to the king of Assyria. In a similar fashion, the list of royal titles in Isaiah 9 juxtaposes 'mighty God' and 'prince of peace' (Isa. 9:6). As Wildberger notes, 'Isaiah makes use of images commonly used when describing the ideology of kingship, but radically reshapes them to convey his expectations about peace.'[20]

The wisdom connections continue in the third word pair, knowledge (*daʿat*) and fear of Yahweh (*yirʾat yhwh*). This terminology is not generally associated with kingship, although David describes himself as 'one who rules over people justly, ruling in the fear of God' (2 Sam. 23:3). The concept of fearing Yahweh forms an important part of the theology of Deuteronomy (e.g. 6:2; 10:12), including stipulations concerning the monarch (Deut. 17:19). The lack of 'knowledge of God' (*daʿat ʾĕlōhîm*) features in Hosea's indictment of Israel (e.g. Hos. 4:1; 6:6). However, apart from Isaiah 11:2 and 33:6, these familiar concepts are only ever paired together in the book of Proverbs: 'the fear of the Lord is the beginning of knowledge' (Prov. 1:7); 'then you will understand the fear of the Lord and find the knowledge of God' (Prov. 2:5). In both instances, the phrase is part of a description of moral character that includes other qualities found in Isaiah's royal mandate, including wisdom, discernment, justice, righteousness and uprightness (Prov. 1:2–4; 2:1–10).

In Isaiah 11, the prophet's description of the coming king brings together wisdom traditions and those connected to royal ideology to present the picture of someone with the skill and wisdom to govern well and protect his land and his people, and with the attitude of humility and reverence towards Yahweh that will ensure God's continuing presence and protection. Verse 3 sums up this attitude as 'his delighting will be in the fear of Yahweh', or as Leupold puts it, 'all thinking and action will be in total submission to the divine will'.[21] There then follows a curious statement to the effect that the ruler will not judge according to what he sees or hears (v. 3b). The motif of seeing

---

18. Clements, *Isaiah 1 – 39*, p. 123.
19. H. C. Leupold, *Exposition of Isaiah Volume 1* (Welwyn: Evangelical Press, 1968), p. 217.
20. Wildberger, *Isaiah 1 – 12*, p. 472.
21. Leupold, *Isaiah*, p. 218.

and hearing occurs frequently in the book of Isaiah, with both negative (e.g. 6:10) and positive (e.g. 35:5–6) connotations, although here neither seems particularly appropriate. The verse suggests perhaps that the king will act impartially, rather than responding to false accusation or political pressure and gossip. But there is more to it than that, especially if we read it alongside other descriptions of kingship, such as in the book of Proverbs (e.g. Prov. 16:9–13; 25:2–3). The spirit of Yahweh gives his appointed monarch 'a share in God's capacity to see through the disputes which are presented to him, and therefore to arrive at a just judgement'.[22]

The spirit of Yahweh acts

Verses 4 and 5 continue the description of the anointed new ruler and make use of two powerful, and different, images to describe his action in the land.[23] The first concerns the power of the king's word to usher in a reign of righteousness and equity. His mouth will be a rod or sceptre (*šēbeṭ*) wielded against those who have corrupted his land and abused the afflicted (v. 4). The king's sceptre as a sign of his power and authority is evident in Psalm 2:9, and it is also the guarantor of equity in Psalm 45:7. Here Isaiah seems to stress the king's spoken ability rather than his physical might in battle. Lest the threat of killing the wicked in verse 4b seem overly violent, verse 5 reiterates the king's mandate to rule in righteousness and faithfulness. The shift of imagery in this verse is intended to emphasize the centrality of these qualities to his reign. The picture of a flowing robe needing to be securely fastened by a belt or waistcloth (*ʾēzôr*), may suggest that the whole of the king's reign will be girded or marked by his righteous actions. Alternatively the image may be more specific to the kingship, with this reference to the king's robes denoting 'his visible public platform'.[24] Using the same imagery, the royal Psalm 93 describes Yahweh as robed in majesty and girded (*ʾāzar*) with strength (v. 1).

---

22. Otto Kaiser, *Isaiah 1 – 12*, trans. J. Bowden, OTL, 2nd ed. (London: SCM, 1983 [Ger. 1981]), p. 257.
23. As a historically specific oracle addressed to a pre-exilic king of Judah, *hā-ʾāreṣ* undoubtedly signifies the land of Judah. In its later reinterpretation in post-exilic contexts and beyond, the word is given a more universal dimension (hence NRSV's 'earth' here and in v. 9).
24. Brueggemann, *Isaiah 1 – 39*, p. 101.

Peace with animals

With these word pictures, we come to the end of Isaiah's portrayal of the divinely appointed Davidic ruler and the direct results in human society of his reign. What follows is a broader description of a world in which wild animals pose no threat to domestic flocks or human beings. The shift from the concrete political situation of a Judean monarch to an idyllic paradisiacal world has led some scholars to regard Isaiah 11:1–9 as two separate oracles brought together under the hand of an exilic redactor.[25] But there is no reason why a single pre-exilic author should not have combined these two pictures of hope, particularly since both themes – that of an anticipated future ruler[26] and of a golden age of peace with animals[27] – are known from other, much earlier, Ancient Near Eastern traditions.

In Isaiah 11:6–8 the named creatures are linked with great artistry in a series of contrasting pairs and triads, and are intended to depict the scope of the harmony rather than provide a definitive list. The predators that formed an all too frequent part of life in ancient Judah – wolf, leopard and bear – are set alongside their helpless and frail prey – lamb, kid and heifer (vv. 6–7a), the wild untamed strength of a lion contrasts with the harnessed might of an ox (v. 7b), the unpredictability of a snake with the innocence of a small child (v. 8). What is not clear from the passage is whether this peaceful idyll is the result of, or in any way contingent upon, the king ruling justly and wisely, or whether it represents another, different outworking of *rûaḥ yhwh*. For Brueggemann it is the reordering of human relationships in the first part of the chapter that makes possible the transformation of creation.[28] The curse outlined in Genesis 3 and demonstrated in numerous prophetic texts (e.g. Hos. 4:1–3; Amos 8:4–8), in which human violation of God's order leads to disorder in creation, is here reversed and is a sign of the cosmic scope of the Davidic king's reign. Just as in Isaiah 32, it is the coming of God's spirit that provides the conditions for transformation, not just of human society but of the whole of creation.

Some have asked how this picture of harmony among animal species can be squared with contemporary scientific understanding, since predation and the food chain play such a key part in ecological systems.[29] Does it imply

---

25. E.g. Kaiser, *Isaiah 1 – 12*, pp. 253–254; see also Clements, *Isaiah 1 – 39*, p. 122.
26. See the Akkadian Prophecies in *ANET*[3], pp. 606–607.
27. See the paradise myth of Ensi and Nihursag in ibid., p. 38.
28. Brueggemann, *Isaiah 1 – 39*, p. 102.
29. E.g. Ronald E. Clements, 'The Wolf Shall Live with the Lamb: Reading Isaiah

cessation of the 'natural' order of creation, articulated elsewhere in the OT, in which some animals are dependent upon others for food?[30] What are we to make of the biological impossibility of a carnivore eating grass? These are hermeneutical questions without easy answers and there is not space to do more than offer a few comments in the context of 11:1–9 as a whole.[31] First, the whole passage is grounded (one might say rooted!) in Judah's understanding of her identity as God's chosen people as epitomized by the Davidic line (v. 1; see also v. 10).[32] What follows is the prophet's vision of a longed-for ideal: the transforming, Yahweh-empowered potential of Davidic kingship at its best, in place of the weak and ineffectual attempts at leadership provided by the pre-exilic monarchs. This includes the transformation of the relationship between human beings and the natural world, as well as a righting of the wrongs that plague society.

Second, the initiative is God's. As we have already seen, it is Yahweh's spirit that will be the empowering force behind the new ruler, who will himself act from a spirit of the knowledge and fear of Yahweh (vv. 2–3) to bring about justice and righteousness for the poor (vv. 3–5). The fulfilment of divine purpose and the consequent restoration of the fear of Yahweh in the world (vv. 2, 9) form the essential precondition for the reconstruction of society (vv. 4–5) and of the natural world (vv. 6–8). What has hitherto been impossible will now become possible.

Third, for the ancient prophets and their hearers, the two 'problems' addressed in this passage – injustice and violence in society and predation by wild animals – are both intractable, but are equally viewed as subject to Yahweh's control through his earthly representative. Since for many of us wild animals no longer present such a daily threat, it is harder for us to appreciate fully the significance of the hope held out in Isaiah 11 to the ordinary citizens of Judah – freedom from violence and predators, in both human and animal form. Our scientific knowledge means that we are more uncomfortable with the idea of the cessation of predation because it violates 'natural' laws, than with the restoration of justice throughout the world, which we

---

11:6–9 Today', in P. J. Harland and C. T. R. Hayward (eds.), *New Heaven and New Earth: Prophecy and the Millennium* (Leiden/Boston/Köln: Brill, 1999), pp. 83–99.

30. E.g. Ps. 104:21.

31. As well as discussion in the commentaries, see Clements, 'Reading Isaiah'; Emmanuel Nwaoru, 'Building a New World Order: A Perspective from Isaiah 11:6–9', *BN* 119/120 (2003), pp. 132–146.

32. See 1 Sam. 16:1; 2 Sam. 7:8–11.

assume (perhaps presumptuously) can be achieved through human efforts. Isaiah's depiction of perfection is not intended to negate the natural biological processes of the world, but rather to paint a wide picture of the potentiality of the reign of the king on whom the spirit of Yahweh rests.

Isaiah's vision broadens out in verse 9 to encompass the whole of Yahweh's 'holy mountain' – probably symbolizing the whole land, not just Mount Zion (cf. Exod. 15:17).[33] Although some have suggested that this verse forms a later addition to verses 6–8, it is unnecessary to separate it from what precedes it, since it sums up and interprets the description of peace with animals.[34] The knowledge of Yahweh that formed such an important part of the king's empowering (v. 2) now extends to fill the land, a theme repeated by the prophet Habakkuk (Hab. 2:14).[35] The simile 'as the waters cover the sea' is essentially descriptive, evoking the expanse of the oceans as a comparator for knowledge of Yahweh and emphasizing its availability to all.

Isaiah 11 reinterpreted

In the pre-exilic context in which this oracle originated, it served as a reminder to Judah of the continuation of the Davidic line and the coming of a new ruler who, as God's representative, would display the ideal qualities of Yahweh's anointed monarch. The prophet holds out the hope that in his reign the twin evils that plagued everyday life – injustice in society and predation by wild animals – will be overcome. In later centuries, after the destruction of Jerusalem and the end of the monarchy forced a radical reappraisal of earlier traditions, these words were gradually regarded as offering a more eschatological hope for the future. The concept of a Davidic messiah was quite likely already relatively established in Judaism by the start of the Christian era,[36] and was then taken up in early Christian interpretation.[37] As noted at the outset, these verses feature prominently in Christian liturgy; they are less important in Jewish Orthodox traditions, at least in part as a reaction against Christological

33. Clements, *Isaiah 1 – 39*, p. 124.

34. See Wildberger, *Isaiah 1 – 12*, pp. 467–468.

35. A liturgical formula according to Clements (*Isaiah 1 – 39*, p. 124).

36. William Horbury, *Messianism among Jews and Christians* (London/New York: T. & T. Clark, 2003), p. 131.

37. See Robert L. Wilken, et al. (eds.), *Isaiah: Interpreted by Early Christian and Medieval Commentators* (Grand Rapids/Cambridge: Eerdmans, 2007).

readings. However we interpret them today, it is important not to forget what a radical and dynamic message of hope this prophetic oracle would have offered to a hearer in pre-exilic Judah, and how central to this hope was the notion of being anointed with Yahweh's spirit.

13. ISAIAH 48:16: A TRINITARIAN ENIGMA?

Paul D. Wegner

It is somewhat remarkable that a clause of just five Hebrew words at the end of verse 16 can give rise to such a lengthy debate among scholars over the centuries. At issue is a shift in speaker in the middle of the verse with little indication from context as to the identity of this new speaker. This debate over Isaiah 48:16b has continued for almost seventeen hundred years, going back at least as far as Origen of Alexandria (185–254) who argued that the servant (or 'Messiah') is speaking:

> That the Savior and the Holy Spirit were sent by the Father is made clear in Isaiah when, speaking in the person of the Savior, it is said, *And now the Lord has sent me and his Spirit* (48:16). It must however, be recognized that this passage is ambiguous. Either God sent, and also the Holy Spirit sent the Savior, or as we understand it, the Father sent both, the Savior and the Holy Spirit.[1]

However, others, such as Theodoret of Cyrus (or Cyrrhus) (c. 393 – c. 457), have been just as certain that the prophet himself is the speaker:

---

1. Robert Louis Wilken, et al., *Isaiah Interpreted by Early Christian and Medieval Commentators*, The Church's Bible (Grand Rapids: Eerdmans, 2007), p. 360.

> It is the prophet who speaks here. I do not speak in my own name, he says, but as one who has been sent by the God of all and the all-holy Spirit. He clearly shows that there is another being referred to besides the person of God [the Father] . . . For he says *The Lord sent me and his spirit* (48:16).[2]

This debate has continued throughout church history and it is not uncommon for modern scholars to suggest that the speaker in this passage is 'the Servant' who turns out to be Messiah. A good example is E. J. Young, who argues as follows:

> The speaker is the Servant *par excellence*, already introduced in 42:1ff., and about to be brought more prominently into the picture in the chapters forty-nine, fifty, and fifty-three. Here he declares that God had sent him, for he is the true instrument who will accomplish the great redemption that alone can bring well-being and peace.[3]

Once scholars have identified the speaker as 'the Servant', it is a natural transition to argue that 'the Spirit of God' is 'the Holy Spirit'. Millard J. Erickson states:

> The expression 'Spirit of God' could well be understood as being simply a reference to the will, mind, or activity of God. There are, however, some cases where the New Testament makes it clear that an Old Testament reference to the 'Spirit of God' is a reference to the Holy Spirit. One of the most prominent of these New Testament passages is Acts 2:16–21, where Peter explains that what is occurring at Pentecost is the fulfilment of the prophet Joel's statement, 'I will pour out my Spirit upon all flesh' (2:28). Surely the events of Pentecost were the realization of Jesus' promise, 'You shall receive power when the Holy Spirit has come upon you' (Acts 1:8). In short, the Old Testament 'Spirit of God' is synonymous with the Holy Spirit.[4]

If 'the Servant' *par excellence* is speaking and if the 'Spirit of God' is synonymous with the 'Holy Spirit', then all three persons of the Godhead are mentioned in this verse.[5] It seems odd, however, that this book would refer to the Trinity,

---

2. Ibid., p. 361.
3. E. J. Young, *The Book of Isaiah: The English Text, with Introduction, Exposition, and Notes*, NICOT (Grand Rapids: Eerdmans, 1972), III:259. See also J. Alec Motyer, *Isaiah: An Introduction and Commentary*, TOTC (Downers Grove: InterVarsity Press, 1999), pp. 304–305.
4. M. J. Erickson, *Christian Theology* (Grand Rapids: Baker, 1985), p. 866.
5. Wayne Grudem states, 'In fact, from a full New Testament perspective (which recognizes Jesus the Messiah to be the true servant of the Lord predicted in

even in such a veiled form, since polytheism was a significant problem during the time of the OT. Israel's religion was monotheistic (Deut. 6:4) and multiple persons in the Godhead would have been construed as polytheism. Even Jesus' claim in the NT to be the 'Son of God' brought a charge of blasphemy because it threatened the early Jews' core beliefs about the nature of God (Matt. 26:63–65; Luke 22:70–71). However, the foundation for this interpretation is built upon the initial identification of the speaker in this verse being 'the Servant', who is fulfilled by Jesus; but if he is not the speaker, then the whole edifice crumbles. Thus this passage is central to our examination of the Spirit in the OT.

The context

Isaiah 48:16 is situated toward the end of the first major section (Isa. 40 – 48),[6] or possibly the middle (40 – 55),[7] in the second half of the book of Isaiah. This section begins with the announcement of the return of the Israelites from Babylon, which serves primarily to praise God for the great deliverance he is initiating. Seven times God proclaims he was the one who brought Cyrus to deliver his people (41:2–4, 25–26; 42:1–9; 44:28 – 45:7; 45:13; 46:11; 48:14–15); he states thirteen times that no idol or other god could have done such a thing (40:18–20; 41:5–7, 21–24, 29; 45:5–6, 16, 20–21; 46:1–2, 5–7; 47:12–15; 48:5). The conclusion appears to be that Israel's God is truly amazing – he did what no other god could do in effecting so great a deliverance.

Chapter 48 continues the theme of Babylon's destruction begun in chapters 46 – 47, with God confirming to the Israelites that he orchestrated this great victory and used Cyrus to deliver them.[8] Yet there has been significant discussion as to whether Isaiah 48 can be considered a structural or thematic

---

Isaiah's prophecies), Isaiah 48:16 has Trinitarian implications: "And now the Lord God has sent me and his Spirit," if spoken by Jesus the Son of God, refers to all three persons of the Trinity' (*Systematic Theology: An Introduction to Biblical Doctrine* [Grand Rapids: Zondervan, 1994], pp. 228–229).

6. Young, *Isaiah*, III:12–13; J. N. Oswalt, *The Book of Isaiah, Chapters 40 – 66*, NICOT (Grand Rapids: Eerdmans, 1998), pp. 8–9.
7. Since the time of B. Duhm this has become very popular (*Das Buch Jesaja* [Göttingen: Vandenhoeck & Ruprecht, 1892, 4th ed., 1922], pp. 18–19).
8. Joseph Blenkinsopp, *Isaiah 40 – 55. A New Translation with Introduction and Commentary*, AB 19A (New York: Doubleday, 2000), p. 293. Both Babylonian and Assyrian records confirm the conquest of Babylon by Cyrus (*ANET*[3], pp. 314–316).

unity.[9] The first sixteen verses exhibit a consistent flow of thought with several elements further explained in later verses; a break then appears in verse 17 with the standard prophetic indicator, 'Thus says the LORD.' However, the abrupt change in speaker right before this in verse 16b gives rise to significant questions regarding its unity.[10] Torrey argued that this phrase suggests the entire passage has been re-read by a glossator, possibly from the circle of 'Third Isaiah'.[11] However, we agree with Blenkinsopp's response that this hypothesis 'would not explain why v. 16b is either a fragment of a longer statement [and how it got separated from the longer section] or [why it is] syntactically awkward to the point of unintelligibility'.[12] Some scholars have suggested that verse 16b should be connected to Isaiah 49:1–6 (and possibly even 50:4–9) where a prophet or redactor also speaks in the first person.[13] However, this suggestion has the same problems as Torrey's, as well as making it more difficult to identify who is speaking, for 49:3 claims that the 'servant' who is speaking is Israel, but in Isaiah 48:16 Israel appears to be the one being exhorted to listen and thus could not be speaking. None of the various emendations in *BHS* improve significantly the meaning of the text,[14] and there is little evidence for any of them.[15] One other suggestion with possible merit

---

9. R. F. Melugin, *The Formation of Isaiah 40 – 55*, BZAW 141 (Berlin: de Gruyter, 1976), pp. 39–41, 137–142; Beuken, *Jesaja*, 2:277–278. John Goldingay points out an interesting parallel structure in ch. 48: 'We have noted the way in which parallelism between whole units such as 42:18–25 and 43:22–28 accompanies parallelism within lines in Hebrew poetry. Here in chapter 48, verses 12–19 stand in a parallel relationship to verses 1–11. They begin with the exhortation to Jacob-Israel to *listen*, and they repeat it twice more as the prophet seeks yet again to grasp Jacob-Israel by the lapels verbally and shake it into a response (John Goldingay, *Isaiah*, NIBCOT [Peabody: Hendrickson, 2001], p. 276).
10. Blenkinsopp, *Isaiah 40 – 55*, p. 292. B. Duhm's argument that this phrase is a gloss (*Jesaja*, p. 365) does little to account for why it aligns so poorly in context; in fact if anything, it is harder to account for it as a gloss.
11. C. C. Torrey, *The Second Isaiah: A New Interpretation* (Edinburgh: T. & T. Clark, 1928), p. 378. See also K. Elliger, *Deuterojesaja in seinem Verhältnis zu Tritojesaja*, BWANT, 63 (Stuttgart: Kohlhammer, 1933), pp. 185–198, 254–258.
12. Blenkinsopp, *Isaiah 40 – 55*, p. 294.
13. C. Westermann, *Isaiah 40 – 66*, OTL (Philadelphia: Westminster, 1969), p. 203.
14. See also Blenkinsopp, *Isaiah 40 – 55*, pp. 292, 294.
15. This reading is supported by 1QIsa[a], partially by 4QIsa[d] (ועתה אד[ני יהו]ה), LXX, Syriac Peshitta, and Latin Vg. It is not found in 4QIsa[c].

is that the statement is a positive response from Cyrus to the mission that Yahweh has for him.[16] In that case verse 16b is an integral part of the passage. The main difficulty is accounting for the switch in voice – verses 14–15 refer to Cyrus in the third person, but in verse 16b Cyrus speaks directly in the first person.

Goldingay points out an interesting parallel structure within the larger unit of Isaiah 48, but he appears to have missed the similar wording of verses 12 and 16 that may act as an *inclusio* by using the repeated commands to 'listen' and 'draw near, listen to this' along with the phrases 'I am the first, I am also the last' and 'from the time it took place I was there'. These phrases enclose the two reasons God can be believed: (1) he formed the universe; and (2) he used Cyrus to deliver his people. Thus the structure is as follows:

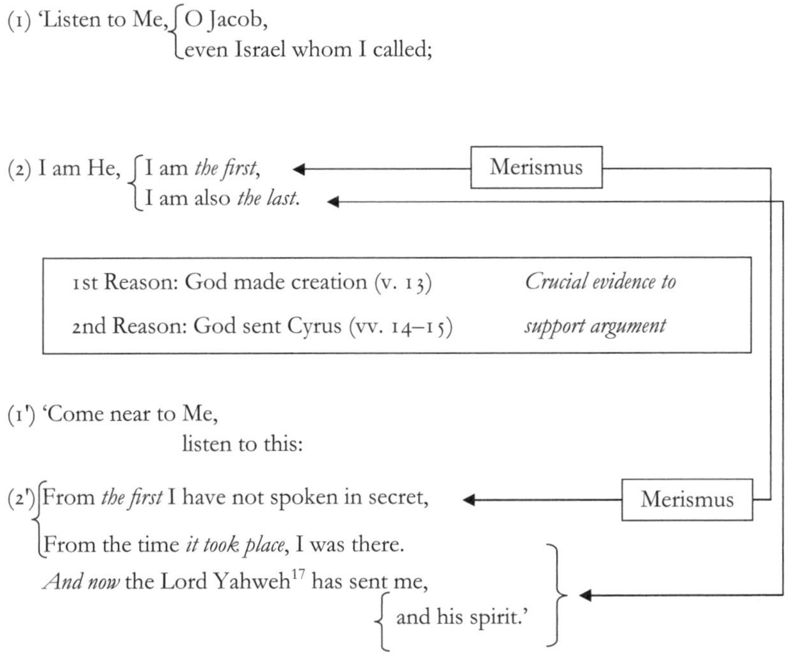

(1) 'Listen to Me, O Jacob,
even Israel whom I called;
(2) I am He, I am the first,
I am also the last.
Merismus
1st Reason: God made creation (v. 13)
2nd Reason: God sent Cyrus (vv. 14–15)
Crucial evidence to support argument
(1') 'Come near to Me,
listen to this:
(2') From the first I have not spoken in secret,
From the time it took place, I was there.
Merismus
And now the Lord Yahweh[17] has sent me,
and his spirit.'

16. J. L. McKenzie, *Second Isaiah: Introduction and Notes*, AB 20 (New York: Doubleday, 1968), p. 99. Blenkinsopp dismisses this possibility, but gives no arguments against such a suggestion (*Isaiah 40 – 55*, p. 294). McKenzie argues as follows: 'It could be attributed to the prophet himself; but Second Isaiah never elsewhere claims the spirit for himself. The connection between the spirit and the person sent is loose, and the syntax is unusual; Yahweh is not said to "put" his spirit upon the one sent.

If this structure is correct, then the final phrase is crucial to the author/editor's argument and is a reasonable conclusion to this section. Verse 16 parallels verse 12, beginning with God speaking. He assures his listeners that he did not hide his plans even from the beginning, and that he has been there all the time even up to their completion. The major question is: what does 'it took place' refer to? 'From the first' could refer to creation (i.e. the first example, v. 13) or when he first told Israel that Cyrus was coming, but either way the key element is that God has continued to make his will known (i.e. from the first he has not spoken in secret). Thus the purpose for the Hebrew word *min* in these phrases is to refer to an extent of time. Then 'from the time it took place' could be God sending Cyrus (i.e. second example, vv. 14–15), or it could refer to both examples, but the crucial element is that God is still there (overseeing the process). Thus 'and now' must contrast to the phrase 'from the beginning' God was overseeing the process 'and now' it is complete (i.e. God has brought me [Cyrus?] and his spirit).

Exegesis of verses 12–16

The unit begins in verse 12 with Yahweh calling Jacob to listen to him and the parallel phrase confirms his addressee. However, the most important part of this verse is God's depiction of himself: 'I am he, I am the first, I am also the last.' These two phrases not only indicate that God is eternal, but the parallel units also suggest that God is personally involved in bringing about all the events of history. He then references two actions that confirm his sovereignty: (1) creating the universe (vv. 13–14a), and (2) bringing Cyrus to deliver his people (vv. 14b–15). It is startling that God chooses these two events to

---

It must be granted that this is not a convincing argument; but if this line be attributed to the prophet, it raises some serious questions about his conception of this own mission. For this reason we make the line the imagined response of Cyrus to the commission which has just been described. The spirit is the charismatic principle of action in men who accomplish Yahweh's purpose; and Cyrus has been given nearly every title of the charismatic agent except the spirit in preceding passages (xli 2–3, 25, xliv 28–xlv 5, xlvi 11). To put these words in his mouth is not a violent departure from the picture of Cyrus which thus emerges' (*Second Isaiah*, p. 99).

17. The compound name for God occurs 302 times in the OT and 26 times in Isaiah (12 times in the first 39 chapters; 14 times in the latter 27 chapters).

underscore his sovereignty, for he puts them both on a par (i.e. creation and bringing Cyrus are both equally miraculous). To drive home his point further, God asks who else could have done these things (v. 14a). The implication is that no-one else could have accomplished such amazing deeds and therefore God deserves praise. God's plan for Cyrus is just as certain as God's action of creation. Verse 16 concludes the section with a call to Israel to listen to him. This refrain is similar to Isaiah 45:19 and emphasizes the fact that God previously declared these events – they were not done in secret. In Isaiah 45:19 God is clearly the speaker with no change of speaker as in Isaiah 48:16. God could have kept his deeds secret, but instead he chose to declare them to anyone who would listen. The emphatic sentence structure of verse 16, beginning with the negation (*lōʾ*) and concluding that unit with the verb, assures us that God never spoke in secret even from the very beginning.[18] 'The first (or beginning)' probably refers to the time God began speaking to his people through the prophets; in fact, the purpose of the prophets was to inform his people of God's plan. What a significant contrast to pagan gods who were clothed in secrecy and whose messages were only for the initiated few. Because of Yahweh's clear revelation, Israel would be without excuse. The next phrase assures us that God was present from 'the time it happened'; the pronoun most likely refers to the events God told his people about up to the most recent deliverance from Babylon. The word 'there' (*šām*) is apparently placed again for emphasis, suggesting God's closeness in watching over these events in their entirety. George A. D. Knight argues that the phrase 'and now' refers to the 'contemporary moment' of Deutero-Isaiah.[19] While this may be possible, this is not how the phrase 'and now' is commonly used (as we will see later) and in context it more likely refers to the time of Cyrus's arrival.[20]

Another important question is if the Lord alone is sending the person, or

---

18. See Young, *Isaiah*, III:258.
19. George A. D. Knight, *Servant Theology: A Commentary on Isaiah 40 – 55*, ITC (Grand Rapids: Eerdmans, 1984), p. 120. Young makes an interesting leap by stating: '*And now* sets forth a significant contrast. As so often employed in the prophecy, these words present the contrast between the old dispensation and the new. It is in looking forward to the new dispensation that they are here employed' (*Isaiah*, III:258–259).
20. Waltke and O'Connor mention an emphatic use that may fit here well, but temporal seems unlikely (B. K. Waltke and M. O'Connor, *Biblical Hebrew Syntax* [Winona Lake: Eisenbrauns, 1990], para. 39.3.4f.); cf. each of the other uses in Isaiah (5:3; 16:14; 28:22; 36:8, 10; 37:20; 43:1; 44:1; 49:5; 52:5; 64:7).

if the Lord and his spirit are doing the sending. It seems most likely that the Lord alone is sending, based upon the arrangement of the Hebrew words in the verse (i.e. generally compound subjects are placed together).[21]

So who is the speaker in verse 16b? If this passage is indeed bound by an *inclusio* (vv. 12–16) as noted above, then God would most likely be the speaker at the beginning of verse 16 as context and the parallel unit suggest. Also in Isaiah 45:19 almost the exact same wording is spoken by God and God is clearly speaking in first person up until this verse. If God is speaking in the first three units of verse 16, then there is a clear change in speaker for the last phrase, for the Lord Yahweh is distinguished from the speaker. The God who is sending cannot also be the one who is being sent. The speaker has been variously identified as: Isaiah,[22] Deutero-Isaiah,[23] Trito-Isaiah,[24] his servant (i.e. the Messiah),[25] or Cyrus.[26] Let's now turn to the identity of the speaker.[27]

His servant (i.e. the Messiah)

Some passages in the second half of Isaiah have been picked up in the NT and applied to Christ (primarily in what are called 'the servant songs'; Isa. 42:1–4 [Matt. 12:18–21]; Isa. 53:1 [John 12:38]; Isa. 53:4–5 [Matt. 8:17]; Isa. 53:7–8 [Acts 8:32–33]; Isa. 53:12 [Luke 22:37]; Isa. 61:1–2 [Luke 4:18–19]),

---

21. Young, *Isaiah*, III:259; R. N. Whybray, *Isaiah 40 – 66*, NCBC (Grand Rapids: Eerdmans, 1975), p. 132. The normal Hebrew order would have the two subjects together joined by a *wāw* conjunction (see examples in GKC, para. 146).
22. *The Targum of Isaiah*, ed. and trans. J. F. Stenning (Oxford: Clarendon, 1949), p. 164; J. Calvin, *Commentary on the Book of the Prophet Isaiah*, trans. W. Pringle, 22 vols., reprint (Grand Rapids: Baker, 1981), VIII:483–484; Oswalt, *Isaiah 40 – 66*, p. 278. Oswalt points out a similar abrupt change in speaker in Zech. 2:12, 13 (ET 8, 9) and in that case it is clearly the prophet speaking – see v. 15 (ET 11).
23. Knight, *Servant Theology*, p. 120; Whybray, *Isaiah 40 – 66*, p. 132; Blenkinsopp, *Isaiah 40 – 55*, p. 294.
24. Elliger, 'Der Prophet Tritojesaja', *ZAW* n.s. 8 (1931), pp. 112–140; Westermann, *Isaiah 40 – 66*, p. 203.
25. Motyer, *Isaiah*, p. 304; Young, *Isaiah*, III:259; B. S. Childs, *Isaiah*, OTL (Louisville: Westminster John Knox, 2001), pp. 377–378.
26. McKenzie, *Second Isaiah*, p. 99.
27. It is grammatically possible for this structure to be an epexegetical *waw* on the last part of the phrase allowing it to be translated 'even his spirit', but this translation would personify the spirit which happens nowhere else in the OT and it would be the only place in the OT that the spirit would be speaking.

but it cannot be assumed that these passages are simply direct fulfilments of the OT passages. NT authors appear to have used a variety of techniques for applying OT passages (i.e. typology, *plēroō*, filling up with more meaning, *pesher* [or midrash], etc.). Still some scholars understand this passage to refer directly to the Messiah. J. Alec Motyer clearly states:

> Once more the word of God is the initial and initiating factor, now seen in the sending of an unnamed speaker. We are told, however, that he is sent by the *Sovereign* L*ORD* (*ʾădōnāy*) and *endowed* with *his Spirit*. The only Spirit-endowed person in these chapters is the Servant (42:1), and in the immediate context the divine designation 'Lord Yahweh' occurs in the third Servant Song as endowing (50:4), directing (50:5) and helping (50:7) the Servant.[28]

Motyer also notes that Isaiah mentions the endowment of the Spirit nine times, five of which refer to the Messiah.[29] However, if we look more closely at these five passages, only one (Isa. 11:2) certainly refers to the Messiah – the rest are doubtful. The most common entity that is endowed by God's spirit is the remnant (32:15; 44:3; 59:21; 63:11), but others are also mentioned (e.g. the servant, 42:1; Isaiah or the Messiah, 61:1). The remnant may be referred to with either singular (44:3; 59:11; see also: 41:9–16) or plural pronouns (41:17; 42:16, 24; 43:6, 10, 12, etc.), but the remnant seems unlikely in this passage since it is not mentioned in context. Another argument that Motyer uses is that the Lord has sent his servant endowed 'with' his spirit. While a *waw* can be used as 'accompaniment',[30] it is a fairly rare usage. We would not assume this interpretation without some hint in context – a conjunction would be more likely here. If the servant is speaking in verse 16b as Motyer suggests, there is no hint from the context and just four verses later Jacob is called 'his servant'. Thus there is reasonable doubt that Isaiah 48:16b refers to the Messiah. The basis of Young's argument that this phrase refers to the Messiah is that the phrase 'and now' refers to a new dispensation, one in which 'A contrast is to be introduced between the prophets of the Old Testament and the Son of the New (Heb. 1:1, 2)'.[31] However, it seems

---

28. Motyer, *Isaiah*, p. 304.
29. Ibid. Motyer indicates that the following passages from Isaiah mention the endowment of the Spirit: 11:2; 30:1; 32:15; 42:1; 44:3; 48:16; 59:21; 61:1; 63:11.
30. R. J. Williams, *Williams' Hebrew Syntax*, revised and expanded by John C. Beckman, 3rd ed. (Toronto: University of Toronto Press, 2009), p. 154, para. 436.
31. Young, *Isaiah*, III:259.

more likely from the context that the 'and now' is contrasted to the temporal elements previously mentioned in the verse: 'from the first' (*mērōʾš*) and 'from the time it took place' (*mēʿēt hĕyôtāh*). The context indicates that God's plan had been well conceived and that even from the time he said he would send Cyrus, he was watching over the events to guide and oversee them. Then God sent the referent and his Spirit to accomplish his plan. Childs argues that chapter 48 is a transition passage from God's agent, Cyrus, to his servant (i.e. Messiah).[32] However, the difficulty is that God's servant is said to be Israel (or Jacob) in 48:20 and 49:3, though there may be a change in the identity of the servant in 49:5 where it states that the servant's mission is to bring Israel back to God.

The author (Isaiah, Deutero-Isaiah, or Trito-Isaiah)

We will discuss these three interpretations together since the same logic applies to each. Oswalt notes that the interpretation of this passage as referring to the prophet Isaiah goes back at least as far as John Calvin:

> This is surely another case of the close identity between God and the prophet. God has been speaking through the prophet. He calls the people to listen because of all he (God) has revealed himself in the events of their lives. Now, the prophet says, God is speaking again through me (the prophet) whom he (God) has inspired with his (God's) spirit. To be sure, God is saying some shocking things, but if past experience teaches anything, it ought to teach you to stop quibbling and believe what I, the inspired prophet, am saying.[33]

A good example of what Oswalt calls a 'close identity between God and the prophet' is found in Isaiah 7:10–14, for verse 10 says that the Lord spoke again to Ahaz and yet it appears to be Isaiah speaking. In verse 13 it becomes very clear that Isaiah must be speaking when he states: 'Is it a little thing for you to try the patience of men, that you will even try the patience of my God?' (my translation). Thus in this passage God and his prophet seem to be intricately related (i.e. when God speaks, Isaiah speaks). This interconnectedness is also seen in God's statement that he has not 'spoken in secret' (v. 16), the implication being that he used the prophet to proclaim his message to his people. However, the interconnectedness between God and the prophet is much less clear in the second part of Isaiah.

---

32. Childs, *Isaiah*, p. 377.
33. Oswalt, *Isaiah*, p. 278.

Blenkinsopp believes the author is Second Isaiah and argues somewhat differently:

> The authorial voice is first heard, appropriately, at the beginning of chs. 40 – 48 and is, significantly, accompanied by other prophetic voices (40:6; . . .). We hear it again at the beginning of the second major section 49 – 54(55) – that is, 49:1–6, in which a prophetic servant of Yahveh speaks of his mission. . .
>
> Though it is discourse of Yahveh, Isa 59:21 deserves mention in this connection since it is addressed to a spirit-endowed prophetic figure who is assured that he will have descendants – meaning, in the context, disciples. The individual prophetic voice is then heard for the last time in 61:1–4, a passage that combines spirit-endowment with being sent on a mission and is therefore closely related to 48:16b . . . These continuities may be explained with reference to a prophetic *diacochē* descending from the inspired figure conventionally referred to as Second Isaiah.[34]

Isaiah 59:21 is an interesting passage, but it appears to refer to Zion mentioned earlier (v. 20). In addition the second-person singular forms continue into the next chapter which clearly refers to Zion (see Isa. 60:10, 'your walls', and 60:11, 'your gates'). Also Isaiah 49:1–4 appears to refer to Israel as God's servant, as verse 3 clearly states. Thus several of the first-person forms suggest other referents rather than the author.

Cyrus

The most likely person to speak is Cyrus, for he is just mentioned in the near context, but this would demand an awkward change in voice from third person to first person. Nevertheless, it is not uncommon for the author/redactor of the second part of Isaiah to refer to a person/nation in the third person and then allow him/it to speak in the first person (e.g. the herald in 40:6; God in 43:1, 10, 14, 16–19; 44:2, 6, 9–20, 24; 45:11, 18–25; etc.; Babylon in 47:10). Verse 15 indicates that Yahweh 'called him' and 'brought him', which certainly suggests the idea of sending (v. 16). The phrase 'and now' in the second part of Isaiah is often used to indicate a summary or conclusion to an earlier statement (43:1; 44:1; 47:8; 48:16; 49:5; 52:5; 64:7). Thus the translation would be 'from the beginning I have not spoken in secret [when he announced Cyrus was coming], from the time it took place [Cyrus's actual coming] I was there, so now [summary] the Lord Yahweh has send me [Cyrus] and his spirit'. This passage begins with God describing the deliverance that

34. Blenkinsopp, *Isaiah 40 – 55*, pp. 294–295.

he will bring about through Cyrus and then appears to end by proclaiming in Cyrus's own words that God has sent him to do a job. In context there are only two people mentioned, God and Cyrus – it seems unlikely that the reader is to assume someone outside the context.

Conclusion

While it is difficult to determine who is speaking in Isaiah 48:16, the most reasonable arguments are for either the author/editor or Cyrus. However, if one argues for the author/editor, then the referent of the first-person pronoun must be obtained from outside the passage. The passage may be a combination of sources brought together into a unity whose flow of thought is difficult to follow, or the author/editor may demand that a reader assume a referent from outside the context. But we believe it is more reasonable to use the context to determine the speaker and in context only two people are mentioned: God and Cyrus. There are a significant number of examples in the book of Isaiah where a person or nation is first described in the third person, followed by a direct discourse in the first person (Isa. 40:6; 43:1, 10, 14, 16–19; 44:2, 6, 16–17, 19–20, 24; 45:11, 18–25; 47:10). Thus we have precedence for this structure in the book of Isaiah. The phrase 'but/and now' appears to indicate that God has declared Cyrus's coming (from the beginning), he oversaw it (i.e. 'I was there'), 'and now' (i.e. as a conclusion) Cyrus has come.

We can now answer the question posed in the title: is Isaiah 48:16 a trinitarian enigma? We have raised serious objections to identifying the speaker in this verse as the Servant (or 'the Son'), thus negating the possibility that this verse refers to the Trinity. Even if the speaker was the 'Son of God' in the person of the Messiah, this would certainly not be how readers at the time would have understood it. In addition, this passage is never quoted in the NT to suggest the Trinity and it would be wise to follow this lead. In the OT 'one's spirit' is a nebulous concept usually connected with one's inner being, power or entity, but when God's 'spirit' is mentioned, it is generally pictured more in what it accomplishes. God's spirit is his power emanating from himself to empower people to do a job. This appears to be exactly what is happening here. God called Cyrus to conquer the Babylonians and God sent his power to make sure that the task is accomplished.

14. JOEL'S PROMISE OF THE SPIRIT

Erika Moore

In Joel 2:28–29 (Heb. 3:1–2)[1] the prophet Joel, son of Pethuel, proclaims, 'And afterwards, I will pour out my Spirit on all people. Your sons and daughters will prophesy, your old men will dream dreams, your young men will see visions. Even on my servants, both men and women, I will pour out my Spirit in those days.'[2] These verses are the only place in the book of Joel where the Spirit is mentioned. The identity of the prophet Joel (whose name means 'Yah[weh] is God'), his father, and the dating of the book are unknown. There is insufficient data to identify the author with any of the dozen or so men by that name in the OT.[3] Furthermore, since the temple is assumed to

1. English versions following LXX and Vg extend ch. 2 to v. 32, thus linking 2:18–27 more closely with vv. 28–32 which form ch. 3 (vv. 1–5) in the MT. This subdivision first appeared in the sixteenth century in the Second Rabbinic Bible. See Hans Walter Wolff, *A Commentary on the Books of the Prophets Joel and Amos*, Hermeneia (Philadelphia: Fortress, 1977), pp. 8, 57. Throughout the discussion English versification will be used with Hebrew equivalents in brackets.
2. Scripture quotations are taken from NIV unless otherwise indicated.
3. See Raymond Dillard, 'Joel', in Thomas McComiskey (ed.), *An Exegetical and Expository Commentary: The Minor Prophets* (Grand Rapids: Baker, 1992), p. 239. LXX, Peshitta and Codex Leningradensis read *Bethuel*, the name of Rebekah's father

be up and operating (1:13–16; 2:15–17), the period of 586–516 BCE can be ruled out as the date for the book. Other factors, including identified enemies (Phoenicians, Philistines, Egyptians, Edomites, Greeks and Sabeans, see 3:4, 6, 8, 19 [4:4, 6, 8, 19]) and unmentioned enemies (Assyrians, Babylonians), lack of any references to the monarchy coupled with the references to elders and priests in leadership roles (1:2, 13; 2:16), lack of any reference to the northern kingdom coupled with the use of 'Israel' as a reference to Judah, the lack of a polemic against idolatry, and the placement of the book between Hosea and Amos have led to suggestions ranging from the ninth century BCE (E. J. Young) to the late fifth to fourth centuries BCE (A. Weiser, H. W. Wolff), to the second century BCE (Duhm).[4] This absence of historical specificity in the book should not be seen as a problem to be solved, but rather as a key to the book of Joel's function in the canon of Scripture. Dillard notes, 'The fact that the Book of Joel resists attempts to date it may in part reflect another important characteristic of the book. Several features suggest that the book of Joel as a whole is either a liturgical text intended for repeated use on occasions of national lament or at least a historical example of one such lament.'[5]

There are two distinct sections to the book. The first half (1:2 – 2:17) recounts a national crisis in which a devastating locust plague has ravished the land. It is not clear whether the descriptions given by Joel are meant to describe a literal locust plague (Cohen, Prior), a foreign army invading the land (Stuart), or an apocalyptic army commanded by God on judgment day (Achtemeier).[6] Crenshaw, following Wolff, argues that the initial reference to

---

(Gen. 22:22–23). See Elizabeth Achtemeier, *Minor Prophets 1*, NIBCOT (Peabody: Hendrickson, 1996), p. 116.

4. See Leslie C. Allen, *The Books of Joel, Obadiah, and Micah*, NICOT (Grand Rapids: Eerdmans, 1976), pp. 19–25; Raymond Dillard and Tremper Longman III, *An Introduction to the Old Testament* (Grand Rapids: Zondervan, 1994), pp. 365–367.

5. Dillard, 'Joel', p. 243. Calvin's sensible observation is worth noting: 'But as there is no certainty, it is better to leave the time in which he taught undecided; and, as we shall see, this is of no great importance' (*Commentaries on the Twelve Minor Prophets*, The Calvin Society, vol. II, trans. John Owen [Grand Rapids: Baker, 2005], p. xv).

6. A. Cohen, *The Twelve Prophets: Hebrew Text & English translation with Introductions and Commentary* (New York: Soncino, 1994), p. 57; David Prior, *The Message of Joel, Micah & Habakkuk*, BST (Downers Grove: InterVarsity Press, 1998), p. 66; Douglas Stuart, *Hosea-Jonah*, WBC (Dallas: Word, 1987), p. 245; Elizabeth Achtemeier, *Minor Prophets I*, pp. 134–135. See also James McKeon, 'Joel', *The New Dictionary of Biblical Theology*, eds. T. Desmond Alexander and Brian S. Rosner (Leicester: Inter-Varsity

locusts does not rule out 'a wider referent to an actual army which is normally associated with coming from the north'.[7] The prophet describes the devastation and urges the people of Judah to respond ('even now', 2:12) with personal (2:12–14) and national (2:15–17) fasting and prayer, and with priestly intervention which was a common practice in response to calamity.

The divine response introduces the second half of the book (2:18 – 3:21 [4:21]). Joel does not record the people's response to his commands, but the fact that the Lord responds the way he does indicates that they had indeed obeyed the prophetic command and repented. There is a further subdivision in this second half between the Lord's reply to the immediate disaster of the locust plague (2:18–27) and his answer to the impending crisis (2:28 – 3:21 [3:1 – 4:21]) that had been predicted in 2:1–11. In response to the immediate disaster, the Lord promises to restore the fortunes of his people. This restoration includes prolific agricultural productivity (2:19, 22–24; see Deut. 28:1–14), protection from the invader (2:20)[8] and the promise that 'never again will my people be shamed' (2:26). This subdivision closes with an expansive recognition formula (v. 27) declaring that the Lord is in the midst of Israel, and a repeat of the promise 'never again will my people be shamed'. Joel invokes the fulfilment of his prophecy as an authentication of his message.[9]

Many understand our verses (2:28–29 [3:1–2]), united by the inclusion 'I will pour out my Spirit', part of the second subdivision (2:28 – 3:21 [3:1 – 4:21]),[10] to shift the focus from the immediate future to a more remote future that is not presently discernible. The *wĕhāyâ* which opens verse 28 (3:1),

---

Press, 2000), p. 239. William Sanford LaSor, David Allan Hubbard and Frederic William Bush, *Old Testament Survey: The Message, Form, and Background of the Old Testament*, 2nd ed. (Grand Rapids: Eerdmans, 1996), p. 377, argue that the actual locust plague metaphorically points to 'a prototype of the day of Yahweh'.

7. James L. Crenshaw, *Joel: A New Translation with Introduction and Commentary*, AB (New York: Doubleday, 1995), p. 62.
8. The identity of the 'northern army' in this verse is uncertain. Prior argues that it could refer to any national threat – military or natural – though the immediate reference suggests a literal locust plague and not a foreign army invading the land (Prior, *The Message of Joel*, p. 66). According to Crenshaw, the term 'functions as a play on a prophetic symbol for the ultimate adversary' (*Joel*, p. 151).
9. The connection between the statement of recognition and the pouring out of the Lord's Spirit which details the signs of the Day of the Lord occurs also in Ezek. 39:28–29.
10. Suggestions to transpose 3:1ff. and 4:1ff. are unconvincing; see Wolff, *Joel*, p. 60.

coupled with the temporal adverbial phrase 'after this' (*ʾaḥărê kēn*; see also Isa. 1:26; Jer. 21:7; 49:6), serves a demonstrative function which, according to Prinsloo, 'focuses attention on events that would only come to pass after the preceding 2:18–27'.[11] Similarly, Wolff comments, 'Not only will earlier conditions be restored (v. 23), they will be exceeded by a second phase of Yahweh's acting, which will occur "afterward."'[12] In other words, the restoration following the locust plague in 2:18–27 is linked as foretaste to fulfilment with the greater salvific acts of Yahweh to come, in which Yahweh pours out his Spirit on Judah in unprecedented fashion and brings an end decisively to the oppression of Judah by her neighbours.

A temporal sequential understanding of 'after this' is a possible but not the exclusive interpretive option.[13] According to VanGemeren, '*ʾaḥărê kēn* ['after this'] may serve a connective purpose, functioning either as a temporal conjunctive, "when" or even an explicative "and".'[14] VanGemeren's approach mitigates an inherent weakness in the temporal sequential approach, the tendency to ignore 'the inner connection of the blessings associated with the new era of God's favor (vv. 18–27), the progressive fulfillment of these blessings ("never again" in vv. 19b, 26, 27), and the connection of vv. 27 and 28'.[15] The blessings envisioned by Joel in 2:18–27 (specifically, agricultural productivity) were never fully realized in the post-exilic period before the outpouring of the Spirit at Pentecost. If the 'afterwards' of 2:28 (3:1) is understood as a parallel to the days of blessing (2:18–27), then the outpouring of the Spirit in 2:28–29 (3:1–2) can be understood as overlapping with this period, as 'complementary

---

11. Willem S. Prinsloo, *The Theology of the Book of Joel* (New York: Walter deGruyter, 1985), p. 80. See also Bruce Waltke and M. O'Connor, *An Introduction to Biblical Hebrew Syntax* (Winona Lake: Eisenbrauns, 1990), p. 539, §32.3.6c.

12. Wolff, *Joel*, p. 65.

13. Passages in which *ʾaḥărê kēn* is used in a temporal sequential sense include Jer. 16:16; 34:11; 2 Chr. 20:35. If *ʾaḥărê kēn* is understood this way in our passage, then 'the era of blessing (vv. 18–27) will precede the era of the Spirit' (Willem VanGemeren, 'The Spirit of Restoration', *WTJ* 50 [1988], p. 84).

14. VanGemeren sees the first words of 2:28 (3:1) as a transition to an explication of 2:27, not sequence. In this view, the eras of blessing recorded in 2:18–27 and 2:28–32 (3:1–5) overlap and the blessings of 2:18–27 are not fulfilled until Pentecost. In support of his interpretation of *wĕhāyâ ʾaḥărê kēn* he discusses several prophetic passages (Isa. 1:26; Jer. 21:7) as well as the similar 'after those days' (Jer. 31:33) (ibid., pp. 85–86).

15. Ibid., p. 86.

and explanatory' of the material blessings of 2:18–27. Both describe the 'new era of covenant renewal' with the outpouring of the Spirit as 'God's guarantee of the fulfillment of his promise-word (the blessings), his close communion with his people, and of the goal of redemptive history, the presence of God among the new community'.[16]

The prophecy opens with the declaration that the Lord will 'pour out my Spirit on all people'.[17] The only other place in the book where 'Spirit' is mentioned, 2:29 (3:2), repeats the phrase 'pour out my Spirit'. *Rûaḥ* is used 387 times in the OT with the basic meanings of 'air in motion, a blowing, breeze, wind, nothingness, spirit, sense',[18] connoting the idea of 'the power to set other things in motion'.[19] It is variously translated as 'spirit' (Gen. 1:2; Judg. 3:10; Ezek. 11:5), 'wind' (Exod. 10:13, 19; Ezek. 1:4; 13:11, 13), 'transitory breeze' (conveying the idea of nothingness, similar to *hebel*; see Job 7:7; Ps. 78:39) or 'breath' as the vitality of life (Job 9:18; Lam. 4:20).[20] Throughout the OT the Lord's *rûaḥ* is a separate entity, or an 'endowment' over which the Lord has control, in the sense that he can pour it out on whom he pleases.[21] Thus 'my Spirit' is 'the self-manifesting activity of God himself, the extension of his personal vitality'.[22]

The verb 'pour out' (*šāpak*, 2:28 [3:1]) is used literally in Scripture of dry goods (Lev. 4:12), blood (as for a sacrifice [Exod. 29:12], or as in murder [Gen. 9:6]), and other liquids (Exod. 4:9). Metaphorically, *šāpak* is used with God's anger (Ezek. 7:8) and the heart (Ps. 62:8 [9]).[23] Joel's depiction of the Lord's Spirit being poured out is employed by other prophets as well (Isa. 44:3; Ezek. 39:29; Zech. 12:10; see also Rom. 5:5).[24] Here, the imagery of God's Spirit

16. Ibid., pp. 87, 89.
17. Targum reads 'my holy spirit'. LXX appears to show the influence of Num. 11:17, 25, 'portions of my spirit'. Aquila and Symmachus agree with MT. See Wolff, *Joel*, p. 56.
18. *HALOT*, II.1197–1201.
19. Bruce K. Waltke, *The Book of Proverbs: Chapters 1 – 15*, NICOT (Grand Rapids: Eerdmans, 2004), p. 92.
20. *HALOT*, II.1197.
21. M. Turner, 'Holy Spirit', *The New Dictionary of Biblical Theology*, eds. T. Desmond Alexander and Brian S. Rosner (Leicester: Inter-Varsity Press, 2000), p. 551.
22. Turner, 'Holy Spirit', p. 558.
23. Crenshaw, *Joel*, p. 164.
24. Duane A. Garrett, *Hosea, Joel*, NAC, 19A (Nashville: Broadman & Holman, 1997), p. 368.

being poured out hearkens back to the picture of abundant showers described in 2:23.[25] God's Spirit, which was given only intermittently in the OT, would someday be abundantly available to all God's people.

Furthermore, the juxtaposition of promises of agricultural abundance (2:18–27) and the outpouring of the Spirit (2:28–29 [3:1–2]) brings to mind apparently similar relationships between the activity of God's Spirit and creation/recreation in other texts (Gen. 1:2; Pss 33:5; 104:30; Isa. 32:15).[26] O. P. Robinson said it this way: 'It should not be surprising then that after Joel's description of the restoration of plants, trees, and animals following the plague of locusts, the Spirit of God enters the picture with distinctive prominence in connection with the rejuvenation of man . . . From this perspective, the second portion of the prophecy of Joel (Joel 2:28 – 3:21) develops naturally out of the first (1:2 – 2:27).'[27] It is important to note, however, that in Joel the only effect directly associated with the Spirit is the manifestation of prophetic gifts: 'it is the relationship to God, then, which has become completely new in the new creation through the pouring out of the spirit.' Or, as Wolff notes, 'Everyone will stand in a relationship of immediacy to God.'[28] While both the agricultural abundance and the general experience of prophetic gifts are God's work, only the latter is said to be specifically brought about by the outpouring of the Spirit.

To whom does 'all people' (*kōl bāśār*, v. 28 [3:1]) refer? Does it embrace all humanity, Jew and Gentile alike (Robertson, Barton), or is it nationally restricted to Israel (Baker, Dillard, Stuart, VanGemeren)? *Bāśār* can refer to animals (Gen. 9:15; Dan. 4:12 [Aramaic]), humankind (Gen. 6:12; Num. 27:16), or it can have a more restrictive meaning ('all the wicked', Isa. 66:16, 23; Jer. 25:31).[29] The Spirit-inspired prophetic actions described in subsequent verses naturally exclude animals[30] and plant life. Is the promise extended to Judah alone, or does it include the Gentiles as well? Arguments in favour of a more restricted interpretation include: the pronominal suffixes '*your* sons and

25. The verb translated 'poured down' in 2:23 (ESV, NASB) is the *hiphil* of *yārad.*

26. Dillard, *Joel*, p. 294. Wolff notes that the promise of the pouring out of the Spirit following the fertile irrigation of dry land also occurs in Isa. 44:2–5 (*Joel*, p. 160).

27. O. P. Robertson, *The Christ of the Prophets* (Phillipsburg: P. & R. Publishing, 2004), pp. 242–243.

28. Wolff, *Joel*, p. 67.

29. Thomas J. Finley, *Joel, Obadiah and Micah*, EBC (Chicago: Moody, 1996), p. 53.

30. Though Prior's admonition not to be adamant about this in light of the incident involving Balaam's ass (Num. 22:28) is accepted (*The Message of Joel*, p. 73).

daughters' (v. 28 [3:1], italics mine); the prophecy contrasts Judah's future salvation with the impending judgment of the foreign nations (3:1–17 [4:1–17]) in the coming Day of the Lord;[31] this oracle is addressed to Judah (2:18–19), whereas the next oracle (3:1 [4:1]) deals with the foreign nations; the same promise is restricted to the house of Israel in Ezekiel (39:29).[32] Arguments in favour of a more universal understanding which would include the Gentiles are: the more restrictive interpretation puts Joel at odds with the approximately forty other usages of the phrase which usually refers to 'all human beings' or 'all living things',[33] Peter's usage of the passage (Acts 2:17–33, 39), and Paul's understanding (Rom. 10:10–13).[34] Crenshaw suggests that in the context of the Pentecost sermon, Peter's use of Joel 2:32 (3:5) broadens the circle of those who 'call upon the name of the Lord' to Diaspora Jews.[35] Acts 2:39 broadens Joel 2:32 further to include the Gentiles. Those who favour a more restricted interpretation counter that Peter's appeal to Joel 2 to explain what was happening at Pentecost was an expansion of Joel's meaning which was not inconsistent with the OT prophet. The arguments in favour of a more restrictive interpretation are persuasive, though perhaps there is an intentional ambiguity that is further clarified by the use of Joel in subsequent revelation.[36]

Joel's prediction centres on the democratization of prophesying as the result of this outpouring of the Lord's Spirit. The pattern in the OT economy was that the Spirit was given to empower a few specific individuals for a few specific assignments. These individuals included judges (Judg. 3:10; 14:6, 19), prophets (Isa. 61:1), kings (1 Sam. 16:13) and specially gifted individuals (Exod. 35:30–31). Prior comments regarding these endowed individuals, 'As

---

31. 'For Zion, the day of Yahweh will become a day of salvation and vindication, whereas the nations will face the full fury of Yahweh in Holy War' (Dillard, *Joel*, p. 294).
32. So Dillard, *Joel*, p. 295; James N. Pohlig, *An Exegetical Summary of Joel* (Dallas: SIL International, 2003), p. 150; Wolff, *Joel*, p. 67. 'This spectacular event will know but one restriction; it will be limited to YHWH's worshippers in Judah' (Crenshaw, *Joel*, p. 171).
33. Barton (following Hulst), 'There seem to be no other places where the meaning is clearly "all Israelites"' (John Barton, *Joel and Obadiah: A Commentary*, OTL [Louisville: Westminster John Knox, 2001], p. 96).
34. Barton conjectures that this startling universalistic proclamation is a secondary insertion into the text of Joel, a prophet primarily focused on Judah (ibid., p. 96).
35. Crenshaw, *Joel*, p. 172.
36. See discussion on Acts 2 below.

a result, or because of their position, they were all leaders in the community . . . For Joel and his audience, therefore, there was an experience (even if only in their past history), but also an expectation, of the Spirit coming on individuals for some expression of leadership among the people of God.'[37] Joel's prediction hearkens back to Moses' plea in Numbers 11, where, during the wilderness wanderings, Moses becomes overwhelmed by the responsibility of leading the nation and the Lord responds that he will give his Spirit to seventy chosen elders who will share the burden of leadership. After the distribution of the Spirit to seventy elders to assist Moses, Joshua is threatened by the Spirit's presence in Eldad and Medad, two elders not among the assembled before Moses. Moses' response to Joshua is the wish for a general outpouring of the Spirit, 'I wish that all the LORD's people were prophets and that the LORD would put his Spirit on them!' (Num. 11:29).

Joel envisions a future when Moses' wish will become a reality. The gift of the Spirit will be lavishly poured out on all, irrespective of factors that mattered in his day: age (old men[38] and young men, v. 28 [3:1]), sex (sons and daughters, v. 28 [3:1]), and social standing (male and female servants, v. 29 [3:2]). What was restricted to a few specific individuals for a few specific assignments would, in the future, be indiscriminately available to all of the Lord's people. All these barriers will be broken as 'The new people of God no longer recognize privileged individuals.'[39] This radical change envisions a 'sociological overhaul'[40] that will affect the entire community. Verse 29 (3:2) begins with the emphatic 'even [*wĕgam*][41] on my servants, both men and women,[42] I will pour out my Spirit in those days'. According to Keil, this is the only case in the whole of the OT of a slave receiving the gift of prophecy.[43] In Israelite society, servants were normally foreigners (though an Israelite could voluntarily sell himself or a family member into slavery to a fellow Israelite for

37. Prior, *The Message of Joel*, p. 70.
38. *Ziknêkem*, translated elsewhere in Joel as 'elders' (1:14; 2:16; 'old men' also in 3:2 [4:2]), refers in this context to elderly men as opposed to young men.
39. Wolff, *Joel*, p. 67.
40. Dillard, *Joel*, p. 295.
41. Waltke and O'Connor, *Biblical Hebrew Syntax*, §39.3.4d.
42. The Hebrew word translated 'female servants' (*šiphâ*) designates a female worker engaged in more menial tasks and less closely assimilated to the employing family than *ʾāmâ* (*HALOT*, IV.1620–1622). Cf. Ruth 2:13; 3:9.
43. C. F. Keil and F. Delitzsch, *Commentary on the Old Testament in Ten Volumes, Minor Prophets*, vol. X (Grand Rapids: Eerdmans, 1980), pp. 211–212.

a limited period of time during times of hardship or to pay off a debt)[44] and here they participate in this outpouring which further enhances the breadth and exclusiveness of Joel's vision of the outpouring of the Spirit. Slave girls will receive the Spirit in similar fashion to the elders of the land as possession by God's Spirit will not be the privilege of the few, but the experience of all (Num. 11:25; 12:6). Dillard cautions, 'It is important that the modern reader not miss the radical character of what Joel announces. In the world of ancient Israel, the free, older Jewish male stood at the top of the social structure; most of Israel's prophets had belonged to this group . . . This statement from Joel must be contrasted with the ancient daybreak prayer of the Jewish male: "I thank you God that I was not born a Gentile, a slave, or a woman."'[45]

In the OT, dreams (Num. 12:6; 1 Sam. 3; Dan. 1:17)[46] and visions (Isa. 30:10; Ezek. 12:27; Hos. 12:10) were accepted prophetic media, in addition to the word of the Lord being actualized for a prophet.[47] The distinction between the two is that dreams were received while asleep, visions while awake. Visions were associated with 'seers' (*rōʾeh*) and did not invoke the same degree of scepticism as with dreams.[48] Both dreaming dreams[49] and seeing visions occurred at the Lord's initiative. In Numbers 12:1–6, a contrast is made between God's revelation to prophets (mediated) and to Moses (direct).[50] The emphasis here in Joel is on the free access that will be enjoyed by 'everyone who calls on the name of the LORD' (2:32 [3:5]). Pohlig states, 'The entire nation will have this intimacy with their God.'[51]

What this general outpouring of the Spirit is meant to accomplish is not

---

44. See G. H. Haas, 'Slave, Slavery', in T. Desmond Alexander and David W. Baker (eds.), *Dictionary of the Old Testament: Pentateuch* (Downers Grove: InterVarsity Press, 2003), pp. 778–783.
45. Dillard, *Joel*, p. 295.
46. Jeremiah's opprobrium towards dreams (Jer. 23:25) was directed at false prophets, not the method of dreams as a means of receiving divine revelation in general. See Crenshaw, *Joel*, p. 165.
47. Joel 1:1, 'The word of the LORD that *came to* Joel' literally reads, 'The word of the LORD that *was to* Joel' in the Hebrew (italics mine).
48. Prior, *The Message of Joel*, p. 75.
49. The expression is a cognate effected accusative in which the dream 'results from the actions the verb describes' (Waltke and O'Connor, *Biblical Hebrew Syntax*, §166–167).
50. David W. Baker, *Joel, Obadiah, Malachi*, NICOT (Grand Rapids: Zondervan, 2006), p. 108.
51. Pohlig, *Exegetical Summary*, p. 152.

specified in Joel. On the one hand, it can be related to Jeremiah 31:33–34. In this case, the general outpouring of the Spirit signifies a new relationship between the Lord and his people. No longer does he deal with his people through specially gifted prophets and teachers. They are no longer needed, because he speaks directly to all his people.

As mentioned above, the general outpouring can also be related to Numbers 11:29. In this case it signifies a change in Israel's calling and service. The Lord enables and equips the people to perform various functions formerly limited to prophets, priests and kings.[52] Dillard says: 'In the OT, the Spirit of God is preeminently the spirit of prophecy. Possession by the Spirit in the OT is the means of prophetic enduement.'[53] The public roles of the prophet – spokesperson, mediator, advocate and prosecutor – are passed on to the people as a whole.

These two outcomes of the Spirit's outpouring are not mutually exclusive. Their relative importance depends to a certain extent at least on how one reads 2:32 (3:5). If the 'saved' and 'survivors' of the latter verse are taken to be those who have already been blessed with the promised Spirit, then the emphasis would appear to fall on the new relationship of the people with the Lord. The outpouring of the Spirit prepares them for the coming deliverance. On the other hand, the 'saved' and 'survivors' of 2:32 (3:5) may include others who subsequently call on the name of the Lord, presumably as a result of being 'called' by the Lord through the prophetic ministry of his newly equipped people. In this case, the text is focusing on the extension of the Lord's salvation via the empowering of his people to be prophets.

Our passage ends with a repetition of the promise, 'I will pour out my Spirit in those days' (2:29 [3:2]). In prophetic texts, 'those days' refers to 'the most recent time indicator' which, in the case of Joel, is the 'afterwards' of 2:28 (3:1).[54] If, as was observed above, the 'and afterwards' is best interpreted as an overlapping between the age of agricultural blessing (2:18–27) and the promise of the Spirit, then the outpouring of the Spirit is 'God's guarantee of the fulfillment of his promise-word (the blessings), his close communion with his people, and of the goal of redemptive history: the presence of God among the new community'.[55] In other words, 'the coming of the great and

52. G. K. Beale, *The Temple and the Church's Mission: A Biblical Theology of the Dwelling Place of God* (Downers Grove: InterVarsity Press, 2004), p. 210.

53. Dillard, *Joel*, p. 295.

54. Baker, *Joel*, p. 101.

55. VanGemeren, 'Spirit', p. 89.

dreadful day of the LORD' (v. 31 [3:4]) will be a day of blessing for those who call 'on the name of the LORD' (v. 32 [3:5]), and a day of divine judgment for the enemies of God.

The verses immediately following our passage employ stock-in-trade eschatological imagery to depict cosmic portents accompanying the outpouring of the Spirit and heralding the 'day of Yahweh', the divine judgment on Judah's enemies to be described in detail in 3:1–16 (4:1–16). As in Isaiah 24 – 25, Zephaniah 1:14 – 3:20 and Zechariah 14, Joel pictures a cataclysmic judgment on the nations accompanied by deliverance for God's people. 'Portents' (*môpětîm*) are extraordinary events; the plagues in Egypt were so designated (Exod. 7:3; Deut. 6:22).[56] As with the coming of the locusts (2:10), the portents of fire, blood, smoke and the darkening of sun and moon hearken back to Exodus-Sinai.[57] They also hint at catastrophes overtaking the nations.[58] Taking all this together, the portents serve as clear signals to Israel that Yahweh is about to deliver her from the nations. If we adopt the reading of 2:28–29 (3:1–2) and 2:32 (3:5) that Israel is being commissioned as prophets to the nations, the portents also serve as confirmations of her prophetic proclamation.

Conclusion

Several NT authors draw on our passage to help explain events in the new era inaugurated by the incarnation. C. H. Dodd underscores the importance of Joel 1 and 2, noting that they 'played a significant part in molding the language in which the early church set forth its convictions about what Christ had done and would yet do'.[59] Also according to Acts 2:14–21, Pentecost is the answer to Moses' prayer and the initial fulfilment of Joel's prediction in which the ascended Christ would give the promised Holy Spirit (Acts 1:5) to mediate his presence. Peter's appeal to Joel 2:28–32 (3:1–5)[60] emphasizes the redemptive

---

56. Wolff, *Joel*, p. 68; Crenshaw, *Joel*, pp. 167–168.
57. Irvin A. Busenitz, *Joel and Obadiah, A Mentor Commentary* (Ross-shire: Christian Focus Publications, 2003), pp. 189–190; Pohlig, *Exegetical Summary*, p. 156.
58. Wolff, *Joel*, p. 68.
59. C. H. Dodd, *According to the Scriptures: The Sub-Structure of New Testament Theology* (London: Nisbet, 1952), pp. 63–64; quoted by Prior, *The Message of Joel*, p. 69.
60. The differences between Peter's citation and the MT are well documented. They include: Peter identifies the slaves as the Lord's; the second half of Joel 2:32 (3:5) is

historical significance of Pentecost as the church is established as the 'new covenant people of God, as the body of Christ'.[61] Crenshaw suggests that in the context of the Pentecost sermon, Peter's use of Joel 2:32 (3:5) broadens the circle of 'everyone who calls on the name of the Lord' (Acts 2:21) to include Diaspora Jews who had come to Jerusalem.[62] The clause 'and for all who are far off – for all whom the Lord our God will call' (Acts 2:39) indicates that the blessing of the Holy Spirit is meant for Gentiles as well.[63] In light of redemptive-historical developments ushered in with the incarnation, Joel's 'all flesh' has been expanded to include all God's covenant people – all Israel now includes both Jew and Gentile. Similarly, Paul uses Joel 2:32 (3:5) in Romans 10:13 as a prooftext to justify his claim that God will save everyone, Jew and Gentile, who believes the good news.

---

lacking in Peter's quotation, but is included later on in Acts 2:39. Peter introduces the citation with 'in the last days' rather than 'and afterwards' (Crenshaw, *Joel*, 172). Prior, *The Message of Joel*, pp. 77–78, observes that the switch from 'afterwards' to 'in the last days' in Acts 2:33 intensifies Joel's historical progression throughout chs. 2 – 3 (2 – 4) (from immediate future to more distant future) to an eschatological pitch, i.e. the giving of the Spirit as a signal that the Pentecost generation is living in the last days.

61. Richard B. Gaffin, Jr, *Perspectives on Pentecost – New Testament Teachings on the Gifts of the Holy Spirit* (Phillipsburg: P. & R. Publishing, 1979), p. 21.
62. Crenshaw, *Joel*, p. 172.
63. 'All that are far off' – i.e. both in terms of time (future generations) and race (Gentiles); cf. Eph. 2:13; 1 Pet. 2:9–10. This understanding fits the architecture of the narrative of Acts presented in 1:8 and carried out in relation to the Samaritans (Acts 8:14–17) and Gentiles (Acts 10:44–48) (Prior, *The Message of Joel*, pp. 78–79).

PART 6: THE SPIRIT AND LEADERSHIP

15. THE SPIRIT AND LEADERSHIP: TESTIMONY, EMPOWERMENT AND PURPOSE

David G. Firth

Although there is no one word in Hebrew that equates to our word 'leadership', this is an area that is of great importance to the OT.[1] We do not find the writers of the OT reflecting on leadership as a general phenomenon, but we do find many instances where it is described, analysed and criticized. That is, the OT clearly recognizes the need for leadership, though its default position is that all leadership is exercised under Yahweh's authority. All forms and functions found in human leadership only have validity to the extent that the leaders understand that Yahweh's authority is greater. Yahweh remains the one from whom all leadership is derived and is at the same time the one who provides the pattern for all human leadership.[2] It is because of Yahweh's leadership that the OT is able to adopt a critical posture regarding all human leaders. Leadership is necessary, but it is measured and valued in terms of its

1. *NIDOTTE* 5:117 lists some twenty terms as falling into this semantic field, and a comparison of their own cross references shows this could be expanded considerably. For example, Ancient Near Eastern kings often styled themselves as 'shepherds', a motif that the Bible as a whole also employs.
2. Looking specifically at the example of the 'shepherd' leader, see Timothy S. Laniak, *Shepherds After My Own Heart: Pastoral Traditions and Leadership in the Bible* (Nottingham: Apollos, 2006), pp. 77–87.

expression of faithfulness to Yahweh.[3] The starting point for any valid expression of leadership is therefore that the leader's authority must derive in some way from Yahweh. How that leader's authority might derive from Yahweh is an open question, as it may be demonstrated in a variety of ways. The process of ordination described in Leviticus 8 – 9, for example, authorizes Aaron and his sons to act as priests through a process of consecration which in turn depends upon the instructions principally laid out in Exodus 29, something emphasized by the refrain that it was done 'as Yahweh had commanded' (e.g. Lev. 8:4, 9, 13). In this instance, the authority of the leader depended upon the faithful adoption of commands previously given. After David, the kings of Israel and Judah could be judged on the basis of their faithfulness in worship and the extent to which they led others into faithfulness, but it is a standard position in the book of Kings that Yahweh was unwilling to act against the kings in Judah because of his promise to David. Thus, although Abijam is judged to have 'walked in all the sins his father committed before him' (1 Kgs 15:3), Yahweh still granted him a son because of David (1 Kgs 15:4), a clear reference back to the Davidic covenant in 2 Samuel 7:1–17, even if it is here nuanced by David's failures in the Uriah incident in 2 Samuel 11. But in other instances, authority derives from the evidence of Yahweh acting through someone, and a particularly important stream within this group represents those who are empowered in some way by Yahweh's Spirit. Perhaps the most obvious example of this is seen in David, on whom the Spirit is said to come at his anointing (1 Sam. 16:13), preparing us for the refrain that marks his rise, that 'Yahweh was with him' (first uttered by Saul's attendant in 1 Sam. 16:18).

Although one might suggest that (in Weber's terms) only this third approach is 'charismatic'[4] and that the others are, in some senses, institutional, the reality is that charisma and institution are much closer together in Israel precisely because it is Yahweh's authority that supports all forms of leadership. Nevertheless, it is worth noting that some leadership's authority derives from that which Yahweh has already given, whether in his word or other actions, whereas that which is associated with the Spirit represents something new in Israel's experience. This does not mean that leadership associated with an experience of the Spirit cannot be institutionalized – after all, the Davidic kings

---

3. This is not restricted to Israelite leaders – see e.g. Dan. 5:13–28.
4. For Weber this does not have to be associated with God's Spirit but rather the heroic character of the leader. On the possibilities and limits of Weber's model, see Rodney R. Hutton, *Charisma and Authority in Israelite Society* (Minneapolis: Fortress, 1994), pp. 3–9.

become an institution in Judah – but it does mean that the ongoing authority of that leadership is dependent upon the faithfulness of those empowered by the Spirit to what Yahweh has already given. As we shall see, leadership in the OT is empowered by the Spirit to enable those called by Yahweh to fulfil his purposes, but (as with Saul) the presence of the Spirit does not validate such leadership for ever. There remains the need for leaders to remain faithful to Yahweh, but the Spirit's presence is an important way in which a new strand of leadership can be validated and empowered. In particular, Spirit language is an important mechanism for pointing to Yahweh's presence with the leader.

The Pentateuch

In comparison with the Former Prophets, there are comparatively few references to the Spirit in the Pentateuch, though those that occur are foundational for the general themes we note elsewhere in the OT. Perhaps more importantly, we note here the first evidence that the text allows that Spirit empowerment can exist without having to mention it directly. Some experience of the Spirit is possible before someone moves into a position of leadership, but it is normally the case that the Spirit's presence is mentioned at the point where leadership is initiated. The notable exception to this is Moses, though, as we shall note, in his case there is other terminology that is equivalent to reference to the Spirit.

Joseph

The first possible reference to the Spirit and leadership occurs in Genesis 41:38, though there are some important ambiguities here. The verse recounts a comment made by Pharaoh to his attendants after Joseph has interpreted his two dreams and suggested that a suitable person be appointed to oversee the collection of stores of grain from the good years before the seven years of famine so there can be enough during that period. Joseph's proposal pleased Pharaoh, who then said to his attendants, 'Can we find a man like this in whom is the Spirit of God/spirit of the gods?' Several difficulties are immediately evident for any understanding of the work of the Spirit here. Most obviously, since Pharaoh speaks from the perspective of polytheism, something we can also assume for his attendants, when he uses the words *rûaḥ ʾĕlōhîm* it would seem the most obvious interpretation that he refers to the 'spirit of the gods'.[5] But against this we should note that in 41:39 he speaks

5. So, e.g., NEB renders the phrase 'one who has the spirit of a god in him'.

directly to Joseph and asserts, 'God has shown you this.' In doing so he again uses *ʾĕlōhîm*, but rather than using a plural verb he employs the hiphil infinitive construct of *ydʿ*. Of course, one effect of using the infinitive absolute is that it has neither person nor number and so is suitably ambiguous. For an Israelite it would be consistent with the claim that Yahweh alone is God, and indeed in 41:16 Joseph has insisted that rather than interpreting the dream himself, it would be God who gave Pharaoh a favourable answer. There Joseph had also used *ʾĕlōhîm*, but had matched it with a masculine singular verb,[6] which is how the OT typically indicates that it is referring to Israel's God rather than using *ʾĕlōhîm* as a generic term referring to 'gods'. If Joseph's statement has influenced Pharaoh to that extent, then it is perfectly possible to render *rûaḥ ʾĕlōhîm* as 'Spirit of God'.[7] A third possibility exists which is that the text is deliberately ambiguous.[8] Joseph's speech is clear and uses *ʾĕlōhîm* to refer to God rather than gods generally, but Pharaoh's speech actually leaves open the possibility that *ʾĕlōhîm* could refer to 'gods' generically or that there is only one 'God' in accordance with Joseph's speech. We have thus an instance of an ambiguity where a detail can be effective in multiple ways.[9] Pharaoh can indeed speak as a polytheist, but the ambiguity in his speech is such that the biblical writer can present it so that readers sensitive to Israel's traditions can appreciate the possibility of him meaning more than he actually says. For the narrator of Genesis, therefore, it is not necessary to determine exactly what Pharaoh might have meant, because the ambiguity of his speech is such that it can still be understood as a reference to the Spirit of God. What is more remarkable about this passage, then, is not that Pharaoh attributes Joseph's ability to interpret his dreams to the work of the Spirit but rather the quality of the counsel he gives in advising him what to do in light of it. As we have noted, Joseph attributes his ability to offer an interpretation of the dreams to God, but his advice in 41:33–36 might appear as the practical wisdom that might be expected of a courtier rather than something that has its roots in

6. Qal imperfect, third-person masculine singular of *ʿnh*.

7. E.g. NIV, ESV. For a defence of this view, see Victor P. Hamilton, *The Book of Genesis: Chapters 18 – 50* (Grand Rapids: Eerdmans, 1995), p. 501.

8. NASB attempts to recognize this by rendering the phrase as 'divine spirit'.

9. This draws on the theory of ambiguity developed by William Empson, *Seven Types of Ambiguity*, 3rd ed. (Harmondsworth: Penguin, 1960). On the possibilities provided by Empson's analysis, see David G. Firth, 'Ambiguity', in David G. Firth and Jamie A. Grant (eds.), *Words and the Word: Explorations in Biblical Interpretation and Literary Theory* (Nottingham: Apollos, 2007), pp. 151–186.

the presence of God. But Pharaoh's speech discerns something more, so that this wisdom is itself seen as deriving from the Spirit. Joseph's appointment to a position of leadership is thus rooted in an expression of wisdom, but this wisdom is itself evidence of the work of the Spirit of God. Wisdom and the work of the Spirit are thus not alternatives, but rather parallel expressions of how God's ways are known. Genesis 39:21 had insisted that 'Yahweh was with Joseph', a phrase we will see is often used of leaders associated with the Spirit in the OT, and this presence is recognized by Pharaoh, but it is recognized in the terms of the Spirit of God because this is the point where a new phase of leadership is initiated.

Moses and the seventy elders

Since Moses is in many ways the paradigm leader for the OT, it is no surprise that his ministry is associated with the Spirit, though in his case the association with the Spirit is not made until later in his ministry, when Yahweh was empowering seventy elders to 'bear the burden' of the people with him (Num. 11:17). The chapter as a whole is filled with reference to the *rûaḥ*, though it is not until 11:29 that it is made explicit that the reference is to Yahweh's Spirit. As will be seen, this narrative provides a retrospective understanding of Moses' leadership as led by the Spirit, while also initiating the subsidiary leadership role of the seventy elders.

The account of the elders is part of a larger narrative (Num. 11:4–35) that integrates the people's complaint about the lack of meat in their diet (having only manna) and the sharing of Yahweh's Spirit. Although attempts have been made to separate the element of leadership and the sharing of the Spirit as a later accretion,[10] it is preferable to consider it as a whole piece,[11] because, although a complete story can be made about the meat without the issue of leadership, it is actually the theme of leadership that is central. In terms of the plot of the story, the issue of meat becomes the presenting issue that actually provides entry into what will be a major theme up to Numbers 20 where there

---

10. Thus Benjamin Sommer, 'Reflecting on Moses: The Redaction of Numbers 11', *JBL* 118/4 (1999), p. 601, claims the two elements are 'entirely unrelated'. Philip J. Budd, *Numbers* (Waco: Word, 1984), pp. 126–127, considers it an addition to core material from J, but prefers to see it as coming from a separate source that was integrated by J rather than from E as suggested by many.
11. Thomas B. Dozeman, 'Numbers', in *NIB*, vol. 2, p. 105, considers the whole account 'a pre-priestly complaint story, in which the subordinate theme of leadership is the central problem'.

are various challenges to Moses' leadership. By foregrounding the theme of leadership here, the narrative is able to provide a key to understanding Moses' authority in terms of the Spirit, while also drawing on Exodus 33:7–11. Read in this way, this story demonstrates that the special experience that Moses was said to have with Yahweh in Exodus 33:11 is to be understood in terms of the Spirit. Nevertheless, it is clear that just because Moses' leadership is marked in this way it is not necessarily perfect, and when the 'rabble' complain to him about their lack of meat (Num. 11:4–6) he in turn complains to Yahweh (Num. 11:11–15). The rabble blames Moses and he blames Yahweh.

Yahweh, however, responds by directing Moses to gather seventy elders and bring them to the tent of meeting where he will 'take from the *rûaḥ*' that is upon Moses and give it to the elders so that he need not bear the burden of the people alone. It is not clear at this point whether *rûaḥ* is a reference to the Spirit of Yahweh or to Moses' own character as a leader. However, when Moses gathered the elders to the tent and the *rûaḥ* was placed upon them, they 'prophesied', though not continually (Num. 11:25). This experience clearly indicates that the *rûaḥ* is not simply Moses' character, but rather points to the divine endowment he has from Yahweh to lead the people. Moreover, even though two of the elders, Eldad and Medad, had not even come out to the tent, they too prophesied and, when challenged about this by Joshua, Moses responded by wishing that Yahweh would put his Spirit on all his people (Num. 11:29). At this point the possible ambiguity about the identity of this *rûaḥ* is resolved and we see that it is Yahweh's Spirit who enables these elders to function in their role and so to assist Moses. The implication is clearly that although they were already recognized as elders, they were not able to assist Moses without the experience of the Spirit. Hence it is the work of the Spirit to initiate them into a new area of leadership, so that it is the Spirit who empowers them for their work while also marking them as those recognized by Yahweh for leadership, whether present in the initial gathering or not. Their 'prophesying' indicates Yahweh's presence with them and attests this to the community, while it is also the Spirit whose presence now means they are able to fulfil their role. Equally, the experience of Eldad and Medad shows that the work of the Spirit cannot be controlled.[12] The Spirit marks out those chosen by Yahweh, but the processes by which the Spirit works cannot be restricted.

But what of Moses? He had clearly come into a position because of Yahweh's call (Exod. 3), but there is no reference there to any experience of

---

12. Ibid., p. 107.

the Spirit. If Moses is the paradigm leader for the OT, would we not expect some association with the Spirit? The obvious answer is that although the Spirit's presence commonly marks those called to leadership at the initiation of their role, there is no need for this always to be recorded. It is certainly the case that it is often said of those leaders who have a marked experience of the Spirit that Yahweh is 'with' them, as for example Joseph (Gen. 39:23) and David (1 Sam. 16:18). Since Yahweh also promised to be with Moses (Exod. 3:12), it is arguable that this is equivalent in some way to a statement of the Spirit's presence. It would perhaps be unwise to press this point too far in that one could put this the other way round and say that mention of the Spirit is merely another way of speaking of Yahweh's presence, but one should also note that mention of the Spirit most commonly occurs in a setting where there needs to be a public testimony of Yahweh's presence with someone in initiating their role. This is clearly not relevant in Moses' call, and rather than mention of the Spirit Moses was given two signs that pointed to Yahweh's presence with him. That is, the context of his call meant that mention of the Spirit could not serve its normal function in that the element of testimony was absent. However, that Moses' ministry has been marked by the Spirit's presence is now indicated retrospectively by this passage, and we are probably to assume that he was imbued with the Spirit from the time of his call, though it is not a central theme within the Pentateuch.[13] If so, then we already see a hint here that leaders empowered by the Spirit could still make major errors, a theme that will become especially important with the judges, Saul and David.

Joshua

Following Moses' and Aaron's sin in Numbers 20:1–13, it became necessary to identify new leaders who would take Israel into the land. Aaron's replacement

13. Wilf Hildebrandt, *An Old Testament Theology of the Spirit of God* (Peabody: Hendrickson, 1995), p. 108, argues that Isaiah 63:7–14 makes explicit the Spirit's presence throughout Moses' ministry. Leon J. Wood, *The Holy Spirit in the Old Testament* (Grand Rapids: Zondervan, 1976), p. 24, seems to offer a similar interpretation. Although the general point can be conceded, the text does not actually describe any specific experience of the Spirit on Moses' part. Claus Westermann, *Isaiah 40 – 66* (London: SCM Press, 1969), p. 389, argues that the 'Spirit' language here refers to God's miracle working power in history. This is perhaps overly restrictive, but this approach does emphasize that the language here refers to what Yahweh has done during the time of Moses rather than to Moses' personal experience of the Spirit.

with Eleazar is reported almost immediately (Num. 20:22–29). Since there is no association with the Spirit in priestly ministry in the OT,[14] it is no surprise that there is no mention of the Spirit in this passage. The validity of priestly ministry is indicated by the process of ordination rather than experience of the Spirit, so that the ordination service functions as the public testimony of the priest's authority.[15] One cannot therefore conclude that priests lacked any endowment of the Spirit, but it is certainly the case that their status did not depend upon evidence of such endowment. But we have already noted when Moses' leadership was shared with the seventy elders that the text provides retrospective evidence of the presence of the Spirit with Moses. Because an experience of the Spirit was necessary for these leaders to share Moses' role and initiation into it, it is no surprise when Moses is about to be replaced by Joshua in Numbers 27:12–23 that we see evidence of the work of the Spirit, though like Moses the reference to Joshua does provide evidence of the work of the Spirit in him already. Nevertheless, the Spirit's presence is only mentioned at this point where he is about to take over the leadership of the people, so even though we are aware that his earlier ministry can be read in light of the work of the Spirit, it is the presence of the Spirit that particularly validates his appointment.

Emphasis upon the *rûaḥ* begins in Moses' prayer in 27:16, where he describes Yahweh as the 'God of the spirits of all flesh', a phrase used elsewhere only in Numbers 16:22 where it points to Yahweh's sovereignty over all creation. A similar thought is probably intended here, but the prayer is specifically focused on Yahweh's sovereignty being employed to identify the appropriate person to continue to lead the nation towards the land, though the language employed has military connotations, even if it is not solely military.[16] But in a context concerned with the person who would lead the people to the land in place of Moses, it is difficult to avoid the sense that military leadership is intended in references to 'going out and coming in' as well as

14. This is not to say that priests cannot be empowered by the Spirit, but this is for other types of ministry. For example, the priest Zechariah is 'clothed' with the Spirit in 2 Chr. 24:20, but this is to enable him to make a prophetic announcement.

15. Note, for example, that in Lev. 9:22–24 after the ordination of Aaron and his sons he not only blesses the people, but Yahweh sent fire that consumed the offering, thus offering a public testimony for this ordination; cf. Nobuyoshi Kiuchi, *Leviticus* (Nottingham: Apollos, 2007), p. 172.

16. Cf. Deut. 31:2–3; and Timothy R. Ashley, *Numbers* (Grand Rapids: Eerdmans, 1993), p. 551.

the analogy of the shepherd (Num. 27:17) which is a frequent royal motif in the Ancient Near East, and which can have military overtones.[17] As such, it is clear that the model of leadership envisaged for Moses' successor is narrower in scope than Moses' own.

In response to Moses' prayer, Yahweh directs him to take Joshua. The only quality mentioned for Joshua is that 'the Spirit is in him'. The presence of *rûaḥ* language here provides an obvious link to Moses' prayer, but it also points to the divine endowment that Joshua has to lead the people. Unlike the seventy elders whose experience might be temporary, this is apparently a permanent experience.[18] As Moses' long-term assistant, Joshua has occupied a position of leadership for some time, so we are not here concerned with the Spirit's presence as the point of initiation. Rather, it is the only necessary basis for the choice of Joshua, though of course the Spirit's presence is itself a gift from Yahweh and so points to Yahweh's prior preparation of Joshua for this role. That Moses' prayer was for a military leader is also significant given Joshua's earlier military success (Exod. 17:8–13) and faithfulness in the spy narrative (Num. 14:6–9, 30, 38), though of course he has assisted Moses more broadly than that. Since Yahweh's answer also draws on military language (Num. 27:21b), it is clear that the reference to the Spirit is here specific to that role. Since, however, Joshua is already a recognized leader the Spirit's presence is evidence only for Moses, and a public commissioning to his new role is carried out as Moses lays hands on him in the presence of Eleazar (Num. 27:19–23). Since an experience of the Spirit is not here appropriate to validate Joshua's leadership publicly, the commissioning service now fulfils this function.

There may be a subsequent reference to Joshua's experience of the Spirit in Deuteronomy 34:9 where he is said to be filled with the '*rûaḥ* of wisdom' because of Moses laying hands on him, a reference back to Numbers 27:18–23. However, the reference here probably equates Joshua's wisdom with the 'authority' Moses passed on, and so is probably not principally a reference to the Spirit of God, though as we noted with Joseph wisdom can be evidence of the Spirit's enabling. But as Christensen observes, it is a 'divine gift',[19] so the exact sense of *rûaḥ* here has a certain ambiguity. Nevertheless, although

---

17. Laniak, *Shepherds*, p. 65, provides examples.

18. Hildebrandt, *Theology*, p. 109, argues that Joshua's endowment with the Spirit occurs in Num. 11, but there is no evidence there that Joshua is included with the seventy elders, and in many ways his experience is distinguished from theirs.

19. Duane L. Christensen, *Deuteronomy 21:10 – 34:12* (Nashville: Thomas Nelson, 2002), p. 872.

Joshua's role in administration does appear, the dominant concern is with him as a military leader in Deuteronomy 31:1–8, 14–24, and it is this theme that continues in the book of Joshua, so that the principal significance of the Spirit's presence in Joshua is to point to his divine equipping to be a military leader. Reference to the Spirit is thus both retrospective, in that it points to what Joshua has already done, and prospective, preparing for his principal role in the conquest narratives.

Main themes within the Pentateuch

Although the number of references to the Spirit and leadership within the Pentateuch are relatively small, they do provide the paradigm for this topic for the balance of the OT. As such, it is worth drawing together the themes that emerge within it. First, we should note that it is not always necessary to refer to the enabling of the Spirit and that in some instances phrases such as 'Yahweh was with [proper name]' are equivalent to a reference to the Spirit. Reference to the Spirit is thus a mechanism for pointing to the presence of God, though a retrospective note can be needed to make this clear. However, this presence is not an end in itself, and Spirit language is associated with Yahweh enabling those who have an experience of the Spirit to lead in some way. The mode by which this is demonstrated varies considerably, but is relevant to the specific needs of the people at that time, though in Joseph's case this also needs to include other peoples. Thus Joseph provides wisdom needed by Pharaoh, the seventy elders take on administrative work and Joshua succeeds Moses in providing military leadership. Moses' leadership encompasses all these things and more, exceeding all others who have only a portion of his authority and role, but he fulfils all these roles because of the specific need of the people at the time. Finally, reference to the Spirit can be made to those who are being initiated into a leadership position and serves to provide a public testimony of Yahweh's choice of those concerned, pointing to both his presence and his empowerment of those called. Reference to the Spirit is thus an important mechanism for recognizing those called to lead, though this only happens when other mechanisms for public recognition are either not required or inappropriate.

The Former Prophets

Whereas references to the Spirit are comparatively rare in the Pentateuch, there is a significant body of them in the Former Prophets, though only in the books of Judges and Samuel, and this is often to someone whose experience of the Spirit is associated with their call to a leadership position.[20] Indeed, the books of Joshua and Kings never refer to the Spirit with reference to leadership, and although Kings does use *rûaḥ* language in terms of prophecy,[21] it is not always clear that it does so with reference to the Spirit of Yahweh. In view of the concentration of Spirit language in Judges – Samuel, this is significant and requires some consideration, and this will be the focus of the balance of this chapter. Although we cannot explore it in detail here, it seems that the reason for this distribution of language lies in the role of the Spirit in publicly validating new leadership. The book of Joshua recounts the period of Joshua's leadership, and his endowment with the Spirit has already been established in the Pentateuch. Since Joshua has no nominated successor there is no need for other references to the Spirit. The absence of Spirit language in Kings is largely explained by the fact of the dynastic promise to David in 2 Samuel 7:11b–16. There is no need for a public validation of David's successors because the dynastic promise has already indicated that they are Yahweh's choice.[22] As such, the paradigm established by the Pentateuch means there is no need for reference to the Spirit initiating leadership in either Joshua or Kings, whereas both Judges and Samuel describe the beginning of several new periods of leadership and Spirit language is an important element in confirming their validity. Hence we shall see that the Former Prophets develop the Pentateuchal paradigm in terms of the Spirit's role in initiating leadership, but also that they continue to explore the Spirit's role in terms of Yahweh's presence which enables those called to fulfil the role he has for them. Nevertheless, Spirit endowment is no guarantee of success

20. A convenient table summarizing these texts can be found in Daniel I. Block, 'Empowered by the Spirit of God: The Holy Spirit in the Historiographic Writings of the Old Testament', *SBJT* 1 (1997), p. 61.

21. E.g. 2 Kgs 2:9, 15.

22. Such a conclusion does not wholly depend upon a synchronic reading of the passage. For a defence of the importance of the promise there, see David G. Firth, 'Speech Acts and Covenant in 2 Samuel 7:1–17', in Jamie A. Grant and Alistair A. Wilson (eds.), *The God of Covenant: Biblical, Theological and Contemporary Perspectives* (Leicester: Apollos, 2005), pp. 79–99; and Michael A. Avioz, *Nathan's Oracle (2 Samuel 7) and Its Interpreters* (Bern: Peter Lang, 2005), pp. 25–31. A diachronic reading which identifies several redactional strata within the passage has been proposed by Petri Kasari, *Nathan's Promise in 2 Samuel 7 and Related Texts* (Helsinki: Finnish Exegetical Society, 2009), pp. 21–109, but he still finds the promise of a successor in his earliest layer (p. 243).

without faithfulness, and sometimes the Spirit may operate to prohibit actions contrary to Yahweh's purposes.

The judges

There are a significant number of references to the Spirit within the book of Judges, but they are not equally distributed, with all occurring in the stories of the judges themselves in chapters 3 – 16. What is particularly noteworthy is that seven[23] out of ten occurrences of *rûaḥ* are in a construct form with Yahweh as the absolute noun, as opposed to two instances where it is an absolute noun referring to someone's state of being[24] and one referring to a baleful spirit sent from God between Abimelech and the people of Shechem.[25] This contrasts significantly with the Pentateuch where such forms are definitely in the minority, but perhaps surprisingly in that the noun *rûaḥ* is never in a construct relationship with Yahweh there, though it is clear that the pronominal suffix on *rûaḥ* in Numbers 11:29 refers to Yahweh and there are a number of references where it is in a construct relationship with *ʾĕlōhîm* ('God'). The books of Samuel also have a high proportion of such construct relationships, though they divide more or less evenly between Yahweh and *ʾĕlōhîm* as the absolute noun. This may point to a stylistic feature of Judges, but the preference may be important within a book where the worship of other gods (*ʾĕlōhîm*) is such a major problem, making clear that the Spirit's source is Yahweh and thus removing any potential ambiguity.

In noting that the experience of the Spirit occurs only in the stories of the judges we should note that not all judges are said to have an experience of the Spirit and the timing and exact nature of this experience varies, though there are certainly common points. Thus only Othniel, Gideon, Jephthah and Samson are said to have an experience of the Spirit. Since we have no narrative associated with any of the minor judges we cannot judge their experience of the Spirit, but we should note that there is no statement about the Spirit for either Ehud or Deborah. It is important to note the reasons for the absence of reference to the Spirit in these cases, and once again the paradigm from the Pentateuch provides an explanation in terms of the public validation of their role. In the case of Ehud it is said that Yahweh had raised him up as a deliverer, but there is no indication that this was yet generally recognized by the

---

23. Judg. 3:10; 6:34; 11:29; 13:25; 14:6, 19; 15:14. The last of these is absent from the Targum, but the weight of evidence favours retaining MT.
24. Judg. 8:3; 15:19.
25. Judg. 9:23.

people when they sent tribute to Eglon by him. Ehud is in many ways a liminal character, a trickster,[26] and he does not stand out as an obvious deliverer, though this is in fact a general trend with the judges. In Ehud's case it seems he worked alone, taking the opportunity to prepare his sword once he was assigned to take the tribute to Eglon, whom he assassinated. Ehud appears to have been recognized as leader only after he had escaped after killing Eglon (Judg. 3:26–29), so in his case it seems it is the assassination that demonstrates him as a leader and thus proves his claim that Yahweh had given Moab into their hand (Judg. 3:28). But since his status has been demonstrated in this way there is no need to refer to the Spirit. Without being a trickster, something similar can be said about Deborah, who was already recognized as a prophetess (Judg. 4:4) and thus already acknowledged as a leader and not requiring the public validation that would be provided by a reference to the Spirit.

Although there are reasons why there is no mention of the Spirit in the case of Ehud and Deborah we still need to note the variations that are present in the experience of those judges for whom the Spirit is mentioned. As Butler has noted, the stories of the judges themselves gradually focus more and more on the problems of each judge,[27] but it is still the case that the brief account of Othniel (Judg. 3:7–11) provides the pattern against which the other judges are measured, perhaps because this story is itself drawn almost entirely from formulae in Judges 2:11–19.[28] As Webb observes, there is 'no dialogue, no reported speech of any kind, no dramatization of events, no scenic presentation'.[29] This means it is difficult to know what is meant by the Spirit 'coming' (*hyh*) upon Othniel, though it is certainly a colourless way of expressing this. Othniel is not introduced for the first time here, having been mentioned in Judges 1:12–15 when he captured some springs and so married Caleb's daughter, a passage that essentially repeats Joshua 15:16–19. There is no mention of the Spirit in these earlier passages, distinguishing the account of him as a judge. What we can observe is that his experience of the Spirit here comes after the people have cried out to Yahweh following their oppression by Cushan-Rishathaim.

---

26. Susan Niditch, *Judges: A Commentary* (Louisville: John Knox Press, 2008), p. 57.
27. Trent Butler, *Judges* (Nashville: Thomas Nelson, 2009), p. 57.
28. Ibid., pp. 62–63. For a Bakhtinian exploration of the possibilities this opens, see Susanne Gillmayr-Bucher, 'Framework and Discourse in the Book of Judges', *JBL* 128 (2009), pp. 687–702, though to claim that the dialogue within the book is 'unfinalizable' (p. 702) is to underplay the art with which the narrative is developed.
29. Barry G. Webb, *The Book of the Judges: An Integrated Reading* (Sheffield: Sheffield Academic Press, 1987), p. 127.

Although Othniel has clearly been a leader to some extent before this, his experience of the Spirit marks him as the one Yahweh shall use to deliver his people, while the statement that he 'judged' Israel points to his role as a military leader since that is how the verb is typically used in the accounts of the judges.[30] Thus reference to the Spirit indicates that he was empowered to provide the military leadership necessary for the nation before providing the rest for the land that typically follows the exploits of a judge. Since he was already a local figure it would seem that reference to the Spirit was also necessary to indicate his status as one chosen by Yahweh, though it also initiates a trend that runs through the accounts of Gideon and Jephthah, where a leader can already be active before any reference to the Spirit's coming is made.

That Israel's experience in the period of the judges is more complex than it might have seemed from just the story of Othniel is clear from the account of Gideon. Where Othniel is presented in largely colourless terms and with no insight into his own struggles, Gideon is a much more developed character.[31] There is, for example, considerable irony when Gideon is called by the angel of Yahweh (Judg. 6:12) and not only assured of Yahweh's presence, but also called a 'mighty man of valour' while he was threshing wheat in a wine press so as to hide it from the Midianites (Judg. 6:11), making the threshing almost completely useless. Of course, there are still strong echoes of the Othniel story – Israel had again done evil in Yahweh's sight and so been sold into a period of oppression before they cried out to him (Judg. 6:1–7). But instead of a judge, this time Israel received a prophet who brought a message of condemnation (Judg. 6:7–10), so when the angel of Yahweh initially appears to Gideon we do not know that he is definitely the one who will save Israel. Indeed, apart from the irony of the initial address by the angel, Gideon himself gives good reason to wonder about his suitability when he insists on a series of tests to confirm that it really was Yahweh who was calling him (Judg. 6:15–24). Only then does he begin the process of saving Israel as the angel had promised (6:14) when he follows the directive to tear down his father's Baal altar, though acting secretly with only ten servants because of his fear (6:25–27). Although this was hardly an inspiring moment, it does indicate the point where Gideon began to act in leadership, even if only in a small way, and

30. There is an exception in Judg. 4:4–5, where Deborah does appear to have acted to assess legal matters.

31. On static versus developed characters, see Meir Sternberg, *The Poetics of Biblical Narrative: Ideological Literature and the Drama of Reading* (Bloomington: Indiana University Press, 1987), pp. 344–346.

even though he still required his father's intervention to prevent his townspeople from executing him for this (Judg. 6:28–32). It is only at this point, after Gideon has begun to act but before he was generally recognized as a leader, that the Spirit came upon him. The contrast with Othniel is indicated by the use of the verb *lbš* ('clothed'), an altogether more picturesque term, though in Judges it probably has no functional difference in meaning.[32] The timing of the statement is, however, important. Before this, Gideon has not been especially effective in rallying support, but from now he is able to summon people from across the northern tribes to join him against Midian (Judg. 6:33–35), though he still needs another sign from Yahweh that he will indeed deliver the nation through him (Judg. 6:36–40). The experience of the Spirit has thus been crucial in testifying to the nation of Yahweh's call of Gideon while also empowering him to achieve this purpose, though this experience has not changed his fundamental character. But that he is recognized by the nation as a whole is apparent from the account in Judges 7, where the huge numbers that now followed him had to be trimmed down to only three hundred men before they defeated Midian. His victories continue in Judges 8, but he remains a conflicted character, one who is prepared to attack his own people who had not supported him (Judg. 8:13–17), one who refuses kingship but who still made an ephod that led the nation to sin (Judg. 8:22–28), though he did still bring rest to the land for the same period as Othniel.

The issues that begin to emerge in Gideon continue in the Jephthah narrative (Judg. 10:6 – 12:7). Israel has again sinned by going after other gods and this time is sold into the power of the Philistines and Ammonites (Judg. 10:6–9), though it is the Ammonites who dominate the story. When Israel cries out to Yahweh there is a message not dissimilar to that given by the prophet before Gideon's call (Judg. 6:8–10), though this time the emphasis is more upon the recent deliverances leading to the shocking directive that Israel should call out to those gods (Judg. 10:10–14). Yahweh's response to this is to be 'short' (*watiqṣar napšô*) with their trouble. This is often read positively as 'he could bear their misery no longer' (NASB), but given that a similar phrase in Judges 16:16 refers to Samson's impatience at Delilah's nagging, it is perhaps more likely that Yahweh was impatient over their misery (ESV).[33] If so, Israel faced a new Ammonite threat without evidence of a deliverer, and so sought

32. Being 'clothed' with the Spirit in Chronicles refers to enablement for prophetic activity (1 Chr. 12:18; 2 Chr. 24:20), but there is no evidence of any allusion to prophecy here.

33. Cf. Webb, *The Book of the Judges*, p. 47.

out Jephthah, who, though a warrior, was also associated with some 'sons of Belial', a phrase in the Former Prophets describing those whose lives are contrary to the will of Yahweh. Where Gideon was an unlikely deliverer because he lacked military skill, Jephthah is chosen by the people because he has military experience even though his life is contrary to the ways of Yahweh. In spite of this, the elders and Jephthah both invoked Yahweh at the point where he began to lead, though this involves more than a whiff of religious formalism and convenience (Judg. 10:17 – 11:12). The remarkable thing is that, rather than leading the people in battle, Jephthah immediately sent negotiators to the Ammonites seeking to avoid battle, offering a potted history of Israel's story to date to explain why they posed no threat to Ammon, though the Ammonite king was not persuaded, perhaps because of Jephthah's final claim that Yahweh would act as judge of the situation (Judg. 11:12–28). It is only at this point that the Spirit comes (*hyh*) upon Jephthah as he passes through the trans-Jordan to battle Ammon. As with Gideon, Jephthah has already begun to lead when the Spirit comes upon him, though it is notable that it is only when he has confessed that Yahweh is the judge that we finally reach a point where Yahweh recognizes Jephthah. Reference to the Spirit here is thus recognition of the point where Jephthah is validated as a legitimate leader by Yahweh and empowered to lead the people. But like Gideon, Jephthah remains fundamentally conflicted, as is apparent from his vow and subsequent sacrifice of his daughter along with the tragic death of forty-two thousand because of their inability to say 'shibboleth'. Moreover, even though Jephthah judges the people, there is no statement of him bringing rest to the land, an omission that will continue with Samson.[34]

The elements of individual conflictedness and the absence of rest for the land come to their climax in the story of Samson, though there are more references to the Spirit in his story than elsewhere in Judges. Whereas for Othniel, Gideon and Jephthah there is only one reference to the Spirit, there are four references for Samson, and new verbs used to describe this experience. Samson's story begins in the familiar way by recounting the nation's sin, but instead of a repentance narrative[35] we have instead a birth narrative telling

34. Alice Logan, 'Rehabilitating Jephthah', *JBL* 128 (2009), pp. 665–685, offers a more sympathetic reading of the story where Jepthah is caught up in forces beyond his control. Although there is some truth in this, it seems more probable that Jephthah is attempting to manipulate Yahweh through his vow and reaps the bitter fruit of such actions.

35. On the ways in which Judges varies standard forms, see Robert B. Chisholm,

how the angel of Yahweh appeared to a woman and her husband Manoah to announce his birth and seeming to imply that he was to be a Nazirite for life (Judg. 13),[36] though most of Samson's life will be spent acting in ways specifically prohibited for a Nazirite. Like Gideon (Judg. 6:22), Samson's parents are convinced they will die because they have seen Yahweh (Judg. 13:22–23), though where Yahweh had reassured Gideon, Samson's parents recognize that the acceptance of their offering meant they would live. Thus Samson was born and blessed in some way by Yahweh and, in some way, the Spirit began to direct[37] him (Judg. 13:25), though his physical maturity is not matched by his character. This first statement about the Spirit is in the context of his family life, but it is from this point that he commences his role of beginning to deliver Israel. However, as is typical of the Samson story, things never quite happen as we expect, except that we no longer anticipate things being as straightforward as they were with Othniel. Hence, rather than an act of delivery, we are told of Samson's desire to marry a Philistine woman. Though against his father's wishes, the narrator makes clear this was Yahweh's will as a means of overcoming the Philistines (Judg. 14:4). As Samson travelled to Timnah he was attacked by a lion, but the Spirit 'rushed' (*ṣlḥ*) upon him, a term that implies a powerful experience, and he therefore overcomes the lion. The significance of this is not initially made clear beyond the fact that he did not tell his parents, but its importance becomes clear in the subsequent account of collecting honey from its corpse and his riddle (Judg. 14:8–18). After his new wife disclosed the riddle's answer, the Spirit again rushed upon Samson so that he killed thirty men from the Philistine city of Ashkelon (Judg. 14:19). It is clear that the two instances in this chapter mutually interpret one another because the first experience of the Spirit is the necessary condition (in terms of the narrative) for the second. However, both are clarified by the narrator's comment in 14:4. By the end of the chapter Samson has nothing he wanted,

---

'What's Wrong with this Picture? Stylistic Variation as a Rhetorical Technique in Judges', *JSOT* 34.2 (2009), pp. 176–178.

36. Exactly what Samson's status was in relation to the Nazirite vow is much disputed, though with Mark Greene, 'Enigma Variations: Aspects of the Samson Story (Judges 13 – 16)', *Vox Evangelica* 21 (1991), p. 59, it seems clear that it is Samson's hair that is of particular interest to the narrator.

37. The verb *pʿm* occurs four other times, always with the sense of 'to disturb, trouble', though this is the only instance of the Qal. It is difficult to draw clear conclusions from such a limited sample, but it is possible that it is chosen here to suggest that the direction of the Spirit was not Samson's own choice.

but through the enabling of the Spirit has begun to fulfil Yahweh's purposes for him.

Nevertheless, Samson's role as a leader (of sorts) has not been recognized by his own people because all these events have taken place in Philistine territory. Hence in Judges 15 we not only read of him taking his personal revenge on the Philistines (Judg. 15:1–8), we also see the Philistines seeking him within Judah so that the men of Judah are prepared to surrender him to the Philistines for their own safety (Judg. 15:9–13). Again, as the Philistines came to him, the Spirit rushed upon him so that he tore off his bonds and slew a thousand at Ramath-Lehi. The importance of this is that this experience of the Spirit is not only evidence of Yahweh's presence with Samson, but it also attests his status to his people. Samson has been acting as a leader for a while (albeit without obvious intent) before this experience of the Spirit, but it is necessary not only because it empowers him to achieve Yahweh's purposes, but also because it confirms his status to the people. Hence Samson can be recognized as a leader because of the Spirit's presence, though apart from the fact that he kills Philistines Samson spends his time doing other than what he wants. That Samson's story continues to subvert our expectations is apparent from the fact that we have a statement of the period he judged Israel in Judges 15:20, but we then have the story of his relationship with Delilah and then death in Judges 16. In addition, although Samson's final experience of the Spirit validates his status to the people, he is the only judge who does not then raise an army to overcome the foe apart from Othniel, for whom we lack any significant information. In spite of his earlier victories, it is only as the Philistine leadership dies with him that he begins to deliver his people. Samson's experience of the Spirit is one where Yahweh's purposes are being fulfilled through him, though Samson himself seems to have little interest in these things. He remains, to the end, deeply flawed, though his flaws mirror those of the people. He is, as Judges 13:25 says, directed by the Spirit, and though it is a direction that is often at odds with the path Samson himself would choose, it is through this that Samson achieves Yahweh's purposes. In the end he dies as 'the naïve victim of his own weaknesses',[38] and yet paradoxically it is through these weaknesses that the Spirit works.

The judges who have an experience of the Spirit thus follow, but also extend, the paradigm established by the Pentateuch. Although it is arguably implicit in the Pentateuch, it becomes clear with the judges that the experience

---

38. Chisholm, 'What's Wrong', p. 179.

of the Spirit is generally not when they begin to lead but when their leadership needs to be recognized. Only as the judges engage with Yahweh's purposes do they experience the Spirit's enabling, something that simultaneously empowers them to deliver the people but also testifies to Yahweh's choice of them. It is notable that in no case does this mean that the Spirit-enabled individual had their fundamental character changed. Although the information about Othniel is too brief to draw any conclusions, each of the other judges is a conflicted individual and there is no evidence that this changes. Indeed, in the case of Samson it is his experience of the Spirit that is in some senses at the root of his conflicted state. Nevertheless, it is the Spirit that enables them to achieve those purposes that Yahweh has for them, even when that means leading them into paths they would not choose themselves.

Kingship

There are no more references to the Spirit until we come to the call of Saul to be Israel's first king.[39] Perhaps the most remarkable thing is how similar Saul's experience of the Spirit is to the judges, though just as there are developments that can be traced between the Pentateuch and the judges, so also there are developments between the judges and the experience of Saul and David, most notably in David's enduring experience of the Spirit (1 Sam. 16:13).

Saul's experience of the Spirit comes at the end of the initial stages of his rise to the throne after he has been anointed by Samuel and told that the Spirit 'rushing'[40] upon him will be the climax of a series of signs that confirm him as the one chosen by Yahweh to save his people from the Philistines while also restraining[41] the people (1 Sam. 9:16–17). This coming of the Spirit indicates to Saul that he would 'prophesy', which here seems to mean 'have an ecstatic experience', and be turned into 'a new man' (1 Sam. 10:6), a phrase which appears to mean both that he is equipped for Yahweh's purposes and that this demonstrates his election by Yahweh.[42]

---

39. There is an important movement in Samuel from speaking of *nāgîd* ('leader' or 'designate') to *melek* ('king'), but for convenience 'king' shall be used as the general term here.
40. As with Samson, the verb *ṣlḥ* is used for both Saul and David's experience of the Spirit.
41. On this translation of *ʿṣr*, see David G. Firth, *1 & 2 Samuel* (Nottingham: Apollos, 2009), p. 119.
42. David Toshio Tsumura, *The First Book of Samuel* (Grand Rapids: Eerdmans, 2007), p. 288.

This combination seems to be borne out by the fact that he is told to 'do what his hand finds to do', a phrase which in Judges 9:23 means to launch an attack, and in the context of reference to a Philistine garrison here suggests he was meant to attack it.[43] The experience of the Spirit is meant both to empower Saul and also to offer a public testimony to his status so that others will follow him. The only sign of importance to the narrator is the experience of the Spirit, the others being assumed, because although Saul does indeed 'prophesy' and receives a new 'heart' from God (1 Sam. 10:9–10), he does not initiate an attack on the Philistine garrison. Saul has been empowered, but unlike the judges he does not act. Instead, we hear only the origins of the proverb 'Is Saul also among the prophets?' Saul has received the promise of the Spirit, but his behaviour generates a level of ambiguity that the people find difficult to pierce, an uncertainty that to some extent is still present following his experience of the Spirit in defeating Nahash (1 Sam. 11:6). Nevertheless, Saul's experience of the Spirit is clearly meant to initiate a new point in Israel's experience of leadership, but where the judges might fail personally after they have delivered the nation, Saul's failure seems to lie at the outset. Spirit empowerment is just that – empowerment – but the Spirit never compels leaders to act, and neither does this empowerment prevent them from making serious errors.

We do not read again of the Spirit in relation to Saul until after David has been elected as the next king after Samuel's visit to Bethlehem, resulting in the Spirit rushing 'upon David from that day onward' (1 Sam. 16:13). Samson's story has already hinted that experience of the Spirit might be sporadic, but the note of David's enduring experience of the Spirit immediately distinguishes him from Saul. Immediately after this we are told of the Spirit of God leaving Saul so that he is afflicted by the grievous spirit instead. In terms of being Yahweh's chosen king, only one can experience Yahweh's Spirit, and that is never again Saul, although he will once again 'prophesy' when he and some of his men attempt to arrest David in 1 Samuel 19:20–24, again raising the question 'Is Saul also among the prophets?' What is clear from Saul's experience of both the Spirit of God and the grievous spirit is that the Spirit works to enable God's servants to do his will, and this means both empowering those who are called to lead and disabling those who attempt to work against the divine purpose.

Nevertheless, we should note that the contrast between David and Saul's

43. V. Phillips Long, *The Reign and Rejection of King Saul: A Case for Literary and Theological Coherence* (Missoula: Scholars Press, 1989), p. 207.

experience of the Spirit is more than just the fact that David's experience is enduring rather than episodic. It is never said that David 'prophesied' and there is no directive given requiring him to attack any Philistines.[44] If 1 Samuel 17 is chronologically prior to 1 Samuel 16,[45] then there is no need to defeat any Philistines as he has already done so, though of course he does so under Saul's leadership. But even if the narrative sequence is the chronological order, then one could still note that Saul is still legally the king so David cannot be expected to lead an attack. But the absence of any reference to David 'prophesying' is perhaps more significant. David's experience of the Spirit is not ecstatic, and David is never out of control in the way Saul is. Indeed, after Saul's second time of 'prophesying' (1 Sam. 19:23) we do not have another reference to the Spirit until 2 Samuel 23:7.[46] We are thus to understand the whole of David's rise and reign as something directed by the Spirit, and we may have further evidence for this in the repeated refrain that 'Yahweh was with David', since a key aspect of the Spirit's role was to point to Yahweh's presence. David's story therefore indicates once again that those empowered by the Spirit may both be powerful in achieving Yahweh's purposes and yet also be capable of appalling mistakes, such as we see in 2 Samuel 11. However great these failings might be, David remains Yahweh's chosen king, and his 'last words' in 2 Samuel 23:1–7 are portrayed as a Spirit-led oracle which is also a reflection on the nature of leadership. Where Saul's prophesying was an ecstatic experience, David's experience of the Spirit results in a reflective oracle that points the way for those leaders who would follow him. It suggests that leadership, even that initially validated by the Spirit, does not endure for ever unless it manifests justice and the fear of God. But within those constraints, leaders can continue and even establish a dynasty. David's reflection thus addresses an important gap from previous experiences of the Spirit in Israel's history, showing that the experience of the Spirit need not only be something that marks the beginning of leadership, but rather that through the Spirit rulers (and even rulers who fail badly) can continue and learn to be more effective as leaders.

---

44. See Keith Bodner, *1 Samuel: A Narrative Commentary* (Sheffield: Sheffield Phoenix Press, 2008), p. 171.
45. See Firth, *Samuel*, pp. 179–181.
46. There is an ambiguous reference in 2 Sam. 22:16, and though *rûaḥ* there is best understood as the 'blast' from Yahweh's nostrils, it can still shade into a reference to the Spirit, and in any case in Hebrew is one of the key links between the two poems at the centre of the Samuel Conclusion (2 Sam. 21 – 24).

Conclusion

David's final note thus prepares the way for understanding the work of the Spirit in a more continuous way than was evident in earlier narratives with the possible exception of Moses. Clearly, the narratives of the OT understand the Spirit as both empowering those called by God to lead, and testifying to the people of who is called to lead. It is frequently, though not universally, the case that those who experience the Spirit have already begun to work as leaders before their empowerment by the Spirit, though in those cases the emphasis is more upon the element of the Spirit's presence being a testimony to the people of those called by Yahweh. In both empowering and attesting the Spirit does not prevent leaders from making major mistakes, but it is the work of the Spirit to enable leaders to fulfil those purposes Yahweh has for his people. In light of this, David's final note (2 Sam. 23:2) points the way forward, so that leaders can explore how the experience of the Spirit can continually enable them beyond their initial empowerment. It is this that provides the model for Zechariah's assurance to Zerubbabel that the building of the second temple would be achieved by the Spirit, while also preparing for the hope that eschatological leaders (e.g. Isa. 11:2; 42:1; 61:1) would have a special experience of the Spirit. Once the enduring experience of the Spirit can be understood, then there is hope for leaders who can be so much more than those who have provided the earlier models.

16. THE SAMSON SAGA AND SPIRITUAL LEADERSHIP

Eugene H. Merrill

Introduction

The purpose of this chapter is to address the role of the Spirit[1] of God in the life and leadership of Samson, a judge of Israel in the late pre-Monarchic era (c. 1124–1084 BCE).[2] The Samson narrative (Judg. 13 – 16) is fraught with difficulties from beginning to end, not least of which is the apparent

---

1. The term 'saga' in the title should not be understood in the technical sense of a purely legendary account of a hero-figure, but connotes the larger-than-life (because miraculous) experiences of its central protagonist, in this case Samson. For a definition of the term in literature in general, see *Merriam-Webster's Encyclopedia of Literature* (Springfield: Merriam-Webster, 1995), pp. 982–983. Likewise, the use of capital 'S' for 'Spirit' throughout is not intended to be construed as suggesting deity but only conformity to common usage in the commentaries and other literature.
2. For justification of these dates, see Eugene H. Merrill, *Kingdom of Priests: A History of Old Testament Israel*, 2nd ed. (Grand Rapids: Baker, 2008), pp. 192–194. The importance of dating the events is to ground them in a relative chronology that sheds light on questions of compositional priority and dependence, especially in the interest of the theological principle of progressive revelation.

paradox of God's powerful work through Samson against the backdrop of his obvious moral and spiritual failings. How could God's blessing through his Spirit be squared with the behaviour of a narcissistic adolescent who at every turn seemed unwilling or unable to comport himself in a holy, upright manner?

The answer lies ultimately in the sovereignty of God who demands and requires no prerequisites in the execution of his will on earth. That is, God is independent and self-reliant, in no need of assistance, yet condescends to call and equip humankind to cooperate with him in the carrying out of his creative and redemptive mission. Thus Samson, like clay in the potter's hand, was carefully moulded to become a vessel through which the Spirit could do his work (cf. Isa. 45:9; Jer. 18:5–6; Rom. 9:21).

Overview of the Samson Saga[3]

Samson, the last of a dozen or more judges who provided leadership to Israel between the time of Joshua and the rise of the Monarchy, was, like his contemporary Samuel, the child of a barren woman who (though granted in her case a son through divine initiative) pledged to devote her son to the LORD in gratitude for his gracious bestowment (cf. 1 Sam. 1:11, 20, 27–28). Unlike Samuel, Samson was characterized by profligate self-indulgence, seeking always to satisfy his carnal appetites despite his status as a Nazirite. His churlish manner towards his parents, his wife and his in-laws (Judg. 14:1–4, 16–18; 15:1–2), his lustful dalliances with women of every kind (14:1–2; 16:1, 4), his uncontrollable fits of rage (14:19; 15:3–5, 7) – all these set Samson in diametrical opposition to the calm and generous spirit of Samuel (1 Sam. 3:4, 6–7; 7:9; 8:6, 21; 9:19; 10:1, 24; 12:3–5, 20–23; 16:1). Yet Samuel is never said to have been energized by the Spirit of God, whereas Samson was thus blessed no fewer than four times (Judg. 13:25; 14:6, 19; 15:14). Clearly the appearance of the Spirit or the lack thereof seems to have had little to do with personal disposition and behaviour. All one can surmise from the respective narratives is that the Spirit acted arbitrarily in contexts of mighty, heroic deeds.

---

3. A good study of the Samson material as a whole is James L. Crenshaw, *Samson: A Secret Betrayed, a Vow Ignored* (Atlanta: John Knox, 1978).

The Angel of the Lord

The story of Samson cannot be fully understood apart from identification of the Angel of the Lord, because the Angel and the Spirit, though not synonymous, appear cooperatively in Judges 13, suggesting a divine manifestation that offers interpretive help with regard to the topic of this chapter.[4] Canonically and chronologically prior to our narrative, the Angel appears in several clusters of texts offering hints as to his identity (Gen. 16:7–13; 21:8–21; 22:9–19; Num. 22:22–41).[5]

Though strangely absent from the book of Joshua, the Angel of the Lord is very much present in two of the most important narratives of Judges, those of Gideon and Samson. The density of reference to both the Angel and the Holy Spirit in these two accounts cannot be by happenstance and will have much to contribute to the study at hand. Gideon (c. 1200–1160 BCE), who preceded Samson by about a century, was called by the Lord to deliver Israel from the devastating ravages of the Midianites who had oppressed them for seven years. As suddenly as he would appear later to Samson's father and mother, the Angel of the Lord visited Gideon at his home and immediately made it clear that God was calling him to some high and holy purpose (Judg. 6:11–24). Described at times as the Angel of the Lord (vv. 11, 12, 21, 22), at others as the Lord (vv. 14, 16, 23), and at still others as the Angel of God (v. 20) or Lord God (v. 22), the intermixing of the epithets is sufficient by itself to make the case that they are

4. Rene Lopez, 'Identifying the "Angel of the Lord" in Judges: A Model for Reconsidering the Referent in Other Old Testament Loci', *BBR* 20/1 (2010), pp. 1–18. See also Stephen L. White, 'Angel of the Lord: Messenger of Euphemism?' *TynBul* 50/2 (1999), pp. 299–305; Gary Simmers, 'Who Is the "Angel of the Lord"?' *Faith and Mission* 17/3 (2000), pp. 3–16; Norman R. Gulley, 'Trinity in the Old Testament', *JATS* 17/1 (2006), pp. 80–97.

5. Later revelation on the matter is deemed irrelevant to interpreting the Samson narrative in its own historical and cultural context. See Walter C. Kaiser, *Toward an Exegetical Theology* (Grand Rapids: Baker, 1981), pp. 134–140. For the earlier narratives, see L. Daniel Hawk, 'The God Who Sees: Genesis 16:1–13', *ATJ* 41 (2009), pp. 1–4; Claus Westermann, *Genesis 12 – 36. A Commentary*, trans. John J. Scullian (Minneapolis: Augsburg, 1985), p. 247; Gerhard von Rad, *Genesis. A Commentary*, trans. John H. Marks (London: SCM, 1961), p. 228; Gordon J. Wenham, *Genesis 16 – 50*, WBC 2 (Dallas: Word, 1994), p. 110.

interchangeable and are to be understood as referring to the same entity or at least to his surrogate.[6]

A similar analysis of the Samson story yields a quite different distribution. The Angel of the Lord appears by name only in Judges 13 (vv. 3, 13, 15, 16, 17, 20, 21), never in the remainder of the narrative. 'Angel of God' occurs twice (vv. 6, 9), enough and in such contexts to establish that they are one and the same. Moreover, the statement that 'God listened to Manoah, and the Angel of God came to the woman' (v. 9) suffices to show that God and his Angel are, for all practical purposes, to be equated, at least functionally.

The person and work of the Spirit of God (in the Old Testament)

Despite the well-nigh universal consensus that Christian trinitarianism is absent in the OT, a number of texts as early as Torah and Judges hint in that direction.[7] This does not mean that every occurrence of 'spirit', even with 'God' or 'Lord', should be construed as a reference to the Holy Spirit. Usage, context and theological development must be brought to bear in making such interpretive decisions. For example, the creation narrative (Gen. 1:1 – 2:3), in anthropomorphic or zoomorphic terms, describes the Spirit of God 'hovering over' the surface of the deep (1:3).[8] Nothing here compels any understanding beyond the spirit being an effluence of God or even a synonymous term for God himself. Even the use of the first-person plural pronoun ('us') in verse 26 is not persuasive of a 'trinitarian conversation', an interchange without parallel elsewhere. Nor should an appeal to the plurality of *ʾĕlōhîm* add weight to the argument for a trinitarian interpretation, or even for one that claims the ontological existence and deity of the spirit. In summary, no case can be made exegetically for the personality of the spirit in Genesis 1, though certainly a full biblical theology is not incorrect to see the ideological

6. Block elegantly describes the Angel here as 'Yahweh's alter ego'. Daniel I. Block, *Judges, Ruth*, NAC 6 (Nashville: Broadman & Holman, 1999), p. 259.
7. For support of the presence of the Trinity in the OT, see Gulley, 'Trinity in the Old Testament', pp. 89–97. An interchange on the matter may be seen in Eugene H. Merrill and Alan J. Hauser, 'Is the Doctrine of the Trinity Implied in the Genesis Creation Account?', *The Genesis Debate*, ed. Ronald F. Youngblood (Grand Rapids: Baker, 1990), pp. 110–129 (Merrill, yes; Hauser, no).
8. Kenneth A. Mathews, *Genesis 1 – 11:26*, NAC (Nashville: Broadman & Holman, 1996), p. 136; cf. Deut. 32:11; Jer. 23:9.

basis for later OT (and even NT) truths latent in these texts (cf. also 6:3 and 41:38).[9]

Exodus 31:3 (cf. 35:31) pictures Bezalel as 'filled with the spirit of God', thus enabling him to undertake the task of building the Tent of Meeting. Here the spirit seems equivalent to the wisdom, knowledge and understanding requisite to carry out the work (cf. v. 35 where Bezalel and others are said to be filled with wisdom, thus suggesting that wisdom and the spirit are one and the same). Stuart suggests that 'being filled with the Spirit' is a biblical idiom for 'having from God the ability to do or say exactly what God wants done or said'.[10]

Numbers 11:16–30 is replete with references to the spirit or 'God's spirit' (7x in vv. 17, 25, 26, 29), all in the context of the installment of seventy elders empowered to assist Moses in the leadership of the community. Verse 17 reads literally, 'I will take from the spirit that is upon you and set [it] upon them.' The actualization of this appears in verse 25 which relates that the Lord descended in the cloud and 'took from the spirit that was upon him [Moses] and gave it to the seventy'. The result is that the 'spirit rested upon them and they began to prophesy'. The same verb occurs in verse 26 to speak of the spirit resting upon Eldad and Medad, two elders who had remained in the camp. Finally, Moses chastened Joshua, who had resented Moses' sharing of the spirit with the seventy, and lamented that all of God's people were not given God's spirit (v. 29).[11] Clearly 'set upon' and 'give' are synonymous, the result being 'resting upon' in both cases.[12]

In as much as Judges and Samuel were composed no later than the time of the United Monarchy, only they require attention. Of the fifteen references

---

9. Stephen G. Dempster, *Dominion and Dynasty* (Downers Grove: InterVarsity Press, 2003), pp. 231–234; Merrill, *Genesis Debate*, pp. 125–127.

10. Douglas K. Stuart, *Exodus*, NAC 2 (Nashville: Broadman & Holman, 2006), p. 651.

11. Ironically, Joshua later was not just empowered by the spirit but was 'filled' (*mālēʾ*) by the spirit (Deut. 34:9). This same verb occurs elsewhere in the Torah only with reference to Eldad and Medad (Exod. 31:3; 34:31; see above). In fact 'spirit' and 'fill' are limited to these two examples alone in the OT, a matter worth exploring in another study.

12. Jacob points out, however, that 'from the first traces of theological reflection about *ruach* as a divine power it was connected with Yahweh; a celebrated passage in the book of Isaiah [31:3] shows that in the eighth century the spirit and Yahweh denote the same reality' (Edmond Jacob, *Theology of the Old Testament* [New York: Harper & Row, 1958], pp. 123–124).

to the spirit in these two books (not including the 'evil spirit from the LORD'), four say simply that the spirit of the Lord *was upon* a given person, thus yielding little information about either the identity of the spirit or his/its relationship to the gifted individual (Judg. 3:10; 11:29; 1 Sam. 19:20, 23). In one important instance, the spirit of the Lord is said to have 'clothed [himself]' with Gideon, a figure of speech to be addressed more fully below. With respect to Samson, the spirit began to stir or trouble him in the camp of Dan (Judg. 13:25), moving him to a course of action.[13]

Most commonly (7x), the verb describes the forcible coming of the spirit upon someone (Samson in Judg. 14:6, 19; 15:14; and Saul in 1 Sam. 10:6, 10; 11:6; 16:13). This suggests perhaps a certain unwillingness or lack of preparedness on the part of the recipients whom the Lord nevertheless is determined to employ in his service.

Space limits forbid a sustained discussion of the phenomenon of the 'evil spirit' sent from the Lord. Only Saul was thus afflicted (1 Sam. 16:14, 15, 23; 18:10; 19:9). In the first instance the spirit of the Lord departed from Saul and an 'evil' (better, 'troubling') spirit began to bother him (1 Sam. 16), even forcibly coming upon him (1 Sam. 18, 19). The powerful spirit came therefore for both good and ill. The clue to his identity, or at least certainly his function, is clear from 1 Samuel 16:14 in which the spirit that blessed and empowered Saul to reign left him to make way for the spirit that troubled him and presaged his loss of kingship and the kingdom. In neither case is Saul said to be possessed by the spirit, but only controlled by him/it.[14]

Exegesis of the relevant texts in Judges 13 – 16

Judges 13:24–25

The broader context of this passage consists of an encounter between the Lord and the childless couple Manoah and his wife. No record exists of their having prayed for a son as in the birth narrative of Samuel (1 Sam. 1:10–11).[15] Indeed, the explanation for the giving of a son was that the child might be the 'saviour' of Israel from the oppression of the Philistines (Judg. 13:5). Such

13. *HALOT*, 952, s. v. חלל.
14. David M. Howard, Jr, 'The Transfer of Power from Saul to David in 1 Sam 16:13–14', *JETS* 32/4 (1989), pp. 473–483.
15. Benjamin J. M. Johnson, 'What Type of Son Is Samson? Reading Judges 13 as a Biblical Type-Scene', *JETS* 53/2 (2010), p. 274.

an assignment demanded that he be a Nazirite from birth with all the restrictions of dedication and purity attendant to that ministry (Num. 6:1–21). This would not happen by his parents' choice or even of his own free will; rather, he would be made a Nazirite by the Lord himself. Cartledge helpfully makes a distinction between Nazirites from birth (such as Samson and Samuel [?]), and those who took upon themselves Nazirite vows (Num. 6:1–21), the latter being voluntary and temporary.[16]

Manoah's remarkable encounter with the Angel of God prompted him to invite his guest to dinner. The likely double entendre of the offer led the Angel to reject the meal but to suggest that Manoah could offer the young goat to the Lord as a burnt offering. In this manner the Angel put beyond doubt that he was more than a mere human messenger. He refused to eat dinner precisely because he was superior to mortal man and, in fact, as the emissary of the Lord God was worthy of receiving sacrificial homage on the Lord's behalf. Sensing even more strongly the superhuman character of this strange guest, Manoah, like his wife before him, asked him his name, learning only that it is 'wonderful'.[17] His credentials were immediately apparent when, in the midst of the ceremony of sacrifice, the Angel did a 'wonderful thing', namely, he ascended 'to the sky' in the flame of the altar (v. 20). Overcome by this glorious manifestation of deity, the couple prostrated themselves, knowing now they had conversed with the Angel of the Lord, who, Manoah said, was God himself (v. 22).[18]

Samson and the Spirit

The Samson story – the lengthiest of the narratives of the judges save that of Gideon – occupies ninety-six verses, only four of which mention the person and work of the Spirit (13:25; 14:6, 19; 15:14). Each of these will be treated individually and then brought together in search for exegetical and theological syntheses contributory to the topic of the chapter.

16. Tony W. Cartledge, 'Were Nazirite Vows Unconditional?', *CBQ* 51 (1989), pp. 409–422.
17. Thus MT; Q reads (correctly) *pelî'*.
18. Keil and Delitzsch go so far as to propose that the Angel of the Lord was 'of one nature with God'. C. F. Keil and F. Delitzsch, *Joshua, Judges, Ruth*, Biblical Commentary on the Old Testament, trans. James Martin (Grand Rapids: Eerdmans, n. d. repr. 1960), p. 408.

Judges 13:21 – 14:4

'Then the spirit of the LORD began to disturb[19] him in Mahaneh-Dan, between Zorah and Eshtaol' (Judg. 13:25).[20] As observed already, Samson was the much-awaited son of parents who had promised the Lord to rear him as a Nazirite. Moreover, he would be the deliverer of his people from Philistine oppression (Judg. 13:5). The problem with being committed to a course of life and action before his birth is that he has nothing to contribute to the decision. This may be what is in view in this passage. Perhaps Samson rebelled during his adolescent years, implicitly refusing to abide by both his Nazirite vows and his calling to be a saviour. By the time Samson was twenty years old,[21] the Spirit of the Lord began to disturb him from his lethargy and towards an encounter with the Philistines.

The encounter could hardly have been more inauspicious or surprising. After being shaken to action by the Spirit, Samson wended his way the short distance between his home and the Philistine village of Timnah in the Sorek Valley, no more than seven miles away.[22] His immediate infatuation with a young Philistine woman led to his demand of his parents that they make arrangements for the two to marry. Unknown to them, or anyone else for that matter, the Lord 'was seeking an occasion[23] against the Philistines' because 'at that time, the Philistines were ruling over Israel' (Judg. 14:4).

---

19. The verb *pāʿam* is rendered variously (CSB, ESV, NASB, NIV, RSV, 'stirred', 'stir'; HCSB, 'direct'; JPS, NKJV, 'moved'; NEB, 'drive hard'; NET, 'control'; NLT, 'take hold of'). The form occurs only here in the Qal/Piel, but 3x in the Niphal (Gen. 41:8; Ps. 77:5; Dan. 2:3) and once in the Hithpael (Dan. 2:1). In all instances it has to do with either insomnia or dreamingomnia, especially troubled sleep. This meaning fits well in our passage.
20. The specifications of the locale – between Zorah and Eshtaol – argues strongly for Mahaneh-Dan as a place name rather than 'camp of Dan' or the like (thus ESV, NASB). For the location, see Yohanan Aharoni and Michael Avi-Yonah, *The Carta Bible Atlas*, 4th ed., Anson F. Rainey and Ze'ev Safrai (Jerusalem: Carta, 2002), p. 65. Another place with this name was located just west of Kirjath-jearim (Judg. 18:12). The two can hardly be the same.
21. For the chronology of Samson's life, see Merrill, *Kingdom of Priests*, pp. 168–169.
22. Now Tell Batash. For the excavation and identification, see George L. Kelm, *Timnah: A Biblical City in the Sorek Valley* (Winona Lake: Eisenbrauns, 1995).
23. The noun *tōʾănâ* conveys the idea of 'an opportunity for confrontation'. Michael A. Grisanti, אנה, *NIDOTTE* 1:628, p. 453. In strongly anthropomorphic terms, the Lord is looking to 'pick a fight'.

The role of the Spirit here is readily apparent – to prepare the way for Israel's deliverance through the young Nazirite Samson. But who or what is the Spirit? The text says only that 'the Spirit of the LORD began to trouble him' (Judg. 13:25). We have already noted the strange language of Judges 6:34: 'The Spirit of the LORD clothed [or dressed] with Gideon' (cf. also 1 Chr. 12:18; 2 Chr. 24:20). That is, the Spirit is likened to a person dressing himself, this time Gideon being the garment. If this is the proper interpretation, this is as close as one can get in the OT to the notion of being filled by or with the Spirit, an image that loses its significance if the Spirit is viewed as anything or anyone other than a personality.[24] However, this rendering requires the verb to be reflexive (perhaps Piel or Niphal), not Qal as here. That is, the better translation says merely, 'The Spirit of the LORD clothed Gideon.' How or with what is not forthcoming. Thus it seems best to see the idiom as an expression of the Spirit's wrapping Gideon with his power and glory.[25] The intent in our Samson text also is to portray the Spirit as almost an emanation of God that disturbed Samson from his lassitude and pushed him into service as a deliverer of Israel from Philistine hegemony. Thus the immediate confines of our narrative yield no more information than that 'the [otherwise indefinable] Spirit of the LORD' disturbed him.

Judges 14:5–18

Further evidence of the Spirit's presence with Samson is not long in coming in the narrative. In what apparently was an initial solo trip to Timnah for unexpressed reasons, Samson met a Philistine girl and, smitten by her, returned home to inform his father and mother that he wanted to take her as his wife. On a second visit, this time accompanied by his parents, Samson encountered a lion which he easily slew following the forcible intervention[26] of the Spirit

---

24. Block proposes that the idiom means that 'the Spirit took possession of the man'. However, this seems not to do justice to the vividness of the imagery of being clothed. Block, *Judges, Ruth*, p. 272. The Greek tradition (subluciana I followed by Vetus Latina) employs the verb *endyō*, 'dress, clothe', in the same figurative manner. See BDAG, 2nd ed., p. 264.
25. See e.g. *TDOT* 7, p. 464, s. v. לבשׁ; *NIDOTTE* 2, p. 758, s. v. לבשׁ.
26. As suggested above, the verb *šāsaʿ* contains an inherent aspect of violence. Here as elsewhere it suggests that the Spirit forced himself/itself upon Samson, enabling him to have supernatural strength and to accomplish supernatural deeds (cf. Judg. 14:19; 15:14; 1 Sam. 10:6, 10; 11:6; 16:13).

of the Lord.[27] Some time later Samson went to Timnah to fetch his bride and en route found and ate honey from the carcass of the lion.

The work of the Spirit here is most central to the focus of our study. It is complicated by Samson's violation of two clear Torah restrictions, namely, intermarriage with a non-Israelite (Exod. 34:16; Deut. 7:3; cf. Josh. 23:12–13) and, as a Nazirite, contaminating himself by touching a dead body (Num. 6:6–7; cf. Judg. 13:7). As suggested already, the conundrum is to understand and justify the empowering by the Spirit of the Lord of such an unworthy candidate as Samson. On what grounds can the opposing notions of perfection and imperfection, purity and impurity, righteousness and unrighteousness be reconciled? Soggin suggests that 'the only virtue which the spirit seems to have given Samson is physical strength pure and simple – certainly not wisdom or ethical consistency'.[28] Thus it is clear that the Spirit could be (and was) bestowed on persons without respect to their spiritual or other qualifications (1 Sam. 10:10; 19:20). He/it enabled ordinary persons to do extraordinary things or, to the contrary, to be immobilized in their efforts to do harm.

In the present instance, the overwhelming Spirit empowered Samson for one task only, the slaying of the lion. David, too, would later kill a lion and a bear (1 Sam. 17:34), but the verb here (*šāsaʿ*) in the Piel means to tear to pieces (cf. Lev. 1:17; 1 Sam. 24:8), a violent act made possible by a violent empowering by the Spirit. Thus it seems that the Spirit in this case bespeaks an exercise of divine power with no clear suggestion of its personhood. In David's case, though the Spirit is not mentioned in the slaying of the lion, the bear and even Goliath, on the occasion of his being anointed as king 'the Spirit of the Lord rushed upon David [Heb. *ṣālaḥ*] from that day forward' (1 Sam. 16:13). That is, there was no need for a special display of the Spirit from time to time, since the Spirit empowered and blessed him as a matter of course.[29]

---

27. The order of events here is confusing in that the text implies that Samson's father and mother are with him and yet they know nothing of the slaying of the lion. *BHS* (and most scholars) simply suggests that the reference to the parents be deleted. However, as Keil and Delitzsch sensibly proposed long ago, all that need be said is that the parents were not eyewitnesses of the episode with the lion. The trio made the same trip but not necessarily close together. See Keil and Delitzsch, *Joshua, Judges, Ruth*, p. 410.
28. J. Alberto Soggin, *Judges*, OTL (Philadelphia: Westminster, 1981), p. 236.
29. The verb here, as in Judg. 14:6, 19; 15:14, connotes the idea of the Spirit forcing himself upon someone; cf. *HALOT*, p. 1026. That is, the recipient need not always

Judges 14:19

After the wedding celebration Samson taunted his male guests with a riddle they could not interpret. Their inability to do so may be partly explained by the fact that by the seventh day of a drunken orgy their capacity to reason was seriously impaired.[30] Under threat of life and limb from the clamorous crowd, Samson's wife revealed the answer to the riddle, thereby setting Samson off into a torrent of rage. The enactment of vengeance for such humiliation and loss was beyond Samson's capacity so 'the Spirit of the LORD overwhelmed him' just as he/it had when Samson encountered the lion. This time he went on to Ashkelon where he struck down thirty Philistine men whose clothing he took to pay the wager he had made about the riddle. No weapon is named, so one is free to speculate that he might have torn them limb from limb just as he had dispatched the lion.

Judges 15:14

In Samson's absences from his wife, her father had given her to another man as wife (Judg. 15:1–2). Infuriated, Samson (absent any reference to the Spirit) tied foxes' tails together, ignited them and turned them loose in the Philistine wheat fields. They retaliated by burning the house of Samson's wife, so he attacked and killed many of them (again, no reference to the Spirit). Threatened by the Philistines, some Judean men came to Samson to persuade him to let them bind him and turn him over to the Philistines. Strangely (or so it seems) Samson allowed the binding provided the Judeans would not kill him themselves (v. 13). The arrangement clearly was a ploy by Samson that allowed him access to the Philistines, who would suppose that his binding was indicative of his weakness. Thus he would be in a position to do them harm. However, no sooner had the moment come when Samson's life seemed about to end, than he broke the bonds and with the jaw-bone of an ass slew a thousand men (vv. 15–16).

The secret of his prowess once more was Samson's overwhelming endowment by the Spirit of the Lord. His vindictiveness and seeming barbarity notwithstanding, God unleashed his Spirit upon Samson as a display of his

---

be compliant because the decision that the Spirit should come upon a person was God's decision alone.

30. John Gray, *Joshua, Judges, Ruth*, NCBC (Grand Rapids: Eerdmans, 1986), p. 329. The term for 'feast' here is *mišteh*, 'a drink', usually of wine. Again, the irony of God's empowerment of not only a drunkard but the breaker of a Nazirite vow is most striking.

mighty power. Surprisingly, perhaps, in Samson's climactic act of prowess in which he caused the collapse of the Dagon temple with the loss of three thousand lives (Judg. 16:23–31), the narrative is silent about the Spirit of the Lord, although it is obvious that Samson relied upon the Lord for supernatural strength (v. 28). Perhaps the note that explicitly states that Samson 'did not know that the LORD had departed from him' (v. 20) is a way of speaking of the Holy Spirit, in this case as synonymous with the Lord himself. That the Spirit came upon individuals and then departed from them is clear from the transition between Saul and David (1 Sam. 16:14). He came at the bidding of God to accomplish whatever needed to be done and he withdrew when the task was accomplished.

Conclusion

By way of summary, the following conclusions are proposed:

- The Samson narrative, though comparatively replete with references to the Spirit/spirit of God, can hardly by itself prove the deity of the spirit, to say nothing of his existence as the third person of the triune God.
- The spirit appears to be an effluence or emanation from the Lord that serves as a kind of surrogate on his behalf, especially in times of great need.
- No clear evidence exists to support the NT idea of a permanently indwelling Holy Spirit or even a temporary embodiment. The seeming exception in Judges is the case of Gideon, of whom it is said that the Spirit 'clothed [himself]' in Gideon, that is, used Gideon's body as his own. However, this understanding of the idiom is based on an incorrect use of the verb form and therefore adds no support to the notion of an incarnation of the Spirit.
- The work of the Spirit in Judges 13 – 16 is never conditioned on the state of belief or unbelief or of obedience or disobedience of Samson. He seems to have been only a divine instrument in God's hands.
- A holistic theology from the Christian and NT perspective must take into account OT imagery and narrative that form the seedbed of a synthetic, integrative and comprehensive understanding of the full revelation of God. Therefore, it is theologically legitimate to see glimpses of God in his trinitarian glory in Judges 13 – 16 as revealed through reference to his Spirit, though it remains exegetically

questionable to understand these texts in such a manner in their cultural, literary and conceptual contexts.

17. IS SAUL ALSO AMONG THE PROPHETS? SAUL'S PROPHECY IN 1 SAMUEL 19:23

David G. Firth

In 1 Samuel 19:23 we encounter one of the most peculiar passages related to the Spirit in the OT. Throughout 1 Samuel 18 – 19 Saul has been attempting various strategies to kill David. In 1 Samuel 18 his method was largely indirect (though not always – see 1 Sam. 18:11), preferring to allow the Philistines to kill him even as he offered David the opportunity to marry his daughters Merab and Michal. Although David declined the opportunity to marry Merab, he accepted the invitation to marry Michal for the bride compensation[1] of one hundred Philistine foreskins. An important theme that emerges through 1 Samuel is Saul's inability to defeat David, and though this is one of its first intimations, the assurance that Yahweh was with David (1 Sam. 16:18) means it is no surprise that David not only survived to make the required payment, he actually provided two hundred Philistine foreskins.[2] In 1 Samuel 19 Saul

1. The meaning of *mōhar* is uncertain, at some points seeming to refer more to a dowry and at others to a bride-price. See Christopher J. H. Wright, *God's People in God's Land: Family, Land and Property in the Old Testament* (Grand Rapids: Eerdmans, 1990), pp. 191–194.
2. LXX, agreeing with 2 Sam. 3:14, has only one hundred foreskins. However, the reference in 2 Sam. 3:14 is to the price stipulated by Saul, not to the actual payment David made, so it is likely that LXX is here a scribal correction to the expected sum.

therefore moved to a more direct mode of attack, directing his servants to kill David (1 Sam. 19:1), only to be dissuaded by Jonathan (1 Sam. 19:4–6). He later sent messengers to arrest David in his house, only to be fooled by Michal, who enabled David to escape (1 Sam. 19:11–17). David then fled to Samuel at Ramah, staying in some shepherds' huts there.[3] But although Saul is never able to capture David, he will prove adept at finding where he has gone, so David's presence with Samuel is duly reported to him (1 Sam. 19:19). This time there was no chance of one of his children preventing him capturing David and so he sent messengers to arrest him. But when they saw a band of prophets prophesying with Samuel at their head, the Spirit of God came upon them and they prophesied. Two more groups of messengers met the same fate (1 Sam. 19:20–21)[4] and with none of them therefore able to arrest David, Saul finally came himself. Confirming that David was still at the huts in Ramah, Saul went there only for the Spirit to come upon him. Unlike his messengers who merely prophesied, when Saul prophesied he stripped off all his clothes, lying naked all day and night before Samuel. Thus we are told that it was said, 'Is Saul also among the prophets?'[5]

Contemporary readers coming to a passage like this are likely to be perplexed for several reasons. One fairly obvious question relates to the origin of the proverb, since 1 Samuel 10:12 has seemingly provided a more positive account of its origin. In addition, anyone used to the idea that prophecy is largely a verbal phenomenon will be surprised by the sort of ecstatic behaviour described here, and one can be fairly sure that when the apostle Paul encouraged the pursuit of spiritual gifts and especially of prophecy (1 Cor. 14:1) he did not have this passage in mind. Finally, the experience of the Spirit here is negative, a judgment on Saul, something that is distinct from most experiences of the Spirit in the OT, let alone the NT. Yet it is also true that it is Saul's negative experience of the Spirit that protects David and thus continues to

---

3. Many ET (e.g. NIV) take *nāyôt* as a proper noun, 'Naioth'. But this would make Naioth a place in its own right, though it is clearly in Ramah. P. Kyle McCarter, *1 Samuel: A New Translation with Introduction and Commentary* (Garden City: Doubleday, 1980), p. 328, argues persuasively that it is a common noun, related to where shepherds stay, rendering it 'camps'. But something more permanent seems implied, so 'huts' is probable.
4. This becomes something of a literary trope, a 'type-scene' in Alter's terminology. See Robert Alter, 'Biblical Type-Scenes and the Uses of Convention', *Critical Inquiry* 5 (1978), pp. 355–368. For another example of the type, see 2 Kgs 1:1–16.
5. All translations are my own unless otherwise indicated.

demonstrate Yahweh's presence with him so that the text can be seen to work at multiple levels. Indeed, it will be argued here that awareness of the levels in which the Spirit's work is understood within the text represents a key insight, but that to understand this we need also to appreciate the issues of the origins of the proverb and the nature of prophecy as it is understood here. This is because the narrator has created a world in which we experience the confusion of bystanders to Saul's experiences while also receiving the narrative insight necessary to understand it. To achieve this we first need to trace the narrative of Saul's experience of the Spirit from the point of his anointing and the various points at which he is said to have prophesied, including a consideration of the 'evil spirit' which afflicts him. From this will emerge a view of the Spirit which stresses that the Spirit's work in these chapters is intimately linked with the purposes of Yahweh, purposes that both enable and sustain kingship which is loyal to him while disabling that which is opposed to him. This therefore means that the Spirit also works both to prevent that which is inconsistent with Yahweh's purposes and to enable those who work with them.

Is Saul among the prophets? The origins and function of a proverb

As we have noted, this is not the first instance of the proverb 'Is Saul among the prophets?' In 1 Samuel 9:1 – 10:16 we have an irony-laced narrative where Saul goes off seeking some of his father's donkeys who have strayed, only to find a kingdom, partly because he has a lad with him who seems much more resourceful than he is. Indeed, it is not Saul but the lad who suggests they inquire of an initially unnamed man of God[6] and who provides the means of payment that was apparently expected.[7] Whether or not they knew that this prophetic figure was Samuel, neither Saul nor his lad knew that Yahweh had indicated to him that he would send a man from Benjamin whom Samuel was to anoint as ruler.[8] When Saul appeared before Samuel, Yahweh confirmed

6. On this label for prophetic figures and its link to the 'seer' (*rōʾeh*, 1 Sam. 9:9, 11), see David L. Petersen, *The Roles of Israel's Prophets* (Sheffield: JSOT Press, 1981), pp. 35–50.
7. The sum (a quarter shekel) is quite small, enough at best for a few days' food. On payment for prophetic services, see Samuel A. Meier, *Themes and Transformations in Old Testament Prophecy* (Downers Grove: InterVarsity Press Academic, 2009), pp. 182–193.
8. The exact sense of *nāgîd* is uncertain, perhaps intentionally imprecise, though the use of anointing is certainly suggestive of royal associations.

that Saul was the one to be anointed and who would save the people from the Philistines and also restrain them.[9] Following his anointing Saul was promised a series of signs, the last of which was that he would meet a group of prophets and that the Spirit of Yahweh would rush (*ṣlḥ*) upon him and that he would prophesy (1 Sam. 10:6). The importance of this sign is evident from the fact that where it is simply reported that the other signs happened, this one is narrated in full.

Consideration of the narrative suggests an ambiguous assessment of Saul's status as a result of this experience. From Saul's own perspective it is clearly positive, confirming the promises of his election made to him by Samuel. But the meaning of the sign was unclear to others. Hence we have here a discussion reported where some express their curiosity about Saul, asking, 'What has happened to the son of Kish? Is Saul also among the prophets?' The response given to this ('And who is their father?') is perhaps related to the identity of prophetic bands as 'sons of the prophets', so the 'father' could then be the prophet who was the head of the group. Kish is apparently not known as a prophet, but Saul is known only as his son. The implication appears to be one of uncertainty on the part of those viewing the scene, with the proverb 'Is Saul also among the prophets?' thus employed to indicate a point of uncertainty about what the Spirit of Yahweh is doing. The situation in which it originates is more positive for Saul, but the proverb itself remains ambiguous because situations in which the Spirit of Yahweh is active are not necessarily easy to interpret.

This ambiguity helps also explain the use of the proverb in 1 Samuel 19:23. This time the Spirit is simply said to have come upon (*hyh*) Saul, distinguishing this experience from 10:6, 10, which speak of the Spirit 'rushing' (*ṣlḥ*) upon him. When used of the Spirit of God, 'rushing' is preparatory for a powerful work to be achieved (Judg. 14:6, 19; 15:14; 1 Sam. 11:6; 16:13). That this is an overwhelming force is also apparent in Saul's experience of the grievous spirit in 1 Samuel 18:10. Although the Spirit's 'coming' (*hyh*) can also signify a powerful act (Judg. 3:10; 11:29) or word (2 Chr. 15:1; 20:14), the shift to a more neutral verb here is surely significant. Saul is not about to do something mighty by the presence of the Spirit. Rather, it is the Spirit who is mightier and thus prevents him from acting against David. Nevertheless, the meaning of Saul's actions remains opaque to those who view him since they do not

---

9. Most ET (e.g. NIV) render the verb *ʿṣr* as 'rule', a sense it has nowhere else. With ESV, 'restrain' is preferable, perhaps to indicate a degree of ambiguity about Saul. See David G. Firth, *1 & 2 Samuel* (Nottingham: Apollos, 2009), p. 119.

know all that the narrator reveals to us as readers. What they see is their king overpowered by the Spirit of God and 'prophesying' before Samuel. Thus, although this narrative describes a negative experience for Saul, it provides a consistent usage for the proverb where it is clear that the Spirit is active, but the meaning of that activity is not immediately apparent, thus contrasting with other experiences of the Spirit in the OT where the ability of onlookers to understand is central to the Spirit's role in providing testimony of Yahweh's election of a leader. For the narrator, this is further evidence of Saul's rejection by Yahweh and that Yahweh was indeed with David,[10] so that the proverb's recurrence can demonstrate this. It is important, however, to distinguish here between the use of the proverb in the mouths of those who witnessed Saul prophesying naked on the ground and the narrator. Nevertheless, the original sense is still important for the narrative in that it demonstrates that one can only interpret the work of the Spirit through awareness of the wider context. By locating the proverb within these two passages the narrator is thus able to provide the information necessary for readers to interpret these two experiences of the Spirit, while also demonstrating that individual experiences of the Spirit are not easy to interpret.

Saul and the 'evil' spirit

The difficulties in interpreting the work of the Spirit are also apparent in that Saul not only experiences the Spirit of Yahweh/God, he also experiences an 'evil' spirit in 1 Samuel 16:14–16, 23; 18:10 and 19:9. Indeed, one reason for the surprising nature of 1 Samuel 19:23 is that since his anointing and defeat of Nahash (1 Sam. 10:10; 11:6), Saul has only experienced the 'evil' spirit, so a clear reappearance of the 'Spirit of God' in 1 Samuel 19:23 is itself remarkable. This is especially important in light of the comment in 1 Samuel 16:14 that the Spirit of Yahweh had left Saul.

Saul's affliction with the 'evil' spirit has long troubled both commentators and general readers of the OT, though part of the problem is with the translation of *rāʿâ* as 'evil', since in English this implies something which is morally flawed and the association of 'evil' with God is inconsistent with the wider biblical portrayal of the character of God. But since *rāʿâ* can also

10. This is a recurring refrain from 1 Sam. 16:18 onwards which is validated in various ways throughout the long rivalry narrative between David and Saul in 1 Sam. 16 – 2 Sam. 1.

refer to the way something is experienced, it is preferable to translate it here as 'grievous'[11] and thus highlight the fact that the emphasis is upon Saul's experience of Yahweh's judgment on him rather than on its moral character, though Routledge has argued that the OT does allow for the possibility of forces which might be opposed to God participating in the divine council.[12] However, the central point here is to demonstrate Yahweh's rejection of Saul in favour of David,[13] so that whatever the character of the spirit itself Saul's experience of it points to him being disciplined by Yahweh since it is Yahweh who sent the spirit. That this was experienced negatively by Saul is evident from the fact that this spirit is said to have 'terrorized' (*bʿt*) him. Where the coming of the Spirit of Yahweh had previously marked out Saul as one chosen by Yahweh, the presence of the grievous spirit marks him out as one judged by Yahweh.

The essential nature of this spirit is outlined in 1 Samuel 16:14–23, though the primary goal of this passage is to explain David's entry to Saul's court. The spirit in some way terrorized Saul, though it was possible that his experience could be improved through music, which was why David was brought in. Initially, Saul was refreshed[14] when David played his lyre and the spirit departed from him. However, it is clear that just as David was said to have an enduring experience of the Spirit of Yahweh (1 Sam. 16:13), so also Saul's experience of the grievous spirit is an enduring one, since this spirit's departure from Saul can only ever be temporary if David has constantly to play his lyre and bring relief. The contrast between David and Saul here is of vital importance in establishing their relative position before Yahweh, a point driven home when one of Saul's own servants notes that 'Yahweh is with him' (1 Sam. 16:18) in indicating why David would be a good person to bring to the court. David's enduring experience of the Spirit points to Yahweh's presence, whereas Saul's experience of the grievous spirit demonstrates his rejection by Yahweh.

Although 1 Samuel 16:14–23 is a crucial passage in understanding Saul's experience of the grievous spirit, there are two more occasions when the narrative highlights the work of this spirit. In 1 Samuel 18:10–11 and again

---

11. See Firth, *1 & 2 Samuel*, p. 187.
12. Robin Routledge, '"An Evil Spirit from the Lord" – Demonic Influence or Divine Instrument?', *EQ* 70 (1998), pp. 3–22.
13. David M. Howard, 'The Transfer of Power from Saul to David in 1 Sam 16:13–14', *JETS* 32 (1989), pp. 475–476.
14. Note the wordplay here between 'spirit' (*rûaḥ*) and 'relief' (*rāwaḥ*).

in 1 Samuel 19:9 we again encounter the grievous spirit, though here we have a host of important critical issues to note. Perhaps the most important of these is that 1 Samuel 18:10–11 is absent from LXX; indeed LXX offers a considerably shorter text for the whole of this chapter than MT,[15] one that is also considerably more positive about Saul. The issues surrounding this chapter are in part a continuation of the radically different texts we find in 1 Samuel 17, and to some extent the absence of some of the text in the LXX is a logical continuation of the shorter text there.[16] I have argued elsewhere that the LXX of 1 Samuel 17 is an attempted editorial solution to the problems posed by the narrative difficulties in relating 1 Samuel 16 and 17, but that the conclusions which lead to the shorter LXX text occur because of a failure to understand the narrative techniques being employed.[17] This allows us to see that the verses absent from LXX represent two different, though linked, sets of problems. Once it is recognized that the text of 1 Samuel 17 is critical of Saul, it becomes more likely that the criticisms found in the MT of chapter 18 are likely to be original too. Klein defends LXX here,[18] but his argument depends upon a psychological assessment of David as to why he would have declined to marry Merab which is not altogether convincing. Grønbaek posits several redactional levels on the basis of this evidence, but once it is accepted that MT represents the original text and that LXX is an attempt to improve this, then the need for these falls away.[19]

The closely parallel nature of these two experiences of the grievous spirit might also suggest that we are dealing with variant accounts of the one event. Klein, though regarding 18:10–11 as secondary, believes it is modelled on 19:9–10.[20] But the important differences between the two accounts suggest rather that we have discrete events. Thus, although both mention the grievous spirit and Saul attempting to kill David with his spear, in the first Saul is said to be 'prophesying' under the influence of this spirit, something not said in 19:9–10, though this element is effectively deferred to the end of the chapter.

---

15. LXX lacks 1 Sam. 18:1–5, 6a, 10–11, 12b, 17–19, 26b and 29b–30.
16. This is true of 18:1–5 and, to some extent, 18:6b.
17. See David G. Firth, '"That the World May Know." Narrative Poetics in 1 Samuel 16 – 17', in Michael Parsons (ed.), *Text and Task: Scripture and Mission* (Milton Keynes: Paternoster, 2005), pp. 24–26, and summarized in Firth, *1 & 2 Samuel*, pp. 194–195.
18. Ralph W. Klein, *1 Samuel* (Waco: Word, 1983), p. 187.
19. J. Grønbaek, *Die Geschichte vom Aufstieg Davids (1. Sam 15 – 2. Sam 5); Tradition und Komposition* (Copenhagen: Prostant apud Munksgaard, 1971), pp. 100–109.
20. Klein, *1 Samuel*, p. 188.

Further, David is playing his lyre in accordance with his normal custom in 18:10–11, whereas in 19:9–10 his status as the one leading the Israelite troops is reflected in the absence of this information. We also note that Saul has an internal monologue in 1 Samuel 18:11, whereas no such insight is given in the second account. However, there is probably no distinction in meaning between affirming that the spirit is from God (1 Sam. 18:10) or from Yahweh (1 Sam. 19:9).[21] Taken as a whole, we should see a development intended between these two events reflective of the diptych nature of 1 Samuel 18 – 19 in which a series of events are paralleled with one another while also allowing for Saul's attacks on David to become more overt.[22]

Granted this context, it is therefore possible to explore these events as independent but narratively related occurrences. In the first of these, the note that Saul is 'prophesying' (*wayyitnabbēʾ*)[23] stands out because of the way it parallels his earlier experience at 1 Samuel 10:10 while also preparing for 1 Samuel 19:23. We will consider the nature of that prophetic experience shortly, but the important point to note is that his 'prophesying' did not prevent him from making independent decisions for which he remained responsible. Thus, as David played his lyre, now no longer able to soothe him, he threw his spear at him not once but twice with the aim of pinning David to the wall. Whatever is meant by Saul 'prophesying', he was not disabled by the experience with the result that he was still able to attack David. In the second experience of the grievous spirit Saul does not prophesy, but the presence of his spear is a sure sign that he is likely to cast it at someone and David is his preferred target. Thus, whether or not he 'prophesies', Saul is able to make independent decisions while under the influence of the grievous spirit, though his utter inability to hit anyone with his spear is apparently independent of this because he also misses Jonathan when he throws the spear at him in 1 Samuel 20:33.

21. Similarly David Toshio Tsumura, *The First Book of Samuel* (Grand Rapids: Eerdmans, 2007), p. 493. For a contrasting opinion see Daniel I. Block, 'Empowered by the Spirit of God: The Holy Spirit in the Historiographic Writings of the OT', *SBJT* 1 (1997), p. 51. We should also note that LXX here reads *pneuma theou* ('spirit from God'), so the textual basis for making such a contrast is also uncertain.
22. See Firth, *1 & 2 Samuel*, pp. 214–215.
23. Many ET (e.g. ESV) render this as 'raving', but this underplays the parallels with 1 Sam. 10:10 and 19:23 and seems more likely to be motivated by a desire to suggest something qualitatively different in Saul's experiences here.

This background with the grievous spirit thus also contributes to the problems faced by any bystanders who see Saul's experience in 1 Samuel 19:23, and to a lesser extent the three groups of messengers who also prophesied rather than arresting David in 1 Samuel 19:19–21. However, although the messengers are unable to arrest David because their experience of the Spirit of God leads them to prophesy, it is never said that they lay on the ground all night and stripped off their garments. Saul's experience is thus presented as escalating theirs, but also as one that contrasts in one crucial sense with his previous experiences of the grievous spirit. Although he could experience that spirit and even prophesy, it is only now that the Spirit of God disables him so that he cannot act as he wishes. Where he could make independent decisions that would appear contrary to the will of Yahweh when under the influence of the grievous spirit, he is unable to do so when under the influence of the Spirit of God. An important distinction between the grievous spirit and the Spirit of God is thus drawn, though in fact in both cases Yahweh's decision that David should replace Saul is carried through, even if in the two references to the grievous spirit this depends upon the fact that Saul is a lousy shot with his spear. This background thus helps us to appreciate the confusion faced by onlookers who see Saul's actions in 1 Samuel 19:23, while also demonstrating that the narrator has provided subtle clues as to how to read it.

Variant experiences of prophecy and the problem of semantics

A further complication faced by readers is in understanding what is meant by Saul and his messengers 'prophesying'. Again, this is something complicated for us by the narrative technique of allowing us to experience the confusion of bystanders while also providing information through the larger narrative that guides us in understanding its nature. Of particular importance is the fact that Saul 'prophesies' under the influence of both the Spirit of Yahweh/God and the grievous spirit, and that important parallels between these experiences exist. At the same time, there are subtle distinctions drawn between the Niphal and Hithpael of the verb *nbʿ*. It is important to note that at no point in the books of Samuel does the verb mean 'to proclaim Yahweh's word'. Indeed, it is striking that in the only instance in Samuel where the Spirit is associated with oral proclamation, in David's 'last words' (2 Sam. 23:1–7), we find instead the normal verbs for speech (*dbr*, *ʾmr*) combined with 'oracle' (*nĕʾum*). David's last words are given a clearly 'prophetic' twist, but the verbs used exclude 'to prophesy' (*nbʿ*). In short, the books of Samuel regard 'prophesying' as something other than verbal proclamation,[24] so that a different vocabulary is necessary when prophetic activity employs speech.

An examination of each of Saul's experiences when he 'prophesies' demonstrates that, whether under the influence of the Spirit of Yahweh/God or the grievous spirit, certain elements are present. It is crucial in 1 Samuel 10:10 that his experience of the Spirit marks him out as the one chosen by Yahweh, though the exact nature of both his 'prophesying' and that of the sons of the prophets is left undefined, since the important point for the narrative is that the experience confirms Samuel's announcement of the signs Saul would experience (1 Sam. 10:6). We should, however, note that Samuel's announcement employs the Hithpael of *nbʿ* (1 Sam. 10:6), but in describing the experience the narrator switches between the Niphal (1 Sam. 10:11) and Hithpael (1 Sam. 10:10, 13). The significance of this shift is not immediately apparent, but it does prepare for subsequent usage.

The next time Saul 'prophesies' is under the influence of the grievous spirit (1 Sam. 18:10). Again, we are given little information about this experience, though it begins to look as if what is described is something where the experience of this spirit leads Saul to behave in a way that cannot be considered rational, so that the verb here (in the Hithpael) appears to have the sense of 'a spiritual experience where one is not in complete control of oneself'. This prepares us for 1 Samuel 19:20–24 which maintains a clearer distinction between the Niphal and Hithpael. The prophetic band with Samuel are 'prophesying' (1 Sam. 19:20, Niphal), but when each of Saul's messengers experience the Spirit of God and also prophesy there is a shift to the Hithpael (1 Sam. 19:20, 21 [x2]), a pattern that recurs with Saul (1 Sam. 19:23–24). Wood is probably right to argue that this is not ecstatic behaviour if one means by this something induced by shamanistic activity,[25] but if 'ecstatic' is

---

24. See also Block, 'Empowered', pp. 46–48. It would seem that the earliest reference to *nbʿ* as denoting verbal proclamation is in 1 Kgs 22:8 where Ahab complains about the prophecies of Micaiah. We then find this usage in Amos before it becomes standard in later texts. This suggests that this use of *nbʿ* began as a northern idiom but later came to be the standard term. The retaining of this idiom lends support to the proposal of Antony F. Campbell, *Of Prophets and Kings: A Late Ninth Century Document (1 Samuel 1 – 2 Kings 10)* (Washington: CBA of America, 1986), that much of the books of Samuel derives from a ninth-century northern prophetic source.

25. Leon J. Wood, *The Holy Spirit in the OT* (Grand Rapids: Zondervan, 1976), pp. 90–100.

understood in a narrower sense of 'an overwhelming spirit-induced experience', then it is hard to avoid the conclusion that the Hithpael at least has this sense, though this sense occurs for both the Spirit of God and the grievous spirit. By contrast, the use of the Niphal for the prophetic band may also indicate some form of ecstatic experience, though the Niphal is never used for the grievous spirit. Moreover, the Niphal might not indicate a loss of control which may, with hindsight, be seen in Saul 'becoming another man' (1 Sam. 10:6).[26] The difficulty we face in translation is that we lack a verb in English which can convey these nuances of meaning, but it is clear that in each occurrence Saul's spiritual experience is one where he is overwhelmed by both the Spirit of God and the grievous spirit. By contrast, David's experience of the Spirit is recorded in a less dramatic way after his anointing (1 Sam. 16:13), while his 'last words' suggest his experience of the Spirit was a means of inspiration (2 Sam. 23:2) that moves more towards what would later be described as 'prophetic'.

The Spirit and the mission of God

That readers experience Saul's encounter with the Spirit of God in 1 Samuel 19:23 as confusing is thus no surprise. The narrator has created a text in which we experience the confusion of bystanders who see him disabled by the Spirit and so lying naked and prophesying on the ground. A sense of confusion is an important element created for us by the narrative techniques employed, something hinted at in both the proverb 'Is Saul among the prophets?' and also the comparison between the divine Spirit and the grievous spirit, since Saul 'prophesies' under the influence of both. Yet the narrator also provides readers with guidance to see how the work of the Spirit of God is consistent throughout these texts. Saul is initially changed by the Spirit so he can become Israel's king, and as long as he is committed to this his experience of the Spirit is one of empowerment (1 Sam. 10:1–13; 11:6). David, after his anointing, is also empowered by the Spirit, something indicated in the narrative of his refrain that Yahweh was with him. Saul's experience of the grievous spirit is evidence of his estrangement from the purposes of Yahweh, while his final

26. Wilf Hildebrandt, *An Old Testament Theology of the Spirit of God* (Peabody: Hendrickson, 1995), pp. 160–161, notes objections to the theory of semantic development, but although it is possible to oversimplify this I would argue that the evidence within Samuel points to nuances within its usage.

encounter with the Spirit of God (1 Sam. 19:23–24) sees him disabled because he has set himself against the purposes of God. Thus those who seek to be faithful to God's purposes find themselves empowered by the Spirit, whereas those who oppose them find that the Spirit's power disables them instead. The Spirit's power might be expressed in ecstatic behaviour, but the significance of this power is determined by whether or not the one affected by it is committed to fulfilling Yahweh's purposes.

18. THE 'SPIRIT OF THE LORD' IN 2 KINGS 2:16

Robert B. Chisholm, Jr

After a whirlwind swept Elijah up into the sky, the prophetic guild at Jericho volunteered to send out a search party. They said to Elisha: 'Perhaps the Spirit of the LORD has picked him up and set him down on some mountain or in some valley' (2 Kgs 2:16).[1] Most English versions concur in translating *rûaḥ* 'Spirit' (see e.g. TNIV, NLT, NKJV, HCSB, NJB, ESV) or 'spirit' (Tanakh, NRSV).[2] Yet some interpreters understand the referent as the powerful wind sent by the Lord (cf. v. 11). Montgomery states that the Lord's spirit 'is thought of quite physically and identified with the whirlwind'.[3] Cogan and Tadmor translate 'YHWH's wind' here and identify it with the 'stormy apparition' (vv. 1, 11) that is 'referred to as a mighty wind, through which, at times, the Lord effects his purpose'.[4]

---

1. Unless otherwise identified, Scripture quotations are taken from NIV.
2. See as well M. Van Pelt, W. Kaiser, and D. Block, *NIDOTTE*, 3:1075–1076; and Jeffrey J. Niehaus, *God at Sinai: Covenant and Theophany in the Bible and Ancient Near East* (Grand Rapids: Zondervan, 1995), p. 263.
3. James A. Montgomery, *The Books of Kings*, ed. H. S. Gehman, ICC (Edinburgh: T. & T. Clark, 1951), pp. 354–355.
4. Mordechai Cogan and Hayim Tadmor, *II Kings*, AB (Garden City: Doubleday, 1988), pp. 31, 33. Similarly Marvin A. Sweeney translates 'wind of YHWH', see *I & II Kings*, OTL (Louisville: Westminster John Knox, 2007), p. 266. John Gray

In no uncertain terms, Fabry states that *rûaḥ* 'clearly means wind' here.[5] What exactly did the prophets have in mind? Does *rûaḥ* refer to the whirlwind or to the spirit of the Lord? Furthermore, did they view the spirit/wind as a negative or positive force? Were they envisioning the death of Elijah or just referring to a typical form of prophetic transportation (at least in his case; cf. 1 Kgs 18:12)?

This chapter addresses these questions and seeks to defend the following thesis: in 2 Kings 2:16 *rûaḥ yhwh* refers to the whirlwind sent by the Lord to transport Elijah to heaven. The prophets, however, did not view this wind as distinct from the 'spirit' of the Lord mentioned so often elsewhere in the Former Prophets. They regarded this wind as a power that emanates from the Lord's very person and is associated with his breath. In other words, in this context 'the spirit of the Lord' is actually the Lord's breath, which manifested itself in the form of a whirlwind. The prophets erroneously viewed the spirit in this case as a destructive force that had swept Elijah up into the air and hurled him to the ground. They envisioned finding his corpse lying somewhere on the nearby terrain.

In developing this thesis, we proceed as follows. (1) We begin by examining the usage of *rûaḥ* in general and, more specifically, in the Former Prophets. This survey shows that there is a broad range of usage attested and that spirit, breath and wind, among others, are possible referents of the term. (2) We then examine usage of the phrase 'the spirit of the Lord' in the Hebrew Bible, again showing that there is a broad range of usage, flexible enough to accommodate different interpretations of 2 Kings 2:16. (3) Next we move to the immediate context and argue that two important contextual features favour identifying the whirlwind of verse 11 with 'the spirit of the Lord' in verse 16. (4) We then offer a synthesis that seeks to explain more precisely how these two concepts were related in the perspective of the original speakers and audience. (5) Finally, we address the issue of the prophets' erroneous view of the spirit as a destructive force that they believed had killed Elijah.

---

states that the Lord's spirit 'might refer to the sudden, and to ancients inexplicable, onset of a whirlwind', though he also suggests that the 'ecstatic experience of Elijah' could be in view. See *I & II Kings*, OTL (Philadelphia: Westminster, 1963), p. 426. T. R. Hobbs sees a 'link between the whirlwind and the spirit of Yahweh in keeping with the presentation of the spirit of God in the OT as an instrument of power', see *2 Kings*, WBC (Waco: Word, 1985), p. 22.

5. H.-J. Fabry, *TDOT*, 13:393.

General usage of *rûaḥ*

A survey of the usage of *rûaḥ* reveals that it has a broad range of referents. Both *HALOT* (pp. 1197–1201) and BDB (pp. 924–926) list breath, wind and spirit (of the Lord/God) among their many categories of usage. Both place 2 Kings 2:16 in the divine spirit category.[6]

In the Former Prophets, where 1 – 2 Kings is situated in the Hebrew Bible, a broad range of usage is attested as well. The term has the following referents:

1. Human spirit or breath: in this case the 'spirit' or 'breath' is depicted as the source of human physical and/or emotional strength (Josh. 2:11; 5:1; Judg. 8:3; 1 Sam. 1:15; 30:12; 1 Kgs 10:5). In 2 Kings 2:9, 15 the word is used of Elijah's 'spirit'. In this context it appears to refer to his powerful prophetic persona, which Elisha hoped would be transferred to him. Since Elijah was a prophet, one is tempted to identify his 'spirit' with the Lord's spirit (cf. Mic. 3:8), but the text stops short of stating this. Weisman objects to identifying the spirit of Elijah (vv. 9, 15) with the spirit of the Lord (v. 16). The spirit of the Lord, which is capable of physically transporting Elijah (1 Kgs 18:12; 2 Kgs 2:16–17), 'differs in its nature in that it is an external physical cause acting upon him as on an object and not setting him in motion as a subject undertaking the conscious activities of a prophet'. He explains that the spirit of Elijah is not an 'external force', but 'a personal essence'.[7]
2. A disposition placed in Sennacherib by the Lord (2 Kgs 19:7).
3. The breath of the Lord (2 Sam. 22:16).
4. Wind (2 Sam. 22:11; 1 Kgs 18:45; 19:11; 2 Kgs 3:17).
5. A personal spirit in the heavenly assembly (1 Kgs 22:21–23).[8]
6. An 'evil' spirit sent from the Lord/God (Judg. 9:23; 1 Sam. 16:14–16, 23; 18:10; 19:9).
7. The spirit of the Lord/God energizing an individual (Judg. 3:10; 6:34; 11:29; 13:25; 14:6, 19; 15:14, 19; 1 Sam. 10:6, 10; 11:6; 16:13–14; 19:20, 23; 2 Sam. 23:2; 1 Kgs 18:12; 22:24).

---

6. See *HALOT*, p. 1200, category 8; BDB, p. 925, category 9.
7. Ze'ev Weisman, 'The Personal Spirit as Imparting Authority', *ZAW* 93 (1981), p. 233.
8. It is possible, based on v. 24, to identify this spirit with the spirit of the Lord that energizes prophets.

So, as one can see, general usage of the word, including its use in the Former Prophets, would allow us to see the term in 2 Kings 2:16 as referring to the wind, the spirit of the Lord, or even the Lord's breath.

Usage of *rûaḥ yhwh*

Of course, it would be short-sighted to look simply at the usage of *rûaḥ* in isolation, for collocated with a modifier, as it is in 2 Kings 2:16, it may point to a specific referent or carry a specialized meaning. In 2 Kings 2:16 *rûaḥ* is collocated with the genitive *yhwh*; this combination occurs, apart from our passage, twenty-seven times in the Hebrew Bible. In the great majority of cases, including all of its appearances in the Former Prophets (excluding the debated 2 Kgs 2:16 for the moment), the referent is the 'spirit of the LORD', however envisioned, that energizes human beings for various tasks (Judg. 3:10; 6:34; 11:29; 13:25; 14:6, 19; 15:14; 1 Sam. 10:6; 16:13–14; 19:9; 2 Sam. 23:2; 1 Kgs 18:12; 22:24 = 2 Chr. 18:23; 20:14; Isa. 11:2; 61:1; 63:14; Ezek. 11:5; 37:1; Mic. 2:7; 3:8).[9] However, there are four texts where this does not seem to be the case. In Isaiah 40:13 the 'mind of the LORD' (that is, the seat of his mental faculties) appears to be the referent (note the parallel line). In Hosea 13:15 the 'spirit of the LORD' is appositional to and apparently identified with the 'east wind' that blows in from the desert. Such a hot wind is equated with the *rûaḥ yhwh* in Isaiah 40:7, where it shrivels up the grass and flowers when it blows on them. The *rûaḥ yhwh* also appears to be identified with the wind in Isaiah 59:19, where it has the power to drive a stream. So, as in the case of the general usage of *rûaḥ*, the collocation *rûaḥ yhwh* is not limited to one referent. It most often refers to the Lord's energizing 'spirit', but in three passages it is identified or associated with a powerful wind.[10]

---

9. In 1 Sam. 19:9 the expression is qualified by 'evil'. In Isa. 61:1 the compound title 'Sovereign LORD' appears as the modifier.

10. The occasional association of the Lord's spirit with the wind may explain why the spirit is portrayed as bird-like in Gen. 1:2. In that passage it is depicted as 'hovering', or perhaps circling, over the waters. The verb (*rāḥap*) is used elsewhere of birds hovering, both in the Bible (Deut. 32:11) and in the Ugaritic legend of Aqhat (where the Ugaritic cognate *rḥp* appears; cf. *CAT* 1.18:21, 30; 1.19:32). On the latter see Simon B. Parker (ed.), *Ugaritic Narrative Poetry* (Atlanta: Scholars Press, 1997), pp. 66, 68. The wind is sometimes viewed metaphorically as having wings

Contextual factors

Usage is important when evaluating the meaning of a word or phrase, but context is the determinative factor. There are two contextual features that are particularly significant when trying to pin down the referent of *rûaḥ yhwh* in 2 Kings 2:16.

A first contextual clue is found in verse 11 (see also v. 1), which states that 'Elijah went up to heaven in a whirlwind'. Since the whirlwind picked Elijah up and carried him into the sky, it seems likely that the prophets refer to this in verse 16 when they speak of the *rûaḥ yhwh* lifting him up. However, the term used in verse 11 is not *rûaḥ*, but *sĕʿārâ*.[11] Can the terms be used of the same phenomenon, perhaps even interchangeably? Usage suggests they can.

1. In all eighteen of its appearances in the Hebrew Bible, a *sĕʿārâ* finds its source in the Lord or is closely associated with him in some way. Here in 2 Kings 2 it serves as the Lord's instrument in transporting Elijah (v. 1) and is accompanied by the Lord's horses and chariot of fire (v. 11). In several instances it is an element in a divine theophany in the storm (Job 38:1; 40:6; Isa. 29:6; Jer. 23:19; 30:23; Ezek. 1:4; 13:11, 13; Zech. 9:14). The whirlwind is at the Lord's disposal (Pss 107:25; 148:8) and obeys his command (Ps. 107:29). It is a metaphor for Israel's military strength (Isa. 41:16), which is imparted to them by the Lord (vv. 14–15). It is even identified with the Lord's breath (Isa. 40:24). Given this consistency of usage, it is certainly possible to identify it with the *rûaḥ yhwh* in 2 Kings 2.
2. In six texts *sĕʿārâ* and *rûaḥ* appear together, either in apposition or in poetic parallelism:
   (a) Psalm 107:25: 'and stirred up a tempest [*rûaḥ sĕʿārâ*]';
   (b) Psalm 148:8: 'stormy winds [*rûaḥ sĕʿārâ*] that do his bidding';
   (c) Isaiah 41:16: 'the wind [*rûaḥ*] will pick them up, and a gale [*sĕʿārâ*] will blow them away';
   (d) Ezekiel 1:4: 'I saw a windstorm [*rûaḥ sĕʿārâ*]';
   (e) Ezekiel 13:11: 'violent winds [*rûaḥ sĕʿārôt*] will burst forth';
   (f) Ezekiel 13:13: 'I will unleash a violent wind [*rûaḥ sĕʿārôt*]'.

(2 Sam. 22:11 = Ps. 18:10; Ps. 104:3; Hos. 4:19; Zech. 5:9), a comparison that is natural given the rapid, darting movements of both the wind and birds.

11. According to Luis Stadelmann, this term refers more generally to a 'windstorm' or 'gale', not a 'whirlwind' specifically. See *The Hebrew Conception of the World* (Rome: Biblical Institute, 1970), p. 108.

Given these collocations of the terms elsewhere, it is not surprising that the words appear to be closely associated in 2 Kings 2.

A second contextual clue is that *rûaḥ yhwh* is collocated with the verb *nāśāʾ*, 'to lift up', in verse 16. Only here and in 1 Kings 18:12 does the precise expression *rûaḥ yhwh* appear as the subject of this verb, but the noun *rûaḥ* is its subject in ten other texts. In four of these passages *rûaḥ* refers to a wind that lifts up an object: Exodus 10:13 ('By morning the wind [literally, 'the east wind'] had brought [literally, 'lifted up'] the locusts'), 19 ('changed the wind to a very strong west wind, which caught up the locusts'); Isaiah 41:16 ('the wind will pick them up'); 57:13 ('the wind will carry all of them off'). In seven other passages where *rûaḥ* is the subject of the verb (excluding 2 Kgs 2:16 for the moment), the referent of *rûaḥ* is unclear. The usage in 1 Kings 18:12 should probably be interpreted in line with 2 Kings 2:16. Six times a *rûaḥ* lifts up the prophet Ezekiel. It makes good sense to interpret the referent as a wind, though the context does not allow one to be certain (Ezek. 3:12, 14; 8:3; 11:1, 24; 43:5).[12] Greenberg translates 'a wind'. He distinguishes this from *rûaḥ yhwh*, which he understands as 'the wind from YHWH'. He comments: 'the wind that transported Ezekiel . . . is, to be sure, supernatural in origin, but unattributed'.[13]

In three texts the wind is not the grammatical subject of the verb, but nevertheless the subject is compared to the wind (Isa. 64:6: 'like the wind our sins sweep us away'), is facilitated by the wind (Zech. 5:9: 'two women, with the wind in their wings . . . and they lifted up the basket'), or uses the wind as its agent (Job 30:22: 'you snatch me up and drive me before the wind').

So we can safely say, based on usage, that the appearance of the verb *nāśāʾ*

---

12. NIV in each instance translates 'the Spirit', but this is interpretive; the Hebrew text has simply *rûaḥ* with no article.

13. Moshe Greenberg, *Ezekiel 1 – 20*, AB (Garden City: Doubleday, 1983), p. 70. In 3:12, 14, Daniel I. Block interprets *rûaḥ* as a wind, albeit 'no ordinary wind'. But in 8:3 he interprets it as the divine Spirit. He states: 'However, since the *rûaḥ* seems to be causing him merely to levitate between heaven and earth, it should be interpreted as the divine Spirit' (*The Book of Ezekiel Chapters 1 – 24* [Grand Rapids: Eerdmans, 1997], pp. 133, 280, respectively). However, this is an odd distinction to make, since the wind could both transport and levitate an object. Furthermore, as our subsequent discussion attempts to show, making a sharp distinction between the divine spirit and the wind is often a false dichotomy.

with *rûaḥ* in 2 Kings 2:16 indicates that a strong physical force is in view and suggests that the *rûaḥ yhwh* in this case was the wind.

There is another issue that should be mentioned here, though it actually proves to be a false trail for determining the identity of the referent of *rûaḥ yhwh*. In 2 Kings 2:16 *rûaḥ yhwh* is construed with a masculine singular verb form. This is unusual, but not unique. Masculine singular verb forms are also used with *rûaḥ yhwh* in 2 Samuel 23:2; 1 Kings 18:12; 22:24 (= 2 Chr. 18:23); Hosea 13:15 (though the verb may agree with the masculine *qādîm*, 'east wind', here); and Micah 2:7. In five of the seven examples (1 Kgs 18:12; Hos. 13:15 being the exceptions) the verb form is a suffixed form, which is preceding in four of the five instances. It is far more common to see a feminine singular verb form used with *rûaḥ yhwh* (Judg. 3:10; 6:34; 11:29; 13:25; 14:6, 19; 15:14; 1 Sam. 10:6; 16:13–14; 19:9; 2 Chr. 20:14; Isa. 11:2; 40:7; 59:19; 63:14; Ezek. 11:5), though it is relatively rare to see a feminine suffixed pattern (1 Sam. 16:14; 2 Chr. 20:14; Isa. 40:7), which is preceding in only one of the three examples (2 Chr. 20:14). It appears that the gender of the verb form collocated with *rûaḥ yhwh* is interchangeable, with the masculine form being preferred when a suffixed form is preceding. Furthermore, references to the spirit of the Lord as the source of human enablement can appear with both feminine and masculine (2 Sam. 23:2; 1 Kgs 22:24; Mic. 2:7) verbs. When the *rûaḥ yhwh* is identified or associated with the wind it can be construed with either a feminine (Isa. 40:7; 59:19) or a masculine (Hos. 13:15) verb.

It is also worth noting that when *rûaḥ* is collocated with the verb *nāśā᾿*, as in 2 Kings 2:16, gender appears to be interchangeable. Apart from our text, masculine forms of the verb occur in Exodus 10:13, 19; 1 Kings 18:12 and Isaiah 57:13, while feminine forms appear in Isaiah 41:16 and in the Ezekiel passages (3:12, 14; 8:3; 11:1, 24; 43:5). In the four texts where *rûaḥ* clearly refers to a wind, a masculine form occurs three times (Exod. 10:13, 19; Isa. 57:13) and a feminine form once (Isa. 41:16).

The referent of 'Spirit of the LORD' in 2 Kings 2:16

In light of the evidence examined above, it appears that *rûaḥ yhwh* refers in 2 Kings 2:16 to the gale-force wind that swept Elijah off his feet. The use of the verb *nāśā᾿*, 'to lift up', in verse 16 suggests this, as does the close association of *rûaḥ* and *sĕ῾ārâ* elsewhere. Yet we need not conclude that the prophets viewed this wind as a mere natural element sent from the Lord, distinct from the energizing 'spirit' of the Lord mentioned so often elsewhere. As stated above, the *rûaḥ yhwh* refers in the majority of instances, including all other passages in the Former Prophets, to a powerful force that energizes individuals for various tasks. There is no indication in these texts that the spirit is viewed as a wind, but in three texts in the Latter Prophets *rûaḥ yhwh* is identified with the wind (Isa. 40:7; 59:19; Hos. 13:15). We conclude that the same is true in 2 Kings 2:16.

But what links these various passages conceptually? How can the spirit be simply an energizing power in one set of texts but be associated with the wind in another? Perhaps the key is recognizing that *rûaḥ* can refer to an individual's breath (see above, under the discussion of the general usage of the term). In fact, it is used on occasion of the Lord's breath.

1. Exodus 15:8: 'by the blast of your nostrils the waters piled up'. Here *rûaḥ* refers to the breath that emanates from the Lord's nostrils (*ʾappayim*) and blows the waters into a heap. A similar expression appears in Job 4:9, where *rûaḥ* is collocated with 'nose' (*ʾap*) and describes the destructive power of the Lord's breath.
2. 2 Samuel 22:16 (= Ps. 18:15): 'at the rebuke of the LORD, at the blast of breath from his nostrils'. Here *rûaḥ* is used of the physical breath of the Lord that emanates from his nose (*ʾap*). The collocation used here (*nišmat rûaḥ*) appears in only one other text, where it refers to the 'breath of life' that emanates from the nostrils of all living beings (Gen. 7:22). The noun *nĕšāmâ*, of course, refers to the breath of a living being.[14] In Isaiah 30:33 it describes the hot destructive breath of the Lord. In 2 Samuel 22:16 the parallel noun, *gĕʿārâ*, describes more than a mere rebuke. It is best understood in this context as a loud shout or battle cry in which the Lord's breath is expelled (cf. Job 26:7; Pss 76:6; 104:7).
3. Psalm 147:18: 'he stirs up his breezes, and the waters flow'. The Hebrew text reads literally, 'he causes his breath/wind [*rûaḥ*] to blow, water flows.' One could interpret *rûaḥ* here as 'wind', but even if so, the wind is conceived as the divine breath. The parallel line describes the Lord as sending out 'his word', which melts the ice (cf. v. 17). An instructive parallel text is found in Psalm 33:6, where 'the word of the LORD' is parallel to 'the breath [*rûaḥ*] of his mouth'. In both passages the *rûaḥ* of the Lord appears to be the breath that accompanies his powerful spoken word.

14. *HALOT*, p. 730; BDB, p. 675. See also the discussion in Hans Walter Wolff, *Anthropology of the Old Testament*, tr. M. Kohl (Philadelphia: Fortress, 1974), p. 59.

In the light of this evidence, it is reasonable to assume that the *rûaḥ yhwh* is the breath of the Lord, which on some occasions, such as in 2 Kings 2:16, manifests itself in the form of a powerful wind. This is not to say that the 'spirit' of the Lord is viewed in this manner in all texts, only in those where it is identified with or associated with wind. Furthermore, this is not to say that the wind is viewed typically as the Lord's breath or 'spirit'. Again, this would only be the case when a context clearly draws that connection. We have argued that 2 Kings 2:16 is such a case.

The prophets' view of the Spirit of the Lord

A final interpretive question concerns how these prophets viewed the spirit of the Lord. Did they conceive of it in this case as a positive or negative force? On the basis of 1 Kings 18:12, it is tempting to say that they were referring to a typical (at least for Elijah) mode of prophetic transportation. In that passage Obadiah says to Elijah: 'I don't know where the Spirit of the LORD may carry you when I leave you.' As in 2 Kings 2:16, the verb *nāśāʾ*, 'to lift up', is used. It is unclear if Obadiah conceived of the spirit as being wind-like, but the use of *nāśāʾ* makes this likely. However, even if he did envision Elijah being swept up by the wind, there does not seem to be any notion of harm coming to the prophet. The verb seemingly refers to a mode of transportation, albeit an odd one. Brichto's paraphrase of the passage is amusing, yet appropriate: 'Suppose you – awesome will-o'-the-wisp that you are – are again wafted away by YHWH's spirit or wind.'[15]

The NIV appears to view the prophets' words in 2 Kings 2:16 in this same way. Its rendering, 'Perhaps the Spirit of the LORD has picked him up and set him down on some mountain or in some valley', suggests the spirit lifted the prophet up but then 'set him down', apparently safe and sound, in some other location (cf. also HCSB, 'Maybe the Spirit of the Lord has carried him away and put him on one of the mountains or into one of the valleys').

However, a closer look at the wording of 2 Kings 2:16 makes this unlikely. In this text the prophets speak not only of the spirit picking the prophet up, but also of letting him down. The verb translated 'set down' in NIV is *šālak*, which means (in the hiphil stem) 'throw, fling, cast'.[16] The verbs *nāśāʾ*, 'to

---

15. Herbert Chanan Brichto, *Toward a Grammar of Biblical Poetics: Tales of the Prophets* (New York: Oxford University Press, 1992), p. 133.

16. *HALOT*, pp. 1528–1529; BDB, pp. 1020–1021.

lift up', and *šālak*, 'throw', are collocated in only two other passages. In both cases the second verb suggests throwing an object down with some force, not merely setting it down in a different location. In 2 Kings 9:25–26 the corpse of the assassinated Joram, at Jehu's command, is thrown with contempt on the plot of land that once belonged to the murdered Naboth. In Psalm 102:10 the psalmist laments that the Lord in his 'great wrath' has lifted him up and 'thrown' him 'aside'.

There are six texts where *šālak* is collocated, as in 2 Kings 2:16, with a personal object and the preposition *bĕ-* introducing the location where the object is thrown. In Genesis 37:20 Joseph's brothers propose killing him and then throwing him into a cistern to cover up their misdeed. Disposal of a corpse is also in view in three other passages. As noted above, Jehu threw Joram's corpse into Naboth's field, Joab's troops threw Absalom's corpse into a pit (2 Sam. 18:17), and some Israelites threw the corpse of one of their comrades into Elisha's tomb (2 Kgs 13:21). In the two remaining passages the throwing is done with hostile intention. Jonah contended that the Lord had 'hurled' him 'into the deep, into the very heart of the seas', and overwhelmed him with his 'waves and breakers' (Jon. 2:3). In Nehemiah 9:11 the Israelites recall how the Lord had 'hurled' the Egyptians 'into the depths, like a stone into mighty waters'.

The evidence suggests that the verb *šālak* has a negative connotation in 2 Kings 2:16. In four of the seven texts just surveyed it is a corpse that is thrown down. In the three remaining texts the throwing is done with hostility and in two cases with intent to kill. Apparently these prophets assumed that the whirlwind had swept Elijah up into the air and then hurled him to the earth. Brichto captures their perspective well: 'They know that what goes up must come down. The wind of YHWH, which sucked Elijah into its vortex, was seen headed in one direction. It must have cast (the same word is used for *exposure* of bodies, in contrast with their burial) his body on some barren peak or into some forsaken gully. Is it proper to so neglect the prophet's remains?'[17] Various translations appear to interpret the verb as having this negative connotation (NKJV, ESV, Tanakh have 'cast him upon', while NJB and NRSV translate 'thrown him down').[18]

But why would these prophets think that the wind had killed Elijah? After all, in their earlier comments to Elisha, they gave no indication that Elijah would die violently. They simply asked Elisha: 'Do you know that the LORD is going to take your master from you today?' (2 Kgs 2:3, 5). Furthermore,

---

17. Brichto, *Biblical Poetics*, p. 163.

18. NLT ('left him on') is ambiguous.

the work of the Lord's spirit is usually viewed in positive terms. Granted, the spirit empowered Samson to kill a lion and Israel's enemies (Judg. 14:6, 19; 15:14), but the spirit is never described in the Former Prophets as dishing out death directly.[19] However, it is likely that the sheer power of this wind led them to conclude that it had a destructive purpose and no-one could survive it. After all, the narrator calls it a 'whirlwind', which, as our survey above demonstrated, is typically an instrument of divine judgment and destruction. The presence of a chariot and horses of fire may also have influenced their thinking. Perhaps they thought Elijah was the victim of a divine attack.

Of course, these prophets were wrong. As Elisha saw Elijah swept away before his very eyes, he cried out: 'My father! My father! The chariots and horsemen of Israel!' The appositional construction suggests that Elisha was equating Elijah with the Lord's army (see 2 Kgs 13:14). Elisha understood that Elijah, as the Lord's prophetic spokesman, was tantamount to a one-man army.[20] Brichto explains it this way: 'Elisha perceives in the vision what it is that Elijah has been: in his one person, the armored divisions of Israel and in his representation of God's will to Israel, Israel's first and best line of defense!'[21]

Summary

We have argued that in 2 Kings 2:16 *rûaḥ yhwh* refers to the whirlwind sent by the Lord to transport Elijah to heaven. In support of this we demonstrated that general usage of *rûaḥ*, including in the Former Prophets, and usage of *rûaḥ yhwh*, which is associated or identified with the wind in three other passages, allows for this interpretation. Two contextual factors favour this view, (a) the close association of *rûaḥ* and *sĕʿārâ*, 'whirlwind', both here (see v. 11) and elsewhere, and (b) the collocation of *rûaḥ* and *nāśāʾ*, 'lift up', which in at least four other texts describes the effect of the wind on an object.

---

19. In Isa. 40:7 the spirit, depicted as a hot wind, destroys directly, as it shrivels up the vegetation (see as well Hos. 13:15).

20. In this regard see M. A. Beek, 'The Meaning of the Expression "The Chariots and the Horsemen of Israel" (II Kings ii 12)', OTS 17 (1972), pp. 1–10. For a perceptive and helpful treatment of how the prophets functioned as the Lord's chariots and horses, as it were, see Samuel A. Meier, *Themes and Transformations in Old Testament Prophecy* (Downers Grove: InterVarsity Press, 2009), pp. 151–155.

21. Brichto, *Biblical Poetics*, p. 163.

The prophets did not necessarily view this wind, however, as distinct from the 'spirit' of the Lord mentioned so often elsewhere in the Former Prophets. They probably regarded it as a power that emanates from the Lord's very person and is associated with his breath. In other words, in this context 'the spirit of the LORD' is the Lord's breath, which manifested itself in the form of a whirlwind. In support of this, one can point to texts where *rûaḥ* is identified as the Lord's breath.

The prophets viewed the spirit/wind in this case as a destructive force that had swept Elijah up into the air and hurled him to the ground. This is apparent from their use of the verb *šālak*, which elsewhere has a negative connotation when used in the collocations in which it appears in 2 Kings 2:16. Of course, these prophets were wrong in their assessment. Rather than destroying Elijah, the spirit/breath of the Lord, manifested in a powerful wind, actually gave the prophet, who had served as Israel's one-man army, an appropriate and dramatic send-off.

PART 7: THE SPIRIT AND THE FUTURE

19. THE SPIRIT AND THE FUTURE: A CANONICAL APPROACH

Willem VanGemeren and Andrew Abernethy

Introduction

Nearly fifty years ago, Gerhard von Rad stated that the 'Old Testament can only be read as a book of ever increasing anticipation'.[1] This chapter builds upon this claim by taking a big-picture look at how the Spirit figures into the OT's anticipation of the future. After dealing with several hermeneutical issues, we will consider how each section of the tripartite OT canon creates expectations regarding the role of the *rûaḥ* in the future.

Hermeneutical issues

It will be helpful to begin by addressing several hermeneutical issues that arise when dealing with the topic of Spirit and future in the OT. We will set the stage for this essay by answering three questions: (1) What do we mean by 'future'? (2) How does this understanding of future relate to eschatological language? (3) What method will we use?

---

1. G. von Rad, *Old Testament Theology*, trans. D. G. M. Stalker, vol. 2 (Peabody: Prince, 2005, 1965), p. 319.

The future in the Old Testament

What do we mean by 'future' in the OT? To answer this question, it is perhaps best to deal first with a related one: Where should a reader look to find what the OT has to say about the future? An initial instinct may be to go directly to eschatological passages in the Latter Prophets that forecast the work of the Spirit.[2] While such prophetic texts do contribute to the OT's future vision, a broader approach that includes the entire OT is preferable for several reasons. To begin, the OT narratives of creation, sin and its consequences, and God's redemptive promises are the womb from which expectations of the future in the OT are birthed. These narratives create a sense of anticipation for the future as they depict God making and fulfilling promises in such a way that a surplus of expectation remains as Israel awaits a 'final fulfilment'.[3] Furthermore, the biblical writers confirm this as they draw upon the past as the seedbed for expectations regarding the future. The Prophets, for example, allude to God's work in creation (e.g. Isa. 51:3; Ezek. 36:35; 47:1–12), his revelation at Sinai (Exod. 34:6–7; e.g. Joel 2:13; Jon. 4:2; Mic. 7:8), his salvation at the Sea of Reeds (e.g. Isa. 51:10) and from Egypt (e.g. Isa. 10:24, 26; 11:19; Amos 4:10), and his promises to Abraham (e.g. Isa. 51:2; Ezek. 33:24) and David (e.g. Isa. 9:6; 55:3) in order to conceptualize God's ways in the present and future.[4] Accounts were even clearly written in order to prefigure later acts of God.[5] Finally, there is growing evidence that books and sections of the OT canon were strategically arranged to serve as a theological witness to future

---

2. C. J. H. Wright packages the future of the Spirit by focusing on prophecy. See 'The Coming Spirit', *Knowing the Holy Spirit through the Old Testament* (Downers Grove: InterVarsity Press, 2006), pp. 121–156.
3. On Israel awaiting 'final fulfilment' in the context of promises, see von Rad, *Theology*, pp. 2:319–335, 357–387.
4. M. Fishbane insightfully develops this inner-biblical use of typology in *Biblical Interpretation in Ancient Israel* (Oxford: Clarendon, 1985), p. 351.
5. This is especially true of work on Gen. 1 – 2. See e.g. G. J. Wenham, 'Sanctuary Symbolism in the Garden of Eden Story', in R. S. Hess, et al. (eds.), *'I Studied Inscriptions from Before the Flood': Ancient Near Eastern, Literary, and Linguistic Approaches to Genesis 1 – 11* (Winona Lake: Eisenbrauns, 1994), pp. 399–404; J. D. Levenson, 'The Temple and the World', *JR* 64 (1984), pp. 275–298; W. J. Dumbrell, 'Genesis 2:1–17: A Foreshadowing of the New Creation', in S. J. Hafemann (ed.), *Biblical Theology: Retrospect and Prospect* (Downers Grove/Leicester: InterVarsity Press/Apollos, 2002), pp. 53–65.

generations.[6] Scripture is not simply a deposit of historical information for one original audience. It is a witness to future communities regarding God's nature, what he is up to in the world, and creates a sense of expectation for how God will act in the future. The reader then will dare to live by faith that God's past actions point to how God will act yet again.

It is, then, preferable to see the entire OT (not only the Prophets) as the source for discovering expectations regarding how the Spirit will work. By 'future', we mean any expectation arising pertaining to how the Spirit will work within God's unfolding plan.

The future and eschatological language

How does eschatological language relate to this broad understanding of the future? A broad understanding of 'future' allows for a differentiation between it and 'eschatological' language. While we acknowledge that the entire OT contains futurist elements,[7] the adjective 'eschatological' describes those prophetic texts that use elevated language to 'speak of a future with significant discontinuities from the present'.[8] Such passages envision '*transformation* as the radical victory over evil'.[9] In our use, the terms 'eschatological' and 'future' are not synonymous; rather, eschatological texts are a unique kind of passage that gives rise to future expectations.

G. B. Caird contributes to understanding eschatological language by approaching it as metaphor. Metaphor conveys truth[10] by inviting reflection regarding implicit correspondence(s)[11] between the vehicle ('the thing to which the word normally and naturally applies') and the tenor ('the thing to which it [the word] is transferred').[12] In eschatological language, the biblical

---

6. See e.g. the essay by C. R. Seitz on Isaiah in *Word Without End: The Old Testament as Abiding Theological Witness* (Grand Rapids: Eerdmans, 1998), pp. 113–129.
7. These futurist elements lead some to call the entire OT eschatological. See W. J. Dumbrell, *The Search for Order: Biblical Eschatology in Focus* (Eugene: Wipf and Stock, 2001).
8. D. E. Gowan, *Eschatology in the Old Testament*, 2nd ed. (Edinburgh: T. & T. Clark: 2000), p. 1. On a catalogue of various uses of the term 'eschatology', see I. H. Marshall, 'Slippery Words: I. Eschatology', in *ExpTim* 89 (1977–8), pp. 264–269.
9. Gowan, *Eschatology*, p. xi.
10. G. B. Caird, *The Language and Imagery of the Bible* (Philadelphia: Westminster, 1980), p. 132.
11. Ibid., p. 144.
12. Ibid., p. 152.

authors creatively employ known concepts (vehicles) to serve as lenses for imagining the realities of the future (tenors). Within this framework, Caird presents three helpful propositions for interpreting eschatological passages. First, 'the biblical writers believed literally' that there was a beginning and will be an end of the world. Second, the authors employed 'end-of-the-world language metaphorically to refer to that which they well knew was not the end of the world'. Third, 'some literalist misinterpretation' is likely 'on the part of the hearer', and 'some blurring of edges between vehicle and tenor' is possible 'on the part of the speaker'.[13] The importance of these propositions resides in their recognition of the diverse uses and the ambiguous nature of eschatological language. In Caird's terms, the prophets exercise 'bi-focal vision' as they could speak of near events with an eye toward the ultimate eschaton.[14]

The prophets often employ 'eschatological' language to express their anticipation of the end of one era and the beginning of a new era.[15] As a new era begins (e.g. return from exile), the discontinuities between the eschatological promises and the experience of the people point forward to 'an even grander fulfillment of [God's] promises'.[16] As history unfolds, the eschatological language applies to each subsequent generation who anticipate new eras of God's work of redemption until the final fulfilment takes place. As we will see, the Spirit ushering in a new era appears in several eschatological depictions of the future.

Methodological approach

What method will we use? Some are interested in the historical development of the Spirit in Israel's history.[17] Others take a literary-synchronic approach in examining the portrayal of the Spirit in various passages, books[18] or the entire

---

13. Ibid., p. 256.
14. Ibid., p. 258.
15. W. A. VanGemeren, *Interpreting the Prophetic Word* (Grand Rapids: Zondervan, 1990), pp. 88–89.
16. Ibid., p. 89.
17. L. Neve, *The Spirit of God in the Old Testament* (Seibunsha: Tokyo, 1972); W. Ma, *Until the Spirit Comes: The Spirit of God in the Book of Isaiah* (Sheffield: Sheffield Academic Press, 1999).
18. J. Robson, *Word and Spirit in Ezekiel* (London: T. & T. Clark, 2006); D. I. Block, 'The Prophet of the Spirit: The Use of *rwh* in the Book of Ezekiel', *JETS* 32 (1989), pp. 27–49.

OT.[19] In this chapter, we will employ a literary-canonical approach to discern how the OT as a whole creates expectations regarding the *rûaḥ*. This requires an investigation of the three sections of the Tanakh (Torah, Prophets, Writings) as they associate with one another to provide a theological witness to the future work of the *rûaḥ*.[20]

Spirit and the future in the Old Testament

The task of exhaustively accounting for how the entire OT gives rise to expectations regarding the work of the *rûaḥ*[21] exceeds an essay of this length. In what follows we provide some indications for how each section of the tripartite OT canon contributes to a sense of anticipation regarding the *rûaḥ*.

Spirit and the future in the Torah

The Torah sets in motion the plot and framework for the rest of the Bible. The activity of the *rûaḥ* in the Torah creates patterns of expectation regarding his role throughout the OT and beyond.

Creation and salvation

We encounter the important cosmic dimension of the *rûaḥ* in Genesis 1:2. 'Now the earth was formless and empty, darkness was over the surface of the deep, and the *rûaḥ* of God was hovering over the waters.'[22] While the term *rûaḥ* does not occur in Genesis 1 other than in this verse, later passages identify God's *rûaḥ* as actively involved in carrying out God's purposes in creation (Ps. 33:6–8; cf. 104:30). The canonical sense is that Genesis 1:2 describes the conditions from which God through his *rûaḥ* creates a good,

---

19. W. Hildebrandt, *An Old Testament Theology of the Spirit of God* (Peabody: Hendrickson, 1995).
20. On association within the Tanakh, see S. B. Chapman, *The Law and the Prophets: A Study in Old Testament Canon Formation*, Forschungen zum Alten Testament (Tübingen: Mohr Siebeck, 2000); C. R. Seitz, *The Goodly Fellowship of the Prophets: The Achievement of Association in Canon Formation* (Grand Rapids: Baker Academic, 2009).
21. We will use *rûaḥ* (Heb. transliteration of term meaning 'wind', 'breath', 'spirit', etc.) instead of 'Spirit' in our analysis to retain its ambiguity within OT usage.
22. Unless otherwise identified, Scripture quotations are taken from NIV.

ordered cosmos.[23] The story of Scripture then begins with God's *rûaḥ* serving as his instrument in mastering the dark, watery, unformed creation to make an ordered heavens and earth. Within this good and ordered world, the divine Creator takes up residence, blessing creation and his image-bearers who are to represent him within this creation.

The *rûaḥ* as God's agent in mastering water appears again in Genesis 8:1b. With the deluge destroying the earth due to human wickedness, 'God remembered Noah and all the wild animals and the livestock that were with him in the ark' (8:1a). The remembrance of 'all the . . . animals' and 'the livestock' echoes back to Genesis 1:25–26 where God creates animals and beasts. In fact, the entire flood account alludes to Genesis 1. Genesis 6:20 and 7:14 stress the preservation of the animals and creeping things 'according to their various kinds' (Gen. 1:11, 12, 21, 24, 25). Additionally, God's blessing of both animals and humans after the flood to 'be fruitful and increase in number and fill the earth' (Gen. 9:1; cf. 8:17) directly parallels Genesis 1:22, 27. The sense one gathers from these parallels is that through the flood God is attempting to restart creation due to the depravity of humanity.

This prepares a reader for the second half of Genesis 8:1. After remembering the creatures he is preserving, '[God] sent a *rûaḥ* over the earth, and the waters receded.' It is no coincidence that again the work of the *rûaḥ* deals with conditions of water (*mayim*) on the earth as in Genesis 1:2.[24] The *rûaḥ* clears the way so that God's plan for 'restarting' creation may progress.

With Genesis 1 – 11 functioning as a prologue to the Pentateuch and the entire Bible, the instances of the *rûaḥ* at work in Genesis 1:2 and 8:2 create expectations for the future. In Genesis 1, we encounter the *rûaḥ* of God as an agent in bringing about creation. Due to the spread of sin and its effects in Genesis 3 – 6, God floods the earth, but sends a *rûaḥ* to subdue the waters in order to 'start over' with creation. The implied hope is that the remnant (Noah's family) will lead to a community characterized by righteousness like Noah (Gen. 6:5–9). Unfortunately, sin persists after the flood leading to

---

23. For a helpful overview of debates on the *rûaḥ* in Gen. 1:2, see K. A. Mathews, *Genesis 1 – 11:26*, NAC (Nashville: Broadman & Holman, 1996), pp. 131–135.

24. For examples of commentators who see a connection between Gen. 1:2 and 8:1, see Mathews, *Genesis 1 – 11:26*; G. J. Wenham, *Genesis 1 – 15*, WBC (Waco: Word, 1987); N. M. Sarna, *Genesis :[Be-reshit]: The Traditional Hebrew Text with New JPS Translation*, JPSTC (Philadelphia: Jewish Publication Society, 1989). See also A. D. Sargent, 'Wind, Water, and Battle Imagery in Genesis 8:1–3' (PhD diss., Trinity International University, 2010).

increasing alienation. With the links between Genesis 1 and 6 – 9, this prologue sets forth a pattern of a God who employs the *rûaḥ* for purposes of (re-)establishing God's creational intentions. With sin continuing to ravage the cosmos after Noah (Gen. 9 – 11), a reader wonders whether God will again act with the *rûaḥ*.

As the narrative progresses, God makes promises to Abraham with the expressed hope that his offspring will be a righteous people (Gen. 18:19) as was desired with Noah. With Exodus introducing Abraham's seed as fruitful, multiplying, and filling the land of Egypt (Exod. 1:7; paralleled only in Gen. 1:27; 9:1), the impression is that Israel is a token of the hoped-for 'new humanity'. As God acts to save this people from the clutches of Egypt, the *rûaḥ* once again appears in order to master waters for God's salvific purposes. As the Egyptian army pursues Israel, 'Moses stretched out his hand over the sea, and all that night the LORD drove the sea back with a strong east *rûaḥ* and turned it into dry land. The waters [*mayim*] were divided' (14:21). By describing the *rûaḥ* as coming from the east,[25] the *rûaḥ* here seems meteorological. The poetic interpretation of this event, however, views the *rûaḥ* in a more theological sense. 'By the *rûaḥ* of your nostrils the waters [*mayim*] piled up . . . You blew with your *rûaḥ*, and the sea covered them [Egyptians]' (Exod. 15:8, 10). The poet envisions the *rûaḥ* as God's own breath that carries out his saving purposes. Just as a *rûaḥ* mastered waters in order for God's 're-creation' plan with Noah to develop (Gen. 8:1), so God's *rûaḥ* tames waters in order to preserve the new humanity God was creating in Israel. The problem, however, is that as the Torah progresses Israel's seed shows signs that they will fail (like Noah's descendants) to be the righteous, new community that God desires.[26]

The Torah sets a pattern regarding the *rûaḥ* acting to fulfil God's creational purposes. The *rûaḥ* brings order to the watery unformed creation (Gen. 1:2) and acts to master waters in order to fulfil God's plans in establishing a righteous 'new humanity' with Noah's offspring (Gen. 8:1) and Abraham's seed (Exod. 14:21; 15:8, 10). With the drama of God's redemption of creation just beginning to unfold in the Torah, a reader wonders whether God's *rûaḥ* will again act to further fulfil his promises of cosmic redemption.

---

25. It occurs twelve times. See e.g. Exod. 10:13; Job 15:2; Ps. 48:8; Jon. 4:8.

26. E.g. Exod. 32 – 34; Num. 11; 14; Deut. 9:7.

Leadership
The *rûaḥ* also associates with the notion of leadership in the Pentateuch. The first link between leadership and the *rûaḥ* emerges from Pharaoh's lips. Regarding Joseph, he asks, 'Can we find anyone like this man, one in whom is the spirit of God?' (Gen. 41:38). This stems from Joseph's insight into Pharaoh's dream and the wise plan he suggests for dealing with the famine. Pharaoh attributes this to the presence of God's *rûaḥ* in Joseph.

Moses also is a leader with the *rûaḥ* of God. Amidst complaints for meat in the wilderness, Moses asks God why he has to care for all Israel. As a result, God takes away from his *rûaḥ* which is on Moses and places it upon seventy elders (Num. 11:17, 25) with the result that these elders begin to prophesy. Two of the elders who skipped the meeting even receive the *rûaḥ* within the camp and start prophesying (11:26–27). While Joshua wants Moses to stop them, Moses expresses his desire that all God's people would be prophets, 'that the LORD would put his *rûaḥ* on them' (11:30). There are a number of important insights to note here. First, the *rûaḥ* of Yahweh links with prophecy.[27] Second, while the *rûaḥ* of God results in prophecy, the ultimate purpose of the *rûaḥ* in this context is to enable leaders to provide societal governance. Third, the emphasis on democratization as it relates to the *rûaḥ* of God is significant. Moses envisions a future where the *rûaḥ* will not be limited to one leader. This gives the impression that God's *rûaḥ* will be present among his people with the specific purpose of providing divine order to society.

While the *rûaḥ* of God spreads to a group of leaders, the Torah focuses on the transition from Moses to Joshua. In Numbers 27:18, though Joshua already possesses the *rûaḥ* of God, Moses lays his hands upon him to invest him with authority. In Deuteronomy 34:9, the narrator looks back on this event and indicates that Joshua was full of the *rûaḥ* of wisdom due to the laying on of hands by Moses. This ends the Torah with the expectation that God's *rûaḥ* will enable Joshua to be a wise leader in Moses' stead for God's people.

The anticipation of a future prophet in Deuteronomy 18:15–22 figures into this future role of the *rûaḥ* with leaders. Moses expects God to raise up and put his words in the mouth of a prophet or prophets like him. Since the Torah presents Moses as a prophet anointed by the *rûaḥ* and also links prophecy with

27. For an overview on possible meanings of prophecy, see R. Dennis Cole, *Numbers* (Nashville: Broadman & Holman, 2000), pp. 192–196; Jacob Milgrom, *Numbers =[Ba-midbar]: The Traditional Hebrew Text with the New JPS Translation*, JPSTC (Philadelphia: Jewish Publication Society, 1989), pp. 380–383.

the reception of the *rûaḥ* (Num. 11), it is likely that the anticipation of future prophets in the line of Moses involves the expectation of the continued involvement of the *rûaḥ*.

There is also an interesting interface between God's *rûaḥ* in leadership and in creation.[28] God gives his *rûaḥ* in Exodus (31:3; 35:21) to several individuals who have the important task of building the tabernacle. With the likelihood of creation paralleling the tabernacle,[29] it appears that the role of the *rûaḥ* of God in mobilizing leaders for tabernacle building also parallels its role in creation (Gen. 1:2; Ps. 104:30). God, then, is endowing his people with his *rûaḥ* in order to carry out his new creation purposes in tabernacle construction.

In summary, there are several major concepts with which the *rûaḥ* of God intersects in the Torah. The Pentateuch presents a pattern of God's *rûaḥ* acting to create the world (Gen. 1:2) and to re-create a new community (Gen. 8 – 9; Exod. 14 – 15). This results in the expectation that the God of Abraham, Isaac and Jacob will use his *rûaḥ* in similar acts in the future to further fulfil his promises of world redemption. Additionally, the association between the *rûaḥ* of God and leadership is also important. With the *rûaḥ* of God transferring to the seventy elders and most notably to Joshua, God's people anticipate the continued role of the *rûaḥ* of God in mobilizing leaders to bring order to society.

Spirit and the future in the Former Prophets

The *rûaḥ* of Yahweh continues to play a role especially with leaders in the Former Prophets (Joshua – 2 Kings).[30] The text is silent regarding the succession of God's Spirit from Joshua to future leaders. The *rûaḥ* of Yahweh, however, comes on Othniel (Judg. 3:10), Gideon (6:34), Jephthah (11:29) and Samson (13:25; 14:6, 19; 15:14, 19) to act in powerful ways. Though the *rûaḥ* of God enables these judges to perform mighty feats, most of these judges fail as religious leaders. Within the framework of Judges, Israel goes from bad to worse. She struggles initially with foreign gods and foreign warfare, but the book ends with them manufacturing domestic idols and engaging in intertribal warfare. The refrain that structures the conclusion aptly reinforces the book's message: 'In those days Israel had no king; everyone did as he saw

---

28. Hildebrandt, *Theology*, pp. 194–195.

29. Levenson, 'Temple'; Wenham, 'Symbolism'.

30. For an overview on the uses of *rûaḥ*, see D. I. Block, 'Empowered by the Spirit of God: The Holy Spirit in the Historiographic Writings of the Old Testament', *SBJT* 1 (1997), pp. 42–61.

fit' (Judg. 17:6; 21:25; cf. 18:1; 19:1).[31] The book yearns for a king who will bring order to society under God's rule. With the *rûaḥ* of God mobilizing even corrupt judges in saving ways, there is an emerging hope for a godly king who will wield the *rûaḥ* of God for redemptive purposes.

Following from Judges, the link between kingship and the *rûaḥ* arises in the book of Samuel. With the *rûaḥ* rushing on Saul around the time of his anointing, there would have been great hope that he would order Israel under God's kingship (1 Sam. 10:10). With Saul's failure and rejection, the transfer of the *rûaḥ* to David leads again to increasing hope (1 Sam. 16:13–14). An oracle at the end of David's life gives insight into both the role of the *rûaḥ* of Yahweh and ideal kingship. The poem begins with the phrase 'The *rûaḥ* of the LORD spoke through me' (2 Sam. 23:2), and here one finds a clear example of God's *rûaḥ* playing a role in communicating God's will. It is important to reflect on the kind of things the *rûaḥ* proclaims. He recounts the blessings of one who rules justly and in the fear of the Lord. While David certainly did not live up to this ideal or experience these blessings (cf. 2 Sam. 11 – 22), this poem presents an ideal that elicits hope that future kings will carry out God's justice on the earth with the world experiencing blessing as a result. Thus, while Judges ends hoping for a king who would rule under God's Lordship, Samuel presents David as a ray of light awaiting the dawn of an anointed king who would reign justly and in the fear of the Lord without faltering.

Spirit of God in the Latter Prophets

The Latter Prophets generally do not make an appeal to the *rûaḥ* to bolster their claim that their words are divinely inspired.[32] Nor do they authenticate their special status as prophets by appealing to the *rûaḥ*.[33] The prophets are marked by a strong awareness of the transcendent deity and of his claim on Israel, Judah and the nations of the world.[34] They claim to be messengers of Yahweh and frequently use the messenger formula ('says the LORD') to authenticate this claim.

It has been assumed that the prophetic teaching on the *rûaḥ* is a distinct

31. K. L. Younger, *Judges and Ruth*, NIVAC (Grand Rapids: Zondervan, 2002), pp. 30–48.
32. S. Mowinckel, 'The "Spirit" and the "Word" in the Pre-exilic Reforming Prophets', *JBL* 53 (1934), pp. 199–227.
33. Ezekiel, as 'a prophet of the Spirit', seems to be an exception. See D. I. Block, *Ezekiel*, NICOT, 2 vols. (Grand Rapids: Eerdmans, 1997–8), 1:50.
34. J. Lindblom, *Prophecy in Ancient Israel* (Philadelphia: Fortress, 1962), pp. 413–414.

exilic/post-exilic development.[35] There is a close connection, however, in the canon between the *rûaḥ* in Moses' ministry and that of the prophets. The process of prophetic association with Moses is such that the legacy and ministry of Moses find their continuity and fulfilment in the prophets (Deut. 18:15–18; Mal. 4:4 [3:22]).[36] This suggests that the canon invites a reader to interpret the role of the *rûaḥ* in the Prophets in relationship to canonical associations beginning especially with Moses instead of in relationship to historical-critical strata.

In what follows, we consider expectations that arise in Isaiah, Jeremiah, Ezekiel and the Twelve pertaining to the work of God's *rûaḥ*.[37] While doing so, there will be an effort to consider how the witness of the Latter Prophets associates with Moses and the Torah.

Isaiah

The book of Isaiah presents a multifaceted and synoptic perspective on the *rûaḥ* of God. Our interest in this section resides more in how the final form of Isaiah presents the theme than in tracing its historical development.[38] At the heart of Isaiah is Yahweh's holiness, glory and universal kingship (ch. 6). Isaiah looks beyond God's judgment upon Israel via Assyria and Babylon to a time where God comes to judge, save and reign in Zion (35:4; 40:10; 52:7). As Israel struggles to grasp God's opaque ways, she is reminded that God's *rûaḥ* is beyond human comprehension (40:13). Isaiah invites the godly to 'wait' in faith for God to establish his kingdom. In our understanding, the *rûaḥ* plays a fundamental role in executing God's plan to establish his kingdom. We will begin our analysis by considering the significant role of the *rûaḥ* in carrying out God's plan. We will then explore how this intersects with the notions of agency.

Yahweh's plan and the *rûaḥ*

The prophet in Isaiah stands between *two* eras as God's spokesperson (42:9). He confronts the corrupted world of the present, comforts the weary and

35. Ma speaks of the move from the ecstatic Spirit to the leadership Spirit (*Until*, p. 152). See also Mowinckel, 'The "Spirit"', *JBL* 53 (1934), pp. 199–227; 56 (1937), pp. 261–265.

36. See above, under 'Spirit and the future in the Torah'.

37. While Jeremiah makes no reference to the *rûaḥ*, his oracles speak of Yahweh's dramatic and monergistic opening of a future for Israel.

38. See Ma, *Until*, for a study on the topic with historical-critical interests.

looks ahead to a time of judgment and the establishment of God's kingdom. As Isaiah envisions Yahweh's plan, the *rûaḥ* is Yahweh's agent enacting this plan within the world. While the book of Isaiah does not support a trinitarian perspective, it certainly builds a bridge toward a trinitarian theology.

In Isaiah 40, the prophet addresses an exilic audience that wonders if God is neglecting his people (v. 27). As the poet invites the reader to imagine God's grandeur to remedy their despair, he asks, 'Who has understood the *rûaḥ* of the LORD, or instructed him as his counsellor [*'ēṣâ*]?' (v. 13). This verse suggests that the *rûaḥ* of Yahweh is a very part of his own thoughts and plan. This notion of the *rûaḥ* as part of Yahweh's plan also appears in Isaiah 30. There Yahweh addresses his apostate children who 'do counsel [*'ēṣâ*], but not mine; who pour out libation, but not of my *rûaḥ*' (30:1, our own translation). In this verse, 'but not mine' parallels 'but not of my *rûaḥ*'. This suggests that God's *rûaḥ* is perhaps a representative of God who knows and conveys his will. For Isaiah the *rûaḥ* is present and active wherever Yahweh reveals and enacts his wise plan.

The lament in Isaiah 63 provides a glimpse into Isaiah's expectations regarding the work of the *rûaḥ* in establishing Zion. The prophet draws upon Exodus. He recalls how the exodus community grieved the holy *rûaḥ* (63:10). Though this resulted in God's punishment (63:10b), God remembered Moses and his people (63:11). The holy *rûaḥ* led the exodus community to find a resting place (63:12). Reflection on the past events raise the question, 'Where is he who set his holy *rûaḥ* among them?' (63:11). By appealing to God's past actions by his *rûaḥ*, the prophet is calling on God to again show his steadfast love to his people (63:7) and act with his *rûaḥ* to restore and renew Zion (63:17ff.). The lament reflects back and also anticipates a day of deliverance where Yahweh, his *rûaḥ*, and possibly a *rûaḥ*-endowed agent (like Moses) may bring sinful Israel out of her exile.[39] God's answer to this prayer is his promise of a new creation for his faithful servants.

The motif of the *rûaḥ* enacting God's plan often relates to reversal of situations as the *rûaḥ* had done in the exodus (63:11ff.; Exod. 14 – 15) and in the creation traditions in the Torah (Gen. 8:1). Isaiah similarly identifies the *rûaḥ* as carrying out God's plan of reversal in the world. For example, after Edom's judgment, the *rûaḥ* re-creates the Edomite territory according to

39. Joseph Blenkinsopp comments, 'It was inevitable that Christian readers and hearers would give this plea a messianic interpretation . . . and so interpreted . . . it came to be used in the Advent liturgy' (*Isaiah 56 – 66: A New Translation with Introduction and Commentary* [New York: Doubleday, 2003], p. 263).

YHWH's command (34:16–17). A prime example of this reversal by the *rûaḥ* occurs in Isaiah 32. Within the larger context of Isaiah 28 – 35, several woes announce that judgment will come upon the proud (28:1), the unjust, those trusting in foreign nations (30:7; 31:1) and those acting in ways that do not accord with God's *rûaḥ* (30:1, 9). This is because Yahweh's rule is characterized by 'the spirit [*rûaḥ*] of justice' (28:5–6). There is hope, however, due to Yahweh's grace and compassion (30:18) for those who fear and wait for him (30:15).

Amid the tension between proclamations regarding Yahweh's judgment against the rebellious and hope for a peaceful era beyond this judgment (29:17–21; 30:19ff.), Isaiah introduces an image of a seemingly secure city. While joyous and secure, it will soon be a sullen wilderness (32:9–14). The prophet, however, indicates that this wilderness will be transformed when the *rûaḥ* is poured out from on high (32:15). As a result of the outpouring of the *rûaḥ*, a new society emerges with the qualities of justice, righteousness, peace, solitude and rest (32:16–20). In conjunction with Isaiah 33, this vision of a society of justice, righteousness and peace centres in Zion (33:5). The hope is that God will again act by his *rûaḥ* to care for Zion. Yahweh will transform all earthly structures through his *rûaḥ* in order to establish his kingdom (Zion) as a symbol of the security of his people, who walk with him in integrity and depend on him for their refuge in adverse circumstances (33:15–16).

Due to the parallel in phraseology between 29:17 and 32:15, the addition of the role of the *rûaḥ* in transforming reality in chapter 32 clarifies that God's plan to transform society will be enacted by the work of God's *rûaḥ*. Childs observes that these two verses (29:17 and 32:15) link together chapters 28 – 35 to create a larger textual world with eschatological and messianic expectations.[40] God's *rûaḥ* plays a significant transforming role in establishing God's kingdom ideals.

In summary, it is essential to recognize that God's *rûaḥ* is a representative of God, if not God himself. He reveals and executes Yahweh's plan within the world. This is evident by recognizing the links between the *rûaḥ* and Yahweh's plan.[41] It is also clear as one notices the central role that Isaiah anticipates

---

40. B. S. Childs, *Isaiah*, OTL (Louisville: Westminster John Knox, 2001), pp. 241–242; G. K. Beale, 'The Old Testament Background to Paul's Reference to "the Fruit of the Spirit" in Galatians 5:22', *BBR* 15 (2005).

41. The role of God's word in Isaiah performs a similar function of accomplishing God's plan (cf. Isa. 40:8; 55:11). With word paralleling counsel (8:10; 44:26) and

the *rûaḥ* will play in bringing about a new creation, a second exodus and the restoration of Zion (chs. 28 – 35).

Rûaḥ-filled agents of Yahweh's kingdom

With the *rûaḥ* as the representative of Yahweh who executes God's plan, there is an important intersection between him and the empowering of agents for God's kingdom agenda.[42] The Davidic agent (chs. 1 – 12) and the Mosaic-prophetic-like servant of the Lord (chs. 40 – 66) serve as two models of *rûaḥ*-empowered agency in Isaiah. Importantly, the *rûaḥ* is primary in this relationship.

The Davidic model of kingdom agency is set within the canonical context of chapters 1 – 12. In this section, the rebellion of Israel and Judah crystallizes in Ahaz's response to a particular historical situation: the Syro-Ephramite crisis (734 BC). Ahaz lacks faith as he persists in fear as Aram and Israel threaten Jerusalem. Amidst this portrait of feeble Davidic leadership, Isaiah projects several visions of the ideal Davidic agent (Isa. 9:1–7; 11:1–6). With the term *rûaḥ* appearing four times in 11:2 and with several plays on that word in 11:3–5, we focus our attention upon Isaiah 11.

The vision of the ideal Davidic agent in Isaiah 11 is best understood in contrast with both Ahaz (see above) and Assyria and its king in chapter 10.[43] Isaiah 10 concludes with tree imagery depicting the destruction of arrogant Assyria and its king (10:17, 33–34). In contrast, Isaiah 11 employs arboreal imagery to envision the emergence of a Davidic king. 'A shoot will come up from the stump of Jesse; from his roots a Branch will bear fruit' (11:1). The *rûaḥ* of God rests upon this Davidic king resulting in four characteristics: wisdom (counsel, justice, righteousness, and faithfulness), strength (valour, power), a fatherly care for the oppressed and judgment on the oppressors, and a reconciling peace (11:1–9; cf. 9:5–6 [ET 6–7]; 16:5; 32:1; Ps. 72). Just as the *rûaḥ* brings about a just and peaceful society in chapter 32, so the

---

rûaḥ also paralleling counsel (40:13; cf. 30:1), it is possible that God's word and *rûaḥ* serve a similar performative purpose.

42. H. G. M. Williamson, *Variations on a Theme: King, Messiah and Servant in the Book of Isaiah* (Carlisle, Cumbria: Paternoster, 1998).

43. A. M. Beuken, '"Lebanon with its majesty shall fall. A shoot shall come forth from the stump of Jesse" (Isa 10:34 – 11:1). Interfacing the Story of Assyria and the Image of Israel's Future in Isaiah 10 – 11', in F. Postma, et al. (eds.), *The New Things. Eschatology in Old Testament Prophecy. Fss. for Frank Lenne* (Maastricht: Shaker, 2002), pp. 17–33.

rûaḥ establishes similar characteristics through the king. This portrait of the Davidic king certainly contrasts Ahaz's feebleness (ch. 7), the Assyrian king's man-made wisdom (10:13) and Judah's social justice (e.g. 1:15–17, 21–23; 5:7; 10:2). Isaiah 11, then, creates expectations regarding a Davidic agent who is empowered by God's *rûaḥ* to wisely bring about an era of justice and peace within society. The results of the *rûaḥ*'s empowerment of this king accord with God's general goal of establishing a community of righteousness and peace.

Hezekiah (chs. 36 – 39) displays characteristics of these messianic expectations in contrast to Ahaz in Isaiah 7. He is one who wisely trusts in the Lord and brings about peace to Judah (39:8; see chs. 36 – 38). It is clear, however, that Hezekiah falls short of the ideal in Isaiah 11 due to his questionable political ambitions hinted at in Isaiah 39. Isaiah looks beyond Hezekiah for a *rûaḥ*-endowed Davidic agent through whom God will establish his kingdom.

The second model of kingdom agency that intersects with *rûaḥ* is the servant of the Lord. The theme of the servant develops in Isaiah 40 – 66. Much has been written on the nature and identity of the servant of the Lord.[44] It is not our intent to review the literature, except to point out the connections between the *rûaḥ* and the servant (42:1), the *rûaḥ* and the prophet (48:16; 61:1), and the *rûaḥ* and the new community of God's people ('the servants of the Lord').[45] Given the prophet's focus on Yahweh as the only Saviour (59:16), the servant of the Lord is an agent of salvation who freely uses people to accomplish his purposes.

In Isaiah 42:1, Yahweh declares that God's *rûaḥ* is upon his servant. This servant is to play the specific role of bringing justice to the nations (42:1). While Israel emerges as an unfaithful servant due to her rebelliousness (43:22–28), the ideal of a servant (corporate and/or individual) emerges who will embody these kingdom ideals and serve as Yahweh's faithful agent to the world.

The prophet as a servant of the Lord also emerges as he describes God's *rûaḥ* enabling him. In Isaiah 48:16, God's *rûaḥ* anoints him to provide instruction for the people. Later, the prophet proclaims: 'The *rûaḥ* of the Sovereign LORD is on me' (61:1). The purpose of this anointing is to commission and endow with power the speaker to proclaim the good news for the broken and

---

44. Bernd Janowski and Peter Stuhlmacher (eds.), *The Suffering Servant: Isaiah 53 in Jewish and Christian Sources*, trans. Daniel P. Bailey (Grand Rapids: Eerdmans, 2004).

45. See the articles on Isa. 11:2 (Hilary Marlow) and Isa. 48:16 (Paul Wegner) in this volume.

to establish a community of righteousness (61:2–3). These characteristics correspond both with the ideal role of the servant (42:1) and also with the Davidic king (9:1–7; 11:1–6; 16:4).

Not only are the servant and the prophet endowed with the *rûaḥ*, their offspring will be also. On the one hand, the unworthy servant (=Israel) has a history of rebelliousness (43:22–28). On the other hand, Yahweh promises to redeem his servant and to transform his offspring by his *rûaḥ* so that generation upon generation will know him and will serve him (44:1–5; 59:21; 60:21–22).[46] The prophetic legacy finds continuance in the ministry of the *rûaḥ* in the lives of the servants of the Lord and of their descendants. The servants of the Lord (cf. 56:6) come from all nations. They are the true heirs of Zion (57:13b). Theirs is the vision of the New Jerusalem (65:19; see ch. 60), of the new creation (65:19–25) and, indeed, of God's salvation and comfort of his people (40:1 – 66:24).[47] As a multitude joined Israel in leaving Egypt during the first Exodus, the New Exodus will be so magnificent that the presence of God among his people will attract non-Israelites to know the God of Israel (44:5; cf. 56:1–8). The prophetic mission will transcend that of the prophet as it will continue from generation to generation.

Thus the role of the *rûaḥ* in empowering agents to establish God's kingdom is significant in Isaiah's expectations. There are a number of commonalities between the Davidic and Servant-Prophetic models of agency. The most significant commonality is the role of the *rûaḥ* in establishing justice and righteousness in society. As Isaiah's message unfolds, agency democratizes to the point where the entire community and future generations are endowed with God's *rûaḥ* to establish the social ideals found in the Davidic and Servant/Prophetic models. The prophetic vision corresponds with that of Moses, the servant of the Lord (Deut. 34:5), who hoped in the democratization of the *rûaḥ* (Num. 11) and the empowerment and wisdom of the *rûaḥ* in mobilizing leaders and prophets (see above). The *rûaḥ* brings about God's plan, and the servants of the Lord, including the Davidic agents, depend upon the *rûaḥ* to carry it out.

The prophetic variation in Isaiah reveals dramatic movements. The book of Isaiah gives little rest to its readers as they connect the many themes together in a synoptic way. The ministry of the *rûaḥ* of God is diverse as he works at many different levels. We have indicated above that the *rûaḥ* plays a central role in executing Yahweh's plan. Within this plan, the *rûaḥ* mobilizes

46. See Ma, *Until*, pp. 84–85.

47. See Beale, 'Old Testament Background', pp. 1–38.

agents, such as the prophet and his community, Davidites, the servant(s) of the Lord, and even Cyrus.

Jeremiah

Jeremiah speaks of a new covenant that God will monergistically establish while changing the heart of the people (chs. 31, 32). Unlike his near contemporary, Ezekiel, he does not refer to the role of the *rûaḥ* in this process.

Ezekiel

Daniel Block briefly observes the theological significance of the *rûaḥ* under the heading 'The Enduring Theology of Ezekiel'.[48] He makes a penetrating remark that catches the import of the person of Ezekiel: 'Ezekiel not only spoke of the power of the *rûaḥ*; he embodied the *rûaḥ*'s power in his own person.'[49] The *rûaḥ* empowers the prophet (2:2), brings him into the presence of the Lord, and shapes Ezekiel into a ready servant of the Lord. Ezekiel is not only called 'son of man'; he becomes the model of humanity in his standing before the Lord. Called to divine service, Ezekiel is faithful in his ministry, suffers for the sake of his people, and ministers in word and in symbolic acts. Under the empowerment of the *rûaḥ*, Ezekiel is transfigured into the model of humanity.[50]

Ezekiel's persona

Ezekiel stands as a mediator between Yahweh and Israel in exile. He becomes another Moses,[51] but with an important difference. Moses merely forewarned Israel that her sin would lead to her being scattered among the nations and away from Yahweh's presence (Deut. 28). What Moses had spoken of was taking place during Ezekiel's ministry. Ezekiel ministers to an exilic community whose history of disobedience resulted in experiencing these curses and necessitated the departure of the glory of the Lord (ch. 10). As the *rûaḥ*

48. Block, *Ezekiel*, 1:47–60.

49. Ibid., 1:50; see also 'The Prophet of the Spirit'.

50. Block opines that Ezekiel, like Jeremiah, may have been a reluctant prophet (*Ezekiel*, 1:12), whose ministry was transformed by the Spirit of God. In contrast, see T. Collins, who argues that 'Ezekiel is robed in the mantle of Elijah and Elisha' (*The Mantle of Elijah: The Redaction Criticism of the Prophetical Books*, The Biblical Seminar 20 [Sheffield: JSOT Press, 1993], pp. 100–101).

51. Henry McKeating, 'Ezekiel: "The Prophet like Moses"?', *JSOT* 61 (1994), pp. 97–109.

of God had empowered Moses to bring rebellious Israel to the point where they would inherit Canaan under the leadership of Joshua (Deut. 34:9–12), so Ezekiel is empowered to bring a transformed Israel into a vision of a transformed land, a transformed Jerusalem and a transformed Davidic kingship.

The vision of the transformation of a community where the glory of the Lord is evidently present (48:35) is Yahweh's revelation to Ezekiel. Neither Ezekiel nor Israel can effect such a radical transformation. It is Yahweh's plan, and Ezekiel entrusts this future to Yahweh's *rûaḥ*.

Word and *rûaḥ*

The close connection between word and spirit is the subject of James Robson's recent work, *Word and Spirit in Ezekiel*.[52] He argues 'that the prophet himself is a prescriptive paradigm of the transformation necessary for the addressees of the book'.[53] Ezekiel's obedience to the Lord, his questions, experiences and prophetic declarations serve 'as a model for the addressees of the book'.[54] The use of the first person in the description of the prophet's experiences with God/the *rûaḥ* has a rhetorical function of drawing the audience into the prophetic world, i.e. the book of Ezekiel.[55] The close connection between the prophet and the book elevates Ezekiel into a 'prophetic persona'.[56] Ezekiel, who received and obeyed the word by the empowerment of the *rûaḥ*, becomes a vehicle for Israel to enter into a new and transformed relationship with Yahweh. Robson concludes, 'In the face of the trauma of exile, Ezekiel mirrors for his readers, in his questioning of Yahweh and in his oracles, the puzzled but necessary realization that Jerusalem fell because of Yahweh's judgment.'[57] The prophetic ministry of announcement and explanation of the fall of Jerusalem vindicates the prophetic experiences and message. The prophet's experiences and the divine revelation, especially the report on Jerusalem's fall, authenticate his message; more than that, they are intended to transform the intended readers by calling for an appropriate response to the prophetic model and message.[58]

Robson further argues that the prophetic descriptions of the transforming

52. Robson, *Word and Spirit*.
53. Ibid., p. 25, cf. p. 273.
54. Ibid., p. 24.
55. Ibid., pp. 271–273.
56. Ibid., p. 25.
57. Ibid., p. 273.
58. Ibid., pp. 170; 275–276.

empowerment by the *rûaḥ* of God are to make Israel aware of her history of disobedience that has led to her exile (death) and to follow the prophet Ezekiel as a 'model of obedience'.[59] The purpose of the *rûaḥ* is to open the people to the future. The past is a story of failure, but the future lies open before them. The *rûaḥ* who opened Ezekiel's eyes to see the reasons for Israel's failure and death also revealed the possibility of a new future. By appeal to the import of the prophetic persona, Robson closely identifies the future of Ezekiel's audience with the paradigmatic role and 'the vision of the future' of the prophet.[60] Ezekiel leads his followers to confess their guilt and to be open to Yahweh's initiatives by asking, 'How then can we live?' (33:10).

In response, Yahweh promises to transform Israel into a new community characterized by purification (holiness), the empowerment of his *rûaḥ*, obedience and blessing. He is with them as their covenant God who commits himself to transform Israel. The verbal phrases italicized in the following verses bring out the monergistic emphasis:

> *I will give* you a new heart and *put* a new spirit in you; *I will remove* from you your heart of stone and *give you* a heart of flesh. And *I will put* my *rûaḥ* in you and *move you to follow* my decrees and *be careful* to keep my laws. You will live in the land I gave your forefathers; you will be my people, and I will be your God. *I will save you* from all your uncleanness. *I will call* for the corn and *make it plentiful* and will not bring famine upon you. *I will increase* the fruit of the trees and the crops of the field, so that you will no longer suffer disgrace among the nations because of famine. (36:26–30; cf. 11:19; 18:31)

Yahweh's promise of restoration is not contingent on Israel's response. Yahweh takes responsibility for both Israel's transformation and the future covenant relationship and blessings: '[Israel's] renewed obedience . . . is part of that restoration.'[61] Yahweh's transformation of the community opens up the bridge to the future as developed in the Vision of the Dry Bones (37:1–14). When the prophet is transported by the *rûaḥ* to the valley, he, like Moses, reveals Israel's future. Looking at the dead bones, Ezekiel is obedient to Yahweh's command to speak to the bones. He witnesses the reconnection of these bones into bodies. The second command brings life (*rûaḥ*) into the bodies. Two observations are in order. First, the intentional play on the word *rûaḥ* marvellously brings out the ambiguity of the polysemy

---

59. Ibid., pp. 180–193.
60. Ibid., pp. 211–212.
61. Ibid., p. 223.

entailed by the word 'spirit'. It may be rendered as spirit, breath and wind, as in the NIV:

> Then he said to me, 'Prophesy to these bones and say to them, "Dry bones, hear the word of the LORD! This is what the Sovereign LORD says to these bones: I will make *breath* enter you, and you will come to life"' . . . Then he said to me, 'Prophesy to the *breath*; prophesy, son of man, and say to it, "This is what the Sovereign LORD says: Come from the four *winds*, O *breath*, and breathe into these slain, that they may live."' So I prophesied as he commanded me, and breath entered them; they came to life and stood up on their feet – a vast army. (37:4–5, 9–10)

Second, many exegetes have observed the connection with the two stages in the creation of Adam: the formation of the body and the imparting of the breath of life (Gen. 2:7).[62] However, in the case of Ezekiel, the two acts of re-creation are not only consecutive; they are two aspects of the restoration process.[63] As the prophet had been obedient to Yahweh's commands while awaiting the judgment on Jerusalem and Judah, so the exiles will have to wait for Yahweh's renewal by the *rûaḥ* and respond accordingly in obedience. Robson presses for the paradigmatic connection between Adam, Ezekiel and the exilic community when he concludes, 'If the prophet is the paradigm of the people in his experience of the divine *rûaḥ* (Hb.), then he can be seen as the first human in Yahweh's new work of creation among the exiles.'[64] The exiles must repent, but their response arises not out of an inner change or volition, but solely from the work of God's *rûaḥ*. He puts his *rûaḥ* in them (36:26; 37:14); i.e. he pours out his *rûaḥ* upon them (39:29).[65] This spiritual transformation has radical implications. It assures the perpetual loyalty of the new community as well as their future as the people of God. Instead of Yahweh pouring out his wrath on Israel, they will receive the renewing, vitalizing and blessedness of the *rûaḥ* of his presence: 'I will no longer hide my face from them, for I will pour out my *rûaḥ* on the house of Israel, declares the Sovereign LORD' (39:29).

The persona of Ezekiel keeps two worlds before his audience. On the one

---

62. See ibid., pp. 225–226.

63. See Robson's restatement of the argument by T. Renz (*The Rhetorical Function of the Book of Ezekiel*, *VTSup* 76 [Leiden: Brill, 1999], pp. 206–207) in ibid., pp. 227–229.

64. Robson, ibid., p. 240; see also Block, *Ezekiel*, 2:379.

65. See Robson's extensive discussion on the essential synonymity of these two expressions, ibid., pp. 252–262.

hand, he portrays a world through the *rûaḥ*'s revelation of Israel's disobedience, judgment, exile and death. On the other, the *rûaḥ* reveals a world where Yahweh's presence and glory are restored amidst a vital, blessed, transformed and obedient Israel. Ezekiel's experiences and revelatory word provide a bridge to Israel's past as well as to her future. The same *rûaḥ*, who had revealed the word of judgment (chs. 1 – 33), reveals the word of restoration (chs. 34 – 39; 40 – 48).

Israel will undergo a transformation from curse to blessing and from the outpouring of Yahweh's wrath to the outpouring of his *rûaḥ*. The God who had poured wrath on his people (chs. 1 – 33) will pour out his *rûaḥ* on them (36:16 – 37:14), dwell with them (37:15–28), protect them from adversity (35:1 – 36:15; 38 – 39) and reveal his glory (40 – 48). As the exile involved a geographical translocation, the Spirit reveals that restoration includes the presence of God with his people in space and in time.

Geographical theology

The *rûaḥ* brings Ezekiel into the sacred space of God's earthly throne from which he looks at a restored world (43:5–7). Ezekiel's Jerusalem is like that of the past, but at the same time so different. It is a holy city where Yahweh alone is King (see Rev. 21:3). As people and kings have rebelled against Yahweh and experienced the shame of exile, so king and people are painted with the same brush stroke. They will have to leave their unclean ways and become obedient to Yahweh. The king and the people and all the tribes are connected to the holy space from which God rules as the Benefactor and King. No tribe can lay claim on Jerusalem. It is Yahweh's city. Renz speaks of Ezekiel's geographical vision as an expression of 'Yahweh's kingship in territorial rhetoric'.[66]

The *rûaḥ* creates a world where Yahweh is King and Benefactor. Yahweh 'constructs' the temple (Jerusalem), transforms creation and blesses his people together with righteous Gentiles (chs. 40 – 48). Neither the temple nor the city is closely connected to the Davidic dynasty.[67] The Davidic king is relegated to a leadership role, but without enjoying the full benefits of the Zion tradition.[68]

The presence of Yahweh as King and Benefactor of people and kings dwarfs the import of the Davidic dynasty, privileged classes, tribal identity or social status. Each tribe has equal access to the city, as each of the city's twelve

---

66. Renz, *Rhetorical*, p. 128. Leslie Allen speaks of 'a new geographical configuration of tribal territories' (*Ezekiel 20 – 48*, WBC [Waco: Word, 1990], p. 213).
67. See Renz, *Rhetorical*, p.127.
68. Allen, *Ezekiel 20 – 48*, p. 213.

gates is named after one of the tribes. Jerusalem is not the city of David, nor is the temple a royal edifice. Jerusalem comes to its own as an intertribal city where 'the holiness of God was to be a paramount principle, and its outworking was to permeate both the structure and the procedure of the temple'.[69] Jerusalem becomes the city of God where his justice rules. It has no place for intertribal disputes and oppression. It excludes the prominence of the tribe of Judah, but it embraces foreigners who reside in the tribal territories (47:21–23).

Ezekiel's portrayal of the *rûaḥ* and the future is like a series of portraits, rather than a movie. He does not want his audience to be misled by temporal or spatial conditions. The imagery is of such a nature that it is in time and out of time. It is in space (the Promised Land) and out of space. It is what Daniel Block calls 'a literary cartoon, with many unreal and bizarre features'.[70] Ezekiel gives rise to expectations regarding the important role the *rûaḥ* will play in creating a new community of obedience. The prophet serves as an example of this transformation, and provides glimpses through the *rûaḥ* of both the judgment and glorious transformation that lay ahead.

The Twelve

The theme of the *rûaḥ* of God in the Twelve is of minor importance, except for the promise of the outpouring of God's *rûaḥ* in Joel.[71] Micah speaks of Yahweh's *rûaḥ* as evidence of his character (2:7). The prophet claims to be filled with the *rûaḥ* and he specifies the nature of the *rûaḥ*'s effect on his ministry, as he states God's case against the people with 'power . . . justice and might' (3:8).[72] Haggai encourages the remnant with a typological connection of their situation with the time of the exodus from Egypt. In so doing, he confirms that the *rûaḥ* of God is with them in this new situation. As God's *rûaḥ* had strengthened Joshua and the judges, so he is with the leaders (Zerubbabel and Joshua) and also the remnant of the people (2:4–5). As evidence Haggai reports on the work of the *rûaḥ* in motivating the leadership and people to rebuild the temple (1:14). Finally, the familiar text in Zechariah resonates with

---

69. Ibid.

70. Block, *Ezekiel*, 1:57.

71. See W. A. VanGemeren, 'The Spirit of Restoration', *WTJ* 50 (1988), pp. 81–102. See also the chapter in this volume on Joel 3:1, 2 (ET 2:28, 29) by Erika Moore.

72. Francis I. Andersen and David Noel Freedman suggest that 'The attributes of power, judgement and might come from (or with) the spirit of Yahweh' (*Micah*, AB 24E [New York: Doubleday, 2000], p. 377).

Micah's connection of the *rûaḥ* with might by distinguishing between human might and the power of the *rûaḥ*: 'Not by might nor by power, but by my *rûaḥ*' (4:6). Zechariah's final prophetic word on the *rûaḥ* associates the *rûaḥ* with eschatology and the messianic era and connects the OT hope with the proclamation of the apostles in the NT that the new era of the *rûaḥ* is present in Jesus' ministry, both before and after the cross.

Spirit of God in the Writings

There are several ways in which the Writings elicit expectations regarding the continued work of the *rûaḥ* in God's redemptive plan. First, the *rûaḥ* of God intersects with prophecy in Chronicles (2 Chr. 15:1; 20:14; 24:20).[73] In two such instances, King Asa (2 Chr. 15:8) and King Jehoshaphat (20:18) obey the message of prophets who are clothed by God's *rûaḥ* (15:1; 20:14) and experience blessing as a result (15:19; 20:22–27). In another instance, Joash and his people reject God's prophets (2 Chr. 24:19) and even kill the *rûaḥ*-anointed prophet Zechariah (24:20). As a result, they are defeated by Syria (24:24). A pattern surfaces in these accounts. Cursing and blessing for the nation directly relates with their response to the *rûaḥ* of God's message spoken through the prophets (cf. 20:20; 24:19; 36:16). As a message crafted to help the post-exilic community understand God's ways, it seems that the Chronicler anticipates that the audience will face the same scenario: will they believe the *rûaḥ*-inspired message of God's prophets?[74] The Chronicler hopes for a new community that embraces God's messages conveyed by the *rûaḥ*.

Second, the *rûaḥ* figures into the eschatological schema of the Psalter. Holding to a strategic post-exilic arrangement, many scholars note the transition from Davidic kingship (Pss 1 – 72, 89) to divine kingship (Pss 90 – 150, esp. 93, 95 – 99 and 144 – 146).[75] While divine kingship is indeed prominent

73. For a brief discussion regarding how the pattern of responding to prophecy in Chronicles speaks to future generations, see H. G. M. Williamson, *1 and 2 Chronicles*, NCB (Grand Rapids/London: Eerdmans/Marshall Morgan & Scott, 1982), pp. 32–33. For a helpful overview of Chronicles as recounting history in order to shape a post-exilic community, see R. K. Duke, 'Chronicles, Book of', in B. T. Arnold, et al. (eds.), *Dictionary of the Old Testament Historical Books* (Downers Grove: InterVarsity Press, 2005), pp. 161–181.

74. See also a similar concern with responding to *rûaḥ*-anointed prophetic instruction in Neh. 9:20, 30. Nehemiah and the Chronicler then go beyond Kings by linking prophetic instruction with the *rûaḥ* (2 Kgs 17:13).

75. On the move toward divine kingship, see Gerald Wilson, 'The Structure of the

in the message of the Psalter, hope endures that God will be faithful to rise up a Davidic king who will bring blessing through a just and righteous rule.[76] As it relates to the *rûaḥ* and Davidic kingship, David rejoices in the first part of the book that God's *rûaḥ* saved him (18:15 [16]; cf. Exod. 15:8, 10) and pleads that God not take away from him the holy *rûaḥ* (51:11 [13]). While David's prominence fades in Book III and the Psalter laments the rejection of the Davidic dynasty (Ps. 89:38), there are glimmers of hope regarding God's continued commitment to his anointed in Books III – V (Pss 86; 101; 110; 132:17). David proclaims that he cannot flee from God's *rûaḥ* (139:7) and calls on God's *rûaḥ* to guide him (143:10). The Psalter holds out hope that the divine King will not neglect to send his *rûaḥ* to the Davidic king to accomplish his purposes.

While there are other instances of the *rûaḥ* of God in the Writings,[77] we have indicated several ways in which this portion of the Tanakh elicits anticipation regarding the future work of God's *rûaḥ*. The Chronicler expects the continued opportunity for humanity to respond in obedience to the message of God's *rûaḥ* through the prophets. The Psalter envisions a scenario where the *rûaḥ* will once again lead and anoint a Davidic king.

Accordance with the New Testament

The NT depicts a new era in the work of God's Spirit. Though this new era differs from OT expectations, the NT writers understand this work of God's Spirit as having accordance with the OT witness in several ways.[78] First, God's Spirit anoints Jesus – a Davidic king and servant agent – and is at work enabling him to bring healing, justice and righteousness to the world

---

Psalter', in D. Firth and P. Johnston (eds.), *Interpreting the Psalms: Issues and Approaches* (Downers Grove: InterVarsity Press, 2005), pp. 229–246. See also D. M. Howard, *The Structure of Psalms 93 – 100* (Winona Lake: Eisenbrauns, 1997).

76. D. C. Mitchell highlights this persisting Davidic hope in *The Message of the Psalter: An Eschatological Programme in the Book of Psalms* (Sheffield: Sheffield Academic Press, 1997).

77. See the assumption of God's continual involvement with creation through the *rûaḥ* in the Psalter (33:6; 104:30; 147:18) and Job (33:4; 34:14).

78. For a brief discussion on this way of understanding the two Testaments' relationship, see B. S. Childs, *Biblical Theology: A Proposal* (Minneapolis: Fortress, 2002).

(e.g. Luke 3:22, 4:18–19; Acts 10:38; cf. 1 Sam. 16:13–14; Isa. 11:1–9; 61:1–2). Second, God's Spirit acts to mobilize leaders to serve as God's spokesmen and prophets (e.g. Acts 4:8, 31; 19:6; cf. Num. 11). Third, the democratization of the *rûaḥ* that the OT anticipates (Num. 11:30; Isa. 59:21; Joel 3) corresponds with the inclusive nature of the Spirit in establishing the new community (e.g. Acts 2:38; 10:44). This community is mobilized to continue the work of Christ (e.g. Acts 4:30; 24:25; Rom. 14:17; 1 Cor. 12:9). Finally, the Spirit of God in the NT also accords with the general involvement in bringing about a new creation. The gift of the Spirit is the token of adoption and of the inheritance of Jesus Christ. The Spirit works in all believers to await the resurrection of the body and the new creation (e.g. Rom. 8:21–25; 2 Cor. 5:5; cf. Gen. 1:2; 8:1; Isa. 32:15ff.). While not exhaustive, we have indicated several ways in which the work of God's Spirit in the NT accords with OT expectations.

Conclusion

The entire OT canon elicits a variety of expectations regarding the work of God's *rûaḥ*. The Torah, Prophets and Writings all associate with one another to elicit anticipation and hope pertaining to God acting by the *rûaḥ*. The most prominent expectations pertain to the Spirit's role in carrying out God's creative-redemptive plans and in equipping prophets, kings and people to restore God's order in society and to participate in and await the coming of the new creation.

20. THE SPIRIT AND THE FUTURE IN THE OLD TESTAMENT: RESTORATION AND RENEWAL

Robin Routledge

Introduction

The activity of the Spirit, in the eyes of the OT writers, is the activity of God. Through the Spirit, God is active in his world and among his people.[1] This volume explores the role of the Spirit of God in creation, including breathing life into human beings, and also in relation to the equipping and enabling of God's people as they seek to serve him and live out what it means to belong

1. See e.g. Robin Routledge, *Old Testament Theology: A Thematic Approach* (Nottingham: Apollos, 2008; Downers Grove: InterVarsity Press, 2009), pp. 112–113. See also Michael Green, *I Believe in the Holy Spirit* (London: Hodder and Stoughton, 1975), pp. 30–31; Norman H. Snaith, *The Distinctive Ideas of the Old Testament* (London: Epworth Press, 1955), p. 153. John Goldingay describes references to the Spirit as 'a First Testament way of describing God's activity in the world'; see John Goldingay, *Old Testament Theology 1: Israel's Gospel* (Downers Grove: InterVarsity Press; Milton Keynes: Paternoster, 2003), p. 794. He suggests, though, that the OT writers also have other ways of referring to the presence and activity of God, which in the NT are subsumed in references to God's Spirit; see John Goldingay, 'Was The Holy Spirit Active In Old Testament Times? What Was New About The Christian Experience Of God', *Ex Auditu* 12 (1996), pp. 14–28 (18).

to him. However, while the Spirit has an important part to play in the ongoing life and witness of the people of God, the OT writers also look forward to a new age,[2] to which God's activity in the past and present points. In that coming era of salvation God's purposes for creation will finally be fulfilled; God will bring all opposition to himself to an end, will restore his people and establish his reign over the whole earth. In the OT, as in the NT, that new age is closely linked with the Spirit of God; and it is to the relationship between the Spirit of God and this future age that we now turn.

For the OT writers, future hope lies at the far side of divine judgment. Israel was chosen and called into a unique relationship with God as his own special people (e.g. Exod. 19:5–6; Deut. 7:7–8). According to the OT, this special relationship was embodied in a series of divine covenants – in particular the covenant with Abraham in which God committed himself to an individual and to his offspring (Gen. 15; 17:7; cf. 22:16–18), and the covenant at Sinai (Exod. 19:5) where God confirmed that relationship with the nation descended from Abraham (Exod. 6:3–8; cf. 3:6–8). From God's side, that relationship entailed taking this people to be his own special possession – as indicated by the recurring covenant formula: 'they will be my people and I will be their God'.[3] Israel's response was to acknowledge Yahweh as their only God, to be obedient to his law and to allow their special relationship with Yahweh

2. In speaking of the future, I have not used the term 'eschatology'. In the NT and Jewish apocalyptic writings eschatology concerns 'the final consummation that will bring history, the cosmos and the present world order to an end' (Routledge, *OT Theology*, p. 272), indicating a fundamental discontinuity between the present world order and the eschatological future. In the OT, however, God's breaking into human affairs to establish his kingdom will take place within history, and so there is a greater degree of continuity between the present and the future. Thus, when applied to the OT, 'eschatology' requires a wider definition, and to avoid the possibility of reading a Christian understanding of eschatology into the OT I have used different language. For further discussion see Routledge, *OT Theology*, pp. 272–280; see also e.g. Donald E. Gowan, *Eschatology in the Old Testament* (Philadelphia: Fortress, 1986); E. Jenni, 'Eschatology of the OT', in *IDB* 2:126–133; Th. C. Vriezen, 'Prophecy and Eschatology', *Congress Volume, Copenhagen 1953*, *VTSup* 1 (Leiden: Brill, 1953), pp. 199–299.

3. E.g. Jer. 24:7; 32:38; Ezek. 11:20; 14:11; 37:23; cf. Exod. 6:7; Lev. 26:12; Jer. 31:33. Unless otherwise stated all biblical references are from the NIV. For further discussion see Rolf Rendtorff, *The Covenant Formula: An Exegetical and Theological Investigation* (Edinburgh: T. & T. Clark, 1998).

to be expressed in their life together. The result would be a people set apart, whose life as a community would bear witness to the surrounding nations of the blessings of living in God's presence, and so draw those nations to God.[4] The prophets in particular, though, emphasize Israel's failure to live up to her high calling; and because of her persistent idolatry and false worship, disobedience and injustice within society the nation came under God's judgment. The result was defeat and exile: for the northern kingdom to Assyria; for Judah, the southern kingdom, to Babylon.

However, while the exile was a national disaster it was also a theological necessity. It was needed to bring the people (or a remnant of them) to their senses; to a point where they were willing to turn back to God. It was a death from which the rebirth of the nation could take place.[5] In this discussion I want to focus on key aspects of that rebirth, all of which are closely related to the work of the Spirit of God. First, it involves the restoration of the nation – including the return of the scattered exiles to their land, the re-establishment of the covenant relationship between God and his people, and the promise of future blessing. Second, and crucially, the OT writers point to the spiritual renewal that will result in the transformation of the people, to enable those who had been disobedient in the past to be obedient and so to ensure that the restoration will be permanent. It should be noted, however, that while passages may focus primarily on one or other of these aspects of Israel's future

4. There is debate about whether the OT points primarily to the future restoration and blessing of Israel, with other nations, at best, subservient to Israel, or is more universalistic, envisaging the sharing of the nations as equal partners with Israel in the blessings of the coming age. While there are some difficult passages, it is my view that the latter better reflects the overall emphasis of the OT. See Robin Routledge, 'Mission and Covenant in the Old Testament', in Rollin G. Grams, I. Howard Marshall, Peter F. Penner and Robin Routledge (eds.), *Bible and Mission: A Conversation between Biblical Studies and Missiology* (Schwarzenwald: Neufeld Verlag, 2008), pp. 8–41; Routledge, *OT Theology*, pp. 319–333; see also Richard Bauckham, *Bible and Mission: Christian Witness in a Postmodern World* (Milton Keynes: Paternoster; Grand Rapids: Baker, 2003), pp. 27–54; James Chukwuma Okoye, *Israel and the Nations: A Mission Theology of the Old Testament* (Maryknoll: Orbis, 2006); Christopher J. H. Wright, *The Mission of God: Unlocking the Bible's Grand Narrative* (Downers Grove: InterVarsity Press; Leicester: Inter-Varsity Press, 2006).

5. See e.g. Routledge, *OT Theology*, pp. 265–272; R. E. Clements, *Prophecy and Covenant*, SBT 43 (London: SCM, 1965), p. 118; Christopher R. Seitz, 'Ezekiel 37:1–14', *Int* 46.1 (1992), pp. 53–56.

hope, and this chapter will consider them separately in order to draw out those different nuances, there is also considerable overlap between them. Passages that focus on restoration often include implicit references to renewal; and renewal takes place within the context of, and to ensure the permanence of, restoration. Both are also closely related to the re-establishment of God's covenant with his people. Alongside these important aspects of the work of the Spirit, I want to consider another key element. The restoration and renewal of Israel is viewed also in terms of a new creation, and as such affects not just one nation, but the whole earth. And this, too, is linked with the Spirit of God.

The Spirit and restoration

In Ezekiel 37:1–14 the restoration of Israel is described in terms of breathing life into those who are long dead. This reflects a common understanding of human personality in the OT: human beings are made up of flesh animated by God's Spirit (*rûaḥ*).[6] A classic example of this is Genesis 2:7: 'the LORD God formed the man from the dust of the ground and breathed into his nostrils the breath of life, and the man became a living being.' While the Hebrew word for 'breath' here is *nĕšāmâ* rather than *rûaḥ*, these two terms overlap in meaning and elsewhere in similar expressions, *rûaḥ* is used.[7] The divine *rûaḥ*, then, gives life to lifeless human flesh. This idea underlies Ezekiel 37:1–14. In these verses, *rûaḥ* occurs ten times and has different meanings, reflecting the varied usage of the term. In verse 1, 'the Spirit of the LORD' transports

---

6. See on 'The Spirit and creation' in this volume; see also Routledge, *OT Theology*, pp. 143–147.
7. *Nĕšāmâ* occurs in parallel with *rûaḥ*, in Job 27:3; 32:8; 33:4; 34:14; Isa. 42:5; 57:16. In the expression 'breath of life', *nĕšāmâ* is used in Gen. 2:7, while *rûaḥ* appears in Gen. 6:17; 7:15 (P) and they occur together in Gen. 7:22 (J), maybe in an intentional editorial attempt to link the expressions together. Walther Eichrodt, *Theology of the Old Testament*, 2 vols. (London: SCM, 1961–7), 2:142, suggests that *nĕšāmâ* may be a poetic synonym for *rûaḥ*. For further discussion, see also R. Albertz and C. Westermann, '*rûaḥ*', in *TLOT* 3:1202–1220; H. Lamberty-Zielinski, '*nĕšāmâ*', in *TDOT* 13:65–70 (67); T. C. Mitchell, 'The Old Testament Usage of Nešāmâ', *VT* 11.2 (1961), pp. 177–187; M. V. Van Pelt, W. C. Kaiser and D. I. Block, '*rûaḥ*', in *NIDOTTE* 3:1073–1078 (1074); Snaith, *Distinctive Ideas*, pp. 144, 150; S. Tengström and H.-J. Fabry, '*rûaḥ*', in *TDOT* 13:365–401 (377–378); John W. Yates, *The Spirit and Creation in Paul* (Tübingen: Mohr Siebeck, 2008), p. 25.

Ezekiel into the valley full of dry bones.[8] Here the divine *rûaḥ* is parallel to God's 'hand',[9] and appears to refer to God's dynamic power at work in the life and ministry of the prophet. In verse 9, *rûaḥ* is used in the plural: 'from the four winds [*rûḥôt*]' – that is, from every direction. This use of the term occurs elsewhere in Ezekiel's prophecy, though usually in the context of judgment: because of their rebellion God's people will be scattered to the 'winds' (e.g. 5:2, 10, 12; 12:14; 17:21). In 37:9, though, the emphasis is on restoration, and the use of *rûaḥ* may intentionally echo the earlier language in order to indicate the future reversal of divine judgment. There is also a play on words: what comes from the *rûḥôt* is the *rûaḥ* that brings new life. And that latter understanding of *rûaḥ* – as the breath that animates lifeless flesh – predominates in this passage (explicitly in six of the remaining seven occurrences and, by analogy, also in the seventh). As noted already, this is linked with the idea of *rûaḥ* as the 'breath of life' (cf. Gen. 2:7). It is worth noting that the prophetic word is addressed, here, directly to the *rûaḥ*, and it is the *rûaḥ*, rather than God, that then breathes on the dead and causes life-breath to enter them. This may be stylistic. Ezekiel also prophesies to the bones, and these clearly do not have the power to effect their own resurrection. The language may also echo God's creative word in Genesis 1: emphasizing both the divine power that is released through prophecy, and also the importance of prophecy for the future hope of the nation.[10] The idea of the *rûaḥ* already present in the world may further echo Genesis 1, where the Spirit of God who hovers over the chaotic waters appears to play some role in bringing order and life to the cosmos,[11] and so points to the possibility of a new beginning. We will discuss this further below.

There are other examples of resuscitation in the OT,[12] but on nothing

---

8. Other instances of the *rûaḥ* transporting the prophet are Ezek. 3:12, 14; 8:3; 11:1, 24; 43:5 (cf. 2:2; 3:24). See further, Daniel I. Block, 'The Prophet of the Spirit: the use of *rwḥ* in the Book of Ezekiel', *JETS* 32.1 (1989), pp. 27–49 (33–34).

9. Ezekiel also refers to God's 'hand' being on him (1:3; 3:14, 22; 8:1; 33:22; 37:1; 40:1). This probably points to God's control over him, and is closely related to the activity of the Spirit (e.g. 3:14; 37:1; cf. 3:22–24; 8:1–3).

10. While it is clear, here, that only God can give life to dry bones (note the prophet's response in v. 3), and God's agent of revival is *rûaḥ*, it is clear, too, that the role of the prophet, particularly his word and its effect, is also crucial.

11. See Leslie C. Allen, *Ezekiel 20 – 48*, WBC 29 (Dallas: Word, 1990), p. 185.

12. E.g. 1 Kgs 17:17–24; 2 Kgs 4:32–37; 13:21. Breathing new life into the dead in Ezek. 37:1–14 is taken as a metaphor for the nation's resurrection. This is not individual physical resurrection beyond the grave, though this passage, along with

like this scale, and not with people as long dead as these clearly are. So when Yahweh asks the question, 'can these bones live?' (v. 3) there would be little doubt in Ezekiel's mind that such a thing was impossible. However, God, whose word created the cosmos and whose Spirit breathed life into lifeless flesh, is able to transform what seems to be an impossible situation. In verses 11–14, Ezekiel's experience in the valley of dry bones is then related to the hopeless situation of Israel in exile.

> Then he said to me: 'Son of man, these bones are the whole house of Israel. They say, "Our bones are dried up and our hope is gone; we are cut off." Therefore prophesy and say to them: "This is what the Sovereign LORD says: O my people, I am going to open your graves and bring you up from them; I will bring you back to the land of Israel . . . I will put my Spirit [*rûaḥ*] in you and you will live."' (Ezek. 37:11–14)

The people in exile felt that they were as good as dead – seemingly without a future and without hope.[13] One reason for that may have been the commonly held view that when one nation defeated another it was because its gods were stronger. Since God's people had been defeated by the Babylonians, did that not therefore indicate the superior strength of the gods of Babylon? This raised the question of whether God could restore them even if he wanted to. To counter that view, the prophets emphasized that defeat and exile have come not because of God's weakness; rather, God brought it about as a result

---

others, such as Isa. 26:19 and Hos. 6:1–2, may have provided a basis for the future development of the idea of resurrection seen more clearly in Dan. 12:2. See e.g. Daniel I. Block, *Ezekiel 25 – 48*, NICOT (Grand Rapids; Cambridge: Eerdmans, 1998), pp. 383–387; Jon D. Levenson, *Resurrection and the Restoration of Israel: The Ultimate Victory of the God of Life* (New Haven; London: Yale University Press, 2006), pp. 156–165; Christopher J. H. Wright, *The Message of Ezekiel*, BST (Leicester: Inter-Varsity Press, 2001), pp. 309–311; for further discussion of afterlife in the OT see Philip S. Johnston, *Shades of Sheol: Death and Afterlife in the Old Testament* (Leicester: Apollos; Downers Grove: InterVarsity Press, 2002); Robin L. Routledge, 'Death and Afterlife in the Old Testament', *JEBS* 9.1 (2008), pp. 22–39; *OT Theology*, pp. 306–309.

13. Block (*Ezekiel 25 – 48*, pp. 377–378) suggests that the fact that the bones in Ezek. 37:1–14 were unburied indicates that they were under a covenant curse, and that Ezekiel saw the condition of the people in those same terms (cf. Deut. 28:25–26; Jer. 34:17–20). That is not directly indicated in Israel's cry of despair, but it is not impossible, and would heighten the nation's sense of abandonment by God.

of the people's sin. That, however, led to a second possible reason for the exiles' despair: that God had abandoned them. This sense of despair is also seen in Isaiah 49:14: 'But Zion said, "The LORD has forsaken me, the LORD has forgotten me."' The prophet's response is to contrast God's power (e.g. Isa. 40:12–31; 44:24–28; 45:12–13) with the weakness of Babylon's gods, who are mere idols, and without the help of their human makers cannot even prevent themselves from toppling over (Isa. 40:20; 41:7), and also to demonstrate God's unfailing commitment to restore his people (e.g. 41:8–10; 43:1–7; 54:4–8).

It is the same commitment to restore his people that we see in Ezekiel 37:1–14. Here the desperate plight of the people is likened to death. However, God can and will revive them. The new life given to dry bones by the infusion of *rûaḥ* is a metaphor for the political and spiritual rebirth of the nation, and this is emphasized in the final reference to *rûaḥ* (v. 14), which is now clearly identified as belonging to God: 'I will put my *rûaḥ* in you and you will live.' It is tempting to see two parts to the national restoration described in verses 11–14. The reference to bringing the people out of their graves and establishing them in their own land (vv. 12–13) corresponds to Ezekiel's initial prophesying to the dry bones. However, the return from exile is not enough, and there is also the need for spiritual renewal (v. 14): only then will the nation be fully restored. While that interpretation is both attractive and theologically correct, it is more likely that these are two ways of saying the same thing: the first giving a dramatic illustration of what God intends to do for those who feel themselves to be as good as dead, the second pointing to the vital role of the Spirit in God's future plans for his people.

The restoration of God's people following judgment is also the subject of Ezekiel 39:21–29. These verses emphasize that the exile was a result of Israel's sin, and demonstrated God's holiness to the nations (vv. 23–24). Similarly, his action on behalf of his people, which includes restoring his relationship with them, is also a demonstration of his holiness (vv. 25, 27) and glory (v. 21). This also provides a link between these verses and the Gog passage that immediately precedes it (cf. 39:7).[14] In the coming days God will intervene decisively on behalf of his people to defeat their (and his) enemies and give them security in the land. Though there is no specific reference to 'covenant' in these verses, the language is covenantal and, in particular, '[they] will know that I am the

14. For discussion of the relationship between Ezek. 38:1 – 39:20 and 39:21–29, see Daniel I. Block, 'Gog and the Pouring out of the Spirit: Reflections on Ezekiel xxxix 21–29', *VT* 37.3 (1987), pp. 257–270.

LORD their God' (vv. 22, 28) echoes the covenant formula, 'they will be my people and I will be their God'.[15] This restoration, both of the people to their own land and of the relationship that has been broken by sin, is again closely associated with the divine *rûaḥ*: 'I will no longer hide my face from them, for I will pour out my Spirit on the house of Israel, declares the Sovereign LORD' (v. 29). There are explicit references to covenant (*bĕrît*) in 37:26, also in the context both of Israel's security in the land (37:25) and of God making himself known through his restoration of Israel (37:28); and the covenantal language of 39:21–29 appears to reaffirm the continuance of the renewed covenant relationship, which includes Israel's presence in the land, in the face of the threat posed to it by Gog's invasion.[16] In this context, the 'pouring out' (*šāpak*) of the Spirit,[17] which stands in stark contrast to the 'pouring out' (*šāpak*) of divine wrath,[18] may be seen as a seal, a guarantee, both of God's covenant commitment to his people, which includes the reversal of judgment, and the promise of restoration and of continuing peace and security of the coming age.[19]

The hope of future blessing after the devastation of judgment is also the theme of Isaiah 32:9–20. Verses 9–14 focus on judgment, while verses 15–20 point to the restoration, blessing and peace associated with the coming age. The turning point is the pouring out of a *rûaḥ* from on high (32:15),[20] which is generally taken to refer to God's Spirit.[21] As a result of sin, the fruitful

15. On the covenant formula, see above, n. 3.
16. See e.g. Allen, *Ezekiel 20 – 48*, pp. 208–209; Block, 'Gog and the Pouring out of the Spirit', pp. 269–270; Wright, *Ezekiel*, pp. 316–317.
17. The Hebrew word used here (*šāpak*) is also used in Joel 2:28. Isa. 32:15 and 44:3 use different words, *ʿārâ* and *yāṣak* respectively. In relation to the pouring out of the Spirit, these verbs express a similar idea. See Block, 'Prophet of the Spirit', p. 47.
18. The same verb is commonly used in the context of divine judgment (Ezek. 7:8; 9:8; 14:19; 20:8, 13, 21, 33–34; 22:22, 31; 30:15; 36:18; cf. 16:38).
19. Block sees the Spirit here as 'a permanent seal of the "covenant of peace" (*bĕrît šālôm*) and "eternal covenant" (*bĕrît ʿôlam*) mentioned in 37:26' (*Ezekiel 20 – 48*, p. 488); see also 'Gog and the Pouring out of the Spirit', p. 270; cf. Walther Eichrodt, *Ezekiel*, OTL (London: SCM, 1970), p. 529.
20. The Hebrew word for 'pour out' is *ʿārâ* (see n. 17 above).
21. See e.g. Brevard S. Childs, *Isaiah*, OTL (Louisville: Westminster John Knox, 2001), p. 241; R. E. Clements, *Isaiah 1 – 39*, NCB (Grand Rapids: Eerdmans; London: Marshall, Morgan & Scott, 1980), p. 263; Otto Kaiser, *Isaiah 13 – 39*, OTL (London: SCM, 1974), pp. 333–334; John N. Oswalt, *Isaiah 1 – 39*, NICOT (Grand Rapids: Eerdmans, 1986), pp. 587–588; John Goldingay, *Isaiah*, NIBCOT (Peabody:

landscape becomes a barren wilderness.[22] However, God remains committed to his people and as a result of the pouring out of his *rûaḥ*, nature will be transformed, the wilderness will become fruitful again and the people will know prosperity, peace and security in the land. However, verse 16 indicates that the barren wilderness is also a metaphor for the spiritual condition of the nation, and the pouring out of the Spirit here is linked not just with restoration, but also with renewal. The physical restoration of Israel will be accompanied by the presence of justice and righteousness,[23] and it is that transformation in the life of the people, brought about by God's Spirit, that makes lasting peace and security possible (v. 17).

Restoration and renewal are also closely related in Isaiah 44:1–5. Here, too, the Spirit is described as being 'poured out',[24] in this case like the showers and streams that bring refreshment to dry ground and enable it to bear fruit (v. 3). This, again, is a metaphor for the condition of Israel and, again, it points not only to national restoration but also to spiritual renewal reflected in the people who were earlier identified as rebels (Isa. 43:27) recognizing and acknowledging God (v. 5).

Another important passage related to the pouring out of the Spirit is Joel 2:28–29.[25] This, too, is set in the context of judgment and restoration. Against the background of the devastation caused by a locust swarm that presages the coming judgment of God on the people, the prophet calls for national repentance. This culminates in a lament (2:17) which God answers, and the scene changes in 2:18 to the promise of restoration. This includes physical restoration: making good the damage caused by the locust swarm and offering an abundant harvest (2:18–27). The expression of hope is, again, couched in covenantal language,[26] indicating, as in earlier passages, the link between

---

Hendrickson; Carlisle: Paternoster, 2001) prefers 'breath (rather than Spirit) of God' (p. 182).

22. Cf. Isa. 5:5–6; 7:23–25; 24:4–11; Jer. 4:26; see also e.g. Lev. 26:32; Deut. 28:38–42.

23. These terms carry a double sense. Righteousness in the sense of right conduct and the proper operation of justice indicates two necessary elements in society. In the past these have been absent, but as a result of the work of God's Spirit they will be restored, thus transforming society. The terms may also refer to the vindication that God brings to his oppressed people; see e.g. Routledge, *OT Theology*, pp. 105–106.

24. Heb. *yāṣak* (see n. 17 above).

25. Heb. *šāpak* (see n. 17 above).

26. E.g. references to God's presence in the midst of his people and recognizing Yahweh as the people's only God (2:27). Willem A. VanGemeren, 'The Spirit of

God's covenant commitment to his people and his intention to re-establish his covenant relationship with them, and the promise of future blessing. This promise of renewed physical prosperity will also be accompanied by the pouring out of the Spirit (2:28).[27] Though not stated specifically, there may be an intended connection here between the rain (2:23) that will refresh the land and the Spirit who will bring spiritual refreshment of the people. The most significant feature of this passage, though, is that the Spirit will be poured out on 'all flesh'. This might be an oblique allusion to the Spirit's role in animating human flesh, or to the contrast between frail human flesh and God's power.[28] It seems more likely, though, that the expression just means 'everyone' or, in this context, 'all God's people'.[29] The coming era of salvation, then, will be

---

Restoration', *WTJ* 50 (1988), pp. 81–102 (83 n. 10), describes this verse as 'the climactic affirmation of Yahweh's covenant presence'. The covenantal link is also emphasized by e.g. Leslie C. Allen, *The Books of Joel, Obadiah, Jonah and Micah*, NICOT (London: Hodder and Stoughton, 1976), pp. 95–96; Block, 'Gog and the Pouring out of the Spirit', p. 268; Douglas Stuart, *Hosea–Jonah*, WBC 31 (Waco: Word, 1987), p. 260. The hope of restoration is, further, based on an orthodox confession of Israel's faith (2:13; cf. Exod. 34:6–7; see further Routledge, 'Mission and Covenant'). We see here, too, the restoration of covenant blessing following the curse associated with the people's rebellion (2:23–24; cf. Lev. 26:3–4; Deut. 11:13–15; 28:11–12).

27. Many commentators take 'afterwards' in v. 28 to indicate that the pouring out of the Spirit is a further stage in the process of restoration; see e.g. Stuart, *Hosea–Jonah*, p. 260; Hans Walter Wolff, *Joel and Amos*, Hermeneia (Philadelphia: Fortress, 1977), p. 65. Allen suggests that material restoration (vv. 18–27) is imminent, while the 'deeper gifts of God's grace' represented by the pouring out of the Spirit are for the more distant future (*Joel*, p. 97). VanGemeren's argument that 'afterwards' does not indicate a subsequent stage in the process, but that vv. 18–27 and 28–32 give complementary descriptions of the future era ('Spirit of Restoration', pp. 84–89), is not persuasive, though he is right to emphasize the close relationship between material and spiritual blessings. David Allan Hubbard, *Joel and Amos*, TOTC (Leicester: Inter-Varsity Press, 1989), p. 68, suggests that 'afterwards' is sequential, but moves not from material to spiritual, but from the 'restoration of old damage' to 'the inauguration of a new era'. The general outpouring of the Spirit belongs to that new era. However, if the damage caused by the locust swarm presages future judgment, physical restoration may also presage future as well as imminent material blessing.
28. So Allen, *Joel*, p. 98; Hubbard, *Joel and Amos*, pp. 69–70; Wolff, *Joel and Amos*, p. 66.
29. In Ezek. 39:29, the Spirit is poured out 'on the house of Israel' (cf. Isa. 44:3) and

characterized by a general outpouring of divine *rûaḥ* – with the result that all God's people, regardless of age, gender or social status, will prophesy. Prophecy is a sign of the Spirit's presence,[30] and its significance here points to the availability of the Spirit's power within the lives of all believers, rather than being limited to select individuals as in the past. It may also denote a new intimacy with God (cf. 2:27). Prophets had special access to the divine presence (e.g. Jer. 23:18, 22; cf. 1 Kgs 22:19), and in the coming days, as God restores his people and renews the covenant, the Spirit's presence among them will ensure that all will have that same direct relationship with God (cf. Jer. 31:34).[31]

The Spirit and renewal

While in part a punishment for sin, the exile was also intended to refine the people and to bring forth a chastened and faithful remnant. It is possible that all the exiles really wanted to do was to go home. However, if the people were to fulfil their calling, it was not just the political situation that needed to change. The exile was a crisis in the life of the nation, but it was not long before those who eventually returned to the land were falling into the same sins as their forefathers.[32] The trauma of defeat and captivity did not result in the change in attitude and behaviour that was necessary to make political restoration more than a temporary respite. That change could come about only through an inward renewal that would enable the people to overcome the sin and disobedience that had characterized their relationship with God in the past, and had led to divine judgment.

As we have noted, passages that point to the role of God's Spirit in the future restoration of Israel's national life also include elements of renewal

---

the similar context in Joel 2:28, and the designation of the recipients as 'your sons', 'your daughters', etc. suggests that God's people are in view (cf. 2:27); see Allen, *Joel*, p. 98; Hubbard, *Joel and Amos*, p. 69; VanGemeren, 'Spirit of Restoration', pp. 90–91; Wolff, *Joel and Amos*, p. 67.

30. E.g. Num. 11:25–29; 24:2; 1 Sam. 10:6, 10; 19:20, 23; cf. Hos. 9:7. See further, 'The Spirit and prophecy' in this volume.

31. See e.g. Allen, *Joel*, p. 99; Wolff, *Joel and Amos*, pp. 66–67. The Spirit is closely linked with the presence of God in Pss 51:11; 139:7; see also the parallels between Exod. 33:14 and Isa. 63:11, 14.

32. See e.g. the religious and social issues faced by Ezra and Nehemiah after the return from exile; cf. Isa. 56 – 66.

(e.g. Isa. 32:9–20; 44:1–5). The people face divine judgment because of their disobedience, and in order for that judgment to be reversed and for the people to once again experience the blessings of being in covenant relationship with God, the people need, again, to be obedient – and that implies inward transformation. We turn now to passages that deal more directly with the spiritual renewal of God's people.

An important passage in this regard is Ezekiel 36:26–27: 'I will give you a new heart and put a new spirit [*rûaḥ*] in you; I will remove from you your heart of stone and give you a heart of flesh. And I will put my Spirit [*rûaḥ*] in you and move you to follow my decrees and be careful to keep my laws.' Here, again, *rûaḥ* is used in different ways. First, it refers to the human spirit, which primarily denotes human disposition. This may include mood and inclination, but, particularly when paralleled with 'heart' (*lēb*), indicates a deliberate orientation of mind and will.[33] As a result of divine renewal, the people will receive a new heart and a new spirit (cf. Ezek. 11:19) and so will have the whole of their inner lives transformed. In these verses *rûaḥ* also refers to God's Spirit, which will be put within human beings. On this occasion the divine *rûaḥ* denotes not primarily life-giving breath, but the power by which human beings are enabled to do what in their own strength would be impossible. The exile came about because of disobedience; the people failed to live up to the demands of their covenant relationship with God. However, God's ongoing commitment to his people results in the promise not only of forgiveness and restoration, but of the renewal that is necessary to enable them to be obedient in the future.

In Jeremiah's vision of the future this renewal is linked with the promise of the new covenant (Jer. 31:31–34), which will be accompanied by putting God's law within his people and thereby creating new people with the ability to be obedient (cf. Jer. 24:7).[34] Ezekiel does not specifically mention a new covenant in chapter 36.[35] However, his use of the covenant formula, 'you will be my people and I will be your God' (v. 28; cf. Jer. 31:33),[36] sets the promise

---

33. *Rûaḥ* may refer to what moves and motivates a person's life (cf. Snaith, *Distinctive Ideas*, p. 148). When paired with *lēb* the reference is to the whole of a person's inner life; see e.g. van Pelt, Kaiser and Block, '*rûaḥ*', in *NIDOTTE* 3:1074–1075; Routledge, *OT Theology*, pp. 144–145; see also Block, 'Prophet of the Spirit', pp. 45–46; Wright, *Ezekiel*, p. 296.
34. For further discussion of the new covenant, see e.g. Routledge, *OT Theology*, pp. 269–272.
35. Ezekiel does, though, refer to a new covenant relationship in 16:60; 34:25; 37:26.
36. See above, n. 3.

within a covenantal framework. There are enough similarities between the language of Jeremiah 31:33 and Ezekiel 36:26–27 to suggest that Ezekiel may have been influenced by Jeremiah.[37] However, in this renewal of the covenant relationship between God and his people, Jeremiah focuses on God's law (*tôrâ*), which the people have failed to keep and which will in the future be written on human hearts – effecting a change of mind, will and nature,[38] whereas Ezekiel emphasizes the role of the Spirit.

In the light of Jeremiah's general unwillingness to refer to God's Spirit in his prophecy, it is not surprising that he does not mention the Spirit on this occasion either. The reason for Jeremiah's apparent reluctance to mention the Spirit and his appeal, instead, to direct encounter with God as the basis for his prophetic authority is unclear. One possibility is that he wanted to distance himself from false prophets, whose ecstatic behaviour might have been taken, wrongly, as evidence of the Spirit's activity and therefore of divine authority.[39] Rather than engage in a fruitless debate about who truly possessed the Spirit of God, Jeremiah chose to focus instead on the message itself – revealed to him in the council chamber of Yahweh (Jer. 23:18, 22). Or it may be that in emphasizing the significance of God's word, Jeremiah had no need to set out a theology of the Spirit. In either case, there is nothing to suggest a negative view of the role of the Spirit. Thus, while Jeremiah 31:33 and Ezekiel 36:26–27 reflect different emphases, from a biblical theological perspective they are complementary rather than contradictory, and the similarities between them allow us to attribute the transformation of God's people associated with the new covenant also to the work of God's Spirit. The Sinaitic covenant marked the birth of Israel as a nation. As the people looked back, they recognized the presence of the divine Spirit among them during that formative time in

37. See e.g. Block, 'Prophet of the Spirit', p. 39; *Ezekiel 25 – 48*, p. 356; John B. Taylor, *Ezekiel*, TOTC (Leicester: Inter-Varsity Press, 1969), p. 232.

38. According to Gerhard von Rad, *Old Testament Theology*, 2 vols. (Edinburgh: Oliver & Boyd, 1962–5), 2:213–214, 'What is here outlined is the picture of a new man, a man who is able to obey perfectly because of a miraculous change in his nature.'

39. This is not to suggest, as does S. Mowinckel, 'The Spirit and the Word in the Pre-exilic Reforming Prophets', *JBL* 53.3 (1934), pp. 199–227, that classical prophets were suspicious of the role of the Spirit. Jeremiah's concern may be over the misrepresentation of the view of the Spirit. See also e.g. J. D. G. Dunn, 'Spirit, Holy Spirit', in *IBD*, 3:1478–1483; Goldingay, 'Was the Holy Spirit Active', p. 17; J. Lindblom, *Prophecy in Ancient Israel* (Oxford: Basil Blackwell, 1962), pp. 177–178.

their history (Isa. 63:11–14; cf. Neh. 9:20),[40] though they were aware, too, that their relationship with God was marred by rebellion, which grieved the Spirit. Nevertheless, on the basis of God's commitment to his covenant promises,[41] his Spirit will remain among his people (e.g. Hag. 2:5) to bring about the inward renewal that will overcome their rebellion and enable them to fulfil their covenant obligations. The result will be a new covenant relationship which will not be broken by the people's sin and which, therefore, may be described as 'everlasting' (e.g. Jer. 32:40; Ezek. 16:60; Isa. 55:3).

There is a further close link between Spirit and covenant in Isaiah 59:21. This verse concludes a chapter that outlines Israel's sin (vv. 1–8), confession (vv. 9–15a) and redemption by God, coming as the divine warrior to defeat his enemies and bring vindication[42] to his people (vv. 15b–20). The reference to God's covenant with the people and the presence of his Spirit among them, in verse 21, then adds a final assurance of his commitment to them.[43] In the

---

40. Richard J. Sklba, '"Until the Spirit from on High Is Poured out on Us" (Isa 32:15): Reflections on the Role of the Spirit in the Exile', *CBQ* 46 (1984), pp. 1–17, suggests that during the exile earlier traditions, including those relating to the Spirit, were reinterpreted and reapplied to the exilic community. In the absence of the cult, emphasis was placed on the Spirit as 'a vital and powerful expression of the divine presence' (p. 15). Against this background, Isa. 63:11–14 and Neh. 9:20 represent a retelling of the exodus story, giving prominence to the Spirit (p. 13), who will also take an active role in Israel's coming restoration.
41. God's commitment to his people is closely linked with his *ḥesed*, which expresses love and faithfulness within the context of a (covenant) relationship. On the basis of this *ḥesed*, God preserves the relationship with his people and promises a new covenant; see further, Robin Routledge, '*Hesed* as Obligation: A Re-Examination', *TynBul* 46.1 (1995), pp. 179–196; *OT Theology*, pp. 108–110, 279–280.
42. In this context, 'justice' and 'righteousness' (vv. 15b–16) refer to God's activity on behalf of his people; see n. 23 above. However, one of the reasons for judgment is the absence of both of these in society (e.g. 56:1), indicating that in order to receive justice and righteousness from God these need to be present within the life of the nation; see e.g. Childs, *Isaiah*, pp. 490–491; John N. Oswalt, *Isaiah 40 – 66*, NICOT (Grand Rapids; Cambridge: Eerdmans, 1998), p. 519.
43. Some see no link between v. 21 and the rest of ch. 59; see e.g. Claus Westermann, *Isaiah 40 – 66*, OTL (London: SCM, 1966), p. 427; R. N. Whybray, *Isaiah 40 – 66*, NCB (London: Oliphants, 1975), pp. 228–229. Childs, though, emphasizes the need to interpret the verse within its canonical context (*Isaiah*, p. 490–491); see also Oswalt, *Isaiah 40 – 66*, pp. 530–531.

preceding chapters there are references to the Noahic (54:9–10), Davidic (55:3) and Sinaitic (56:6) covenants. Within the context of Isaiah 56 – 66, the reference in 59:21 is probably to the renewal of the Sinaitic covenant. Chapters 56 – 59 refer to the failure of the people to practise true religion, including sacrifice (57:5–6), fasting (58:3–5), looking after the weak in society (58:6–10) and observing the Sabbath (58:13–14) – all of which are associated with the law given at Sinai.[44] That failure has led to judgment. However, in accordance with his covenant commitment to his people, God will redeem, restore and renew those who are willing to repent (59:20).[45]

Significantly, this indictment of the nation is set after the return from exile, reinforcing the view that the events of the exile itself were not enough to bring about the change that God requires in his people. That change can only be brought about by God and here, again, it is associated with the work of his Spirit. The direct result of the Spirit's activity is that the people will be enabled to speak God's word. This is similar to the democratizing of prophecy in Joel 2:28 (cf. Num. 11:29, which provides another link with Sinai) and may, as there, indicate a renewed intimacy with God. The reference to God's words being in the mouths of the people also has another important significance for the prophecy of Isaiah. When confronted by the holiness of God, Isaiah acknowledged that the uncleanness of sin made him and the nation unworthy to speak God's word (Isa. 6:5). For Isaiah himself, repentance opened the way for forgiveness and for the cleansing that would enable him to fulfil his divine commission (vv. 6–8); and what God did for Isaiah, he can do for the nation.[46] Those who repent will be redeemed (59:20) and, like the prophet, will be divinely equipped to speak his word and so, also, to fulfil their divine calling. Again, this renewal and new enabling to serve God will be made possible by the Spirit.

While God may bring renewal directly through his Spirit, he also works

---

44. Childs suggests that the reference to 'covenant' functions to set the call for justice and righteousness within the context of the Sinaitic covenant (*Isaiah*, pp. 490–491).

45. The call to repentance is also prominent in Joel 2. In other passages it is less prominent, not because it is unnecessary, but because in those passages the main emphasis is on the *possibility* of restoration and renewal. Having set out the future hope for the nation, passages such as Isa. 59:20 and Joel 2:12–17, 32 describe what the people must do to appropriate it.

46. Oswalt suggests that Isa. 1 – 5 describes the sinful condition of the nation, and the prophet's call, in ch. 6, which includes his forgiveness and recommissioning, provides the pattern for what the rest of the book seeks to achieve, namely the fulfilment of Israel's hitherto failed calling as God's servant (Oswalt, *Isaiah 1 – 39*, pp. 174–175).

through other agencies. We have seen, for example, the significance of the prophetic word in Ezekiel 37:1–14. An important agent of spiritual renewal in the book of Isaiah is the Servant of the Lord.[47] The identity of this figure is unclear. On several occasions Israel is identified as God's servant (e.g. Isa. 41:8–9; 43:10; 44:1; 49:3), with a role in relation to the non-Israelite nations, as a witness to what God has done in her history (Isa. 43:10–13; 44:8). However, Israel has failed in that role and seems oblivious to God's saving activity (Isa. 42:19–20; 43:8). As a result God has appointed another Servant, referred to in the so-called 'Servant Songs' (Isa. 42:1–4;[48] 49:1–6; 50:4–9; 52:13 – 53:12). In addition, the speaker in Isaiah 48:16, who is sent with the Spirit,[49] is sometimes identified with the Servant,[50] and some also take Isaiah 61:1–3, which seems to echo the language of the Servant Songs (cf. Isa. 42:1–4), to refer either to the Servant,[51] or to one who sees himself continuing the Servant's ministry.[52] Called because of Israel's failure, this Servant 'is the embodiment of what Israel was intended to be'[53] and will also be the means by which Israel

47. For further discussion of the Servant of the Lord, see Routledge, *OT Theology*, pp. 291–296; see also e.g. John Goldingay, *God's Prophet, God's Servant* (Exeter: Paternoster, 1984); Christopher R. North, *The Suffering Servant in Deutero-Isaiah* (Oxford: Oxford University Press, 1948); H. H. Rowley, *The Servant of the Lord and Other Essays on the Old Testament* (Oxford: Blackwell, 1965), pp. 3–88.

48. Some extend this 'song' further; see e.g. S. D. (Fanie) Snyman, 'A Structural Historical Exegesis of Isaiah 42:1–9', in David G. Firth and H. G. M. Williamson (eds.), *Interpreting Isaiah: Issues and Approaches* (Nottingham: Apollos; Downers Grove: InterVarsity Press Academic, 2009), pp. 250–260 (250–253).

49. The text does not make it clear whether the Spirit is alongside God as the sender, or accompanies the speaker, though the latter seems more likely; see Oswalt, *Isaiah 40 – 66*, p. 274 n. 61; Westermann, *Isaiah 40 – 66*, p. 203; Whybray, *Isaiah 40 – 66*, p. 132.

50. E.g. Childs, *Isaiah*, pp. 377–378.

51. E.g. Oswalt, *Isaiah 40 – 66*, pp. 562–563; see also Jacob Stromberg, 'An Inner Isaianic Reading of Isaiah 61:1–3', in Firth and Williamson (eds.), *Interpreting Isaiah*, pp. 261–272.

52. See W. A. M. Beuken, 'Servant and Herald of Good News: Isaiah 61 as an Interpretation of Isaiah 40 – 55', in J. Vermeylen (ed.), *The Book of Isaiah*, BETL 81 (Leuven: Leuven University Press, 1989), pp. 411–442; Childs, *Isaiah*, pp. 502–506; Goldingay, *Isaiah*, pp. 345–346.

53. Routledge, *OT Theology*, p. 292. This seems the most likely explanation of Isa. 49:3, 5–6, where the Servant is identified with Israel *and* has a ministry to Israel; see e.g. Childs, *Isaiah*, pp. 383–385; Oswalt, *Isaiah 40 – 66*, p. 291.

will, finally,[54] be restored and renewed (Isa. 49:5–6; 53:10–12; cf. 61:1–3). This aspect of Israel's renewal can be seen by examining a possible narrative substructure of the book of Isaiah.[55] At his call the prophet received an overwhelming vision of God's glory, which filled the whole earth (Isa. 6:3), and it is possible to see within the book the working out of a divine purpose to reveal that glory to the nations.[56] Israel has a key role within that purpose as the one through whom God's glory will be displayed (Isa. 43:7; 49:3), but has failed because of sin, particularly in the form of rebellion.[57] The spiritual renewal that will enable Israel to fulfil her divine calling (e.g. Isa. 60:1–3; 66:19) is brought about through the ministry of the Servant, who is equipped for his task by the Spirit of the Lord (Isa. 42:1; cf. 48:16; 61:1).

The Spirit and new creation

As we have noted, Ezekiel 37:1–14 portrays the Spirit, who brings national and spiritual renewal, in terms of the breath that animates human flesh. This echoes the creation of human beings in Genesis 2:7 and could be seen, therefore, to present Israel's future restoration as a re-creation.[58] The idea of re-creation is also evident in Ezekiel 36:33–36, where Israel's renewal is linked with the restoration of creation and a return to Eden,[59] and we see it too in passages that associate the pouring out of the Spirit with the rain that refreshes the land, and with renewed prosperity and blessing (e.g. Isa. 32:9–20; 44:1–5; Joel 2:18–28).

---

54. The Servant's identity is debated. In my view, while there are historical figures who may have contributed to Israel's restoration and renewal, including Cyrus and the prophet himself, the Servant's role is essentially future, connected with the era of salvation – and is ultimately fulfilled in Christ.
55. See Robin Routledge, 'Is There a Narrative Substructure Underlying the Book of Isaiah', *TynBul* 55.2 (2004), pp. 183–204; *OT Theology*, pp. 48–50.
56. E.g. Isa. 40:5; 43:7; 49:3; 59:19; 60:1–3; 66:19; see Routledge, 'Narrative Substructure', pp. 194–195.
57. For Isaiah, rebellion against God appears to lie at the heart of the nation's sin. Oswalt notes that the book begins and ends with rebellion (1:2; 66:24), and suggests that this is 'a conscious placement on the part of the final editor(s)' (*Isaiah 1 – 39*, p. 38); see also Childs, *Isaiah*, pp. 543–544.
58. E.g. Levenson, *Resurrection and the Restoration of Israel*, pp. 159–160.
59. See Yates, *Spirit and Creation in Paul*, pp. 33–34.

There is a further connection between the Spirit and new creation in the close relationship between the restoration and renewal of Israel, and the re-establishment of God's covenant relationship – which in turn links the return from exile with the exodus.[60] Just as God brought Israel out of Egypt and, through the Sinaitic covenant, established them as his own people, so he will act again to bring his people out of Babylon. In describing the return from exile, exodus imagery sometimes appears alongside imagery associated with creation.[61] Thus the exodus is viewed as a creative act by which God brought Israel into being as a nation, and the return from exile, portrayed as a second exodus, is linked with God's renewed creative activity. This is further seen in the depiction of the exile as a return to the pre-creation 'chaos' described in Genesis 1:2.[62] On that occasion, the Spirit of God 'hovered' over the waters,[63] a term that also describes an eagle hovering over its young (Deut. 32:11) and suggests watchfulness and readiness for action. The nature of that action is not clear,[64] but appears to point to divine control over the chaotic waters in preparation for the creative acts that follow.[65] As a corollary, when God's Spirit is withdrawn as a result of sin (Gen. 6:3), those chaotic waters, in the

---

60. The view of the return as a second exodus is seen primarily in Isa. 40 – 55 (e.g. Isa. 43:16–19; 48:20–21; 51:9–11), though exodus imagery also occurs in Jer. 31, in the context of the new covenant. See also David W. Pao, *Acts and the Isaianic New Exodus* (Tübingen: Mohr Siebeck, 2000), pp. 51–59.
61. E.g. in Isa. 51:9–11, making a road for the redeemed to cross over (v. 10) alludes to the exodus, while cutting Rahab into pieces and piercing the dragon (v. 9), and 'waters of the great deep' (v. 10), appear to allude to mythological imagery that depicts creation as God's victory over the waters of chaos at creation. For further discussion, see Routledge, *OT Theology*, pp. 137–138; 'Mission and Covenant in the OT', pp. 17–20.
62. Jer. 4:23 refers to the devastated earth following God's judgment as *tōhû wābōhû* ('formless and empty'), the same expression that appears in Gen. 1:2. Zeph. 1:2–4 also appears to present God's judgment as the reversal of creation.
63. In my view *rûaḥ ʾĕlōhîm* should be translated 'Spirit of God'; see e.g. Victor P. Hamilton, *Genesis 1 – 17*, NICOT (Grand Rapids: Eerdmans, 1991), pp. 111–114; cf. Gordon J. Wenham, *Genesis 1 – 15*, WBC 1 (Milton Keynes: Word UK, 1991), pp. 16–17. On the translation of *mĕrāḥapet*, see Hamilton, *Genesis 1 – 17*, pp. 114–115; see also 'Spirit and creation'.
64. Job 26:12–13; Ps. 33:6–7 also point to the role of God's *rûaḥ* in creation.
65. See e.g. Hamilton, *Genesis 1 – 17*, p. 115; John E. Hartley, *Genesis*, NIBCOT (Peabody: Hendrickson; Carlisle: Paternoster, 2000), p. 43.

form of the flood, return.[66] Similarly, when chaos again threatens, this time in the form of the exile, the Spirit is again instrumental in God's continuing victory and the redemption and new creation that will transform the situation of his people. And the OT writers recognize, too, that this does not only affect Israel. Their God and Creator is the God and Creator, too, of the world, and that future transformation will also include the redemption and re-creation of the whole earth.[67]

Another link between the Spirit and the new world order is through the Messiah (Heb. *māšîaḥ*, 'anointed one').[68] Explicit references to the Messiah in the OT are rare, but Isaiah 11:1–9 is widely regarded as referring both to the reign of the Messiah (vv. 1–5) and to the future messianic kingdom (vv. 6–9). That kingdom is characterized by peace. The verses again suggest a return to Eden, and point to the reversal of the effects of the fall and the restoration of the harmony in creation that was broken by sin. Significantly, the Messiah is equipped for his task by the Spirit of Yahweh (v. 2). In the OT kings were anointed with oil, symbolizing both God's choice and the enabling of the Spirit, though there is no specific mention of the Spirit's anointing after David. This may indicate the general failure of the monarchy when compared to the Davidic ideal. However, the hope remained of a future descendant of David who would be all that David had been and more – and he, like his predecessor, would be permanently endowed with the Spirit.[69]

---

66. Links between Gen. 6:1–4 and vv. 5–8 indicate that the whole passage forms a unified introduction to the flood narrative; see Sven Fockner, 'Re-opening the Discussion: Another Contextual Look at the Sons of God', *JSOT* 32.4 (2008), pp. 435–456; Wenham, *Genesis 1 – 15*, pp. 136–138. This in turn implies that the withdrawal of God's Spirit in v. 3 is directly related to the flood. In part this involves the withdrawal of the 'breath of life' (Gen. 6:17; 7:15, 22; cf. 2:7), though 'my Spirit' may also point back to Gen. 1:2 – the only other occasion in the primeval history where the Spirit is designated as belonging to God. This suggests that the Spirit in Gen. 6:3 has, also, a cosmic function: as the presence of the Spirit in Gen. 1:2 holds the waters of chaos in check, so the withdrawal of the Spirit in 6:3 allows the waters to return.
67. See Routledge, *OT Theology*, pp. 136–138.
68. See ibid., pp. 280–289.
69. When he was anointed the Spirit came upon Saul (1 Sam. 10:1–13), but left when he was rejected (1 Sam. 16:14). At David's anointing, the Spirit came upon him 'from that day forward' (1 Sam. 16:13), suggesting the more permanent endowment that is evident also in Isa. 11:1–5.

We have already noted that the Servant of the Lord is also endowed with the Spirit, and a comparison between Isaiah 11:1–5 and 42:1–4 suggests a close relationship between the Messiah and the Servant.[70] Isaiah 61:1–3 may well also be linked with the Servant and refers, too, to one anointed with the Spirit, thus providing a further possible connection between the two figures. And, of course, the NT writers see both fulfilled in the person of Jesus.

Hope fulfilled?

Israel's hope of restoration and renewal needs to be set against the general theological background of future expectation within the OT. The NT writers interpret that hope in the light of Christ's first coming, ministry, death, resurrection and coming again, and thereby give us a deeper insight into the wider purposes of God. As Christians we need to look at what the OT says in its own right, and be wary of reading later theological understanding back into it. However, as Christians, too, we are concerned about how the divine promises in the OT relate to and may be appropriated by the church.

The clearest reference to the fulfilment of the OT promise of the future pouring out of the Spirit is Peter's quotation of Joel 2:28–32 in his sermon on the Day of Pentecost (Acts 2:17–21). As we have noted, Joel's prophecy is couched in covenantal language and points to the availability of a new, more direct relationship with God. In other passages the link between the Spirit and the renewal of God's covenant relationship with his people is even clearer. Isaiah 59:21, for example, directly brings together covenant and the universal bestowal of the Spirit; and the reference to this resulting in God's words being in the mouths of his people, as well as mention of the driving wind (Isa. 59:19), suggests that Luke may have seen an allusion to this passage in the events of Acts 2.[71] Through the Spirit believers will have a new intimacy

70. See e.g. Richard Schultz, 'The King in the Book of Isaiah', in Philip E. Satterthwaite, Richard S. Hess and Gordon J. Wenham (eds.), *The Lord's Anointed: Interpretation of Old Testament Messianic Texts* (Carlisle: Paternoster, 1995), pp. 141–165.

71. See Jon Ruthven, '"This Is My Covenant with Them": Isaiah 59.19–21 as the Programmatic Prophecy of the New Covenant in the Acts of the Apostles (Part I)', *JPT* 17 (2008), pp. 32–47; '"This Is My Covenant with Them": Isaiah 59.19–21 as the Programmatic Prophecy of the New Covenant in the Acts of the Apostles (Part II)', *JPT* 17 (2008), pp. 219–237.

with God and, further, because God will put his Spirit within them, God's people will be enabled to be obedient and so to live up to their calling in a way they failed to do in the past. The restoration of Israel is thereby portrayed as a new exodus, offering a new beginning, and in the light of that, the Day of Pentecost may have been a particularly appropriate occasion for the pouring out of the Spirit. Although there is little in the OT to support the view, in later Jewish writings Pentecost, or the Feast of Weeks, came to be regarded as the anniversary of the Sinaitic covenant. It is uncertain when that association was made, though the implicit link between covenant and the pouring out of the Spirit, and the more explicit parallel between the three thousand people killed after the worship of the golden calf (Exod. 32:28) and the three thousand added to the church on the Day of Pentecost (Acts 2:41), indicates that Luke may have been aware of the connection.[72] This suggests that the OT promise of a people restored to covenant relationship with God, and characterized by the renewing and enabling presence of the Spirit,[73] has been fulfilled in the birth of the church. Paul further emphasizes the relationship between the Spirit and the new covenant (2 Cor. 3:6), and the link with OT expectation is seen, too, in the view of Jesus, who fulfils the roles of Servant and Messiah and shares their endowment with the Spirit (Luke 4:16–21), as the one through whom the new covenant is mediated (Luke 22:20; 1 Cor. 11:25; Heb. 9:15; 12:24).

The OT expectation of a new world order is also echoed in the NT (e.g. 2 Pet. 3:10–13; Rev. 21:1–8). In the OT, this includes prosperity and blessing in a transformed political and physical landscape, something that is less in evidence in the NT. However, the new order will again be characterized by righteousness (2 Pet. 3:13; Rev. 21:8; cf. Isa. 32:16–17), and so like the OT envisages the inward renewal of God's people. In the NT, though, that new creation may be seen as already present (2 Cor. 5:17; Gal. 6:15).[74] Believers have already been made new in Christ and are presently experiencing the ongoing, renewing power of the Spirit (e.g. Rom. 8:12–13; 2 Cor. 3:18; Gal. 5:16–24), though that process of renewal will not be complete until Jesus comes again (e.g. 1 John 3:2). This highlights a significant difference in the view of the future

72. See e.g. Moshe Weinfeld, *Normative and Sectarian Judaism in the Second Temple Period* (London: T. & T. Clark, 2005), pp. 268–278; cf. Jubilees 6:17.

73. E.g. Pao, *Acts and the Isaianic New Exodus*, pp. 115–116.

74. The Spirit is not directly linked with Paul's references to the 'new creation', though Yates argues that the importance of the Spirit is implied in Paul's argument (*Spirit and Creation in Paul*, pp. 118–119).

in the Old and New Testaments. In the OT, Israel's restoration and renewal is associated with a single event, when God will break into human history to defeat his enemies and establish his kingdom. The NT writers recognize that the kingdom of God has arrived in the person of Christ, but the kingdom will only be established in power, and its blessings will only be fully evident, when Jesus returns. Meanwhile, the OT hope of restoration and renewal associated with the Spirit is partly fulfilled: through the Spirit, who has now been poured out, believers have the first-fruits of what has been promised (Rom. 8:23; 2 Cor. 1:22; 5:5; Eph. 1:14) and may begin, now, to experience the blessings of the kingdom. The full revelation, though, is, as then, still to come.

PART 8: THE SPIRIT AT QUMRAN

21. THE HOLY SPIRIT AT QUMRAN

Geert W. Lorein

At the end of this volume we want to give some attention to the intertestamental period. Admittedly, the texts from the library of Qumran are not representative for this period (in fact, the Pharisees constitute the main current), but they offer a quite extensive and relatively homogenous collection,[1] which was at least known to the people of NT times.[2] And when we understand the intertestamental times better, we will also have a better impression of the background of the NT and of the possible interpretations of the OT.

We will study the texts in chronological order and limit ourselves to texts where the (or a) 'holy spirit' is mentioned, since it is this term that is used in the NT.

---

1. I consider all texts found at Qumran as fitting into the theology of the Qumran Community, whether they are written by them, or only accepted in their library. For my understanding of the history, see G. W. Lorein, 'Een gebed tegen Jonathan de Makkabeeër', *Nederlands Theologisch Tijdschrift* LIII (1999), pp. 265–273 (270–272).
2. Cf. n. 147.

The texts[3]

Instruction

The oldest text comes from the Instruction. Its origin is situated before there was any token of a Qumran Community, even somewhere in the third century,[4] but it was much respected by the Community[5] and was copied many times (1Q26; 4Q415–418, 418a, 418c and 423), until the first century AD.[6] The text where a 'holy spirit' is mentioned is situated in 4Q416 fr. 2 ii 6–7.

בכל הון אל תמר רוח קודשכה 7 כי אין מחיר שוה

Do not exchange[7] your holy spirit for any possession, as there is no equivalent price (for it).

---

3. The texts come from F. García Martínez, E. J. C. Tigchelaar, *The Dead Sea Scrolls Study Edition* (Leiden: Brill, 1997–8), except for 1QH (H. Stegemann [†], Eileen Schuller, *1QHodayot^a*, DJD XL [Oxford: Clarendon, 2009], including their numbering) and the Greek text of the Levi testament (H. Drawnel, *An Aramaic Wisdom Text from Qumran. A New Interpretation of the Levi Document*, *JSJSup* LXXXVI (Leiden: Brill, 2004), p. 354.
4. A. S. van der Woude, 'Wisdom at Qumran', in J. Day, et al. (eds.), *Wisdom in Ancient Israel*, Fs. J. A. Emerton (Cambridge: Cambridge University Press, 1995), pp. 244–256 (255); A. Lange, *Weisheit und Prädestination*, STDJ XVIII (Leiden: Brill, 1995), pp. 46–47; E. D. Reymond, 'The Poetry of 4Q416 2 III 15–19', DSD XIII (2006), pp. 177–193 (193); E. Puech, 'Resurrection: the Bible and Qumran', in J. Charlesworth (ed.), *The Bible and the Dead Sea Scrolls II. The Dead Sea Scrolls and the Qumran Community* (Waco: Baylor University Press, 2006), pp. 247–281 (265 n. 24); cf. T. Elgvin, 'Early Essene Eschatology: Judgment and Salvation according to Sapiential Work A', in D. W. Parry, S. D. Ricks (eds.), *Current Research and Technological Developments on the Dead Sea Scrolls*, STDJ XX (Leiden: Brill, 1996), pp. 126–165 (133): 'representative of the wider Essene movement'.
5. G. W. E. Nickelsburg, 'Response: Context, Text, and Social Setting of the Apocalypse of Weeks', in G. Boccaccini (ed.), *Enoch and Qumran Origins. New Light on a Forgotten Connection* (Grand Rapids: Eerdmans, 2005), pp. 234–241 (240).
6. 4Q416–418; see F. García Martínez, A. S. van der Woude, *De rollen van de Dode Zee. Ingeleid en in het Nederlands vertaald I* (Kampen: Kok; Tielt: Lannoo, 1994), p. 406.
7. תמר hiphil jussive 2 sg.m.; מור.

As the Spirit of the Lord cannot normally have a possessive pronoun with it, this text speaks about a human spirit,[8] which needs to be holy – that is, needs to be oriented to God in a special[9] way.

Words of the Luminaries

As Baillet dates the manuscript 4Q504 in 150 and this manuscript is a copy, the redaction of the Words of the Luminaries (4QdibHamme'orot) has to be earlier. Baillet situates it in a Chasidic milieu, at a time when the Essenes did not yet form a separate group, let us say in 175.[10] In a prayer of thanksgiving, the author says (4Q504 xvi [*olim* frr. 1–2 v] 15–17):

כיא יצקתה את רוח קודשכה עלינו 16 להביא ברכותיכה לנו לפקודכה
בצר לנו 17 וללחש בצקון מוסרכה

> For You[11] have poured out Your holy spirit over us, to bring us Your blessings, so that we would look for You in our distress and would murmur[12] in the dispensation[13] of Your discipline.

At the beginning it seems that the author's days are considered to be the time of fulfilment of Isa. 44:3. In lines 16–17 words of Isaiah 26:16 are used.

In another fragment (4Q504 iii [*olim* fr. 4] 5, also found in 4Q506 frr.

---

8. This is confirmed by l. 17, where we find 'your soul' (נפשכה) instead of 'your (holy) spirit': J.-S. Rey, *4QInstruction: sagesse et eschatologie*, STDJ LXXXI (Leiden: Brill, 2009), p. 83.
9. And *positive*; for the opposite, see חרם.
10. M. Baillet, *Qumrân grotte 4 III (4Q482 – 4Q520)*, DJD VII (Oxford: Clarendon, 1982), p. 137; D. K. Falk, *Daily, Sabbath, and Festival Prayers in the Dead Sea Scrolls*, STDJ XXVII (Leiden: Brill, 1998), p. 61; A. S. van der Woude, 'Prophetic Prediction, Political Prognostication, and Firm Belief. Reflections on Daniel 11:40 – 12:3', in C. A. Evans, S. Talmon (eds.), *The Quest for Context and Meaning*, Fs. J. A. Sanders, Bibl. Interpretation XXVIII (Leiden: Brill, 1997), pp. 63–73 (69 n. 14).
11. It is a prayer, God is addressed: cf. ll. 8–9: 'For You are the living God.'
12. Probably in the sense of 'praying silently'.
13. Cf. E. Qimron, *The Hebrew of the Dead Sea Scrolls*, Harvard Sem. St. XXIX (Atlanta: Scholars, 1986), §500.3. The derivation of the other root צוק ('to press someone') is possible too. Cf. J. R. Davila, *Liturgical Works*, Eerdmans Commentaries on the Dead Sea Scrolls VI (Grand Rapids; Cambridge: Eerdmans, 2000), p. 261.

131–132 10–11), which was originally positioned at a later point in the document by Baillet, but was, according to its inner logic, reallocated more forward in the document by Puech,[14] we read that God is omniscient,[15] and that

אלה ידענו באשר חנואתנו רוח (ה)קודש

we know these things because You have gifted[16] us with a (the[17]) holy spirit.

Here things are different. In the first text the spirit was clearly coming from God, and was something specific for him, while in this second text it has more of a human spirit, which of course is owing to God, as all things are owing to him. This can be interpreted differently in the version of 4Q506, which is a much later copy (AD 50).[18] There it seems that the holy spirit is more independent.

Testament of Levi

The manuscript 4Q213a (4QtLevi[b] ar) gives a part of the text of the Aramaic Testament of Levi. We can situate this text as a whole, physically[19] as well as textually,[20] in the first part of the second century. So we are in the same

14. The 'Luminaries' are probably the lights in the firmament (Gen. 1:14–18), which are responsible for the days of the week. As we have in this composition one prayer for each day of the week (albeit a long one for the Sabbath), the Sunday prayer (4Q504 fr. 8 1 – fr. 4 15) should come before the Friday prayer (4Q504 fr. 1–2 v). Baillet, who edited this text in DJD, was aware of this problem, but did not consider himself responsible for solving the problem. See further Davila, *Liturgical*, pp. 240, 248, 260; Falk, *Prayers*, pp. 59, 63–66, 68.
15. With wordings of 1 Sam. 2:3.
16. חנואתנו qal perf. 2 sg.m. + suffix 1 pl. of חנן (normally without א).
17. 4Q506 has the article; 4Q504 has not.
18. Baillet, *Qumrân grotte 4*, pp. 57–58, 168, 170, 184.
19. G. Bonani, et al., 'Radiocarbon Dating of the Dead Sea Scrolls', *'Atiqot* XX (1991), pp. 27–32 (30).
20. F. García Martínez, A. S. van der Woude, *De rollen van de Dode Zee. Ingeleid en in het Nederlands vertaald II* (Kampen: Kok, 1995), p. 383; Cana Werman, 'Qumran and the Book of Noah', in Esther G. Chazon, M. E. Stone (eds.), *Pseudepigraphic Perspectives. The Apocrypha and Pseudepigrapha in Light of the Dead Sea Scrolls*, STDJ XXXI (Leiden: Brill, 1999), pp. 171–181 (179–180); H.-J. Fabry, 'Die Messiaserwartung in den Handschriften von Qumran', in F. García Martínez, *Wisdom and Apocalypticism in the*

Chasidic milieu as with the Luminaries. This explains that we find a version of this testament at Qumran as well as in the better-known Pharisaic Testaments of the Twelve Patriarchs (T. XII P.), most probably written in Egypt.[21] The exact words that are interesting for us are absent in the Qumran manuscript, but can be confidently supplied from additions to a Greek manuscript of T. XII P., so we will study them here, along with the texts that are actually found at Qumran. Again we have the text of a prayer, and again the omniscience of God is mentioned. Then a double demand follows (4Q213a fr. 1 i 12–15).

ארחק 13 . . . באישא וזנותא דחא 14 . . . חכמה ומנדע וגבורה 15 . . .
לאשכחה רחמיך קדמיך

Μάκρυνον ἀπ' ἐμοῦ, Κύριε, τὸ πνεῦμα τὸ ἄδικον καὶ διαλογισμὸν τὸν πονηρὸν καὶ πορνείαν, καὶ ὕβριν ἀπόστρεψον ἀπ' ἐμοῦ. Δειχθήτω μοι, Δέσποτα, τὸ πνεῦμα τὸ ἅγιον, καὶ βουλὴν καὶ σοφίαν καὶ γνῶσιν καὶ ἰσχὺν δός μοι ποιῆσαι τὰ ἀρέσκοντά σοι καὶ εὑρεῖν χάριν ἐνώπιόν σου.

Keep far from me,[22] O Lord, the unjust spirit and the evil consideration and fornication, and push away hubris from me. Let be shown to me, O Master, the holy spirit, and give me counsel and wisdom and knowledge and strength, to do what is pleasing to You, and to find Your[23] grace before You.

Dead Sea Scrolls and in the Biblical Tradition, BETL CLXVIII (Leuven: UP; Peeters, 2003), pp. 357–384 (368); J. C. Greenfield (†), M. E. Stone, Esther Eshel, *Aramaic Levi Document. Edition, Translation, Commentary*, SVTP XIX (Leiden: Brill, 2004), pp. 19–20.

21. Cf. G. W. Lorein, *The Antichrist Theme in the Intertestamental Period*, *JSPSup* XLIV (London; New York: T. & T. Clark, 2003), pp. 108–110. An Egyptian provenance might look strange as the distance from Qumran to Egypt seems important. One should, however, consider the influence of T. Levi on Sap. Sal. (D. Winston, *The Wisdom of Solomon*, AB [New York: Doubleday, 1979], p. 217). Cf. Devorah Dimant, *Old Testament Pseudepigrapha at Qumran*, in Charlesworth (ed.), *The Bible and the Dead Sea Scrolls*, pp. 447–467 (464 n. 91), about the limited importance of the Qumran documents for T. XII P.
22. Cf. 11QPs[a] xxiv 11 (Ps. 155:12): same form (albeit in Hebrew) and same idea.
23. Aramaic; the Greek simply has 'grace'; although there is a difference between a final kaf and a final nun, a copyist could make a mistake rather easily: see M. E. Stone, J. C. Greenfield, 'The Second Manuscript of *Aramaic Levi Document* from Qumran (4QLevi[b] aram)', *Le Muséon* CIX (1996), pp. 1–15 (15).

The placing together of these two ways of life can be compared to the well-known passage in the Community Rule, on which we will comment later. The combination of counsel, wisdom, knowledge and strength is also found in Isaiah 11:2 (albeit not in the same order[24]), as properties of the 'spirit of the LORD'.

Hymns[25]

The *Hodayot*, or Hymns, offer a long, rather well-preserved text, and are ascribed by most commentators – at least partially – to the True Teacher himself, around 125 BC,[26] when the Community had already found its way to the desert. We read about the spirit of the Lord in 1QH[27] iv 38 (*olim* xvii 26); its central part can also be found in 1QH xv 9–10 (*olim* vii 6–7).[28]

הניפותה רוח קודשך על עבדך ותטהור מכול פשעי חטאותי לבו

> You have sprayed[29] Your holy spirit over Your servant, and You have purified him from all the transgressions and sins of his heart.

The spirit again refers to God's spirit, but who is the 'servant'? The simplest solution would be to think of the True Teacher; another possibility is that every member of the Qumran Community experiences (or at least can experience) a special relation with God through his protecting spirit. This seems to be sustained by 1QH vi 23–24 (*olim* xiv 12–13).

ואני ידעתי מבינתך 24 כי ברצונכה באנוש תגברתה גורלו עם רוח קודשך

---

24. Again the same elements in 1 Henoch 49:3, but again in another order.
25. The official edition prefers *Hodayot*: Stegemann, Schuller, *1QHodayot*[a], p. 1 n. 1.
26. Devorah Dimant, 'Qumran Sectarian Literature', in M. E. Stone (ed.), *Jewish Writings of the Second Temple Period*, CRINT 2 II (Assen: Van Gorcum; Philadelphia: Fortress, 1984), pp. 483–550 (523). Although the main manuscript, 1QH, is quite young (AD 20; Bonani, et al., 'Radiocarbon Dating'), 4QH[b] is much older (75 BC; Eileen Schuller, 'Hodayot', in Esther Chazon et al., *Qumran Cave 4 XX. Poetical and Liturgical Texts, Part 2*, DJD XXIX [Oxford: Clarendon, 1999], pp. 69–254 [74]), and so a redactional date about 125 is sustained also palaeographically.
27. This manuscript has never been numbered.
28. 1QH xv 9–10 (*olim* vii 6–7) סמכתני בעוזכה ורוח 10 קודשכה הניפותה בי בל אמוט : 'You have sustained me by Your power, and You have sprayed Your holy spirit over me, lest I stumble.'
29. הניפותה hiphil perf. 2 sg.m. נוף.

> I know from Your insight that by Your favour towards a man You have multiplied his share in Your holy spirit.

In 1QH viii 20–31 (*olim* xvi 2–13) the spirit is mentioned several times.

ברוח קודשך אשר נתתה בי . . . ולא יוכל אנוש לבקש 21 רוח קודשך . . .
מלוא השמים והארץ . . . כבודך מלוא כול תבל 22 ואדעה כי ברצונך
באיש הרביתה נחלתו בצדקותיך . . . ר אמתך בכול . . . 23 ומשמר צדק
על דברך אשר הפקדתה בו פן ישגה ממצוותיך ולבלתי כשול בכול מעשיו
כי 24 בדעתי בכול אלה אמצאה מענה לשון להתנפל ולהתחנן תמיד על
פשעי ולבקש רוח בינה 25 ולהתחזק ברוח קודשך ולדבוק באמת בריתך
ולעובדך באמת ולב שלם ולאהוב את דבר פיך 26 ברוך אתה אדוני גדול
העצה ורב העליליה אשר מעשיך הכול הנה הואלתה לעשות בי רוב
27 חסד ותחונני ברוח רחמיך ובעבור כבודך לך אתה הצדקה כי אתה עשיתה
את כול אלה 28 ובדעתי כי אתה רשמתה רוח צדיק ואני בחרתי להבר כפי
כרצונך ונפש עבדך תעבה כול 29 מעשה עולה ואדעה כי לא יצדק איש
מבלעדיך ואחלה פניך ברוח אשר נתתה בי להשלים 30 חסדיך עם עבדך
לעולם לטהרני ברוח קודשך ולהגישני ברצונך כגדול חסדיך אשר עשיתה
31 עמדי

> . . .by Your holy spirit which You[30] have given in me . . . and mankind cannot look for Your holy spirit . . . the fullness of the heavens and the earth . . . Your honour the fullness of the whole world. I know that by Your favour towards[31] a man You have multiplied his inheritance by Your signs of righteousness . . . Your truth in all . . . and a righteous guard over Your word that You have ordained to him lest he make a mistake against Your commandments and not to stumble in all his deeds. Because I know all these things, I will find an answer of (my) tongue,[32] in bowing myself down and in asking for mercy continuously for my trespasses and in looking for a spirit of insight and to be strengthened by Your holy spirit, to adhere to the truth of your covenant, to serve You in truth and with a complete heart, and to love the word of Your mouth. May You be praised, Lord, great in counsel and mighty in acts,[33] because everything is Your work. Behold, You have willed to do much kindness in me, and You have been graceful to me by Your merciful spirit and for the sake of Your honour. To You alone belongs the righteousness, because You have done all these

---

30. God is generally addressed in the Hodayoth.
31. The preposition ב can be translated as 'towards': Joüon, §133c.
32. Prov. 16:1bβ.
33. Jer. 32:19a.

(things).[34] Because I know that You have registered[35] a spirit of a righteous one, I have chosen to purify my hands according to Your will, and the soul of Your servant detests every unrighteous act. I know that no human being is righteous without You. I have appeased[36] Your face through the spirit that You have given in me, to complete Your signs of kindness with Your servant for eternity by purifying me by Your holy spirit and to bring me nearer by Your favour according to Your great signs of kindness that you have done to me.[37]

Although this is a relatively well-preserved text, different translations are possible, and although the spirit is mentioned more than once, we can only conclude that most of the times it deals with the spirit of God and that this spirit is essential for contact between God and the praying person.

We continue with 1QH xvii (*olim* ix) 32.

ובאמת נכון סמכתני וברוח קודשכה תשעשעני

With confirmed truth You have sustained me, and by Your holy spirit You have delighted me.

This is once again more specifically intended for the True Teacher.

We read now in our last excerpt of the hymns, 1QH xx 14–15 (*olim* xii 11–12; reconstructed also in 4QH[a] – 4Q427 frr. 2–3 ii 12–13; partly in 1QH v 35–36[38]).

---

34. Jer. 14:22bβ.
35. Qimron, *The Hebrew of the Dead Sea Scrolls*, §500.1; cf. Dan. 10:21. J. Carmignac, 'Les Hymnes', in Id (ed.), *Les textes de Qumrân traduits et annotés I* (Paris: Letouzey et Ané, 1961), pp. 127–282 (165), paraphrases: 'Tu as consigné sur les tablettes célestes les actes qu'il doit accomplir.'
36. ואחלה piel imperf. cons. 1 sg. חלה. For the possibility of consecutive forms, see M. S. Smith, *The Origins and Development of the* waw-*Consecutive. Northwest Semitic Evidence from Ugarit to Qumran*, HSS XXXIX (Atlanta: Scholars, 1991), pp. 35–63; L. Vegas Montaner, 'Some Features of the Hebrew Verbal Syntax in the Qumran Hodayot', in J. Trebolle Barrera, L. Vegas Montaner (eds.), *The Madrid Qumran Congress*, STDJ XI (Leiden: Brill, 1992), pp. 273–286 (284–286).
37. Gen. 19:19b.
38. *Olim* xiii 18–19. With 'your servant' instead of *maśkîl*. That variant is not exclusive either.

ואני משכיל ידעתיכה אלי ברוח 12 אשר נתתה בי ונאמנה שמעתי לסוד פלאכה ברוח קודשכה

> I, one who has/gives insight, I know You, my God, by the spirit that You have given in me, and I have heard something reliable about Your wonderful counsel by Your holy spirit.

The one who prays calls himself someone who has or who gives insight (*maśkîl*[39]). Although several elements can be found in Nehemiah 9:20 ('spirit',[40] 'to give', 'to give insight'), we have to think also of the prophecy of Daniel, for example in Daniel 9:25,[41] 11:33, 35, and 12:3. The one who prays suggests that he understands what is said in Daniel 9:25–27, that he belongs to the group mentioned in 11:33, 35 (even when it is said that they will stumble, but it is more important that they will make the people understand) and in 12:3: he is one of those who will shine like the stars for ever. Although I think that Daniel 12:3 has to be interpreted quite generally,[42] it has been interpreted in a more restricted sense as referring to the martyrs.[43] As far as Daniel 11:33, 35 is concerned, the Chasidim could be considered as a fulfilment of this prophecy. The Qumran Community, however, will have had a more restricted interpretation in both cases, pointing to themselves. We know that the Community had no problem with regarding the True Teacher

39. משכיל hiphil ptc. שׂכל, intransitive as well as transitive causative: cf. Joüon, §54d. In Neh. 9:20 it is of course transitive.

40. In replacement of the Law, as K. vom Orde, *Die Bücher Esra und Nehemia*, Wuppertaler Studienbibel (Wuppertal: Brockhaus, 1997), p. 252, wants it, which would be very similar to what is happening at Qumran, if I understand A. R. G. Deasley, 'The Holy Spirit in the Dead Sea Scrolls', *Wesleyan Theological Journal* XXI (1986), pp. 45–73 (62), well (and, of course, in the NT).

41. This verse is also important for 11Q13 ii 18.

42. Cf. Joyce G. Baldwin, *Daniel*, TOTC (Leicester: Inter-Varsity Press, 1978), p. 206: 'those who demonstrate their Faith and encourage others to Faith, and this the humblest believer can do.'

43. E. C. Lucas, *Daniel*, Apollos Old Testament Commentary (Leicester: Inter-Varsity Press, 2002), pp. 294–295; cf. E. Bickerman, tr. H. R. Moehring, *The God of the Maccabees. Studies on the Meaning and Origin of the Maccabean Revolt*, Studies in Judaism in Late Antiquity XXXII (Leiden: Brill, 1979), pp. 24–26. It could be related to Rev. 20:4–6: cf. M. J. Erickson, *Christian Theology* (Grand Rapids: Baker, 1983–5), p. 1217.

as an extraordinary person, especially after his death.[44] On the other hand, we have to bear in mind that we do not have the article here (he is only *a maśkîl*) and that at Qumran importance was given not only to the True Teacher (who knew his limits: 1QH xi 2 24–26 [*olim* iii 23–25]), but also to the group: it was in the group that truth and wisdom could be found.[45] The solution that fits most of the data seems to be that the True Teacher is speaking about himself here, although he is less exclusive about himself than later generations at Qumran.[46] Maier comments that this holy spirit is not just temporarily in this member of the community, but permanently.[47]

Damascus Document

The Damascus Document was written after the death of the True Teacher[48] but before the Rule of the Community (1QS).[49] It was an important text

44. See 1QS xi 5–6; 1QpHab ii 2, vii 4–5; see further H. M. Barstad, 'Prophecy at Qumran?', in K. Jeppesen, K. Nielsen, B. Rosendal (eds.), *In the Last Days. On Jewish and Christian Apocalyptic and its Period*, Fs. B. Otzen (Aarhus: Aarhus University Press, 1994), pp. 104–120 (107, 119); J. H. Charlesworth, in H. Ringgren, tr. Emilie T. Sander, ed. J. H. Charlesworth, *The Faith of Qumran. Theology of the Dead Sea Scrolls* (New York: Crossroad, 1995²), p. xxi. This specific role of the True Teacher was rejected in rabbinical times: see S. Beyerle, 'Der Gott der Qumraniten. Anmerkungen zum Gottesbild der Qumran-Texte aus der Sicht der Mischna, der Talmudim, frühen Midraschim und des Josephus', *Henoch* XX (1998), pp. 271–289 (278). Cf. CšD i 6, 8; iv 6–7, where God gives visions and prophecies to David; see further G. W. Lorein, E. van Staalduine-Sulman, 'A Song of David for Each Day. The Provenance of the *Songs of David*', *Revue de Qumran* XXII/85 (2005), pp. 33–59 (46–47).
45. See CD iii 12–16; see further E. J. Schnabel, *Law and Wisdom from Ben Sira to Paul*, WUNT 2 XVI (Tübingen: Mohr, 1985), pp. 182, 190–194, 201–203, 222; T. Elgvin, 'Early Essene Eschatology: Judgement and Salvation according to Sapiential Work A', in D. W. Parry, S. D. Ricks (eds.), *Current Research and Technological Developments on the Dead Sea Scrolls*, STDJ XX (Leiden: Brill, 1996), pp. 126–165 (144); G. W. Nebe, *Text und Sprache der hebräischen Weisheitsschrift aus der Kairoer Geniza*, Heidelberger orientalistische Studien XXV (Frankfurt am Main: Lang, 1993), pp. 308–309, 359 (*CWg* is more individual in its outlook than the Qumran writings).
46. But keep in mind: more exclusive than the biblical data allow!
47. G. Maier, *Mensch und freier Wille*, WUNT XII (Tübingen: Mohr, 1971), p. 188.
48. See CD xix 35 – xx 1; xx 14.
49. García Martínez, Van der Woude, *De rollen van de Dode Zee*, vol. 1, p. 226. Note

for the Qumran Community, although some doubt exists about its audience: probably it is a text of the Qumran Community,[50] intended for Essene communities from which they were already separated, but which they hoped to convince nevertheless.[51] The first excerpt we want to discuss is 4Q270 (4QD[e]) fr. 2 ii 10–17 (for the last part together with 6QD – 6Q15 fr. 5 2–4). This text does not exist in the CD manuscript,[52] but probably it belonged to the introduction of the Damascus Document.[53] The text runs as follows.

אין להשיבה וחומשה עליה או י . . . 11 בשמותם לטמא את רוח קודשו
. . . 12 או ינוגע בנגע צרעת או זוב טמאה . . . וכל 13 אשר יגלה את רז
עמו לגואים או יקלל את עמו או ידבר 14 סרה על משיחי רוח הקדש
ותועה ב . . . 15 את פי אל או ישחט בהמה וחיה עברה או אשר ישכב
עם 16 אשה הרה מקיץ דמו או יקרב אל בת אחיו או ישכב עם זכר
17 משכבי אשה

. . . and there is no returning of it and a fifth part of it on top of it or he . . . in their names to defile his holy spirit . . . or he is slain[54] by the plague of leprosy or

---

the carbon dating for 4Q267 (4QD[b]), pp. 194–195; palaeographically 4QD[b] is situated in the second half of the first century of a little bit later. 4Q266 (4QD[a]) is palaeographically situated in the first half of the first century and the carbon dating points to the period from 45 BC to AD 120; A. J. T. Jull, et al., 'Radiocarbon Dating of Scrolls and Linen Fragments from the Judean Desert', *Radiocarbon* XXXVII (1995), pp. 11–19 (14); Charlotte Hempel, *The Damascus Texts*, Companion to the Qumran Scrolls I (Sheffield: Sheffield Academic Press, 2000), pp. 21–23. Have things gone wrong by mixing up old and new numbers (cf. E. Tov [ed.], *The Texts from the Judaean Desert*, DJD XXXIX [Oxford: Clarendon], p. 56), or because dating Qumran scrolls is anyway hazardous (cf. p. 363)?

50. As is confirmed by the mentioning of the True Teacher (CD xx 1) and the quantity of copies found at Qumran (4Q266–273, 5Q12, 6Q15).

51. Cf. J. Murphy-O'Connor, 'An Essene Missionary Document? CD II, 14 – VI, 1', *RB* LXXVII (1970), pp. 201–229 (partly, as the title indicates: see pp. 204–225); A. S. van der Woude, 'Fünfzehn Jahre Qumranforschung (1974–1988)', *Theologische Rundschau* LVII (1992), pp. 1–57 (55), mentions J. M. Boyce, 'The Poetry of the Damascus Document' (diss. Edinburgh 1988), who would defend this position too.

52. As this manuscript was found (already in 1896) in the Genizah of Cairo, it has of course no Qumran number.

53. García Martínez, Van der Woude, *De rollen van de Dode Zee*, vol. 1, pp. 220–223.

54. ינוגע pual.

> an unclean discharge . . . and everyone who reveals the secret of his people to the heathen or who curses his people or who speaks rebelliously against those who are anointed with[55] the holy spirit, or confusingly[56] in . . . the commandment of God, or slaughters a pregnant[57] animal or beast,[58] or who lies with a pregnant woman[59] because of the heat of his blood[60] or comes near to the daughter of his brother or lies with a male the way one sleeps with a woman.

We find here a list of sinful situations, although the construction of the sentence is not clear.[61] In the first instance, we are probably speaking about a human spirit which is considered as holy. In the second instance, we are probably dealing with members of the community who do not behave towards their leaders as they should. So we can conclude that in the author's opinion not paying back, being leprous, revealing secrets, cursing the community, committing sexual sins, is about at the same level as defiling one's spirit, which is considered to be holy, and not to stay in line with the leaders, who are considered to have a special relationship with *the* holy spirit (but is this the Spirit of the Lord?).[62] This necessity of staying in line with the leaders, together with the interdiction of revealing to outsiders, is typical for the sectarian character of the community.[63]

---

55. Lit. 'of' (cstr. state + gen.); cf. 11QpMelch ii 18.
56. סרה . . . ותועה: actually nouns (originated as ptc.fem. of resp. סרר and תעה), objects of [ידבר]; translated as adverbs with [ידבר].
57. According to Qimron, *The Hebrew of the Dead Sea Scrolls*, §500.2.
58. Same principle in 11QT lii 5; cf. Deut. 22:6. See further J. M. Baumgarten, 'A Fragment on Fetal Life and Pregnancy in 4Q270', in D. P. Wright, D. N. Freedman, A. Hurvitz, *Pomegranates and Golden Bells*, Fs. J. Milgrom (Winona Lake: Eisenbrauns, 1995), pp. 445–448.
59. As sexual intercourse serves only procreation: cf. Flavius Josephus, *Bellum* II 161.
60. For another interpretation, see Baumgarten, 'A Fragment on Fetal Life', p. 448.
61. As the word 'transgressors' figures after a *vacat*, it is probably not – grammatically speaking – the predicate of this list of subjects. However, we can consider it as a list of sinful situations.
62. According to H.-J. Fabry, 'Mose, der "Gesalbte JHWHs". Messianische Aspekte der Mose-Interpretation in Qumran', in A. Graupner, M. Wolter (eds.), *Moses in Biblical and Extra-Biblical Traditions*, BZAW CCCLXXII (Berlin: W. de Gruyter, 2007), pp. 129–142 (141), they are to be considered to be prophets.
63. This is confirmed by our translations 'rebelliously' (cf. Jer. 28:16; 29:32) and 'confusingly' (cf. Isa. 32:6), but that could be – at least partially – circular reasoning.

We read as follows in our second excerpt, CD ii 12–13.[64]

ויודיעם ביד משיחי רוח קדשו וחוזי 13 אמת

He[65] taught[66] them by the people anointed with[67] His holy spirit and seers of truth.

This text speaks about the people ('them') that God has elected from mankind, who generally deviate from the right way and will perish. The spirit that is mentioned here is obviously God's spirit. The anointed people are prophets,[68] but who are the seers of truth? Cothenet refers to 1QH xii 11 (*olim* iv 10),[69] where 'seers of deceit' are mentioned. Further on in this line we read the word *ḥălāqôt*, 'easy things', an indication for the teachings of the Pharisees, the adversaries of the Qumran Community. Hereby we may conclude that in CD ii 13 the 'seers of truth' represent the community. Although many translations give a different impression, there is no grammatical determination in 'seers of truth'.

In CD v 11–12 we read:

וגם את רוח קדשיהם טמאו ובלשון 12 גדופים פתחו פה על חוקי ברית אל לאמר לא נכונו

They also pollute their holy[70] spirit and open their mouth with a blasphemous tongue against the commandments of God's covenant by saying: They are not sure.

This incrimination is directed against the 'builders of the wall', the followers of Saw, the Pharisaic leader of the competing group.[71] These people

64. It must have figured also in 4QD[a] (4Q266) fr. 2 ii 12, but now it has to be reconstructed completely in that manuscript.
65. We still have the same subject as in l. 7: God.
66. Lit. 'He made know'.
67. Cf. n. 55.
68. E. Lohse, *Die Texte aus Qumran* (Darmstadt: Wiss. Buchges., 1971^{2}), ad loc. É. Cothenet, 'Document de Damas', in J. Carmignac (ed.), *Les Textes de Qumrân II* (Paris: Letouzey et Ané, 1963), pp. 129–204 (155). Fabry, 'Mose', p. 141.
69. Cothenet, 'Document de Damas', ad loc.
70. The gen. (pro adj.) is a plural.
71. Cf. Lorein, *The Antichrist Theme*, pp. 168–170, 174–175.

nevertheless seem to have (had) a holy spirit,[72] but they pollute it by negating the strict interpretation of laws about marriage and sexuality (CD iv 19 – v 11).

The last text we want to discuss is CD vii 3–4.

ולהבדל מכל הטמאות כמשפטם ולא ישקץ 4 איש את רוח קדשיו כאשר הבדיל אל להם

> . . . by separating oneself from all forms of polluting, according to their judgment, so that nobody will make his holy[73] spirit abominable, according to (what) God has separated for them.

This prescript is one of a long series for people who have come to the covenant (cf. vi 11–14) and who will accordingly leave the temple service in Jerusalem, as concluded from Malachi 1:10.[74] Several words occur also in Leviticus 20:25, but not as one single expression. The most important difference, for our purpose, is the use of 'your souls' in the position where CD has 'his holy spirit'.[75]

Rule of the Community

We situate the writing of the Rule in the year 105 BC.[76] Although many copies have survived, 1QS[77] is the most important one: it is quite old[78] and has probably been written by one of the leaders of the sect.[79] We will first read

---

72. Cf. J. R. Levison, *The Spirit in First Century Judaism*, AGJU XXIX (Leiden: Brill, 1997), pp. 74–76, as a life-sustaining spirit, not as an exceptional, temporary endowment.
73. Cf. n. 70.
74. Cf. G. W. Lorein, 'Maleachi', in Id (ed.), *Geschriften over de Perzische tijd*, De Brug XI (Heerenveen: Groen, 2010), pp. 331–354 (340).
75. Which makes the translation 'throat' in Lev. 20:25 less appropriate.
76. Cf. the introduction of CD, *supra*.
77. It is the manuscript 1Q28, although this name is seldom used, as 1QS was not published in the DJD series.
78. Beginning first century BC (García Martínez, Van der Woude, *De rollen van de Dode Zee*, vol. 1, p. 184).
79. E. J. C. Tigchelaar, 'In Search of the Scribe of 1QS', in S. M. Paul, et al. (eds.), *Emanuel*, Fs. E. Tov, *VTSup* XCIV (Leiden: Brill, 1994), pp. 439–452 (451–452); that was the reason why it was written rather carelessly.

1QS iii 6–8 (the last sentence can also be found in 4QS[a] pap – 4Q255 fr. 2 1–2):

כיא ברוח עצת אמת אל דרכי איש יכופרו כול 7 עוונותו להביט באור
החיים וברוח קדושה (1QS) / קודשו (4Q255) ליחד באמתו יטהר
מכול 8 עוונותו וברוח יושר וענוה תכופר חטתו

> If the ways of a man are in the spirit of the counsel of God's[80] truth, all his iniquities are pardoned,[81] so that he sees the light of life.[82] By the[83] holy spirit for the community, in his truth, he is purified from all his iniquities and by an upright and humble spirit, his sin is pardoned.

Although the syntax of this text is very difficult (and therefore other translations are possible), it is clear that forgiveness of sins has to do with the spirit that can be found in the community.

At the end of the explanation about the struggle of two spirits within man (1QS iii 13 – iv 26), we read (1QS iv 20–21) what will happen at the moment of retribution.

ואז יברר אל באמתו כול מעשי גבר יזקק לו מבני איש להתם כול רוח
עולה מתכמי 21 בשרו ולטהרו ברוח קודש מכול עלילות רשעה ויז עליו
רוח אמת כמי נדה

> And then God, in His truth,[84] will sift all the works of man, and He will purify for Himself (people[85]) from the sons of man, by suppressing every spirit of perversity

---

80. But אל could also be the preposition 'towards, concerning'; cf. Isa. 11:2 for the combination 'spirit of counsel'.
81. יכופרו; a distinct form for 3 pl. fem. does not function regularly any more: Qimron, *The Hebrew of the Dead Sea Scrolls*, §310.128.
82. Cf. Job 33:30b; Ps. 56:14b (and in the NT John 8:12).
83. In 4Q255 'his holy spirit'; in 1QS 'a holy (sanctified) spirit'.
84. P. Guilbert, 'La Règle de la Communauté', in J. Carmignac (ed.), *Les textes de Qumrân traduits et annotés I* (Paris: Letouzey et Ané, 1961), pp. 9–80, ad loc., translates with *fidélité*, which of course is a possible translation of אמת too – and perhaps in some cases even a better one – but for reasons of concordance, we always use 'truth'.
85. But followed by a sg.

> from his carnal members[86] and by purifying him by a holy spirit from all his wicked deeds and He will sprinkle[87] over him a spirit of truth as lustral water.[88]

The 'spirit of truth' is mentioned in the whole explanation, as the counterpart of the 'spirit of perversity'. I am under the impression that the 'holy spirit' is not identical to it.[89] This holy spirit is only mentioned at the end and is not active within man, but comes from the outside as a strong instrument of retribution. From that moment on, there will be no more struggle between the spirit of truth and the spirit of perversity (this struggle will be common until then, even in a pious person), but thanks to the holy spirit, the spirit of truth will be active for 100%. Keep in mind that this will only happen at the end of time.[90] The Qumran Community still awaits this moment, although it believes to be living in pre-eschatological times.[91]

Later on, in 1QS viii 15–16, the order is given to prepare in the desert the way of the Lord (Isa. 40:3), i.e. to study at Qumran God's word. The same text occurs also in 4QS^{d}, 4Q258 fr. 2 i 7–8, albeit rather fragmentarily.[92]

היאה מדרש התורה אשר צוה ביד מושה לעשות ככול הנגלה עת בעת
16 וכאשר גלו הנביאים ברוח קודשו

> This is the study of the Law, which He commanded by the hand of Moses in order to act according to everything that has been revealed from time to time,[93] and according to what the prophets have revealed through His holy spirit.

---

86. תכמים typical for Qumran Hebrew: Qimron, *The Hebrew of the Dead Sea Scrolls*, §500.3.
87. ויז hiphil imperf. 3 sg.m. from נזה; for the forma apocopata, see Qimron, ibid., §310.129b.
88. מי נדה, lit. 'water of (for) defilement', but here obviously 'water for purification'; cf. F. Zorell, *Lexicon Hebraicum et Aramaicum Veteris Testamenti* (Roma: Pontificium Institutum Biblicum, 1968), ad loc.
89. So that we do not need to read the whole passage about the two spirits. Of course, one could refer to John 14:16–17, 26, but that cannot be decisive for 1QS.
90. Cf. Maier, *Mensch und Freie Wille*, pp. 189–190.
91. Lorein, *The Antichrist Theme*, pp. 165, 177.
92. Variant forms of this passage can be found in 4QS^{b}, 4Q256 fr. 8 i 3, and in 4QS^{e}, 4Q259 iii 6, without the mentioning of the holy spirit. It is beyond the scope of this chapter to look for an explanation of these differences.
93. Does this mean that there is progressive revelation, and that the Law of Moses

This does not refer to an activity of the holy spirit in the times of the Qumran Community, but of Moses and the prophets. God's holy spirit is responsible for the inspiration of Scripture.[94] Nevertheless, Guilbert sees a direct relation to the thinking of the Community: this is the way Israel should always have understood the Law of Moses and should always have applied it.[95]

We read about the holy spirit once again in 1QS ix 3–5; this text occurs also in 4QS^{d} (4Q258) fr. 2 ii 4–6:

בהיות אלה בישראל ליחד (4Q258) / ככול (1QS) התכונים האלה
ליסוד רוח קודש לאמת 4 עולם לכפר על אשמת פשע ומעל חטאת ולרצון
לארץ מבשר עולות ומחלבי זבח(ים) ותרומת (ונדבת) 5 שפתים למשפט
כניחוח צדק ותמים דרך כנדבת מנחת רצון

When these things happen in Israel (to the Community[96]), according to (all[97]) these measures,[98] as a foundation of a holy spirit, for eternal truth, to propitiate for rebellious debt and for sinful[99] infidelity, and for favour towards the land, then

---

is not considered to be a monolithical block? Cf. Guilbert, 'La Règle de la Communauté', p. 58 n. 40. If this would be true, it would be in opposition to the view of the Pharisees, who were afraid of the concept of progressive revelation (when would it end?): É. Levine, *The Aramaic Version of the Bible. Contents and Context*, BZAW CLXXIV (Berlin: W. de Gruyter, 1988), p. 75.

94. Cf. the expression 'spirit of prophecy' in the official Targums, where it replaces the Hebrew 'spirit of God'. Levine, *The Aramaic Version of the Bible*, p. 66, thinks this is for anti-trinitarian reasons, but M. Aberbach, 'Prophets and Prophecy in *Targum Jonathan* to the Prophets', in: J. H. Ellens, et al., *God's Word for Our World II*, *JSOTSup* CCCLXXXIX, Fs. S. J. de Vries (London; New York: T. & T. Clark, 2004), pp. 82–97 (83), stresses the relation between prophecy and the divine spirit, and J. P. Schäfer, 'Die Termini "Heiliger Geist" und "Geist der Prophetie" in den Targumim und das Verhältnis der Targumim zueinander', *VT* XX (1970), pp. 304–314, points out that in other (in his opinion later) Targums the term 'holy spirit' is used. For the relation between the spirit of God and prophecy, cf. also Flavius Josephus, *Antiquitates* VI 166.
95. Guilbert, 'La Règle de la Communauté', p. 59.
96. Only in 4Q258.
97. Only in 1QS.
98. תכון typical for Qumran Hebrew: Qimron, *The Hebrew of the Dead Sea Scrolls*, §500.3.
99. Printing error in *DSSSE*, as well in 1QS as in 4Q258.

will, without[100] the flesh of burnt offerings and the fat pieces of sacrifice,[101] the (voluntary[102]) contribution of the lips according to the norm[103] be as a right odour, and integrity on (life's) way as a voluntary goodwill offering.

After the rules about mistakes in the community, it is sketched how at a certain moment, 'when these things will happen' (what things? when?), there will be no more offerings according to the OT prescriptions, but offerings in the spiritual form of praise and a righteous living.[104]

Rule of Benedictions

The Rule of Benedictions (1QSb) is probably an elaboration of 1QS ii 2b–4a,[105] and therefore somewhat younger than the Rule of the Community (1QS), let us say from about the year 100 BC. It contains (1QSb ii 24) a benediction, probably intended for the high priest during the admittance of the newly initiated and the renewing of the vows by the members.[106]

יחונכה ברוח קודש וחסד

May He be graceful to you with a holy spirit and loyalty.[107]

---

100. Or 'more than', but in that case an adjective should precede. Guilbert, 'La Règle de la Communauté', p. 60, even translates with *grâce à*, because he thinks that during the redaction of 1QS the Community was still offering in the Temple (p. 61).
101. 4Q258 pl.
102. Only in 4Q258; נגדבת nifal ptc. st.abs. pl.fem. from נדב.
103. This supposedly deals with teaching of the law with regard to correct behaviour: P. Heger, 'Did Prayer Replace Sacrifice at Qumran?', *Revue de Qumran* XII/85 (2005), pp. 213–233 (223, 226).
104. This makes clear how the Qumran Community evaluated cultic practices at the temple in Jerusalem. We find the same idea in the intertestamental literature in Sirach 35:1–5, and already in 1 Sam. 15:22; Ps. 51:18–19; Prov. 15:8 (quoted in CD xi 21); Jer. 7:21–23; Hos. 14:3; Mic. 6:7–8. See further R. A. Kugler, 'Rewriting Rubrics: Sacrifice and the Religion of Qumran', in J. J. Collins, R. A. Kugler, *Religion in the Dead Sea Scrolls* (Grand Rapids: Eerdmans, 2000), pp. 90–112.
105. M. G. Abegg, '1QSb and the Elusive High Priest', in Paul, et al., *Emanuel*, pp. 3–16 (13, 16).
106. Abegg, 'High Priest', pp. 9, 12; cf. Num. 6:24–27; see especially the first words.
107. For a translation 'and with loyalty', the preposition should normally have been repeated (cf. B. Waltke, M. O'Connor, *An Introduction to Biblical Hebrew Syntax*

As the spirit is not definite, it is possible that this text speaks about the spirit of the high priest, which needs to be holy.

Communal Confession

The Communal Confession of the Fourth Cave of Qumran contains a paraphrase of Psalm 51:11–13 (ET 9–11) (4Q393 1–2 ii 4–7). However, the expression we are studying, and which occurs in Psalm 51:13, is not repeated here. The text is sometimes situated at the beginning of the first century BC.[108]

> הסתר 5 פניך מחטאינו וכול עונותינו מחה ורוח חדשה 6 ברא בנו . . . 7
> . . . ואל רוח נשברה מלפניך תהדף אל

> Hide Your face from our sins and blot out all our iniquities and create in us a new spirit . . . And do not thrust a broken spirit from before You, O God.

On the one hand, we may conclude that the ideas of Psalm 51 are fully accepted; on the other hand, we may also conclude that the expression 'holy spirit' did not have the same meaning for the Qumran Community as in Psalm 51, e.g. because they used these words in a very specific sense. So the usefulness of this Communal Confession is limited.

The theologies

J. Coppens

Already at the *Colloquium Biblicum Lovaniense* of 1956, J. Coppens (1896–1981) held a lecture about the gift of the Spirit in Qumran. He concluded that the Qumran Community believed that the whole community had received the gift of the Spirit, according to 1QS iii 6–8. When in the Hymns the True Teacher speaks in the singular, he is expecting that all members of the community can obtain this same gift.[109] On the other hand, he does not exclude the possibility of a special 'aspersion' on the Last Day: a process that starts

---

[Winona Lake: Eisenbrauns, 1990], §11.4.2). It is possible that חסד is the first word of a new sentence, because the text is broken after this word.

108. Palaeographically, these words of 4Q393 date from about 40 BC: cf. D. Falk, 'Works of God and Communal Confession', in Chazon, et al., *Qumran Cave 4 XX*, pp. 23–61 (46–47).

109. J. Coppens, 'Le Don de l'Esprit d'après les textes de Qumrân et le Quatrième

when one enters the community, and which would come to its fulfilment on the Last Day. He feels obliged to see it this way because of 1QS iv 20–22.[110] There, however, the spirit of *truth* is mentioned, and in my opinion this text speaks about the victory of the good part of man, caused – indeed – by the holy spirit.[111] In any case, according to Coppens, having the gift of the holy spirit is not the same as the inhabitation of the Spirit.[112] According to Coppens, a person (member of the community) receiving the gift of the spirit becomes a holy spirit himself.[113] In my opinion, one could only say that the spirit of a man, his spiritual part, becomes holy. This holy spirit of God can be equated with God's power (1QH xv 9 – in the terms of his days: vii 6), producing superior knowledge;[114] the holy spirit is not a person, he is not even personified.[115]

The sources for this Qumran pneumatology can be found in Ezekiel 36:25–27 and in (the sources of[116]) Wisdom of Solomon 9:17. The concept of wisdom in the latter text would offer most parallels.[117] Coppens mentions John 3:34 as a possible reaction to Qumran theology, but does not underscore it. The parallel of the relation between spirit and life in John 6:63 and in 1QS iii 6 is considered too weak to have any importance.[118]

F. Nötscher

Around the same time, F. Nötscher (1890–1966) studied the concept of holiness at Qumran. His article in the 1960 issue of the *Revue de Qumran* was reprinted with some minor updating in 1962, and we will refer to this edition.[119] In his opinion, there was no real theology about the holy spirit. The

Évangile', in F. M. Braun, et al., *L'Évangile de Jean. Études et Problèmes*, Recherches Bibliques III (Bruges: Desclée De Brouwer, 1958), pp. 209–223 (215).

110. Coppens, 'Esprit', pp. 216–217; cf. pp. 221–223.

111. See our pp. 385–386.

112. Coppens, 'Esprit', p. 217 n. 1.

113. Ibid., p. 218.

114. Ibid., p. 219.

115. Ibid., p. 222. In the same sense Ringgren, *The Faith of Qumran*, p. 89.

116. Sap. Sal. itself dates from the end of the first century BC: M. Gilbert, 'Wisdom Literature', in M. E. Stone (ed.), *Jewish Writings of the Second Temple Period*, CRINT 2 II (Assen: Van Gorcum; Philadelphia: Fortress, 1984), pp. 283–324 (312).

117. Coppens, 'Esprit', p. 220.

118. Ibid., p. 221.

119. F. Nötscher, *Vom Alten zum Neuen Testament. Gesammelte Aufsätze*, BBB XVII (Bonn:

holy spirit was primarily viewed as a power, given by God for the salvation of man (e.g. 1QH xv 9–10 – *olim* vii 6–7),[120] to be free from guilt (e.g. 1QS iii 7–8).[121] Nötscher also[122] identifies the holy spirit and the spirit of truth,[123] erroneously, in my opinion. The spirit is not only directed at salvation, but also at knowledge.[124] The community as a whole as well as the individual members possessed this holy spirit (1QS ix 3). According to Nötscher, the most important activity of the holy spirit is situated in the prophets, with reference to 1QS viii 16 and CD ii 12.[125] These texts, however, speak about the times of the OT prophets, so this activity of the holy spirit is not typical for the Qumran Community. Another aspect is found in the texts where people are said 'to have their holy spirit' (CD v 11; vii 3–4), in relation with the concept of *tāmîm*, not so different from the expression that 'they are holy',[126] a more correct expression than Coppens's. Also for Nötscher, it is clear that the holy spirit is not considered to be a person.[127]

The views of the Qumran Community about the holy spirit can be seen as a development of OT beliefs. Dependence on Iranian religion is unprovable.[128] The Hebrew Testament of Naphtali (10:9[129]) is mentioned

---

Hanstein, 1962), pp. 126–174 (orig. 'Heiligkeit in den Qumranschriften', *Revue de Qumran* II/7 [1960], pp. 163–181, 315–344).

120. In the same sense Ringgren, *The Faith of Qumran*, pp. 89–90.

121. Nötscher, *Aufsätze*, pp. 167, 169–171.

122. As does Coppens, *v.s.*

123. Nötscher, *Aufsätze*, pp. 170, 172.

124. Ibid., p. 171, with reference to 1QH xx 15 (*olim* xii 12) – not so convincing, but texts available after Nötscher's publication would sustain his position (e.g. 4Q213a fr. 1 i 14). For the relation between salvation and knowledge, see also 1QH xix 12–17 (*olim* xi 9–14); see further Ringgren, *The Faith of Qumran*, p. 114.

125. Nötscher, *Aufsätze*, pp. 167, 171.

126. Ibid., p. 168.

127. Ibid., p. 172; it is not clear why he finds Coppens's position '*etwas zu apodiktisch*', while he himself has the same position.

128. Ibid., pp. 173–174.

129. 'Blessed is the man who does not defile the holy spirit of God which hath been put and breathed into him, and blessed is he who returns it to its Creator as pure as it was on the day when He entrusted it (to him).' Translation by R. H. Charles, *The Apocrypha and Pseudepigrapha of the Old Testament II. Pseudepigrapha* (Oxford: Clarendon, 1913), p. 363; Hebrew text in R. H. Charles, *The Greek Versions of the Testaments of the Twelve Patriarchs* (Oxford: Clarendon, 1908), p. 244.

as an interesting parallel,[130] but an early date of this text has never been defended.[131]

A. R. G. Deasley

In 1986, A. R. G. Deasley (b. 1935) wrote an elaborate article about 'The Holy Spirit in the Dead Sea Scrolls' (part of which found its way into his *The Shape of Qumran Theology*[132]). For the prophets, the holy spirit is the source of revelation; for the composer of the Hymns,[133] the holy spirit is the source of his joy, the means of his purification, the source of his guidance. On the other hand, 'holy spirit' can refer to good human attitude, but the holy spirit is its source, possibly even leading to perfection. Eschatological purification is considered to be the most important aspect of the holy spirit in 1QS iii 13 – iv 26. The holy spirit who has inspired the OT prophets also guides the Qumran Community, and more specifically the True Teacher, in interpreting them. The community considered itself to be a community of the spirit (only for full members),[134] living in pre-eschatological times,[135] and outside of which there was no hope for salvation.[136] So 'to enter the community' equals 'to receive the spirit' equals 'being saved'.[137] Deasley does not speak about the essence of the holy spirit or the relation to God.

Deasley looks for origins in the OT, specifically to Psalm 51 (the use of the

---

130. Nötscher, *Aufsätze*, p. 168.

131. H. C. Kee, 'Testaments on the Twelve Patriarchs', in J. H. Charlesworth (ed.), *The Old Testament Pseudepigrapha I. Apocalyptic Literature and Testaments* (New York: Doubleday, 1983), pp. 775–828 (776).

132. A. R. G. Deasley, *The Shape of Qumran Theology* (Carlisle: Paternoster, 2000), pp. 229–234.

133. Who, according to Deasley, 'The Holy Spirit in the Dead Sea Scrolls', p. 56, is not the True Teacher. It is of course impossible to prove that every line of 1QH has been written by the True Teacher, but Occam's razor obliges us to identify the author of the Hymns and the True Teacher.

134. Deasley, 'Holy Spirit', pp. 54–55, 57–58, 60–62.

135. Cf. his pp. 57–59 and our n. 91.

136. Deasley, 'Holy Spirit', p. 60; the statement that the Community was '[r]egarding itself as a replacement Temple' has to be doubted: see e.g. Heger, 'Did Prayer Replace Sacrifice'.

137. Deasley, 'Holy Spirit', pp. 62–63; regrettably Deasley does not become more concrete about how we have to conceive the receiving of the spirit at the moment of (or as condition of?) admittance to full membership.

term 'holy spirit'), Numbers 11:24–29 (the relation to prophecy and the wish that all would be gifted with the spirit) and Ezekiel 36:26–27 (a new spirit for everyone in eschatological times). The people of Qumran knew these texts and lived by them.[138] Deasley does not mention sources or parallels outside the OT.

É. Puech

The latest specific study about the holy spirit in Qumran we will present was authored by É. Puech (b. 1941) and published in 1999. The holy spirit departed from mankind due to the mingling of the sons of God with the daughters of man (Gen. 6:2–3), but returned to the Qumran Community, where he purifies, forgives and informs about the two ways offered to humankind, and about his intention with them. This means that the believer can be assured in his search for the truth. The messianic age, however, is always awaited but never realized.[139] With the remark that in other texts purification is attributed to God directly, Puech seems to give a hint about his opinion on the relation between the holy spirit and God.[140] Indeed, later on he states that '*L'esprit saint n'est jamais distinct de Dieu d'où il provient et dont il est une des manifestations de sa présence dans le cœur de l'homme*' (The Holy Spirit is never distinct from God: He comes thence and is one of the manifestations of His presence in man's heart).[141] The fact that in the texts of the Qumran Community the holy spirit is never subject of an active verb[142] also points to a specific, elusive being/relation.

Although Puech mentions a lot of texts from the OT and apocryphal literature, he returns to Joel 3:1–2 (ET 2:28–29): although the prophecy is not yet definitively fulfilled – it is still awaited – there already seems to be some kind of participation in the spirit for the members of the Community, by

---

138. Ibid., pp. 46–48.
139. É. Puech, 'L'Esprit Saint à Qumrân', *Studium biblicum Franciscanum. Liber annuus* XLIX (1999), pp. 283–297 (288–289, 291). Of course, other people have also studied the question of the holy spirit at Qumran, but we hope to have procured a representative overview.
140. Puech, 'Esprit', p. 288 n. 14.
141. Ibid., p. 291; on p. 290 he says that at Qumran the holy spirit is never a divine hypostasis, as he will be in the NT, but in view of the difficulties of the term 'hypostasis', this does not clarify his viewpoint.
142. As hinted at by Puech, ibid., p. 286, although his reasoning is not completely correct; cf. the texts we have mentioned *supra*.

which they can live a life of perfection.[143] An interesting question concerns the parallels and differences of the teaching on the holy spirit in the NT and the views of the Community of Qumran on the same subject. Puech cites 1 Corinthians 6:11 as being prepared by the description of the function of the holy spirit at Qumran, and 1 Corinthians 3:16–17; 6:19 as being prepared by the Community's self-identification as the temple, foundation of the holy spirit.[144]

Conclusion

One passage in the texts we have studied clearly describes the prophets of the past: 1QS viii 15–16. In the oldest text (Instruction), the term 'holy spirit' refers to an attitude. We find the same situation in the first instance of 4QD^{e} and in CD vii 3–4. Another situation is found in the Hymns: the True Teacher has a special relationship with God through the Holy Spirit. A precursor of this situation occurs in the Testament of Levi. But what is possible for one individual could also be realized for other members. Here we can also refer to the plural in the Luminaries. The fact that the first instance there can best be interpreted as speaking about the Holy Spirit makes us think that this is also the best option for the second instance (and consequently that the article of 4Q506 was the original reading). This seems to be already the case in the Damascus Document (but we have to keep in mind that this text tries to convince other groups), for their own group (positively; second instance of 4QD^{e}) as well as for the Pharisees (negatively; CD v 11–12). We find in different passages of 1QS that the Holy Spirit is still awaited (against Coppens and Nötscher, together with Deasley and Puech). The same can be said of the Rule of Benedictions.

Nötscher's definition as a 'power given by God' might be a nice translation (interpretation) in several instances, but another translation ('soul', 'attitude', 'Holy Spirit') is always possible too.

143. Ibid., pp. 288, 290.

144. Ibid., p. 289. See, however, our n. 136. Here we can ask how interesting it is when we see that the thinking of the NT has been prepared by the Qumran Community: does it prove that the NT is the fulfilment of the OT, as other people reading the OT came to similar conclusions? Or does it lead to the conviction that Jesus did not bring something entirely new, but collected ideas here and there, and also in the Community of Qumran?

While Coppens and Nötscher say that the holy spirit is not a person, Puech stresses the very close relation between God and the Holy Spirit, and we have also mentioned the relation between the Holy Spirit and the Spirit of the Lord in Instruction. Let it be clear that a worked-out pneumatology is only reached in the formative era of Christian theology.

Generally, we find the range of meanings in the texts of the Qumran Community that is normal in the period before Pentecost (i.e. in the OT and an important part of the NT): besides the senses of 'attitude' and 'soul', we find that the Holy Spirit was given to some people for a specific function, possibly limited in time[145] (specifically to prophets, or to the True Teacher), while a new, more generous situation was announced. At this point, the texts from Qumran are not innovative. They are, however, in using the term 'holy spirit' so frequently.[146] Here, the NT seems not to have reacted against the ideas of the Qumran Community,[147] but to have adopted some of its usage.

---

145. J. M. Hamilton, *God's Indwelling Presence. The Holy Spirit in the Old & New Testaments* (Nashville: Broadman & Holman: 2006), pp. 26–27, 50. A. Kuyper, *Het werk van den Heiligen Geest* (Kampen: Kok, 1927; orig. 1888–9), p. 171.

146. Of course, the term occurs also in other texts. Was this usage influenced by the Stoa, as Levison, *The Spirit in First Century Judaism*, pp. 70–71, 77, suggests? Notice that in Seneca, *Ep.* XLI 2 *sacer spiritus* is paralleled by *deus*!

147. Cf. Lorein, *The Antichrist Theme*, p. 149 n. 2; É. Puech, *Les manuscrits de la mer Morte* (Rodez: Rouergue, 2002), pp. 203–215.

AUTHOR INDEX

SCRIPTURE INDEX

OLD TESTAMENT

Genesis

Exodus

Leviticus

Numbers

2 Samuel

1 Kings

2 Kings

Proverbs

Ecclesiastes

Isaiah

Jeremiah

Daniel

Hosea

Joel

Amos

ANCIENT SOURCES INDEX